P9-AGS-575

HILLSBORO PUBLIC LIBRARIES
Hillsboro, OR
Member of Washington County
COOPERATIVE LIBRARY SERVICES

WITHDRAWN

The
ARTS and CRAFTS
MOVEMENT
in the Pacific Northwest

The ARTS and CRAFTS

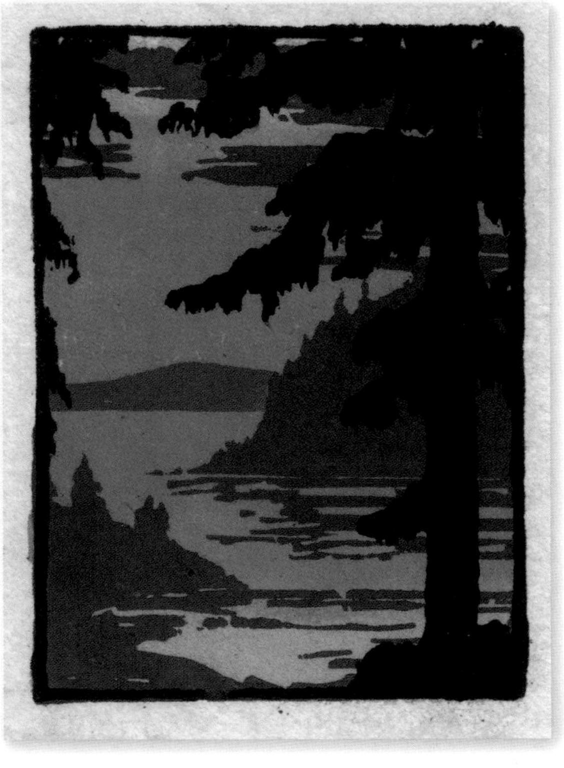

MOVEMENT
in the Pacific Northwest

LAWRENCE KREISMAN
and
GLENN MASON

TIMBER PRESS

HILLSBORO PUBLIC LIBRARIES
Hillsboro, OR
Member of Washington County
COOPERATIVE LIBRARY SERVICES

Frontispiece: *Sunset*, c. 1925, by Elizabeth Colborne. Color woodblock print, 3⅜ × 2½ inches. Bellingham Bay as seen from Bellingham. Art Department, Seattle Public Library.

Copyright © 2007 by Lawrence Kreisman and Glenn Mason. All rights reserved.

Published in 2007 by
Timber Press, Inc.
The Haseltine Building
133 S.W. Second Avenue, Suite 450
Portland, Oregon 97204-3527, U.S.A.
www.timberpress.com

For contact information regarding editorial, marketing, sales, and distribution in the United Kingdom, see www.timberpress.co.uk.

Designed by Susan Applegate
Printed in China

Library of Congress Cataloging-in-Publication Data

Kreisman, Lawrence.
    The arts and crafts movement in the Pacific Northwest/Lawrence Kreisman and Glenn Mason.
        p. cm.
Includes bibliographical references and index.
    ISBN-13: 978-0-88192-849-5
    1. Arts and crafts movement—Washington (State)—History—20th century. 2. Arts and crafts movement—Oregon—History—20th century.
    I. Mason, Glenn (Glenn W.), 1944– II. Title.
    NK1141.K74 2007
    709.795'09041—dc22   2007007302

3689 0902 12/07

Funding by

4

CULTURE
KING COUNTY LODGING TAX

CONTENTS

May health and happi-
ness both be yours,
And fortune smile
on all you do;
And we hope you feel
like wishing us
The same good things
we're wishing you.

ACKNOWLEDGMENTS

THE RESEARCH, WRITING, AND preparation of this book have required the cooperation of many individuals. Their knowledge, diligence, and generosity with time, advice, and research have been invaluable. In addition, their permission to access and document works on paper and objects in public and private collections has resulted in bringing to light a great deal of information about the rich body of Arts and Crafts work produced in Washington and Oregon. We thank each and every one of the persons listed below, and apologize if we have left anyone out.

We were honored to receive one of the first grants established by the Arts and Crafts Research Fund at Bruce Johnson's annual Arts and Crafts Conference from proceeds of a 2004 silent auction. That funding and a Heritage Fund Special Projects Grant from the 4Culture/CDA King County Lodging Tax Fund helped with the significant expense of reproducing historic photographs and taking new photographs of artwork, furniture, and objects. We are grateful for those sources of support for our work on this book.

Eve Goodman, the editorial director at Timber Press, has provided us with exceptional encouragement from the inception

This greeting card, postmarked from Pasco, Washington, in 1912 and published by the Enterprise Novelty Works, Seattle, shows that the Arts and Crafts bungalow was not simply shelter. It was the physical expression of economic security, shared experiences that enriched its owners, and ties made by its families with a community of friends. Mason Collection.

of the project. She and publisher Jane Connor gave us the flexibility to expand the original concept as new materials came to light. We were especially grateful to be able to work with editor Ellen Wheat. We thank her for her extremely thoughtful review, her attention to the broader contextual issues, and her dedication to the smallest details. Susan Applegate's thoughtful book design shows great understanding and respect for the content and images, as well as to the eye of the reader.

To Wayne Dodge and Judith Mason, in particular, we are grateful for all the ways you have supported this project: by bringing your technological and intellectual skills to our aid whenever it was needed, and for your patience, respect, and encouragement when it seemed there was no end in sight.

Ginny Allen
Dennis Andersen
Philip Austin
Stephen Dow Beckham
James Elliott Benjamin
Benton County Historical Society: Judith Sutliff and Irene Zenev
Bosco-Milligan Foundation: Cathy Galbraith
John Brinkmann
Richard Buck
Rose Burch
John Burrows
David Cathers
Erin Condit
Kathy Congdon
Jerry Cook
Coos Historical and Maritime Museum: Annie Donnelly and Vicki Weise
Ron Covey
Imogen Cunningham Trust: Katie Pratt
Randy Dagle
Paul Dorpat
Steve Dotterer
Glee Draper
Paul Duchscherer
Eastside Heritage Center

Ron Endlich
Richard Engeman
Everett Public Library: David Dilgard, Northwest Room
Mike Fairley
4Culture: Flo Lentz and Charles Payton
Steve Franks
Norm Gholston
Betsy Godlewski
Hallie Ford Museum of Art: John Olbrantz
William J. Hawkins III
Bill Henderson
James S. Heuer and Robert Mercer
Historic Seattle Arts and Crafts Guild
Joan Hoffman
Mark Humpal
Ben Hunter
Jackson Street Gallery: James Flury
Brian Johnson
Bruce Johnson
Luci Baker Johnson
Hermon Joyner
Eric Kelly
John Kelly
Dan Kerlee

James Kopp
Mary and Marvin Krenk
Craig Kuhns
Vennard and Jan Lahti
Craig Litherland
Stephen and Cathy McLain
Doug Magedanz
Michael and Barbara Malone
Martin-Zambito Fine Art: David Martin
Michael Maslan
Kathy Monaghan
Sheila Mulligan
Multnomah County Library: Jim Carmin
Museum of History and Industry: Elizabeth Furlow, Leonard Garfield, and Carolyn Marr
Don Nelson
Northwest Museum of Arts and Culture: Rose Krause, Marsha Rooney, and Laura Thayer
Northwest Pottery Research Center: Dick Pugh and Harvey Steele
Jeffrey Ochsner
Oregon College of Art and Craft: Jodie Creasman,

Arthur DeBow, and Bonnie Lang-Malcolmson

Oregon Historical Society: MaryAnn Campbell, Sue Seyl, and Geoff Wexler

Lynn Pankonin

Michael Parsons

Maria Pascualy

Marcella Peterson

Portland Art Museum: Margaret Bullock, Amanda Kohn, Deborah Royer, and Terry Toedtemeier

Jane Powell

Judith Rees

Rejuvenation: Bret Hodgert, Steve Hohenboken, and Bo Sullivan

Tom Robinson

David Sachs

Seattle Art Museum

Seattle Public Library: Jodee Fenton

Bruce Smith

Southern Oregon Historical Society: Carol Harbison Samuelson and Steve Wyatt

Spokane Public Library

Kristine Sproul

Ray Stubblebine

Tacoma Public Library: Brian Kamens

Joe Taylor

Ron Thomas

Timber Press staff

Mark and Karen Timken

Linda Toenniessen

University of Oregon Special Collections and Archives: Heather Briston and James Fox

University of Washington Special Collections: Nicolette Bromberg, Kris Kinsey, Sandra Kroupa, and Carla Rickerson

Jan Vleck

Ken Wagner

Tim Wahl

Thomas H. Wake

Washington State Historical Society, Research Center: Elaine Miller and Edward W. Nolan

Diane Wells

Wessel & Lieberman: Mark Wessel

Western Washington University, Center for Pacific Northwest Studies: Elizabeth Jeffrion

Whatcom Museum of History and Art: Jeffrey Jewel and Toni Nagel

Yvonne Wilber

Scott and Mary Withers

Barry Wong

Linda Yeomans

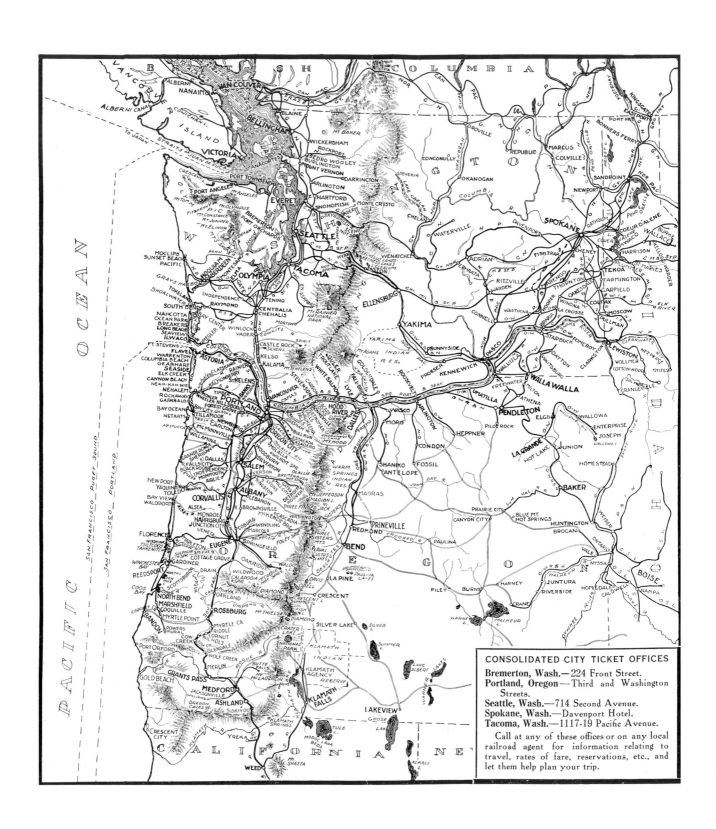

CONSOLIDATED CITY TICKET OFFICES

Bremerton, Wash.—224 Front Street.
Portland, Oregon—Third and Washington Streets.
Seattle, Wash.—714 Second Avenue.
Spokane, Wash.—Davenport Hotel.
Tacoma, Wash.—1117-19 Pacific Avenue.

Call at any of these offices or on any local railroad agent for information relating to travel, rates of fare, reservations, etc., and let them help plan your trip.

PREFACE

THIS BOOK EXAMINES THE IMPACT of the Arts and Crafts design and reform movement on Washington and Oregon in the first quarter of the twentieth century. Our goal is to begin to fill what we perceived was a regional void in the scholarship and literature about the American Arts and Crafts story. Toward this end, we examine products and buildings by regional designers, architects, and artisans in order to convey how the Arts and Crafts movement influenced urban and rural lifestyles. We explore how individuals and companies in these two states were influenced by activities elsewhere in America, Britain, Europe, and Asia in their introduction of new ideas and products. In particular, we seek an answer to the question: How did they adapt designs developed elsewhere to reflect Pacific Northwest climate, topography, indigenous cultures, and influences from Pacific Rim communication and trade?

We discuss fairs and expositions, architecture, interior design, furniture and furnishings, handicrafts, fine art and photography, publishing and printing, and offer numerous and intriguing related back-stories and images. We introduce you to the many

Historic map of Washington and Oregon, c. 1918. This map of railroad lines in Washington and Oregon shows many place names mentioned in the book. The Cascade Range divides the states into two distinct regions—west and east. By the early twentieth century, the many railroads crisscrossing the states minimized the vast distances from such places as Spokane and Baker on the east side to Seattle, Tacoma, and Portland on the west side, and on to Pacific coastal communities like Raymond, Astoria, and Coos Bay. Washington State Historical Society (Tacoma), 2006.80.1.

commercial businesses, cottage industries, and individuals who capitalized on the Arts and Crafts movement by introducing locally produced wares.

Arts and Crafts ideals were a powerful influence in many early twentieth-century Northwest businesses. Regional distributors of furniture, metalwork, and tile made sure that the work of the most significant American companies was shown and promoted in Northwest cities, including Spokane, Wenatchee, Yakima, Walla Walla, Seattle, Bellingham, Portland, Eugene, and Ashland. Department stores, such as Grote-Rankin in Seattle, Portland, and Spokane and Tull & Gibbs in Spokane, had special displays of Stickley and Limbert furniture. Public and private buildings included Tiffany glass, Rookwood and Grueby tile fireplaces, and lighting fixtures from Gustav Stickley's Craftsman Workshop.

The Arts and Crafts movement inspired art instruction and manual arts courses in many of the Northwest's public school systems. The results were students' prolific production of handmade Mission-style furniture, hammered metalwork, lighting fixtures, ceramics, and textiles. Regional architecture clubs organized public exhibitions that showcased the current work of nationally and locally known architects and interior designers. Arts and Crafts societies trained art workers and hobbyists alike. Handicraft and fine arts exhibitions were regularly held in Seattle, Portland, Eugene, and other cities. These exhibitions often preceded and encouraged establishment of regional museums. There were also modest salesrooms organized by art groups in Portland, Spokane, Bend, and elsewhere.

Architects and designers, striving to create environments of domestic comfort, found what they wanted in the stock of locally available Pacific Northwest resources, such as logs and cedar shingles, river rock and stone, for building houses and furnishing them appropriately to fit the ideals and trends promoted nationally.

World War I, along with shifts in social, economic, and cultural priorities, signaled the beginning of the end of the popularity of products of the Arts and Crafts movement in some areas of the country. But in the Pacific Northwest, the styles and ideas of the movement continued to exert a strong influence on residential neighborhoods well into the Depression years, despite the slowdown in new house construction and a sluggish economy.

The rebirth of interest nationally in the Arts and Crafts movement during recent decades has had an impact on the restoration of inner-city housing, new construction in the Craftsman style, and a seemingly endless attraction to objects and accessories that reflect "the simple life." Entrepreneurs whose motives do not necessarily represent the broader moral, aesthetic, social, and reform purposes of the founders of the late nineteenth-century movement nevertheless reinforce some of the movement's teachings in products they bring to market. In particular, they focus on the value of rest and respite to be sought and found in one's home as the pressures and complexities of daily life mount.

A number of today's craftspeople are emulating the ideals of the original movement founders by their commitment to handiwork, to designing and fabricating a work of beauty and utility with one's own skill, and by often marketing these products through a direct buyer/seller connection at key Arts and Crafts conferences and fairs around the country. The work of outstanding current regional artists in ceramics, metal, glass, and wood is grounded in the belief system expressed a century ago by "head, heart, and hand."

Because this book concerns a particular period in social and cultural history, its stories are best related in the words of the period's contemporary writers who documented the architecture, furniture, and fine, decorative, and applied arts, and promoted them to the reading public. Articles from regional and local journals and periodicals, advertising copy from promotional brochures, and graphics and illustrations that appeared in these publications are used in these pages to tell the story wherever possible. These examples reflect the concerted efforts for design reform being forged in Washington and Oregon.

There was a large amount of Arts and Crafts work done in Washington and Oregon during the first quarter of the twentieth century. However, with the exception of buildings, little of that legacy remains and that makes it challenging to study. The local products of the Arts and Crafts movement fell out of favor for a long period. With rare exceptions, museums and historical societies did not collect those items and the generations that inherited them may have thought less of them and discarded them—or used them until they were ready to discard. Since many Arts and Crafts objects are unsigned, it is difficult to assess whether pieces that have survived were originally produced locally or were brought to Washington and Oregon from other areas of the country.

If exhibitions and shop interiors were photographed—and it is clear that some of them were—then the photographic evidence has not been preserved. Many photographs taken by firms for *Pacific Builder and Engineer*, *Bungalow Magazine*, and local newspapers and journals were discarded. Consequently, some images in this book have been reproduced directly from these periodicals. As the only surviving record of important interiors, they are necessary to the telling of the story. We also are left with the teaser of descriptions in local dailies and weeklies or in personal journals, but without the visual evidence of the actual pieces produced. This challenge may be why so little is known about leading artisans in the fine and applied arts in Washington and Oregon during that period and why there has been so little exploration of their legacy. In this book, we have provided birth and death dates when known for significant architects, artists, and craftspeople associated with the Arts and Crafts movement in Washington and Oregon. In captions, we also have credited those who have photographically documented buildings and objects for this book, and have provided sources for public and private collections that are repositories of historic photography by both known and unknown photographers or firms. We have provided dates for historic photographs when known.

A number of buildings, sites, objects, and people representative of regional Arts and Crafts design are not included here because the physical evidence and documentary images either do not exist or have not been found. We were restricted in our study by the limits of available and appropriate visual and written documentation. Unfortunately, that led to heavier coverage of urban centers that tended to be written about and photographed—Seattle, Portland, and Spokane. Wherever possible, we have incorporated other communities in the narrative to support the case that sophisticated Craftsman, Mission revival, and Prairie School civic buildings, social and business clubs, and residences, as well as fine and applied arts that adhered to the tenets of the Arts and Crafts movement, were not simply metropolitan phenomena.

One important component of the Arts and Crafts movement, landscape, has been discussed in its broadest aspects in this book— the park and boulevard systems and the residential neighborhoods developed as City Beautiful ideas that reached the Pacific Northwest. Gardening, the treatment of grounds, and appropriate plantings on residential property were well documented in national magazines and also in monthly articles in Seattle's *Bungalow Magazine*. Many of these articles were syndicated by East Coast authors. Some, though, were by local enthusiasts and included advice specifically directed to Northwest climate and topography. These materials offer rich possibilities for the investigation of regional Arts and Crafts landscape design by those with expertise in the field.

Our initial inquiry, review, and studied interpretation of primary and secondary source materials is intended to lead to more comprehensive and in-depth studies in the future. The limited geographic focus of the Pacific Northwest—Washington and Oregon—does not include study of British Columbia, Idaho, and western Montana (with some notable exceptions), even though there were certainly key links with Washington and Oregon architects, designers, and clients.

We sincerely hope that our efforts in seeking out the role that the Arts and Crafts movement played in the Pacific Northwest will stimulate discoveries in basements, in attics, and in museum storage that will bring to light some of the exceptional work of local artists and craftspeople. We also hope this initial overview will inspire communities to explore further their architectural and design heritage. We will be gratified if this study encourages other researchers to dig deeper into the lives and work of individual craftspeople and artists, and into the creation and development of businesses, institutions, and organizations associated with the broadest interpretation of the Arts and Crafts movement in Oregon and Washington.

Untitled [Mount Baker] (n.d.), by Elizabeth Colborne. Color woodblock print, 1¾ x 1½ inches. Art Department, Seattle Public Library.

PART I Setting the Pacific Northwest Stage

ONE
Arts and Crafts Ideas Move to the Northwest

THE ARTS AND CRAFTS MOVEMENT, as expressed in the writings of John Ruskin (1819–1900) and in the examples set by William Morris (1834–1896), emerged in England in the last half of the nineteenth century as a universal rejection of poorly designed goods mass-manufactured with little regard for beauty or practicality. The movement quickly transcended issues of design, however, to embrace greater social and economic issues arising from the Industrial Revolution. Key thinkers and designers spent great energy discussing, debating, and writing about how work was done, what was being produced, and the powerful impact of new technologies on workers. Impetus for the preservation of craftsmanship, design integrity, and humane working conditions inspired design reformers to establish communities of workers and supporters in Britain, Europe, and North America.

[opposite, clockwise from top left] A publicity brochure for Spokane promoting The City Beautiful was influenced by the teachings of Arthur Wesley Dow in the simplicity of shapes and colors to define landscapes and conventionalized ornament of pine cones. Special Collections, Washington State Historical Society (Tacoma), 1999.122.104.

Rookwood Pottery Company nationally advertised its award-winning status at the Alaska-Yukon-Pacific Exposition (Seattle, 1909) with a color poster. Cincinnati Art Museum. Courtesy of Tile Heritage Foundation.

Spokane's Boulevard Park Addition brochure (c. 1910) encouraged single-family real estate development. Its cover indicates the widespread influence of the aesthetics of artist-educator Arthur Wesley Dow. Northwest Museum of Arts & Culture, Eastern Washington State Historical Society (Spokane), Eph 979.785 J 613b.

Beauty and Utility

Artists and craftspeople sought to embellish the home and workplace with objects that expressed their "joy in labor" and that also moved forward tenets of sound construction, proportion, grace, and simplicity without slavishly borrowing from historic precedents. Some workers rejected new systems of production, while others embraced them successfully.

The initial ideal of the movement—that of individual art workers designing and creating objects of beauty and utility—was, in reality, a short-lived unattainable ideal. One of the key lodestars of the movement, for example, C. R. Ashbee's Guild of Handicraft in Chipping Campden, England, was unable to sustain itself by staying true to the vision of the movement, and fell into bankruptcy in 1908. The British companies that did manage to survive for lengthy periods, such as Shapland & Petter Ltd. in Barnstaple, were able to endure only by embracing and adapting American carving machinery, training workers for specific aspects of fabrication, inlay and marquetry, and assembly, and concentrating on an advertising and marketing network to promote their furniture—many of these practices antithetical to the ideals of the movement.[1]

Americans did not hesitate to be more entrepreneurial, more open to utilizing mechanization and efficient methods of production. Consequently Arts and Crafts furniture, ceramics, and metalwork prospered and were available to a much broader public. The workshops of American designers Gustav Stickley and Louis Comfort Tiffany, and the studios of the Roycroft handicraft community and the Rookwood Pottery Company, became nationally recognized. No longer was one person involved from start to finish with a product. In some cases, the product only bore the name of the company rather than the name of an individual craftsperson, leaving it to a generation of scholars and sleuths to discover these unnamed art workers.

The torchbearers of the movement were often unhappy with the factory system approach. In January 1909, C. R. Ashbee (1863–1942) visited the Pacific Northwest to spread the message of the Arts and Crafts movement, delivering talks in Seattle, Portland, and Eugene. The *Seattle Post-Intelligencer* mentioned his lecture "The Arts and Crafts and Their Stand Against Machinery and Commercialism," on January 8 under the headline "Art Cheapened by Factory Systems: C. R. Ashbee Declared that Profit in True Art is Impossible." Ashbee took the position that imitation of art in factories tended to cheapen the product of the real artist, the factory systems allowing production of but single parts by the workman: "Art is impossible to those who try to exploit it. We who are in the arts and crafts movement must know that profit in true art is impossible, that is, profit such as those of the commercial world would have. Legitimate profit in arts is not possible because the methods used in production are adapted more to the production of art than that of money. For this reason, I say that production, according to the arts and crafts standard, does not pay. Commercialism and machinery demand that consumption keep pace with production while art demands that production keep pace with consumption. Then the commercial man, to keep his large factories going, advertises his wares—to have consumption increased to a high degree."[2]

The topic must have stirred considerable

discussion in Seattle, a city putting the finishing touches on a world's fair that had a goal of increasing investment in the region's natural resources and industry. Of equal importance was the fact that a man of high stature in the arts and considered the heir to Morris and Ruskin in the Arts and Crafts movement would include the Pacific Northwest on his national lecture tour. In the late nineteenth and early twentieth centuries, it was remarkable how quickly ideas about design spread to America, even as far west as Washington and Oregon. With the time-saving devices of telegraph, telephone, the railway, and publications, Americans learned about the activities of British and European designers quickly through design journals and newspapers, visits by Ashbee and other leaders of these movements, and their own travels to the Midwest, the East Coast, and abroad.

Some specific local examples show how this communication of ideas occurred. For instance, William Morris's books, tiles, wallpapers, and textile designs were available in department stores throughout Europe and America and reached Seattle through architects and designers who subscribed to the British journal the *Studio*. Northwesterners also would have been exposed to Morris's work by attending the World's Columbian Exposition in Chicago in 1893 or through East Coast and Midwest decorators commissioned to furnish large houses. Seattle architect Charles Bebb's (1856–1942) earlier work with Chicago architect Louis Sullivan on the Auditorium and other buildings in Chicago surely inspired the ballroom Bebb designed for Frederick Stimson's house on Seattle's Queen Anne Hill in 1903. However, Bebb was likely introduced to Morris wallpapers and

[top] C. R. A. Ashbee rides on a path through the forest with his Seattle hosts, January 1909. Ashbee Journals, King's College Library (Cambridge, England). Courtesy of James Elliott Benjamin.

[above] An upstairs bedroom in the F. Stimson residence, Seattle, 1904, decorated with William Morris wallpaper, was illustrated in a 1906 *Western Architect* article.

fabrics by his association with decorator William A. French of St. Paul, Minnesota, when his firm came west to oversee decoration of Stimson's house and install Morris papers in the bedrooms. French gave Bebb the present of a bound copy of *William Morris and His Art*, published in 1899.

British architects C. F. A. Voysey (1857–

The ballroom of the F. Stimson residence, Seattle, completed in 1904, shows the influence on architect Charles Bebb of Louis Sullivan's principles of ornament. Photograph by Greg Gilbert.

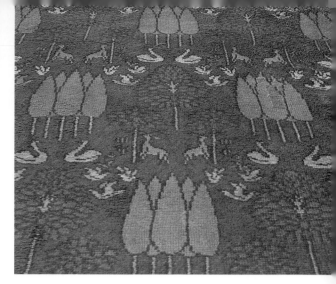

[above] The simple stained exterior of the David Ramsay residence (1904) by Samuel Maclure was complemented by the distinctive decorated porch railing and the crowning finials on its many roofs. Photograph by Lawrence Kreisman.

[above right] An Irish Donegal carpet designed by Charles Voysey was one of two specially ordered for the John Leary residence, Seattle, and installed in 1908. Photograph by Marissa Natkin.

1941) and M. H. Baillie Scott (1865–1945), who were inspired by Medieval-style and English vernacular cottages, influenced American architects to look away from high-style historic eclecticism and seek out and develop a domestic style that responded to the natural surroundings and building materials at hand. The work of these and other British architects was carried into Vancouver and Victoria, British Columbia, in the handsome stone and half-timbered residential work of architect Samuel Maclure (1860–1929). Scotsman David Ramsay and his wife were so impressed by Maclure's buildings during frequent trips to Victoria that they commissioned him in 1903 to design their bungalow residence in Ellensburg, Washington.

Northwest architect Alfred Bodley (1872–?) is believed to have worked for Maclure before partnering with John Graham Sr., accounting for the Arts and Crafts features in the Seattle residences he designed for Pierre Ferry and John Leary on Capitol Hill. At the Leary residence, along with specially commissioned Tiffany windows and Rookwood tile, the interior featured Irish Donegal woven carpets decorated with animals, birds, and trees by leading British Arts and Crafts architect and designer C. F. A. Voysey.

In Portland, architects A. E. Doyle (1877–1928), Joseph Jacobberger (1867–1930), William Knighton (1864–1938), Ellis Lawrence

(1879–1946), Wade Hampton Pipes (1877–1961), and Emil Schacht (1854–1926) were similarly inspired by English country forms for residences. Pipes actually studied at London's Central School of Arts and Crafts during its golden age as a teaching facility for art workers before opening his Portland practice in 1911. He built a reputation on his English Arts and Crafts residences and was still building in the style well into the 1950s.

As part of his 1909 lecture tour to the West Coast, C. R. Ashbee presented two additional lectures in Seattle, one on Arts and Crafts Education and the other on William Morris. Unimpressed by the crowding, pollution, and degradation he had seen in New York, Pittsburgh, and Chicago, he was fascinated and delighted with the West. While his wife, Janet, remarked on the city's cosmopolitanism, its "well appointed restaurants decorated with the latest Arts and Crafts distinction of line and coloring," Ashbee wrote in his journals that Seattle was "the only American city I have so far seen in which I would care to live. All the gold of Ophir would not tempt me to live in one of those smug eastern cities.... Here is a city with a new light in her eyes."[3]

Utopias Realized and Unrealized

Elbert Hubbard's Roycroft community in East Aurora, New York, founded in 1897, predated Ashbee's art workers' community in Chipping Campden by five years. Hubbard, a soap salesman for the Larkin Company in Buffalo, had been inspired by William Morris's Kelmscott Press in 1894 to start his own Roycroft Press, which did artistic press work and also promoted him nationally through his magazines. His community grew to include design-ers of furniture, metal and leatherwork, and other crafts. He traveled throughout America, including the Northwest cities of Spokane, Seattle, Tacoma, Portland, Salem, and Eugene, on lecture circuits. His experiences in cities far and wide were published in the *Fra* and the *Philistine*. As early as 1906, he made a stopover in Spokane, and was so impressed with its people and architecture that he went back to East Aurora and wrote of Spokane as the "model city of America" in the *Philistine*.[4]

Roycroft, Byrdcliffe, and Rose Valley—workers' communities all located in the East—were well publicized and known across the country. The Far West, with its distance from the traditions and restrictions of the East Coast, was highly receptive to ideal and idyllic communities founded on principles of art, utility, comfort, and shared values.

Hubbard was asked to give a lecture at Home, Washington, in 1904. While a number of utopian community experiments flourished in the south Puget Sound area (including the Puget Sound Co-Operative Colony, Equality, and Burley), Home was considered to be the most radical group, having a reputation for anarchism, the liberal Home press, and stories about free love and nude bathing. The individualism of local residents and famous visitors fascinated later journalists and historians.[5] Founded on principles of tolerance and independence, the community grew to 120 residents by 1905. Among the settlers was Richard Bowle, who came to Home from Elbert Hubbard's Roycroft community.[6] James F. Morton, a chief spokesman for Home, commented that there was "probably more in common between Home and the Roycroft community . . . than . . . any other settlement in the world."

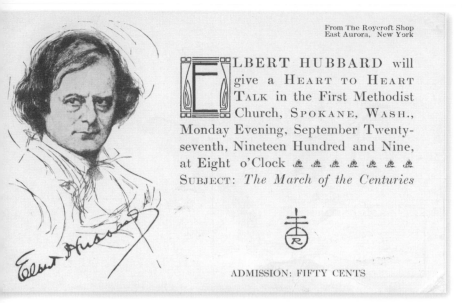

From The Roycroft Shop
East Aurora, New York

ELBERT HUBBARD will give a HEART TO HEART TALK in the First Methodist Church, SPOKANE, WASH., Monday Evening, September Twenty-seventh, Nineteen Hundred and Nine, at Eight o'Clock ☙ ☙ ☙ ☙ ☙ ☙ ☙ SUBJECT: *The March of the Centuries*

ADMISSION: FIFTY CENTS

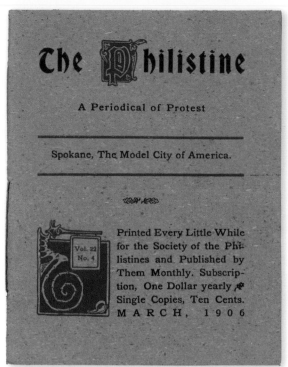

The Philistine

A Periodical of Protest

Spokane, The Model City of America.

Vol. 22 No. 4

Printed Every Little While for the Society of the Philistines and Published by Them Monthly. Subscription, One Dollar yearly ☙ Single Copies, Ten Cents.
MARCH, 1906

[top left] Postcards such as this one from 1909 promoted Roycroft founder Elbert Hubbard's speaking engagements. Mason Collection.

[above] The *Philistine* of March 1906 proclaimed Spokane "the model city of America." EPH 979.7371 H861p 1906, Special Collections, Washington State Historical Society (Tacoma), 2005.45.1.

[left] The *Fra* was serious reading for thousands of Americans from coast to coast, as suggested in this postcard, c. 1910. Mason Collection.

Morton and another Hubbard admirer, L. E. Rader from Olalla, Washington, enticed Hubbard to speak in Home after hearing him lecture in Tacoma. Hubbard spent time at the colony, won over his audience with his charisma, and shared his belief in the need to bring beauty into the world by doing for others. Hubbard praised his "day with the most peculiar community I ever saw—Anarchists."[7] The following year, Morton visited Roycroft and so impressed its residents that Hubbard was said to be considering setting up a shop at Home.

While that was perhaps a gesture of support rather than an actual intent, Hubbard's model was an inspiration to the founders and editors of Burley Colony's *Soundview*, a "Magazinelet Devoted to the Obstetrics of Thought and the Philosophy of Existence." This monthly, of about thirty-six pages, was conceived as the western counterpart of Elbert Hubbard's *Philistine*. It included brief articles, short homilies, anecdotes, comment, and book reviews to broaden readers' knowledge and understanding of social, political, and economic issues. Rader envisioned it as the organ of a new society of men and women called "Evergreens."[8]

The Pacific Northwest's open-minded approach to community prompted Ralph Whitehead, whose first artists' community, Arcady, in Montecito, California, failed to develop during the 1890s, to consider another location farther north. In 1900, with the assistance of writer Hervey White, he planned a commune near Alsea, Oregon, in a spot so remote that self-sufficiency was the only way to stay alive. According to Robert Edwards in his essay *Byrdcliffe: Life by Design*: "A group of musicians was dispatched in the fall to build the colony, but by the time White and Whitehead arrived the following July, the settlers were all quarreling and the commune was abandoned before it began. Whitehead then brought in Bolton Brown, an artist, whose preference for the lower Catskill Mountains in New York State prevailed as the site of the new utopia."[9] This new artists' colony was Byrdcliffe.

Arts and Crafts communities such as Byrdcliffe and Rose Valley were probably known to educated and well-read residents of Portland, Seattle, Tacoma, and Spokane. Nevertheless, it took no elitism to know about Elbert Hubbard or to be exposed to the seeming thou-

sands of publications issuing forth from his Roycroft publishing house. The circulation of the *Fra*, the *Philistine*, and *Little Journeys* was a nationwide phenomenon, and every city library carried copies for those who could not afford the subscriptions.

While there is no direct evidence of a relationship, the formation of the Beaux Arts Society and Workshops by commercial artists Frank Calvert and Alfred Renfro in 1908 nicely coincided with Elbert Hubbard's visits to the Northwest. It also may not be a coincidence that C. R. Ashbee visited Seattle in January 1909. His public lectures while there would have drawn an audience from the newly formed Beaux Arts Society and Workshop, and he certainly would have visited with those whose interests he shared before continuing to Oregon and California.

The workshop at Chipping Campden may have been known to Calvert and Renfro. However, it is more likely that Hubbard's well-promoted Roycroft community and its Arts and Crafts workshops served as models for the two artists in their vision of a fifty-acre forested community on the east shore of Lake Washington, where art workers could live, work, and play together. The emblem of the Beaux Arts Society was the Beaux Arts cottage, an Arts and Crafts bungalow designed along Swiss Chalet lines and constructed partly of logs. According to the founders, the cottage was a refinement of the pioneer cabin of the West, and emblematic of home.

The society and its physical manifestation on Lake Washington were promoted in a beautifully photographed volume, *Homes and Gardens of the Pacific Coast* (1913), which showed off some of the finest architecture and gardens in the Seattle area. In their preface, Calvert and Renfro explained their motivation and vision:

> The Beaux Arts Society was founded in 1908 with the idea of establishing a community in many respects similar to the Garden Villages of England, and to advance the arts and crafts, as related to home building. With this object in view the Society acquired a tract of land on the shores of Lake Washington which was named Beaux Arts Village. This is a beautiful spot which offers unlimited opportunities for the building of such a village. Most of the great trees and natural cover have been preserved, and just enough clearing done to make the roadways. The Society is divided into two branches, the Western Academy of Beaux Arts and the Beaux Arts Workshop: the former having for its aim the educational features and the latter the industrial features and business management. The educational work has been planned along the lines similar to the Chautauqua but confined to arts and crafts work only. The workshop is for the practical demonstration of this study. The work so far has been confined to establishing the village and to putting the institution on a firm financial basis. A magazine to further advance the Beaux Arts idea will soon be published at the village. Workshops are being planned, and there is no doubt that this will be, before long, one of the most interesting places in the West. The establishment of such a village will lead to a greater interest in home building. Gardening and outdoor life will lead to a greater happiness and pleasure in life.[10]

During this period, houses in the Craftsman style began to rise on half-acre lots in the village's woodland setting. The settlement had 1,000 feet of waterfront dedicated to a community park; plans were prepared for studios, workshops, and a community center. Calvert and Renfro were the first to build rustic woodland chalets, and other members followed suit. Unfortunately, Beaux Arts Village soon lost its focus as its "artists" commuted by ferry to Seattle for their 8 a.m. to 5 p.m. jobs, and the workshops, studios, and community centers remained unrealized. The dream altered quickly once the ideals of the bohemian life of the artist were tested against the realities of daily life and making a living.

European Ideas Take Root

Ideas emerging in other countries also found acknowledgment and imitation in the Pacific Northwest. The German word *Gesamtkunstwerk*, in use at the time, described interiors that share a common design vocabulary and provide a sense of ensemble and harmony throughout—a total work of art. The unified interiors of Scottish architect and designer Charles Rennie Mackintosh (1868–1928) were hugely popular on the Continent; they had been exhibited in Vienna and Turin and published in *Die Kunst, Deutsche Kunst und Dekoration, Moderne Bauformen*, the *Studio*, and other art journals. Spokane architect Kirtland Cutter's (1860–1939) exposure to such periodicals must account for the remarkable Glasgow School–inspired interiors he lavished on the ladies' retiring room, one of a complex of restaurant and entertainment rooms, and a private suite designed for Louis Davenport's Pennington Hotel (later called the Davenport Hotel) from the late 1890s, with major improvements in 1903–1904. Similarly, the fame of Mrs. Cranston's Glasgow tea

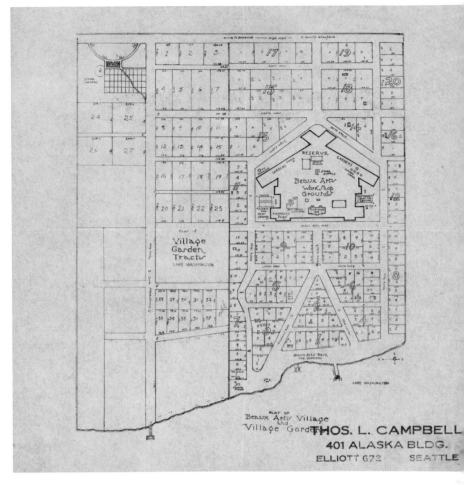

[above] A rendering of a Swiss Chalet–inspired Arts and Crafts home fostered the type of dwelling that fit the Northwest wooded setting of Beaux Arts Village. Eastside Heritage Center (Bellevue).

[above right] The plan of Beaux Arts Village and Village Gardens (1909) shows the workshop grounds laid out in the form of the iconic Beaux Arts emblem and cottage. Eastside Heritage Center (Bellevue).

[right] The ladies' retiring room adjoining Louis Davenport's suite in the Davenport Hotel (c. 1904), Spokane, reveals Kirtland Cutter's borrowing of then popular Glasgow School designs for stylized roses in stained and leaded glass and also for wall and ceiling stencil designs. *Western Architect* (September 1908). Northwest Museum of Arts & Culture, Eastern Washington State Historical Society (Spokane), L84-207.4-31.

[above left] The Frederick & Nelson department store writing room echoed Glasgow School and British Arts and Crafts designs, c. 1910. Special Collections Division, UW 26469z, University of Washington Libraries (Seattle).

[center] The living room of Louis Davenport's private suite (c. 1904), Davenport Hotel, Spokane, Washington. The mantel clock was by Albin Müller, a leading Darmstadt Colony artist. *Western Architect* (September 1908). Mason Collection.

[left] Louis Davenport's private dining room (c. 1904), Davenport Hotel, Spokane, Washington, combined custom woodwork, stained glass, and metalwork. Simple geometries with conventionalized floral designs were tied to stained glass cabinetry and wall stencils. *Western Architect* (September 1908). Northwest Museum of Arts & Culture, Eastern Washington State Historical Society (Spokane), L87-1.5915X-11.

[above] Austrian Secession–inspired terra-cotta embellishments with blue glass tile inserts crown the Seward Hotel, Portland (1908–1909). Photograph by Lawrence Kreisman.

rooms and British Arts and Crafts design assuredly inspired the white painted woodwork and cutouts in the tea room and writing room at the Frederick & Nelson department store on Second Avenue in downtown Seattle.

The works of Germany's active Darmstadt Art Colony and Austria's Wiener Werkstätte, modeled after Ashbee's Guild, also were well known through periodicals and exhibitions. The German and Austro-Hungarian exhibits at the 1904 Louisiana Purchase Exposition in St. Louis offered Americans some of their first actual glimpses of Secession design, the word coined to refer to a group of artists who rejected the conservative traditional arts community and sought to develop and exhibit new art that acknowledged changes in society and lifestyle. The new style was striking in its simplicity, its stylization of natural imagery and attraction to geometry of form, its application of industrial techniques in manufacture, and its effort to develop unified and harmonious environments.

Louis Davenport may have accompanied Kirtland Cutter to the St. Louis Fair and been smitten by the designs of the Germans. He purchased an important clock designed by Albin Müller of the Darmstadt Art Colony, which was on display at the fair. It was the focal point of the fireplace in his private suite above the restaurant in the Davenport Hotel. The remarkably stylish rooms of his quarters were paneled with carved wood inspired by nature, with colored glass stylized roses inset in the doors. The fireplace had a hand-beaten copper hood and stylized copper trees and branches. Lighting fixtures were from Stickley's Craftsman Workshop, complemented by a Tiffany standing lamp. Furniture by Gustav Stickley and by Charles Limbert filled the apartment's large living and dining spaces, open to the street through semiround arched windows with stylized rose leaded glass borders. That, along with the hotel's ladies' retiring room, made Davenport's establishment a showcase for current European and American design ideas.

German and Austrian design was not commonplace in Pacific Northwest cities, though Portland and Seattle restaurants in hotels and department stores were furnished with bentwood chairs likely manufactured by the firm of Thonet or Jacob and Josef Kohn and imported to America in great quantity. In Portland, architect William Knighton (1864–1938) was inspired by Austrian designs in his terra-cotta detailing of the Seward Hotel and its splendid mosaics and stained glass. In his writings, he acknowledged the groundbreaking work of the founders of the Vienna Secession (1897–1918) and their efforts to develop a new nonhistoricist approach to design, a "superb, new ornamental vocabulary that was purely Viennese: spare, compartmentalized, geometric, and bending the serpentine art nouveau line into Secessionist right angles."[11] Immigrants from western and northern Europe who settled in the region brought with them both skills and design ideas from their native land. They became the builders, cabinetmakers, metalsmiths, and tile and glass fabricators whose work defined early twentieth-century towns and cities.

Made by Hand by Native Americans

At the turn of the twentieth century, Northwesterners joined other Americans elsewhere in having heightened regard for the indigenous peoples who were thought to be disappearing in the rapidly developing western frontier. The material culture of the Native tribes reflected indigenous Arts and Crafts ideals, true to the spirit of the Arts and Crafts movement—useful handmade objects of simplicity and beauty. These handicrafts began to be collected and studied.

Period photographs show Northwest Indian women selling basketry items on the sidewalks of Seattle, Spokane, and Portland; at fairs, expositions, and holiday festivities; and on their respective reservations during special celebration days. Indians would have sold their basketry and beadwork at the Pendleton Roundup in eastern Oregon, the interstate fairs in Spokane, the Potlatch parades in Seattle, Fourth of July celebrations, and powwows on any of the Northwest reservations.

The Euro-American's fascination with Native American handcrafted items at the turn of the twentieth century was filled with irony. From the 1840s through the 1880s, many early Anglo settlers in Oregon and Washington perceived the Indians as primitive, childlike peoples who should be contained and/or "converted" to a more "civilized" lifestyle. The U.S. governmental policy of placing Indians on reservations, in the minds of some, eliminated the "threat" of everyday encounter.

With this forced distance came the beginning of a revised public opinion. Artistic and literary expressions of the "Vanishing Race" or the "End of the Trail" addressed with poignancy a perceived dying off of American Indian cultures. Coupled with the disenchantment of many Americans with the tired clutter of the Victorian era and the production of machine-made, mass-produced goods of low quality, the new perception—that perhaps America was losing its purist link to the true

spirit of the Arts and Crafts ideal—helped spark a new appreciation and desire for American Indian handcrafted objects.

In the High Plateau country of eastern Washington and Oregon, this new demand prompted resurgence in the creation of Native baskets, cornhusk weaving, and beaded bags. People living in Salem and Eugene would go to the coast to buy Siletz baskets. Indian women of the Grand Ronde reservation would walk to towns to sell their basketry. Seattle-area collectors traveled to the Makah reservation on the Olympic Peninsula to purchase "made for the trade" baskets. Makah and Quileute basket makers were often seen in Seattle selling their trade or "trinket" baskets.

Consequently, while there was a governmental and religious push for the Indians to abandon their traditional ways, there was a parallel popular desire to acquire their elegant and carefully crafted objects. This strong interest in their art actually helped keep alive many traditions of Indian tribes in Oregon and Washington, as well as in other regions of the country.

Craftsman magazine, Seattle's own *Bungalow Magazine*, and other popular periodicals of the early twentieth century that espoused the Arts and Crafts movement featured illustrations of Washington and Oregon house interiors decorated with Indian baskets, rugs, pottery, and masks. American Indian objects also became part of expected decor in the lobbies of many early rustic lodges, inns, and hotels not only nationally but also in the Cascade Range and Olympic Mountains, along Puget Sound, or on the shores of the Pacific Coast. In Washington and Oregon, where

[top] Indian basket weavers were frequently seen on Seattle streets selling their wares to the growing citizenry. This photo was taken in front of the Frederick & Nelson department store, c. 1910. PEMCO Webster & Stevens Collection, Museum of History and Industry (Seattle), 21,715.

[above] The billiard room of Frederick Stimson's Queen Anne Hill house in Seattle (c. 1904) was decked out with Indian baskets and Navajo rugs. *Western Architect* (1906).

B. B. Rich Curio Store, Portland, Oregon

VISIT YE OLDE CURIOSITY SHOP   EST'D 1899

MOST UNIQUE SHOP IN THE WORLD

1—Whale Jaw Bones, 1 ton each, 21½ feet, largest in U. S.
2—Skull of Alaska Buffalo, largest in the world.
3—Giant Clam Shell, weighs 161 pounds. From Equator.
4—Ivory Tusk of Alaska Elephant (mammoth).
5—Head of Arctic Walrus with ivory tusks
6—Shell, 855 pounds, fired from U. S. Fort Worden.
7—Navajo Rugs, from Navajo Indians.
8—Indian Totem Poles.
9—Saw of a Saw Fish.
10—Indian Cooking Basket.
11—Old Ship Lanterns, brass.
12—Hat worn by Chief Seattle.
13—Alaska Snail, petrified, 67 pounds.
14—Chilcat Blanket from Alaska.

GROUND FLOOR AT COLMAN DOCK ENTRANCE, SEATTLE

[top] The B. B. Rich Curio Store in Portland was stocked floor to ceiling with American Indian goods in expectation of tourist demands related to the Lewis and Clark Centennial Exposition in 1905. Mason Collection.

[above] Ye Olde Curiosity Shop on the Seattle waterfront was a significant retail outlet for Northwest Coast Indian art, seen here c. 1915. Mason Collection.

there were many Native tribes and many art-producing residents, ample opportunities existed for enthusiasts to acquire Indian objects for their Arts and Crafts–inspired interiors.

As Indian craftspeople worked to accommodate demand for their handiwork, their designs began to change. Appearance, rather than function, became paramount. Baskets and woven bags were not going to be used to hold berries or other items; instead, they were going to be displayed on Mission furniture in an Arts and Crafts bungalow or Craftsman house.

To a degree, the buying public influenced designs. There is some evidence that transfer patterns and tracings similar to those used by china painters, leatherworkers, and embroidery workers of the period were adopted as patterns for weaving or beadwork. So at the same time as interest in the handcrafts of the American Indian grew, Indian weavers and bead workers were often adapting conventional, stylized designs that could be found in various sources, including women's magazines. In addition, the availability of new materials (tools, cloth, beads, dyes, paints) influenced their work.

Because of Seattle's role as the distribution point for supplying the Alaska gold rush in the late nineteenth century, many Americans were exposed to the distinctive, often powerful handiwork of the Pacific Northwest Coast Indian peoples all the way up to Alaska. Ye Olde Curiosity Shop, established in 1899 on Seattle's waterfront by Joseph Edward Standley, sold Alaskan and coastal totem poles, masks, and baskets to thousands of tourists, and also to museums, including the Smithsonian.

Soon, polychromed Northwest Coast totem poles, objects of carved horn and fossil ivory, and intricately woven Chilkat blankets began to find their places in the decorating schemes of Arts and Crafts–inspired interiors in the Northwest, along with the work of the local indigenous peoples. Seattle, in particular, seemed to be enamored with Indian objects from the Canadian coast and Alaska. The Alaskan totem pole in Seattle's Pioneer Square became a symbol for the city almost a decade before the Alaska-Yukon-Pacific Exposition of 1909 took place.

Coming of Age with the World's Fairs

The World's Columbian Exposition of 1893 in Chicago gave the Pacific Northwest a venue for showcasing its rugged individuality, abundant natural resources, surviving Native culture, and increasing sophistication. This grand exposition was largely engineered by Chicago architect and city planner Daniel Burnham and other architects who promoted the Classical style. It fostered fairs in other cities, bringing in a new age referred to as the "City Beautiful," in which architecture was thought of more broadly, in terms of urban planning and civic design to formulate modern cities for the twentieth century. As fairs materialized, so, too, did "City Beautiful" plans that encouraged far-reaching physical changes to existing cities. Among these were Seattle's Bogue Plan of 1911 and Portland's City Beautiful Plan, the latter initially involving Burnham and completed by E. H. Bennett in 1912.

Within this environment, the two design reform movements—City Beautiful and Arts and Crafts—found voice in the Pacific North-

M. H. Whitehouse's watercolor of the Arch of Titus in Rome served as the frontispiece to the First Annual Exhibition of the Portland Architectural Club in 1908. While the subject was Classical, the stylized, flat, graphic approach to forms was typical of the Arts and Crafts style. Dennis Andersen Collection.

west during the first quarter of the century. Both were grounded in principles of beauty and artistry as a cure for the rampant unstructured growth of cities. And both were reacting to the unprecedented growth in industry and mechanization and its subsequent impact on the environment. The design vocabulary being promoted may have differed—Beaux Arts eclecticism versus rustic vernacular—but the similar intent was to formulate harmony, dignity, and contextual sympathy in buildings and civic pride in their use. A critical part of both movements acknowledged setting aside significant parks for rest, recreation, and breathing space before the opportunities disappeared.

Since City Beautiful plans were mammoth, costly, and required both a supportive govern-

ment and an approving public willing to be taxed significantly, few of the plans were realized. By contrast, Arts and Crafts reform was capable of proceeding in small increments, beginning with individual artisans and growing through support groups of like-minded individuals within emerging membership organizations. The short-lived but ground-breaking Guild of Arts and Crafts of San Francisco was established in 1894 to encourage "an artistic standard in the future architecture" of the city.[12] Its members and supporters included design professionals whose residential work embraced the call for simplicity, honest materials and construction, and the revival of handicraft. The Boston Society of Arts and Crafts was founded shortly afterward, in 1897, followed by societies in Chicago, New York, Minneapolis, and Detroit. Within a decade, hundreds of societies had formed and were exploring Arts and Crafts ideals and products through exhibitions, salesrooms, periodicals, and classes. A National League of Handicrafts was established in 1908 that comprised twenty-three crafts societies, including one in Portland, Oregon.

The proliferation of Arts and Crafts societies was also occurring north of the border in Canada, most likely the result of the British training of many of its leading architects and design professionals. Through the efforts of R. Mackay Fripp, a fellow of the Royal Institute of British Architects, in 1900 the Vancouver Art Workers' Guild became the Vancouver Arts and Crafts Association. Members of the association held annual exhibitions and sales of work and conducted art classes throughout the year. The Island Arts Club, formed in Victoria on Vancouver Island, British Columbia, in 1909, had the purpose of promoting the development of Arts and Crafts by sponsoring exhibits. The society changed its name to the Island Arts and Crafts Club in 1912. The Provincial Arts and Industrial Institute was formed in 1919 to promote Arts and Crafts in British Columbia, with a focus on the application of craftsmanship to industrial uses. The two groups merged in 1922 under a new name, the Island Arts and Crafts Society. In 1951, this long-lived group became the Victoria Sketch Club.

The British Columbia Art League was incorporated in 1920. The league was committed to the encouragement of art in Vancouver and to the acquisition of an art school and an art gallery for the city. In 1921, arrangements were made with the B.C. Manufacturers Association to stage exhibitions and to house collections that would form the nucleus of a permanent art gallery. In 1925, the Commercial Arts and Crafts School was established, and in 1931 the Vancouver Art Gallery opened. East of Vancouver, in nearby New Westminster, the Fellowship of the Arts was formed in 1914 to promote the appreciation of literature, arts, and crafts. The Fellowship continued to operate until 1968.[13]

Through these means, tastemakers, artisans, and reformers introduced Craftsman ideals to the public. In her excellent study *Art and Labor: Ruskin, Morris, and the Craftsman Ideal in America*, Eileen Boris points out that in American hands, what had been an idealistic movement shifted quickly to commercial exploitation. Early exhibits in Boston and Chicago displayed English examples as well as diverse styles—Medieval, Colonial, peasant, and Native American—all claiming roots in Ruskin and Morris. Crafts societies, workshops, and department store show-

Handcrafted lettering and a ceramic flower vase are elements that tied the bookplate of the Arts and Crafts Society of Portland, organized in 1907, to its mission. Mason Collection.

rooms brought producers and consumers together; they served simultaneously as art exhibits and commercial ventures. Even traditional forms of basketry, weaving, furniture, and pottery became commodities for the tourist trade, a transformation of the Craftsman ideal that also distinguished the New Deal revival of handicraft. Meanwhile, a wide diversity of printed materials carried messages of Ruskin, Morris, and true craftsmanship into twentieth-century America.[14]

Boris hints at why some local guilds and societies eventually failed. While originally organized by professional artists, architects, and art workers, their popularity drew many more members, from amateurs and dues-paying "associates" or patrons, than had the original English crafts groups.[15] Those who pas-

[top] A birds-eye view of the Alaska-Yukon-Pacific Exposition (1909), Seattle, reveals grand axial vistas and the extensive site plan. Several important buildings were retained after the fair to serve the University of Washington. Special Collections Division, University of Washington Libraries (Seattle), Nowell x4000.

[above] Kirtland Cutter's remodel of the Pennington Hotel for Louis Davenport (1900), Spokane, turned a simple building into an exotic Mission Revival–style hacienda with distinctive tile roofs and stepped gables. A 1904 addition (far left) included the signature clock tower, seen here in 1907. The ground floor held a restaurant. The semiround leaded windows on the second floor defined Louis Davenport's private suite of rooms. Northwest Museum of Arts & Culture, Eastern Washington State Historical Society (Spokane), L87-1.2316-09.

sively attended shows and lectures but did not produce products themselves eclipsed the number of actual art workers.

The 1905 Lewis and Clark Centennial Exposition in Portland and the 1909 Alaska-Yukon-Pacific Exposition in Seattle spread Arts and Crafts ideas throughout the Northwest in their exhibits by national and regional artists and craftspeople. The exposition buildings themselves set the stage: in general, they were modeled after the Classicism of the 1893 Chicago fair, but some of the pavilions suggested regional sources. The dramatic forestry buildings at both Portland and Seattle's fairs were constructed of indigenous materials and used visible construction techniques, in spite of the fact that they were designed by architects more closely associated with Beaux Arts commercial and civic buildings—Whidden and Lewis in Portland and Saunders and Lawton in Seattle.

The development of other historic architectural styles, such as the Mission style, also prompted architects to think about what building forms were suitable for the West Coast. Mission forms were explored at the California Midwinter International Exposition held in San Francisco in 1894. As early as 1895, the Mission style appeared, along with the Italian Romanesque, in the walled courtyard and simple stucco façade of San Francisco's Swedenborgian Church, designed in the office of A. Page Brown in collaboration with the Reverend Joseph Worcester. The rustic, intimate interior was highly influential in Arts and Crafts circles, with its simple redwood wainscoting, rough-cut madrona posts and arched supports, and painted landscape friezes. Its straightforward chairs became the

The Nikko Palace Café was a popular gathering place at the Alaska-Yukon-Pacific Exposition in Seattle, 1909. Special Collections Division, University of Washington Libraries (Seattle), Nowell x2994.

prototype for ubiquitous Mission furniture for decades to come.[16]

While never a prevalent design form in the Pacific Northwest, Mission's cement stucco walls, red tiled roofs, and distinctive cornices found expression in a number of churches, schools, city and county buildings, and libraries throughout Washington and Oregon. A prominent early example was Kirtland Cutter's remodel of the Pennington Hotel in 1900 for Louis Davenport of Spokane. What could have been more exotic and evocative for Inland Empire residents than the promise of endless sunshine and warmth that went hand in hand with the Mission style and the fragrance of orange blossoms from potted orange trees edging the building?

Japanese pavilions and teahouses were particular hits at both the Seattle and Portland

[top] Kirtland Cutter's love of Swiss Chalet forms is evident in the design of his own residence, Chalet Hohenstein, Spokane (1887, expanded 1906). Kirtland K. Cutter Collection, Ms. 49. Northwest Museum of Arts & Culture, Eastern Washington State Historical Society (Spokane).

[above] Willatsen and Byrne's house (1914) for the J. C. Black family of Seattle's Queen Anne Hill epitomized Prairie School design principles in its bands of windows and sheltering roof forms. Dennis Andersen Collection.

fairs; they inspired broad appreciation of Far Eastern design. Their simplicity, the implied outdoor and indoor connections, and the surrounding romantic landscape caught the eye of many architects who applied these features to Oriental bungalows with upturned gable ends and wisteria-covered porches. Japanese architecture also inspired the design of civic and commercial buildings, ranging from a YWCA building on the shore of Puget Sound to the streetcar station house at Point Defiance Park in Tacoma to the Tokyo Apartments in Spokane.

Seeking Regional Expression for Architecture and the Applied Arts

The qualities of rustic simplicity, native materials, and hand-built character, as expressed in the forestry buildings at the two fairs, fed the public's interest in vernacular regionalism. This expression was realized in informal entertainment pavilions, summer cottages, and more substantial town houses throughout the area. At the close of the nineteenth and the beginning of the twentieth centuries, regional architects and designers found a large client base drawn to Arts and Crafts design. The aesthetics of the movement stimulated the development of elite residential enclaves for the wealthy and more democratic streetcar suburbs for first-time homebuyers in growing cities, small towns, and rural farms.

Spokane architect Kirtland Cutter's 1887 Spokane home, Chalet Hohenstein, likely inspired the informal vernacular of the Swiss Chalet style of his Idaho Building at the Chicago fair in 1893 and the more sophisticated 1909 Seattle Golf and Country Club in the Highlands gated community. Just back from a trip to Switzerland, Midwest-born Seattle

One family's moving day to its handmade river rock bungalow in the Spokane Valley involved the help of friends and family with available wagons. In the foreground were the leftover stones from the building project. Northwest Museum of Arts & Culture, Eastern Washington State Historical Society (Spokane), L87-1.2109-08.

architect Ellsworth Storey took some ideas from the vernacular Chalet style—but less slavishly than Cutter had done in Spokane—to design two connected houses for his family and his parents. Local river rock and wood shingles, deep roof overhangs, and ribbon windows with his signature cross or angled mullions became distinctive Storey features in many commissions.

Seattle architect Eben Sankey's approach to the design of the house for Captain John Boyer in the city's Montlake neighborhood also incorporated local materials, but in a more robust manner that recalled Richardsonian Romanesque. Massive granite walls with half-timbering and overhanging roofs made for a dramatic composition, which was embellished within by Batchelder and Mercer tile fireplace surrounds in the living and dining rooms.

In Portland, architects Wade Hampton Pipes, Emil Schacht, Ellis Lawrence, and William Knighton designed substantial and sophisticated houses that interpreted the British and the American Arts and Crafts visions in well-to-do residential districts. An excellent example of nonhistorical residential architecture, Francis Brown's design of a house for Wilbur Reid in 1914, reflected Portland's response to the ultimate California bungalows of Greene and Greene. And at the same time as architects Andrew Willatsen and Barry Byrne were doing their signature Prairie School works in Seattle and the Highlands, influenced by their apprenticeship in Chicago architect Frank Lloyd Wright's Oak Park studio, the Portland firm of Bennes Hendricks and Thompson was doing Prairie houses for clients Marcus Delahunt and Aaron Maegley. But specially commissioned, architect-designed residences on this order were only a small segment of a growing industry.

For rich and poor alike, a new American vernacular domestic architectural vocabulary arose to answer the question "What does 'home' mean?" With streetcar lines making it

The *Ladies Home Journal* magazines on the lower shelf of the Mission library table may have inspired the owners of this Spokane residence. Mason Collection. Photograph by W. O. Reed.

possible for people to move farther away from the industrial and commercial areas, fortunes were being made in single-family real estate development. Evocative promotional brochures, such as those for Healy Heights in Portland and Boulevard Park in Spokane, were persuasive. In this new niche, the bungalow found a perfect fit. A broad range of bungalows and Craftsman houses arose in city and suburb and in rural countryside throughout the Northwest. Many of them were complete with characteristic built-in cabinets, Mission furniture, hammered metal lighting fixtures, stenciled walls, and embroidered table covers. In every community, the "American Dream" came to be represented by the Craftsman bungalow, as family after family moved into Arts and Crafts houses.

Coinciding with this period of growth, expansion, and homebuilding, home decoration became legitimized as the activity where domestic science and aesthetics met. A new academic discipline arose for women—home economics—with a focus on teaching art and utility in the home. Home decorating magazines met a growing interest on the part of middle-class women for information and advice. *House Beautiful*, founded 1896, reached a 1906 circulation of 40,000. *Ladies Home Journal* claimed over one million subscribers, featuring house and room designs by Will Bradley, Frank Lloyd Wright, and others influenced by the Arts and Crafts style.[17] The local libraries subscribed to these and other of the nation's most popular magazines, including Gustav Stickley's *Craftsman*. Despite Stickley's belief that his magazine and workshop were the trendsetters during this period, he did have competitors.

Pacific Northwest residents did not need to go to Stickley or to the leading national magazines when they had Seattle architect Jud Yoho and his competitors in their midst. *Bungalow Magazine* was published by Yoho, Seattle's self-proclaimed "Bungalow Craftsman," from 1912 to 1918. Yoho practiced what he preached, living in a 1911 bungalow of his own design in the Wallingford neighborhood. His magazine offered a bungalow a month, with complete working drawings. The periodical helped promote Yoho's construction firm, Craftsman Bungalow Company. In fact, Gustav Stickley threatened to sue Yoho if he did not change the company name, because people might confuse his enterprise with Stickley's own Craftsman Workshop.

Yoho had plenty of competition in the plan-book building industry, including Frank Cruse's Seattle Building and Investment Company, as well as the offices of Victor Voorhees, Frank Fehren, and W. W. DeLong. In Portland, the general public could choose bungalow plans from Roberts & Roberts Plan

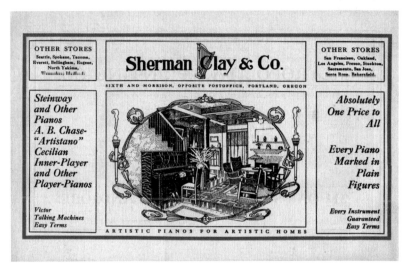

Books, Bungalow Book Publishing Company, Millmade Construction Company, and many others. Hyslop and Wescott, Chamberlin, and the Ballard Plannery were dominant companies in Spokane. And in Eugene, architect D. L. Harden published his own plan book.

Regional plan books were adapted to the hilly topography and cooler climate of the Northwest. Thousands of houses built from these plans, most of them between 1910 and 1930, share features with their counterparts elsewhere in the country: straightforward lines, simple finishes, informal plans, and the use of local materials.

Advertising was an important aspect in selling Arts and Crafts ideas and products nationwide. Seattle's Frederick & Nelson advertised a Bungalow line of furniture in June 1913. There were several local furniture companies, too, including Empire in Seattle, Carman Manufacturing Company in Seattle, Tacoma, Spokane, and Portland, F. S. Har-

[top left] During its first year of publication, *Bungalow Magazine*'s cover uses stylized potted roses and a bungalow landscape from English and European Arts and Crafts imagery that was popular in America by 1912. Seattle Room, Seattle Public Library.

[top right] Portlander E. A. Roberts produced his *Roberts Home Builder* catalog of house plans in 1909. Mason Collection.

[above] A Sherman Clay advertisement in *Roberts Home Builder* (1909) displays a Mission-style oak upright piano in a living room with other appropriate Arts and Crafts furnishings. Mason Collection.

A rendering by Bellingham architects William Cox and F. S. Piper for the Kulshan Club (1906) shows a modified bungalow that takes advantage of a hillside location to include a substantial lower floor. J. W. Sandison Collection, Whatcom Museum of History and Art (Bellingham), 3662.

mon in Tacoma, and Oregon Chair Company in Portland, that could have accommodated furniture orders if purchasers were not buying Stickley, Limbert, or Roycroft items through the local outlets for these companies.

Tull & Gibbs (Portland and Spokane), Grote-Rankin (Seattle, Portland, and Spokane), and other retailers advertised nationally produced Arts and Crafts goods while continuing to carry reproductions of traditional furniture and late Victorian models for those not drawn to the aesthetics of domestic reform. In 1913, Seattle's Standard Furniture Company celebrated its anniversary with a Home Show and erected a full-scale model Craftsman bungalow complete with river rock features, in which to showcase its Mission and wicker lines.

Local businesses dealing with every aspect of interior furnishing profited from the domestic reforms of the Arts and Crafts movement stimulated by contemporary magazines and newspaper coverage. Seattle's Sherman Clay & Company advertised artistic pianos

for artistic homes. Built-ins and disappearing beds joined the furniture market as space savers in new houses.

While Arts and Crafts forms, interiors, and furnishings were most closely identified with private homes, they made their way successfully into civic and commercial buildings, hotels, restaurants, clubs, libraries, transportation gateways, and churches. And it was not simply the major cities that embraced the vocabulary. The Craftsman aesthetic inspired community clubs in Bellingham, Washington, and Baker, Oregon, and seemed a perfect fit for the Pilot Butte Inn in Bend, Oregon, and the White Pelican Hotel in Klamath Falls, Oregon. It was the natural choice for lumber company offices in Onalaska and Winlock, Washington, and found its way into the design of large buildings and small—the natatorium in Tacoma and restrooms at the Oregon State Fairgrounds in Salem.

The geographical diversity of Oregon and Washington lends itself to a variety of outdoor recreational and leisure activities. Inspired by the rustic wood structure and furnishings of Old Faithful Lodge in Yellowstone Park, numerous mountain and lakeside lodges were built with a similar aesthetic—national park structures such as Paradise Inn at Mount Rainier and Crater Lake Lodge. Many of these properties, outfitted with furniture in Mission or rustic Arts and Crafts manners and accented with Native American objects, epitomized the "total art" qualities Gustav Stickley or Elbert Hubbard would have appreciated.

The Northwest mountains, lakes, and seashore provided healthy environments away from the polluted city air for recovery from tuberculosis and other diseases of concern in

the period. Sanatoriums and health resorts were established, and small bungalows or cottages were constructed in forests and along the beaches and coastline. Bungalows were heavily promoted as the ideal solution for people wishing to escape the increasing pressures of urban life. In 1905, Zoe Kincaid, reporter for the *Seattle Mail and Herald,* poetically captured the value of this lifestyle: "People of moderate means build bungalows half hidden by the firs, and but a short distance from the salt water. Some of these homes are of logs and built upon a mountain slope that commands a sweeping view of the water—others are nestled among the shrubbery close down to the tide. To own five acres of woodland and a bungalow is to live a luxurious and independent life. Year after year the owners of the bungalows return to their homes in the woods. Their children grow straight as pines, learned in water, craft and wood lore. Brought up in the shadows of the mountains, they are taught to be true Westerners, men and women of right-living and thinking."[18]

[top right] Portland architect Emil Schacht designed an elaborately detailed bungalow (1907) for the Vaness Lumber Company in Winlock, Washington. It relied heavily on English Medieval-style forms. The open brackets under the barge boards created a half-timbered effect. Mason Collection.

[center] Arts and Crafts architecture and nature meet at Haystack Rock and Needles, Cannon Beach, Oregon (postcard, c. 1940). Mason Collection.

[bottom] W. J. Bernard's Alki Point estate, Fir Lodge, was an Arts and Crafts log bungalow with shingled dormers and a wraparound covered porch for enjoying the nearby water views. The chimney stonework was structurally honest, lightening as it rose from the substantial foundation. Special Collections, Washington State Historical Society (Tacoma), Curtis 5558B. Photograph by Asahel Curtis.

In design terms, the cumulative effects of the Arts and Crafts movement on the Pacific Northwest were significant. Builders no longer looked back romantically at a past not their own to inspire them. They embraced the technical adeptness and know-how that defined America in order to create affordable housing that satisfied the growing population of newly emerging communities. Arts and Crafts values suited the developing temperament of Pacific Northwest cities and towns and created a need that was answered by local craftspeople and industries. As thousands of public and private buildings were shaped by the Arts and Crafts philosophy, craftspeople were stimulated to develop suitable, non-historic furniture and furnishings that adhered to the mission that they be "useful and beautiful."

Artistic Enterprises

Many contemporary craftspeople belonged to societies formed around the ideals of the Arts and Crafts movement. In the Northwest, the Arts and Crafts Society of Portland, founded by Julia Hoffman and fellow Arts and Crafts enthusiasts, took center stage. Hoffman's passion for crafts and her professional connections in Boston led her to initiate a series of exhibitions featuring important American designer-craftspeople from the East and the Midwest. These exhibits included the work of a fledging group of regionally trained workers in metal, textiles, ceramics, leather, wood, and the like. The society also ran a sales shop, along with a regular schedule of exhibitions.

In Seattle, an artists' collective occupied rooms in the Boston Block as early as 1907. While most of the attention of these artists was given to drawing, painting, and sculpture, there were craftspeople among them, including metalworker and painter Jessie Fisken. The nearby Arcade block became home to another group of artists and to the Beaux Arts Institute. But it was the Woman's Century Club that was able to present the work of local artists and craftspeople at its annual Arts and Crafts exhibitions in its clubhouse on Harvard Avenue and, in 1909, in the Manufacturers Building at the Alaska-Yukon-Pacific Exposition. Another arts group, the Fine Arts Society (the forerunner of the Seattle Art Museum), also organized exhibits at the Seattle Public Library Gallery and at William Kellogg's tile showroom. One of the most original of Seattle's art workers was metalsmith Albert Berry, who moved to Seattle from Alaska to open a downtown shop where he displayed and sold his unique hammered copper lamps and accessories adorned with carved pieces of fossil walrus or mammoth tusks.

In eastern Washington, the Spokane Art League trained young people and promoted exhibits of local art and craftwork. In smaller cities, such as Bend, Grants Pass, and Marshfield, arts workers followed the lead of the Portland group by opening art shops.

Many local fine artists and craftspeople received their training in established programs in New York City, Boston, or Chicago under such important artists-instructors as Kenyon Cox, Frank V. DuMond, and Arthur Wesley Dow. When they returned to the Northwest to practice and teach, they introduced these new design ideas to the next generation of creative people.

Regional distributors of tile assured that the work of the most significant American companies was shown and promoted throughout the Northwest. The Kellogg showroom in Seattle

was a major supplier of Rookwood, Grueby, Batchelder, and Mercer tile. The company designed fireplaces, with compositions ranging from typical matte green surrounds with fir tree motifs to Rookwood commissions for special items, such as views of Mount Hood for the Hotel Oregon in Portland or of Mount Rainier for the New Washington Hotel in Seattle. Fred Wagner's studio in Portland also did design and tile installation work far and wide. Ceramic artists applied their craft at Washington Brick, Lime & Sewer Company near Spokane, which produced a line of art tile closely resembling Los Angeles tile maker Ernest Batchelder's products. There were also pottery companies, such as Pacific Stoneware Company in Portland and Clayton Standard Stoneware in eastern Washington.

Edward Bruns in Portland specialized in Arts and Crafts glass designs. The larger firms of Povey Brothers and, in Seattle, C. C. Belknap and Raymond Nyson also provided art glass for homes, churches, and commercial buildings.

[top] Women at Franklin School, Seattle (c. 1914), were occupied with various applied arts projects, including stenciling on textiles, and hand-building ceramic forms. On display behind them were handmade ceramic and metal items and stenciled pillowcases and runners. Special Collections, Washington State Historical Society (Tacoma), Curtis 29982. Photograph by Asahel Curtis.

[above] "The Heart of Reason, The Flame of Soul" banners frame a bucolic view of Mount Hood seen from the Willamette River. This Rookwood tile installation commissioned by the Hotel Oregon, Portland, and designed by William Kellogg was shown at the 1910 Pacific Architectural League Exhibition. Dennis Andersen Collection.

Bungalow Magazine (May 1913), in "For the Amateur Craftsman," featured a library table with working drawings by student M. W. Patten under the direction of Charles McNabney, the manual arts instructor at Queen Anne High School, Seattle. The table and a lamp by Patten brought Mission-style furnishings into the family's Victorian era parlor. Courtesy of Kristine Sproul.

Book designer Will Ransom brought the spirit of Roycroft to his short-lived Snohomish venture, the Handcraft Press, in 1901. While the Northwest was not a center for hand-press publishing, various printing firms in Washington and Oregon incorporated Arts and Crafts typography and design in their production work, even producing mottos of which Elbert Hubbard might have been proud.

Most of Washington and Oregon's design professionals did not gain national recognition, with the rare exception of entrepreneurs on the order of Jud Yoho, whose publications and catalogs reached well beyond the borders of the Pacific states, or W. W. Kellogg and Edward Bruns, whose Seattle and Portland studios did commissions throughout the Pacific and Mountain West, or a small group of artists and photographers, such as Edward S. Curtis and Myra Wiggins. In their time, regional craftspeople such as metalworkers John Nelson Wisner and Albert Berry were well known and featured in the local press; their talent and fame, however, remained a secret shared by the small and dedicated arts communities in which they functioned.

Nevertheless, the Pacific Northwest did play a highly significant role in disseminating information on the Arts and Crafts movement, displaying the most important producers of work in America at its fairs and in its art galleries, and advertising and selling these wares in its shops and department stores. School children of the region were brought up with a respect for handwork and with skills that would serve them well in building houses, making furniture, and shaping metalwork, or doing embroidery, china painting, jewelry, and basketry. Furthermore, a vibrant arts community banded together to support one another, to learn the latest methods of working in clay, metal, glass, and wood, and to produce work that was often on an equal footing with work of important craftspeople in the Midwest, the East, and in California.

TWO
Expositions Open the World to the Northwest

THROUGHOUT THE PACIFIC NORTHWEST, individual experiences in business and social interactions, as well as increasing opportunities to travel outside their own communities, broadened people's knowledge of culture and the arts. Newcomers from Europe, Asia, the American East, Midwest, and California brought with them ethnic and cultural traditions, education, and skills that they shared with their adopted communities. The increasing number of national and regional expositions and the concurrent coverage of these in the press stimulated many people in small towns and large cities to reevaluate their own participation in the economic and cultural developments shaping the twentieth century.

Great Britain's 1851 Great Exposition in London and subsequent fairs in other nations brought forward what were thought to be the most important achievements of the time. The centennial of our country, celebrated with a monumental fair in Philadelphia in 1876, the Centennial Exhibition, signaled the start of a series of

John Paxton's Crystal Palace built for the 1851 Great Exposition in London set the stage for larger and even more elaborate world's fairs in Great Britain, Europe, and America.

great expositions that invited foreign participation but, at heart, were designed to focus attention and excitement on the extraordinary accomplishments of American industry. These expositions were the ultimate in civic boosterism, as witnessed by the number of cities that mounted them.[1]

The 1904 Louisiana Purchase Exposition in St. Louis set the stage for a decade of stellar events. A successful exposition was held in Portland, Oregon, in 1905 to commemorate Lewis and Clark's achievement a century before. The Alaska-Yukon-Pacific Exposition opened in Seattle, Washington, in 1909, followed by the Panama-Pacific International Exposition in San Francisco and the Panama-California Exposition in San Diego, both held in 1915.

Preparing the Northwest Stage

From the 1870s on, many communities in the Pacific Northwest mounted yearly agricultural and county fairs in which handicrafts, furniture making, textiles, and even some decorative oil paintings and watercolors were displayed and awards given. This focus and acknowledgment reflected a growing American middle-class culture heavily oriented toward the domestic and the practical. Domestic arts—handicrafts, fashion, interior decoration, weaving, home economics, and sanitation—were promoted through popular magazines as the women's rights movement grew and found fertile ground in newly developing cities and towns.

In addition, regional expositions were organized to showcase local technological, agricultural, and industrial progress, such as Spokane's North-Western Industrial Exposition of 1890. Domestic reform went hand in hand with technological advances, convenient appliances, and diminishing reliance on servants. The growing middle class aspired to affordable family housing and was encouraged by the many new options available to them. Art and handicraft displays were included in regional expositions, providing important education to a new crop of potential homebuilders and buyers.[2]

While these regional expositions were far more sophisticated than the more common county fair, they could not match the expansive nature of the glittering pavilions and grand boulevards that characterized the world's fairs to come. Those spectacular fairs, from a design standpoint, reflected remarkable efforts to push America away from its rudimentary pioneer image. They encouraged a new definition of architecture based on Greco-Roman traditions of harmony, symmetry, and uniformity of character, and represented the City Beautiful aspirations of its planners. As a result, these expositions inspired a generation of dignified, classically designed civic and commercial architecture in cities throughout America. Washington and Oregon cities followed the lead of the East Coast and the Midwest in adhering to Classicism in their skyscrapers, business blocks, schools, and libraries during the first quarter of the twentieth century.

Within the borders of each classically inspired city within a city, each exposition sought to achieve something else: indigenous design to define distinctive characteristics of the local environment, geography, and earlier settlement patterns. For example, California interpreted its Spanish Mission past in romantic red-tiled and stucco buildings that beckoned visitors.

Kirtland Cutter's Idaho State Building was built for the World's Columbian Exposition in Chicago, 1893. Kirtland K. Cutter Collection, Mo. 49. Northwest Museum of Arts & Culture, Eastern Washington State Historical Society (Spokane).

For the newly formed states on the West Coast, national and international expositions were a particularly important opportunity to acquaint people elsewhere in the nation with the virtues of settling and bringing business to this corner of the world. Despite the huge commitment of funds required by states to have a presence at a world's fair, Washington, Idaho, and Montana built buildings at the World's Columbian Exposition in Chicago in 1893. Spokane architect Kirtland Cutter showed off his personal interest in vernacular buildings derived from the Swiss Chalet tradition in the Idaho State Building, a rustic log chalet for which he created custom-designed decorative fixtures, ironwork, and furniture. Warren Skillings (1860–1939), a newcomer to Seattle from New England, designed a Washington State Building, which acknowledged the timber resources that had already brought many eastern and midwestern lumbermen west. From a log base and stone entrance, the building façade broke into a stucco and half-timbered assemblage of towers, pitched roof pavilions, and bracketed eaves. The building was praised for its unique interpretation of centuries-old wood building traditions.[3] August Heide's wood-frame Washington State pavilion at the 1904 St. Louis fair continued the region's promotion of timber to the rest of America.

Even during its territorial years, Washington had sent trade and crafts exhibits—usually showcasing produce, minerals, and artwork—to major exhibitions from 1875 onward. But the Washington pavilion at the World's Columbian Exposition was a moral and self-promotional necessity as a consequence of the state's recently acquired statehood and its dismal economic circumstances. It was cited as one of the most interesting and largest of the state buildings at that fair, at 140 feet by 220 feet. Within, the "Evergreen State" displayed the largest cedar vase ever turned from one piece of wood; a 208-foot flagpole of red fir; a reproduction of a farm featuring a 20-foot-high wheat pyramid; a 26-ton block of coal; the largest mammoth skeleton ever found; and the largest known yield of oats in the world from a single acre—156 bushels.[4] Washington also sent 150 paintings, including 36 by Harriet Foster Beecher and her students.[5]

The West Coast had a distinct presence at the St. Louis fair a decade later. Some of the attention certainly had to do with the fact that the Washington and Oregon pavilions differed greatly from the Classical buildings surrounding them. The impact of these state buildings was reported enthusiastically in an article "The Inspiring Displays of the States" by *World's Work*, a monthly magazine founded and edited by W. H. Page, which celebrated the American way of life and the expanded role of the United States in the world:

Just beyond the Fisheries Building, its pointed top 100 feet from the ground, is a wooden building that looks like a Chinese pagoda stripped of ornate trimmings. Beams of wood 110 feet long rise from the ground like the poles of an Indian wigwam. In this building, which is the Washington State Building, they meet at a point and form the apex of a very striking piece of architecture. The Lumbermen's Association of Washington furnished the wood. Inside, Washington's resources and products are displayed: woods from the dense forests (Washington last year manufactured more shingles than any other State); fruit from her large orchards; wheat, corn, and hops from her ample fields; coal from her rich mines; and fish from her extensive salmon-canning industry. The office of the Washington State Commission is in the trunk of a fir-tree 12 feet in diameter. With the characteristic spirit of commercial achievement of the Northwest, Seattle and Spokane make effective displays. They show how thriving cities have grown from villages in less than a quarter-century, and how the spirit that makes this possible is the spirit that is developing the empire of the Northwest. It has linked our commerce with the commerce of the Orient, and it has opened up a great trade with Alaska.

The Oregon pavilion is of timber as well, but is historically based. Every twenty-four hours 1,000,000 feet of lumber are sawn in Portland, Oregon. The State pavilion is of wood, therefore, and is a reproduction of Fort Clatsop, the log blockhouse occupied by Lewis and Clark on their famous Northwest expedition in 1805. The logs are Oregon pine. The flags of nearly all the great nations of the world fly from poles made of Oregon fir.[6]

The Lewis and Clark Centennial Exposition, Portland (1905)

While Washington and Oregon were represented in these fairs, it was on their home ground that the two states put their names and their products on the national map, Oregon in 1905, with the Lewis and Clark Centennial Exposition in Portland, and Washington in 1909, with the Alaska-Yukon-Pacific Exposition in Seattle. Both fairs were nationally promoted, and the American press took great pleasure in covering every aspect of the buildings, exhibits, and events. One such example was the coverage given the Portland exposition by *Literary Digest*, quoting the *Philadelphia Ledger*:

> The charm of the Portland fair will consist not only in its exhibits of people of the northwestern genus, but in the displays of the native arts and crafts, the progress of the people of the Pacific coast; what they have achieved in industry, commerce, agriculture, forestry, and in the winning of their West. The place is all so new, the country so lately won from forest and prairie, the people so ingenuous and enthusiastic and hearty and hopeful, that the fair will undoubtedly be worth a trip across the land to see. . . .
>
> Everybody who can afford to go to fairs should go, and every Eastern man, especially, who thinks that life is becoming stale and that the country is in a decline should go to a Far Western fair and there note the mighty enthusiasm of the Western man, woman, and child; the bursting faith in their country; their energy, joyousness, frankness, sincerity, and wholesome genuine good-nature and strong Americanism.[7]

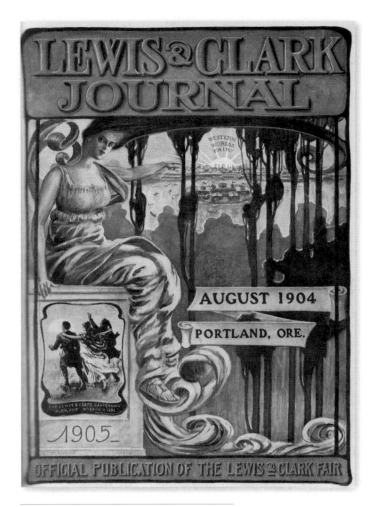

The *Lewis & Clark Journal* covered every aspect of the development and events at the Lewis and Clark Centennial Exposition (1905), Portland, over the two-year period 1904–1905. The art in the publication took design cues from the sinuous female forms and organic, curvilinear nature of Art Nouveau graphics. Seattle Public Library.

The same article also quoted the *Tacoma Ledger*, whose civic boosterism unknowingly anticipated the great Seattle exposition that would occur four years later: "This is the gateway of the Orient and Alaska. This section is destined to become the commercial and industrial center of the Pacific seaboard. Westward the star of empire takes its way, and the celebration of the two hundredth anniversary of the overland expedition of Lewis and Clark will find this Pacific Northwest rivaling in population, commerce, manufactures, and

OFFICIAL MAILING CARD
LEWIS & CLARK CENTENNIAL, 1905
PORTLAND, OREGON.

General View.

PUBLISHED BY B. B. RICH, OFFICIAL STATIONER.

Colored bird's-eye view of the Lewis and Clark Centennial Exposition, Portland, 1905. Don Nelson Collection.

wealth the present centers of the world's trade and industry. The Lewis and Clark Exposition begins today its splendid career of education and promotion not for Portland alone, but for the entire Pacific Northwest."[8]

The Lewis and Clark Centennial Exposition forged new territory as the first major West Coast event of its kind. The fair had broad appeal both as the centennial of Lewis and Clark's incredible expedition and in billing itself as the "American Pacific Exposition and Oriental Fair." The economic impact of the Pacific Rim and the Orient would be fully explored in this venue and, four years later, in Seattle. Through its lobbying efforts, management encouraged sixteen states to mount exhibits, ten of which would construct buildings. Washington and California joined Oregon in building major structures.

The common denominator of this fair and the Seattle exposition to come was the site plans designed by John Olmsted of the prestigious Brookline, Massachusetts, firm of the Olmsted Brothers. In 1903, Olmsted had presented a park plan to the City of Seattle and was about to do the same in Portland. His plan for the Guilds Lake site chosen for the Lewis and Clark fair determined the location of buildings, grading, and landscaping. The local firm of Whidden and Lewis oversaw development of the site, with exhibition buildings designed by a number of local firms in the agreed upon "Spanish Renaissance" style.[9]

Lewis & Clark Journal was published monthly during the period 1904–1905 to keep readers informed of progress and activities surrounding the fair. Despite the dominance of Renaissance-style buildings on the grounds, the journal could barely contain delight at the remarkable Forestry Building: "But for the new hotel which has but recently been completed in Yellowstone Park, composed of giant logs, the Forestry Building in Centennial Park would enjoy the notewor-

THIS GREAT BUILDING WAS MADE OF IMMENSE OREGON LOGS— AN OBJECT OF INTEREST TO TOURISTS.

116. FORESTRY BUILDING, "LEWIS AND CLARK MEMORIAL," PORTLAND, OREGON.

Forestry Building at the Lewis and Clark Centennial Exposition, Portland, 1905. Mason Collection.

thy distinction of containing the biggest log building in the world. Even ranking in second place, it is a wonderful structure, as pre-Exposition sightseers testify. There are two miles of five and six foot Oregon fir logs used in the construction, eight miles of poles and tons of shakes and cedar shingles. The extreme height of the building is 70 feet."[10]

The rustic nature of this building, its ties to the timber that had helped encourage westward expansion, its exposed construction, and its hand-hewn qualities fit the tenets of the Arts and Crafts movement. In a June 1905 article, the regional magazine *Westerner* recognized the significance of an emerging Northwest regional vernacular architecture when its author noted, "The building is constructed after no particular architectural style, but is nevertheless an architectural triumph, since in its sturdy simplicity, its solid strength, it is typical of the mighty forests of the great Pacific Northwest which are estimated to contain 300,000,000,000 feet of lumber."[11]

California's state building offered another notable deviation from European historic prototypes upon which the exhibit buildings were based. Its simplified façades, with their Mission characteristics, piggybacked with the more commonly expressed rustic imagery associated with the Arts and Crafts movement in architecture. *Lewis & Clark Journal* in April 1905 made a point of focusing attention on the romantic architecture of the Golden State's building, which chose a design compounded from four of its twenty-one Franciscan missions. In the shape of a Greek cross, the building prototypes were the missions San Luis Rey and Santa Barbara in Southern California and Delores and Carmel in Northern California.[12]

Mounting a successful exposition was a major achievement for Oregon's leading city. It also fed the ongoing rivalry between Portland and Seattle. In June 1905, *Lewis & Clark Journal* proclaimed that Portland was the un-

A brochure announced the Alaska-Yukon-Pacific Exposition in Seattle, 1909, to be "The World's Most Beautiful Exposition." Mason Collection.

portunities to any city of similar size in the United States."[13]

Alaska-Yukon-Pacific Exposition, Seattle (1909)

Seattle was pushed into the twentieth century by three major events: the rebuilding of Seattle after a major fire in 1889, the direct transcontinental railway connections established to the rest of the country beginning in the 1890s, and the Klondike gold rush in the late 1890s. Major earth moving and fill projects, the development of an up-to-date business district, and the opening up of new neighborhoods proceeded rapidly. The city promoted its potential leadership in the Pacific Rim by mounting the Alaska-Yukon-Pacific Exposition in 1909. With the successes of the Lewis and Clark Centennial Exposition fresh on their minds, Seattle's leading businessmen spent the ensuing four years raising funds, securing commitments, engaging important architects and landscape professionals, and implementing a more ambitious undertaking than their Portland neighbors.

Seattle conceived of an exposition that would turn the forested slope of the University of Washington grounds into a formal setting for monumental buildings offering a south-facing view of spectacular Mount Rainier. John Olmsted, having participated in laying out the grounds for the Portland exposition and having proved invaluable in establishing a park plan for Seattle in 1903, was invited back to the city to plan the fair grounds. John Galen Howard of New York and San Francisco was consulting architect. Architect and engineer Frank P. Allen, who had been in charge of structural work for the Lewis and

questioned metropolis and unrivaled commercial and financial center of the Pacific Northwest: "Not with phenomenal rapidity, but steadily, resistlessly, admirably, and splendidly, from decade to decade, from year to year, it has for half a century maintained its lead over all other places, has grown from a crude village, hewn out of an almost impenetrable forest, to a city of approximately 150,000, and stands today in most respects far superior in advantages, attractions and op-

Northwest Coast Indian and Asian design vocabularies merged in the monumental south entrance gate, one of the tori gates, at the Alaska-Yukon-Pacific Exposition in Seattle (1909). Special Collections Division, University of Washington Libraries (Seattle), Nowell x11690

Clark Centennial Exposition, was appointed director of works.

Following in the tradition of its predecessors, the Alaska-Yukon-Pacific Exposition's major buildings were classically styled. The dominant U.S. Government Building and its subordinate Agriculture and Manufacturers Buildings were temporary for the six-month run of the fair. The art gallery and auditorium were intended for permanent use by the university after the exposition closed.

The A-Y-P Exposition, as it was often called, offered the first opportunity for many Pacific Northwest residents to see objects that came directly from Europe and Asia, including contemporary design and handicraft. While they may have seen illustrations in books or magazines—the Seattle Public Library had acquired substantial holdings in art and design by 1909—locals could gain memorable direct experiences at the fair.

The press carried stories with headlines such as "Foreign Craftsmen Take Much

Space: Occupying the entire left half of the lower floor in the European building is the artistic exhibit of French products, manufactures, and works of art." This article described an exhibit of items from gold jewelry to bric-a-brac: "In the German section is a large space devoted to the exhibit of metal fine art goods, jewelry and ornaments, vases and interior decoration. Silverware and artistic silver jewelry is manufactured in one of the booths of the Austria-Hungary section. There are displays of lamps, statuary, and articles made from brass and bronze."[14] These displays certainly would have had an impact on young designers looking for new ideas.

While European historical styles were the leading force in the architecture of the fair, it was the great "tori gates" that welcomed visi-

[top] The uplifted roof forms of the Japan Building at the Alaska-Yukon-Pacific Exposition (Seattle, 1909) charmed visitors and may have inspired the use of this feature in Northwest bungalows built during and after the fair. Special Collections Division, University of Washington Libraries (Seattle), Nowell x2820.

[above] The Mission Revival appearance of the Spokane Building at the Alaska-Yukon-Pacific Exposition (Seattle, 1909) resembled Kirtland Cutter's remodeling of that city's Pennington Hotel in 1900 and an addition in 1904. Special Collections Division, University of Washington Libraries (Seattle), Lee 20064.

tors to the exhibition. These grand entrances were a combination of both traditional Japanese form and Northwest Coast Indian totems, and reminded attendees that this fair directed attention to the Far North and to Pacific Rim nations. Once on the grounds, visitors could visit Asian pavilions, restaurants, gardens, and tearooms.

The official guide, discussing the Japan Building, explained: "Seattle has the largest Japanese population of any city in the United States, and the Japanese merchants are taking a deep interest in the Alaska-Yukon-Pacific Exposition, and propose that the Japanese exhibit shall be one of the most interesting on the grounds."

In one of a series of *Seattle Post-Intelligencer* articles, a journalist who was clearly won over by the exoticism of Japanese architecture explained the Japanese exhibit:

A Japanese saying goes like this: "Seeing once is better than hearing a hundred times." The Americans, with the exception of a comparative few, have heard much about Japan and things Japanese. But they have seen very little of them. The visitors at the AYPE will have ample opportunity to verify or contradict what they have heard about Japan if they spend a little time in the Japan exhibits building.

It is situated directly below the Cascades, within a cozy grove of fir trees. Painted red and constructed in a peculiarly Oriental style of architecture, the building stands in bold relief to the monotony of the prevailing Occidentalism in the rest of the exhibits buildings. It was built by the Japan Exhibits Association, which was organized under the direction of the Japanese government.[15]

X 2563   FORESTRY BUILDING

The Forestry Building at the Alaska-Yukon-Pacific Exposition (1909) by Saunders and Lawton was a temple in timber.
Special Collections Division, University of Washington Libraries (Seattle), Nowell x2563.

In addition to the classically inspired buildings defining the main axis of the fair and the purposeful inclusion of Asian buildings in the mix, there were also several buildings inspired by Native American and Spanish settlements. The Utah Building was a reproduction of a section of the Hopi adobe pueblo originally built by the Bear and Snake families. The California and Spokane buildings were inspired by Spanish missions.[16]

The essence of the Northwest was represented by the most distinctive building on the campus—the Forestry Building. It had undoubtedly been modeled after Portland's immense timber temple at the Lewis and Clark exposition, yet was more akin to its classical neighbors in the use of brick pilasters and cement stucco for entablatures and pediments. The pavilion extolled the strength and raw power of native timber through an immense columned arcade supporting a balcony along the principal façade that was 320 feet in length and 144 feet in depth, with a total of 124 logs

supporting its roof and two cupolas. By contrast, the Portland building had been considerably smaller at 200 feet by 100 feet, and constructed completely of untrimmed logs.

Another log structure on the grounds was an important reflection of the rustic. The Arctic Brotherhood, designed by Eben Sankey and Axel Edelsvard for a fraternal and benevolent organization, was built of rough logs held together by wooden pegs. The press considered it one of the coziest places on the grounds, with its large fireplaces on the first and second floors and 100 pieces of custom-made furniture of Alaska spruce, red and yellow cedar, and other Alaskan woods.[17]

Farther to the east, on a ridge overlooking Lake Washington, sat a building that fully acknowledged the rising tide of interest in the

products of the Arts and Crafts movement. It was a clubhouse built for the Hoo Hoo, a national lumberman's fraternity, and was known as the Hoo Hoo House. It was designed by local architect Ellsworth Storey (1879–1960), with true half-timbered and stucco walls, and signaled the entry of the lowly bungalow into the realm of public architecture. Its niche was in providing cozy, comfortable, and honest spaces for gathering and community building. While recalling the Stick style, with an exposed timber frame and vertical board-and-batten siding, it featured elements of the contemporary Prairie School in its horizontal massing. In his design of all the building's furniture and many of its appointments, Storey may have been inspired by the ideas of the Chicago Arts and Crafts Society, which he was exposed to during his education and early work experience in 1901 and 1902.[18]

A detailed description of the building and its furnishings was published in *Pacific Builder and Engineer* under the title "The Hoo Hoo House at AYP: A club house of individual architecture—unique ornamentation and appropriate decoration." The building was a showpiece for the use of local resources in construction and interiors:

> Black cats guard the entry. Each side of the doorway has settees, the ends of which carry the scrolled emblem of the fraternity. . . . [The building] serves as an exhibit of Washington fir and spruce, of local architectural effort, of Seattle-made furniture, fixtures, and decorations.
>
> Secretary's rooms are of spruce from Grays Harbor country, manufactured by Slade Lumber Co. and Northwest Lumber of Aberdeen and Hoquiam. Floors are Douglas fir. The color scheme on the club room floor

[top] The Arctic Brotherhood Building at the A-Y-P Exposition (1909) was a sophisticated two-story log house with a covered porch oriented toward lake and mountain views. Special Collections Division, University of Washington Libraries (Seattle), Nowell x1802.

[above] Inside the Arctic Brotherhood Building, Arts and Crafts–style tables and chairs made of clear fir showed off true tenon joinery and floral cutouts. Special Collections Division, University of Washington Libraries (Seattle), Nowell x2891.

is in shades of forest brown and light forest greens. The walls are paneled, with plate rail and candlestick brackets. The ceiling is supported on solid 4 × 10 beams and the beaded ceiling is stained the same brown as walls. On the east side of the clubroom is a Denny-Renton brick fireplace. Large electric candles in massive black iron candlesticks of the primitive style and . . . lanterns are suspended from the beams. . . . The furniture for the house was built largely from one-inch fir stock, along novel lines, yet comfortable and satisfying to the eye. The Seattle Turning & Scroll Works could have had no better exhibit of a product of their shops than this.[19]

The article also mentioned the veranda and open terrace on the east side of the clubhouse, with its scroll panels and window boxes. It described a smoking room finished in redwood with a hand-decorated Washington forests frieze and green lattice-pattern draperies with black cats in appliqué. Weissenborn & Company was credited with the decorative scheme.[20]

[top right] Stretching black cats, the national lumbermen's symbol, guarded the entrance of Ellsworth Storey's Hoo Hoo House (Seattle, 1909) and observed visitors from the peak of the principal gable. Ellsworth Storey Collection, Special Collections Division, University of Washington Libraries (Seattle), UW 1946.

[center] Architect Ellsworth Storey also designed the woodwork and the furniture in the rooms of the Hoo Hoo House (Seattle, 1909). Hand-painted friezes above the wainscoting incorporated the feline emblem. Ellsworth Storey Collection, Special Collections Division, University of Washington Libraries (Seattle), UW 1947.

[bottom] A working drawing of a Hoo Hoo House rocking chair, showing side, front, and back elevations, by Ellsworth Storey (1909). Special Collections Division, University of Washington Libraries (Seattle), UW 26459z.

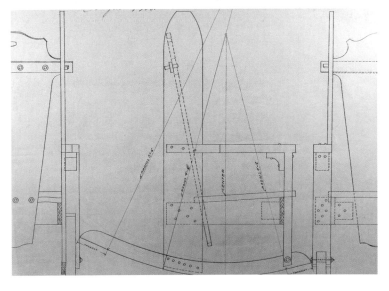

The value placed on wood and its many construction uses also was showcased in the Chehalis Building, built for exhibitions from Lewis County, Washington. Its façade reflected a typical Greek or Roman temple, but instead of Classical sculpted figures within its pediment, the pictorial design in the gable portrayed lumber mills and factories as "The Exchange," where Northwest resources, represented by a train of logs, were traded for the world's gold, represented by an incoming ship.

The interior of the building was finished in highly polished native woods. Displays showed different classes of manufactured shingles, and the structure of the building was itself an advertisement. The roof was supported by trusses, each consisting of one entire timber, eight by eight inches square and fifty feet long, highly polished, and without a knot or blemish. Timbers were bolted together so that truss rods were not required. Despite its emphasis on the local timber business, there was booth space for women's handiwork.[21]

The Role of Women

One building that was significant by its very absence from the Portland fair was a separate Women's Building. Ostensibly, this omission was attributed to the growing suffrage movement and the pressure for equality in society and the workplace. In his article "Woman's Part at the Centennial," Frank L. Merrick explained:

> Women at the Lewis and Clark Centennial Exposition are placed on the same plane with men as competitors in every line—artistic, educational, industrial and economic. It was clearly decided to make no separate exhibit of women's work. No woman's building for exhibit purposes is to stand at the Exposition as a mark of the ancient idea of woman's inferiority to man; but, instead of woman's work being isolated from the classification where it naturally belongs, all products of feminine genius and industry are placed on the same footing as those of the sterner sex. The same conditions and tests, the same standards of excellence that apply to man's work, apply also to the work of women; both are to be judged by the same juries who will alike distribute impartially the diplomas and medals and bestow honorable mention.[22]

The rhetoric of the Portland fair organizers about placing women on equal competitive footing with men, while its concept was progressive, may merely have been a way to argue for not putting money into a Women's Building. One of the great successes of the Chicago world's fair was, in fact, the enormous Women's Building, which showcased the remarkable achievements of women in the arts, industry, science, and in reform and philanthropic work.[23]

The women of Washington state were determined not to let the opportunity for worldwide exposure slip by. Plans for a Women's Building were already in place over a year before the opening of the exhibition. On March 28, 1908, the Seattle papers reported that the A-Y-P Exposition commission had appropriated $10,000 for a building "for exhibit of needlework by the State Federation of Women's Clubs. The building will be constructed and placed in charge of the women's federation."[24] Its interior design and Mission furnishing were turned over to J. S. Wilson.

Elsewhere on the grounds, a clubhouse

sponsored by the American Women's League gave visitors a glimpse of how furniture, textiles, lighting, and stenciled treatments could turn a house into a home. The league had been established in 1907 by Edward Lewis, a progressive businessman in St. Louis. Lewis developed an eighty-five-acre Arts and Crafts community called University City adjacent to the grounds of the St. Louis Fair in 1904. The focal point was a publishing enterprise and an internationally recognized art pottery. His publications included *Woman's Magazine*, *Woman's Farm Journal*, *Woman's National Daily*, *Palette and Brush*, and *Beautiful Homes*, which, beginning in 1908, carried articles on architecture and handicraft. In establishing the American Women's League, he turned over ownership of the Lewis Publishing Company and real estate. He also set up a chapter house program that offered permanent clubhouses in communities in return for a quota of sold periodical subscriptions from his network of nearly 100 magazines.[25]

While intended as a profit-making venture, the program was also meant to provide a place for women to be educated and informed on a wide range of topics such as housing, civic beautification, conservation, cooking, embroidery, arts and crafts, travel, and politics. The chapter houses, six standardized variants of a bungalow, were introduced in the 1909 winter issues of *Beautiful Homes*. Architects Helfenseller, Hirsch, and Watson of St. Louis designed the wood-frame, stucco-on-wood, and brick bungalows; the one at the A-Y-P Exposition was an early completed model. The style of these bungalows was meant to fit contextually into preexisting middle-class residential neighborhoods.[26]

[top] Behind its Classical Revival façade, the main lounge of the Women's Building at the Alaska-Yukon-Pacific Exposition (Seattle, 1909) was furnished with a wide variety of Mission-style chairs. Special Collections Division, University of Washington Libraries (Seattle), Nowell x2975.

[above] The interior of the American Women's League building, A-Y-P Exposition (Seattle, 1909), was outfitted with Mission furniture, leaded and stained glass lighting fixtures, and stenciled wall and curtain treatments. Special Collections Division, University of Washington Libraries (Seattle), Nowell x1905.

Visitors rested on Mission rockers in the grand columned portico of the Washington State Building, Alaska-Yukon-Pacific Exposition (Seattle, 1909). Special Collections Division, University of Washington Libraries (Seattle), Nowell x1700a.

Furnishing the Fairs

Behind the Classical Revival façades of its leading buildings, Alaska-Yukon-Pacific Exposition designers found that Mission oak furniture was a reliable, comfortable, and relatively inexpensive way to furnish the many reception, lounge, and meeting rooms. The Washington Building was one such example, described in detail by the press, with the headline "State Exhibits Solid Comfort: Easy chairs and cool shade at Washington Building are popular": "The Washington State Building with its cool, spacious rooms and comfortable chairs, was one of the most popular

places on the exposition grounds yesterday. There is no exhibit at the Washington building, unless solid comfort is an exhibit, and there was plenty of that. On the porch, where the afternoon shade was the deepest, visitors sat to recuperate from the fatigue of sightseeing. In one chair an elderly woman fell asleep and had a nap undisturbed. . . . The big reception room is decorated with fresh flowers daily and while the room is too spacious to look cozy, there is restfulness in the color scheme of the walls and pillars and genuine comfort in the couches and chairs."[27]

Another pairing of formal architecture and informal furnishings was offered at the New York State Building, destined to become the official residence of the president of the University of Washington after the fair ended. New York was the only state east of the Rocky Mountains that had official representation at this fair with a building for exposition purposes, motivated by the fact that Seattle did over $8 million annually in business with New York. In its 1910 report, the legislative committee from the State of New York to the A-Y-P Exposition described its building, designed by New York City architect Clarence Eluce, who had been responsible for the design and construction of the New York State Buildings at fairs in St. Louis and Portland. The building, a Colonial pavilion, was modeled after the home of William H. Seward at Auburn, New York, an appropriate choice, given Seward's significant role in the purchase of Alaska in 1867 as Secretary of State.

The first floor included a vaulted reception hall with an Ionic colonnade, a banquet hall, and ladies' and gentlemen's reception rooms. There was also a dining room for executive officers and an exposition clubroom. The interiors were finished in pine with Colonial painted woodwork and trim, but locally produced interiors were outfitted with Mission oak furniture supplied by "Frederick & Nelson Company of Seattle under the direction of the hostess, Mrs. Benjamin M. Wilcox. The entire cost of the furniture and furnishings was close to $8,000."[28] While the Seattle department store stocked a wide range of historically inspired furniture at the time, it was also promoting its bungalow line in advertisements, and this is probably what Mrs. Wilcox ordered. Photographs included in the report show Mission library tables, two-sided writing desks, and chairs in both reception rooms, cross-ended settees lining the reception hall, and an assortment of wicker and oak pieces in the exposition clubroom. Iron or brass fixtures with clear pendant globe lights illuminated the interior.

Pacific Builder and Engineer mentioned another repository of Mission furniture at the fair: "The Army and Navy tea room is among the first-class refreshment stands on the grounds. The interior decorations, including Mission furniture, are designed to carry out the military idea."[29] Perhaps the Spartan character of Mission furniture lent itself to this interpretation. In any case, it must have been an enormous facility, as H. Chase & Company was responsible for the furnishings, which included 2,000 settees, each with a seating capacity of six.

Impact of the Fairs

These major Pacific Northwest expositions stimulated regional interest in design, with many examples of persuasive influences, including: Asian architecture and design; Spanish missions that embodied an indigenous architecture Americans might take as their own; and the power, beauty, and utility of local building materials—Douglas fir, clay, and stone—in sophisticated buildings inspired by pioneer traditions. As a teaching tool, the fairs exposed the public to a broader range of design efforts than most had ever seen, bringing together the wealth of Asia, Europe, Alaska, and America.

While only a small number of these products could be considered part of the growing Arts and Crafts movement, nonetheless they were there to see—Tiffany glass, Rookwood and Newcomb pottery, and metalwork, furniture, lighting, and ceramics by professionals, by amateurs, and by students in the progressive manual arts programs in public schools throughout the two states. Visitors to the fairs dined at Mission tables, sat on Mission settees and rockers, and wrote their postcards at Arts and Crafts desks lit by slag (colored and textured) glass lights.

Undoubtedly, visitors to the fairs went home at night dreaming of how to incorporate these new and enticing objects into their current homes. Perhaps they even considered investing in a new bungalow in Irvington, Westover Park, Laurelhurst, or Eastmoreland in Portland; in Ravenna, Wallingford, or Mount Baker in Seattle; in Rockwood, Corbin Park, or Nettleton's Addition in Spokane; and in any number of new and expanding neighborhoods in Oregon and Washington.

In the greater sphere of business, commerce, and social organizations, there was also an acknowledgment that the products of the Arts and Crafts movement were sturdy, reasonably priced, and refreshing alternatives to traditional, historically derived furnishings.

THREE
Embracing the Arts and Crafts Movement

ALTHOUGH RHYSICALLY FAR AWAY from major cities such as New York, Boston, Chicago, Cleveland, Philadelphia, Minneapolis, San Francisco, and other communities that had begun to embrace and interpret Arts and Crafts ideals, by 1900 Oregon and Washington were not isolated from trends in the world of the fine and applied arts.

The completion of mainline railroads during the late nineteenth and early twentieth centuries made it possible for people and products to move easily in and out of the Northwest, allowing for exchange of ideas as well as goods. Trunk lines reached out into the farm and ranch lands, the timber and mining districts, and along the Pacific Coast. West Coast steamship traffic linked San Francisco to Portland and Seattle. With the increasing popularity of the automobile and the mobility it allowed, more Northwest roads were built or improved—the highlight coming in 1916 with the opening of the scenic Columbia Gorge Highway. Interurban rail lines, along with modern streetcar systems, encouraged people to build houses some distance from downtown business centers of their towns and cities.

Enhanced transportation systems, as well as the U.S. Post Office, helped keep Northwesterners informed of the growing American expression of the Arts and Crafts aesthetic. By the early 1910s, most interested people in Oregon and Washington could easily learn more about this widespread national movement through the growing variety of periodicals and trade journals, books on relevant subjects, fairs and exhibitions in major cities, and lectures by national figures involved in the arts. The public could attend an increasing variety of classes and workshops offered by established craftspeople, or connect with those in their community who had ties to national figures in the arts. For young people, Northwest school systems provided opportunities for hands-on experience in manual or domestic art training classes. Art schools, colleges, and universities provided advanced instruction in the fine and applied arts. Regional opportunities for experiencing and participating in the "good life" associated with the Arts and Crafts movement were becoming widely available.

Literature and Libraries

From the latest national periodicals on home furnishing and decoration to how-to books on making Mission-style furniture in a basement workshop, by 1900 a wide array of publications on national design trends was readily accessible to Northwest readers.

Popular women's magazines of the period, such as *Ladies Home Journal*, *Good Housekeeping*, and *House Beautiful*, contained articles on the virtues of the small, compact, labor-efficient bungalow. Needlework patterns in new design styles were featured, encouraging homemakers to create their own beautiful utilitarian items, such as embroidered pillowcases and drapes. The modern woman could take advantage of all sorts of popular handicraft opportunities in keeping with Arts and Crafts ideals. Although similar information on the domestic arts was available during the Victorian period several decades earlier, the growing middle class in the early 1900s was experiencing profound changes: a general trend toward a smaller immediate family and the efficiency of the smaller bungalow allowed women more leisure time to read, to experiment with craft ideas, and to indulge in making their homes pleasant places for their families.

These same periodicals contained thoughtful articles for the reader, whether living in the Palouse farmlands of eastern Washington or in the bungalow section of Portland's Laurelhurst. Women's suffrage and other social movements were covered in considerable detail, as was the latest thinking on creating more attractive communities. These enlightening topics, along with reviews of art exhibitions and the latest books, introduced and stimulated interest in national trends. If handiwork articles in any of the popular magazines of the day sparked a desire to know more about a particular craft and to learn the necessary techniques to do the work themselves, readers could subscribe to craft-specific publications, such as *Keramic Studio* for china painting or *Modern Priscilla* for artistic needlework on textiles.

Myra Ballou, who, in the 1910s, lived on a farm outside of Milton-Freewater in north-

The opening of the Columbia River Gorge Highway in 1916, as celebrated in this promotional brochure, expanded automobile tourism in Washington and Oregon. Mason Collection.

eastern Oregon, exemplified the young person living in a rural area who was trying to keep in touch with all things Arts and Crafts.[1] She had a Gustav Stickley single bed and dresser as well as a butterfly-design Apollo Studio slag glass table lamp. Ballou subscribed to *Craftsman Magazine* and possessed Roycroft publications and a variety of printed ephemera from some of the most important names in the American Arts and Crafts scene.

Her collection included catalogs of work produced by Adelaide Alsop Robineau, Tiffany Studios, Stickley's Craftsman Studios, Clifton Art Pottery, Van Briggle Tile & Pottery Company, and Rookwood Pottery. She also had a Weller Pottery catalog from the Man-

ufacturers Building at the Lewis and Clark Exposition in Portland in 1905, as well as brochures and mailers from Paul Elder's Arts and Crafts Book Company in San Francisco and the Roycrofters of East Aurora, New York. Her handwritten notebook, dated 1952, itemizes several boxes of books that accompanied her move to Spokane. The list includes many books from the Roycroft Press, and there are several pages titled "Elbert Hubbard Books." While her interest may have been more focused than many of her peers, what is significant about her collection is that she assembled it while living in a rural Oregon community more than 200 miles from Portland.

For those who could not afford to purchase periodicals and books, the key to increasing their knowledge about the Arts and Crafts movement was the strength of public library collections. Libraries were growing to meet the needs and requests of resident patrons. Thanks to the generosity of Andrew Carnegie, many towns in Oregon and Washington proudly had their own library. In some smaller communities, women's clubs or civic organizations sometimes sponsored lending libraries.

The larger cities, such as Portland, Seattle, and Spokane, often published annual reports of their library acquisitions, and some sponsored reading lists or announced new title arrivals in the local newspaper's Sunday edition. These activities reveal collection focuses of the libraries and indicate the interest level of readers during the pivotal years when the Arts and Crafts movement peaked nationally. Library holdings served as a template for practical education that might lead to a viable trade, as well as encouragement of personal pursuits in applied and industrial arts.

Among the books on fine and useful arts acquired by the Seattle Public Library during this period were some key texts by American and British architects, artists, craftspeople, academicians, and instructors that opened up the world of design to even the most impoverished and uneducated Northwesterner. Popular subjects acquired during the years 1905 through 1907 included basketry, woodworking, home decoration, pottery, copper metalwork, architectural composition, design, leatherwork, needlework, carpentry, jewelry making, bungalow houses, and bookbinding.[2]

When C. R. Ashbee toured Portland in 1916, two things struck him: "the mountains and the library. The Library, not as a building, but as an object lesson in democratic conviction; the mountains—Hood, Saint Helens, Adams, and far away Rainier, an eternal reprimand."[3] Ashbee described the work of Mary Frances Isom, the head of Portland's library:

> She has under her a staff of 60 men and women, and she has the great work of "making the Library be alive." I've learnt from her a little of what an American library in a great town is. . . . Here it is a huge democratic propagandist institution, with its subsidiary libraries and book stores, and its motor cars, its staff that searches out lonely homes where books are needed and taken, its system of inviting all new immigrants into the Library, and teaching workpeople and the school children how to use the catalogue and what it all means. . . . I try to mark down the difference between our libraries and the American. Ours seem to be afflicted with the property sense. They are public institutions for guarding the public books. Here, as she told me, they act on the hypothesis

[top] *Keramic Studio* offered hundreds of stylized and naturalistic designs to inspire china painters in Washington and Oregon, such as this color page from the December 1916 issue. Seattle Public Library.

[above] Envelope from The Roycrofters addressed to Myra Ballou in Freewater, Oregon, in 1911. Mason Collection.

that it is better for a book now and again to be stolen than for the public not to be using the Library.[4]

Arts and Crafts Organizations, Exhibitions, and Leadership

Upon occasion, libraries in many smaller communities displayed regional artwork and handicrafts through the auspices of organizations lacking physical space for public exhibitions. Although the libraries in Portland, Spokane, and Seattle also hosted handiwork exhibits from time to time, those larger communities began to foster organizations particularly devoted to promoting the Arts and Crafts philosophy through educational classes, instruction, and exhibition of beautiful and artistic handmade objects of high quality.

In 1903, the *Spokesman-Review*, in a long article titled "Arts and Crafts on View," described an exhibition of handicrafts and fine arts sponsored by the Spokane Art League: "The present exhibition is devoted to the arts and crafts as developed in Spokane." Hand-painted china by Miss Lena Eddy was mentioned as work "worthy of a place in any of the ceramic art galleries in the east." Architect Kirtland Cutter lent some candelabra and a Colonial cabinet designed by him. A Miss Green exhibited a plaque, candlestick, dresser box, bowl, and tray, and a Mrs. Hamblen exhibited a bas relief of an Indian head in terra-cotta. The Spokane Art League had been organized in 1892 to encourage arts and crafts endeavors and to advance a wider community appreciation for the arts.[5]

The Walla Walla Art Club, organized in southeast Washington in 1898, and the Artistic Needlework Club of Marshfield, Oregon,

started in 1901 for social amusement and the advancement of handwork, were typical of organizations initiated throughout the Northwest to promote an artistic environment that would foster creative talent. In 1915, that same Artistic Needlework Club donated funds to pay for the Marshfield public library's subscription to *Ladies Home Journal* and *Modern Priscilla*. In 1905, they had won a medal at the Lewis and Clark Exposition in Portland for their artistic needlework display in the Coos County exhibit.[6]

The Lewis and Clark Centennial Exposition in 1905 and the Alaska-Yukon-Pacific Exposition four years later provided the inspiration and impetus for artistic communities in both Oregon and Washington to formally organize groups that would embrace the arts and crafts workers in their respective regions. Fine arts organizations were the norm, and welcoming the applied arts craftspeople into that same fold was sometimes troublesome to those who felt that a hammered piece of copper could not, or at least should not, be considered in the same way as the well-established, although subjective, standards of fine art.

PORTLAND

Nowhere regionally was the controversy of the age-old question "Is it art?" demonstrated so vividly as in correspondence between Frank Vincent DuMond (1865–1951), who had just been appointed chief of the department of fine art for the Lewis and Clark Centennial Exposition, and Henrietta H. Failing, curator of the Portland Art Museum. In April 1905, in response to a question from Failing about including arts and crafts in DuMond's fine art exhibition, DuMond forcefully responded:

The Spokane Art League held classes for students in drawing, painting, sculpture, and handcrafts in the attic of the city hall. Northwest Museum of Arts & Culture, Eastern Washington State Historical Society (Spokane), L2003-14.287.

As to Applied Arts, Arts and Crafts, etc., I am not doing anything as the size and nature of the galleries would not permit a showing of these elements; the pictures and the other objects would produce an effect entirely destructive and undivided. It has been amply proven in this city that to expose Arts and Crafts in a separate and distinct department is necessary. Again, so few really good things are being done in Arts and Crafts that it is, in my opinion, almost impossible to make an interesting showing.

As Chairman of the Art Committee at the National City Club, I have been over the ground most thoroughly and found that the Arts and Crafts are more of an idea and a fad by far than they are a reality, and that for one good production it would be necessary to search the country from end to end, however, this is beside the point. You must readily see that the Galleries are not large enough to make two departments and that it is absurd to think of mixing them up.[7]

Failing must have responded by suggesting that perhaps a case or two of craftwork might be put down the center of the Fine Arts exhibition space. Relying on his "sorry, no more space or money" excuse, DuMond took another jab at any proposed Arts and Crafts presentation in "his" space: "As for the Applied Arts exhibit, I have most reluctantly abandoned the idea as you did not state in your telegram whether there was any room or not available in some one of the other sections, very near the Fine Arts building. As I wrote, Applied Arts cases down through the center of a 25 ft. gallery ruins the effect of everything. I am not speaking from theory but from actual effect as developed in the gallery of the National Art Club which are precisely this same width."[8]

Although DuMond's dictate held up—no applied arts were shown in the Fine Arts exhibition—some national and regional craft workers and pottery companies found venues for exhibiting their handiwork in other buildings throughout the exposition grounds. The Manufacturers Building included an exhibit of the pottery of S. A. Weller and the J. B. Owens Pottery Company, both of Zanesville, Ohio. The Arts Crafts Shop of Buffalo, New York, exhibited enameled silver and copper, brass, and individual jewelry in gold and silver, along with Teco Art Pottery manufactured by Gates Potteries of Chicago and Terra Cotta, Illinois.[9]

The State of Louisiana's exhibit in the Agricultural Building included the work of the Newcomb Art Pottery, New Orleans. The Newcomb entry form listed fifteen pieces, and Robert Glenk, the coordinator for Louisiana's exhibit, wrote that the designs on the items exhibited were "distinctively Louisiana & Creole subjects. No duplicates. Best examples were not available for Exhibition. Demand much greater than production. This pottery ranks third in U.S. & is surely worthy of the highest distinction for its merits."[10] The judges must have agreed, since the Newcomb Pottery was awarded a bronze medal.

Local examples of china painting by members of the Oregon Keramic Club were exhibited in the Women's Court along with a collection sent from the National League of Mineral Painters. Embroidery work was also displayed in that same area.

The sampling of Arts and Crafts items exhibited at the Lewis and Clark Exposition must have piqued an interest among Portland enthusiasts for learning various crafts from trained instructors. Within the next eighteen months, Julia Hoffman, a woman of social standing in Portland with connections to some of the best artisans associated with the Society of Arts and Crafts in Boston, was in correspondence with Failing of the Portland Art Museum about assembling a major exhibition of Boston and other eastern craftspeople. Hoffman also passionately urged Failing to somehow find the resources to bring a nationally known metalwork instructor to Portland to teach a two-month course.

Born in Utah in 1856, Julia Elizabeth Christenson moved to Portland in 1881. She married Lee Hoffman, an engineer and contractor, two years later. In 1895, Lee Hoffman, by then a successful Portland contractor, was killed in a shooting accident. Wishing to educate her two children in eastern schools, Julia Hoffman moved to Boston.

Boston was an active center for handcrafts, particularly metalwork and art pottery. Hoffman took painting classes at the Grundmann Studios of the Boston Art Students' Association. She joined the Copley Society, the Folk Lore Society, and the recently organized Boston Society of Arts and Crafts. She received silverwork instruction from George Gebelein, who became her mentor as well as a long-time friend.

Hoffman returned to Portland in 1904 and had a house built for her family. A year later, she returned to Cambridge, Massachusetts, while her son, Hawley, studied at Harvard and her daughter, Margery, began her coursework at Bryn Mawr in Pennsylvania. In 1906 she moved back to Portland, where she took up permanent residence.

In 1907 Hoffman was again visiting the East Coast during the Boston Society of Arts and Crafts Exhibition. While there, she acted as the curator for an exhibition of quality craftwork to be shipped to Portland for display at the Portland Art Museum. The selection of items was taken largely from objects on display at the Boston Society exhibition. The Portland Art Museum's archives contain a number of letters between Hoffman in Massachusetts and curator Henrietta Failing about the logistics of selecting artwork for the Portland exhibit, including the following: "In view of the great distance and cost of transportation, it would seem best to confine the choice for smaller articles such as weigh comparatively little or can be packed into a small compress. This will exclude such things as furniture, heavy pottery, etc., but metal work, leather and needle work, etc., can be sent at comparatively small expenses."[11]

Failing responded with the recommendation that "it would perhaps be better to attempt a small selection of the best available objects rather than to go to a somewhat excessive expense for a larger number of less artistic value." The two women agreed that there was enough antique metalwork, furniture, large textiles, and other early examples of well-executed handmade objects in the Portland area to supplement the exhibit with a "loan collection" from regional families.[12]

Throughout her correspondence, Hoffman's excitement and dedication to the task is clearly evident. At the same time, another event in Boston captured her interest. Her letters mention a series of meetings she attended as a member of the Boston Society of Arts and Crafts which would soon have a major impact on Portland: "You see by an enclosed clipping that a national society has been formed and will go into effect when ten societies have joined. Have been to most of the meetings.

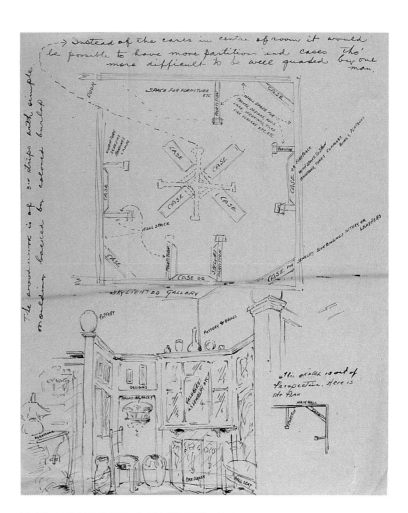

Exhibit layout for applied arts exhibition at the Lewis and Clark Centennial Exposition in Portland, 1905. Oregon Historical Society (Portland).

Its birth was quite a process to an on looker. Most intense interest was shown by all the delegates and the result I think entirely satisfactory."[13] Never missing the opportunity to further the opportunities for the Arts and Crafts, Hoffman must have started thinking about the value of such an organization in her adopted home. By the end of that same year, she would be named to the board of directors of the newly formed Arts and Crafts Society of Portland.

Hoffman's selection of materials from the East, along with the loan of "many of the choicest treasures from Portland homes," opened in an exhibit of applied art at the Portland Art Museum on April 30, 1907. The

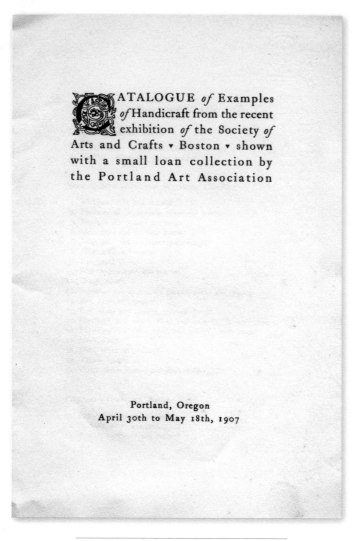

ATALOGUE *of* Examples *of* Handicraft from the recent exhibition *of* the Society *of* Arts and Crafts ▾ Boston ▾ shown with a small loan collection by the Portland Art Association

Portland, Oregon
April 30th to May 18th, 1907

Title page from the catalog of the first Arts and Crafts exhibition in Portland shown at the Portland Art Museum in 1907. Mason Collection.

Oregonian announced, "Art Treasures on Show: A distinct epoch in the history of Portland's movement toward a better appreciation of art and its related interests is marked by the Arts and Crafts exhibit which opened at the Museum of Art yesterday."[14] In a review two days later, the newspaper gave credit to Hoffman for arranging the Boston portion of the exhibit, and said, "The collection is a large one and embraces the work of some of America's best jewelers and silversmiths, which for beauty and originality are distinct."[15]

The names included in the Portland Art Museum's catalog for the exhibition were a virtual "Who's Who" of American Arts and Crafts of the day. Jewelry and metal exhibitors included Elizabeth Copeland, Seth Ek, George C. Gebelein, Karl F. Leinonen, L. H. Martin, Arthur Stone, and the Kalo Shop. Leatherwork and bookplates from Amy Sacker, printed materials lent by Bruce Rogers, and art pottery by Arthur Eugene Baggs also were on display.

The items listed in the loan collection from Portland area families indicated the donors' knowledge of Arts and Crafts work created in other parts of the country. Leatherwork by the Misses Ripley of New York and pottery from Rookwood, Volkmar, Newcomb, Van Briggle, Teco, Grueby, and Dedham were listed as being owned by local individuals. In addition, several pieces of hand-wrought silver and copper work from local artisans John Nelson Wisner and Florence Knowlton owned by Portlanders were exhibited, giving regional workers a big boost. The *Oregonian* singled out one of those works, a hammered silver punch bowl, proclaiming that it "is a beautiful piece of work which suggests the Tiffany ware from the iridescent tints. The bowl was the handiwork of Mr. J. N. Wisner of Oregon City."[16]

The *Spectator* of Portland, in describing the exhibit, said, "The display of the Arts and Crafts includes silver, copper, pewter and jewelry, in charming and unique form; basketry that astonishes with the variety of work; leather, illumined and embossed in fine design and soft tones; volumes showing how beautiful books can be made when art works with craft."[17] The weekly correctly predicted that, "The collection . . . should be the means of encouraging Portland's taste for arts and crafts."[18]

The Oregon Building left vacant after the Lewis and Clark Centennial Exposition (Portland, 1905) was converted into a handicraft shop for metalwork instruction in 1907. Oregon Historical Society (Portland), BL003343.

The time-consuming task of securing items for the exhibit did not deter Julia Hoffman from her interest in having a metalwork instructor in Portland for a two-month residency to conduct summer classes. Having initiated the idea through correspondence with Henrietta Failing in the spring of 1906, Hoffman thought that L. H. Martin, "who, I am told, is one of the best if not the best craftsman in this country," might be a possibility.[19] In February 1907 Hoffman wrote that Martin had increased his amount of desired compensation to such a point that she suggested substituting Mildred Watkins of Cleveland.[20] Failing sent a discouraging response to Hoffman, explaining that there were too many obstacles to overcome, including a lack of sufficient funds, space, proper equipment and supplies; the uncertainty of how many students metalwork classes would attract; and the unsuccessful attempt on her part to find an existing organization or person to oversee the development and management of such a venture.[21]

Hoffman took the news in stride, replying, "Sorry to get your message by wire that no one is willing to take up the Summer School metal work proposition. It will have to come if we want to keep pace with the rest of our country and it is too bad to have any delay." She then interjected a little jolt of friendly rivalry, perhaps to encourage the folks in Portland to continue to pursue the potential of a summer workshop. "I hear Seattle has a Society of A&Cs. Do you know if they [have] any sort of Handicraft School?"[22]

Hoffman's persistence paid off. A 1907 broadside proudly announced that Mildred Watkins would be the instructor for a summer School of Metal Work. The course of study included the making of articles in copper, brass, and silver, "such as bowls, trays, paper knives, boxes, buckles, brooches, pendants, spoons, salt cups, etc."[23] An undated clipping gives more detail about this new endeavor located in one of the buildings remaining at the Lewis and Clark Centennial Exposition grounds: "The commodious and well-lighted room has recently been converted into a well-equipped handicraft shop which for a period of two months is to be under the direction of Miss Watkins of Cleveland, O., whose efforts in metal work and enameling have attracted much favorable recognition alike, from her fellow technicians and from the lay public."[24]

The combined success of the exhibition of work from Boston and the enthusiasm surrounding the workshop and a qualified metalwork instructor, along with Julia Hoffman's strong encouragement, led to the creation of the Arts and Crafts Society of Portland that same year. In a letter dated October 8, Hoffman wrote: "I have been busy on the Arts & Crafts. Today, we had our big meeting—

adopting a constitution, electing officers and getting names for membership. 85 signed for membership. It is a most gratifying outcome. I was asked to be one of the officers, but refused and am one of the directors. I don't want to get too deep in work!"[25]

The *Arts & Crafts Society of Portland, Oregon, Constitution, By-Laws & Prospectus*, printed in 1907, stated the organization's purpose: "The object of this Society shall be to encourage and develop higher artistic standards in the handicrafts; to open and maintain a salesroom and permanent exhibition; to hold occasional exhibitions of ancient and modern works of various crafts; to equip a workshop for the use of members; and to further the cause of handicraft in every manner."[26]

By the following year, the organization had gained enough momentum to sponsor the First Annual Exhibition of the Arts and Crafts Society of Portland. Although this 1908 exhibition featured the work of more local craftspeople, its success was still due to a large amount of work from the East, most of which was on consignment. The group would continue to mount exhibitions, both large and small, including an annual show, for many years. By 1910, it was reported that the Arts and Crafts Society had grown to a membership of over 150 members and that the interest in the work of the organization was growing.[27]

The *Sunday Oregonian* of November 13, 1910, praised the Arts and Crafts Society of Portland for having concluded "a most successful exhibition of local handicraft work." It was, the article said, particularly interesting "for lovers of the beautiful in this line of art to note the many fine examples of metal work, leather and bookbinding, that were shown. The exhibition in itself speaks well for the earnestness of purpose and the artistic ability of local crafters." The writer of the article summarized the growth of the Arts and Crafts movement in relation to Portland:

The great work which has been accomplished in the awakening of the art instincts of the people, and the raising of their standards of taste, not only in handicraft work, but in the output of factories as well, is a testimonial to the arts and crafts movement. Its permeating influence is gradually reaching everywhere. The great power of the educational systems is used to foster the love for well-designed, simple articles for everyday use.

The local society brought to Portland many beautiful examples of Eastern Crafters' work in its former exhibitions, but this is the first display it has essayed of entirely local work.[28]

Besides the annual exhibitions, the society often worked in collaboration with the Portland Art Museum to host shows of mutual interest. One example was an exhibition of the tile work of California's Ernest A. Batchelder held at the museum in December 1915. The *Spectator*, in describing the tiles, said they were "in subtle tones of color, arranged in a great variety of simple but spirited designs of peacocks, roses, forests, castles, figures, ships, and other interesting subjects."[29] Three months later, Batchelder presented a lecture on tile at the art museum that was co-sponsored by the Arts and Crafts Society.[30]

Educational programs, instruction, and a sales shop that could act as an outlet for local members' work, as well as for the consigned work of some of the leading craft workers in America, became important components of the efforts of Portland's Arts and Crafts Society. Lectures were scheduled regularly to broaden interest and awareness in arts and crafts. In only the second year of its existence, the society hosted the leader of the Handicraft Guild of England, C. R. Ashbee, to address its Portland members at the annual meeting.[31]

In March 1909, the *Spectator* announced that the Portland Art Association, the parent organization of the Portland Art Museum, and the Arts and Crafts Society were working together to start a school of design.[32] By that summer, the plan had come to fruition, primarily due to Julia Hoffman's personal pledge to pay for the first year of an instructor's salary, along with the Arts and Crafts Society's promise to pick up any difference in expenses incurred by the new Museum Art School that student tuition did not cover. The art association was to furnish the studios, furniture, and models. Kate Cameron Simmons of New York would be the first instructor.[33]

Simmons was a former student at Pratt Institute and had studied under artist Arthur Wesley Dow at Columbia University. She was a promising choice. At the end of the first week of the instruction, the newspaper announced the design class had an enrollment of nearly fifty students. Classes included drawing, color, and design.[34] The Arts and Crafts Society hosted a welcoming reception that was "the prettiest affair of the sort ever held in Portland. Miss Simmons is a remarkably beautiful and charming girl, and made an attractive picture as she received, standing before a background of chrysanthemums and vividly tinted autumn leaves. She has won many friends during her short stay here, and has already become immensely popular."[35]

The society's Shop of Fine Arts and Indus-

SHOP OF FINE ARTS AND INDUSTRIES

SEVENTH AND SALMON STREETS

Beautiful and Useful Articles in Hand Craft Jewelry, Silver and Furniture
Adapted for Wedding and Anniversary Presents

Exhibition of Important Works of the Noted Painters
DEMING and YARDE

An advertisement for the Shop of Fine Arts and Industries, Portland, in the *Spectator*, November 13, 1909.

tries opened in October 1908 with an exhibit of paintings by the California artist William Keith. In announcing this new venture, the *Spectator* stated, "This shop will afford the people of Portland an opportunity to see and buy the best in art, handicraft work, reproductions, and bookmaking. Many of the notable artists have sent examples of their work and the shop will be at once an exhibition hall of what is really worthy in the fine and applied arts and a salesroom."[36] The shop also served as "the headquarters of the Arts and Crafts Society, which is producing articles in silver, leather work and jewelry."[37]

Throughout the next decade, the Shop of Fine Arts and Industries featured short-term exhibits of items for sale by some of the best known Arts and Crafts workers and artists in America. Beginning with William Keith, over the next few years the shop introduced the work of sculptor A. Phimister Proctor; color prints by Ruth Sypherd Clements, Helen Hyde, Ethel Mars, and Maud Hunt Squire; metalwork by Mildred Watkins, George Gebelein, Dirk Van Erp, and Arthur Stone; paintings and drawings by Josephine Pitkin of New York; leatherwork from the Campañeros of Santa Rosa, California, and the Ripley sisters of New York; Indian photographs by Edward S. Curtis; jewelry by Frank Gardner Hale and Josephine Harwell Shaw; and decorated lampshades by Mary Ludlow of the Swastica Shop of Chicago.

Several times throughout the 1910s, the Arts and Crafts Society issued pleas for more local craftspeople to participate in the sales shop. In a 1915 notice to the society's trustees and consignors, Florence Knowlton, the director of the salesroom, reported that for 1914 the annual sales for out-of-the-region consignors (not members of the society) were more than double the sales for the local craft members. "As it is in the local work that the management is most keenly interested, a most hearty co-operation with the Craft-members is pledged in bringing the sales of their work to an amount equal to that of the non-local consignors." The total annual sales figure for 1914 was $2,002.[38]

The society had the same concern over their popular annual exhibitions. Just two years after the *Sunday Oregonian* had heaped praise on the society for showing local work over East Coast arts and crafts, an April 4, 1912, meeting notice laid out the society's dismay over the lack of participation, cooperation, and support for the organization among the craft workers in Portland. Calling it a meeting at which "the future of the Portland Arts and Crafts Society will be definitely de-

cided," the society attempted to rally local craft worker support:

Our exhibitions have not been as successful as we could have made them, because we have not realized the great good that each and all of us would have received by making a large and diversified display of our work. The exhibition in December was a thoroughly artistic success, but this was due more to the generous consignments from the East than to the showing made by the local members, who, unfortunately, took little interest in the exhibition, although it was the desire and intention of the Society to have the work of local craftsmen predominate.

The Board of Directors feels that we have depended long enough on the display of eastern craft workers for material for our exhibition, and knowing that there is here a super abundance of craft talent, thinks that the time has come when it can produce beautiful craft work of sufficient merit and in sufficient quantity to make fully successful exhibitions of purely local work. The Society desires to encourage in every way the local craftsmen.[39]

By 1918, the Arts and Crafts Society had committed itself to regional craft workers in the annual exhibit, including work from Portland, Grants Pass, and the art department of the Oregon Agricultural College in Corvallis.[40]

Home-front efforts during World War I occupied much of the society members' time, and some activities were suspended for a while. Interest resumed after the war ended in 1918, but the times and interests of the general public had altered, and interest in the Arts and Crafts movement had waned considerably. Nevertheless, the Arts and Crafts

Society of Portland continued through the 1920s. Exhibitions were still mounted and public programs were offered.

The society's salesroom and gallery closed in July 1930. The stated reasons for the closure included an insufficient number of craftsmen consigning work; competitors underselling the gallery; the quality of work not being up to the standards required by the Society; the gallery not being known well enough locally because of insufficient advertising; and the public not being craft-minded.[41] Undoubtedly, the 1929 Stock Market Crash and the ensuing Depression also had a significant impact on the buying public, since crafted items were not necessities.

A 1930 broadside announced that instead of maintaining a continuous salesroom, the Arts and Crafts Society was starting a new venture for the public and for craftsmen: "We anticipate enlarging our field of work and our plan is to hold exhibits and sales at our workshops on the Barnes Road, where we have much larger quarters."[42] Once again, it was Julia Hoffman to the rescue. The workshops the society referred to were actually those Hoffman had built on her own property. The transformed Arts and Crafts Society eventually evolved into what is known today as the Oregon College of Art and Craft, located on Barnes Road just a mile or so away from where Hoffman's workshops had been the lifeblood of survival for the society.

As one considers the impact of the national Arts and Crafts movement on the Northwest, it is clear that the Arts and Crafts Society of Portland, through Julia Hoffman's contacts, passion, and work, made Portland an exemplar of what was happening elsewhere in the nation. Hoffman's efforts to band together communities of arts and crafts workers and the commitment of her own personal funds directly led to a permanent teaching center for the arts and crafts in Portland.

EUGENE

Like Julia Hoffman in Portland, Allen Hendershott Eaton in Eugene was the catalyst of much that happened between 1907 and 1917 related to the Arts and Crafts movement in the southern end of Oregon's Willamette Valley. Eaton, born in Oregon, grew up appreciating the home handiwork of his grandmother and others around him. Later in his career, after he became known for his research and books on American handcrafts in New England and the South, he wrote that his grandmother, Mrs. Hendershott, of Union County, Oregon, proved conclusively British designer Walter Crane's assertion that "needlework is the most domestic, the most delicate and the most beautiful of all handicrafts."[43]

Eaton graduated from the University of Oregon at Eugene in 1902. For a short period of time, he may have been involved with a store selling art in Portland in 1907. In response to Julia Hoffman's arranging to secure a few pieces of Grueby Faience Company's pottery for the Arts and Crafts exhibition planned for Portland in 1907, the firm's representative, Henry Belknap, wrote to the Portland Art Association, "We are sending to you . . . 30 vases, 6 scarabs, 7 single tiles, 8 frames of tiles. . . . A list of prices will follow in a day or two, and those that are unsold are to be delivered at the close of the exhibition to Eaton & Winstanley."[44] Three days later, Henrietta Failing in Portland wrote Julia Hoffman that "Mr. Eaton is now in Eugene & the shop here is closed."[45] Hoffman's response was, "Do you mean that Mr. Eaton has closed his shop permanently? I have been telling consignors of his place and that I would see him about taking unsold articles."[46]

Eaton had relocated to Eugene, because on March 27 he wrote to the Portland Art Association that he had heard from Grueby Faience about the upcoming exhibit. He expressed a wish to be kept informed about upcoming exhibits, explaining, "I would like to take advantage of anything good." He graciously offered to help in any way he could and closed with a question, "Are you planning an exhibit of book bindings?"[47]

He wrote another letter three days later, evidently in response to Failing's reply. "I have not forgotten your suggestions about interesting people to do something or other with—but between politics and business I have been kept busy during the past few months. But, if you ever choose to make an exhibit of Oregon handiwork, I can get you some rather good things in weaving (cotton), embroidery, wood and metal work and bookbinding."[48]

That passage underscored two characteristics of Eaton's interest in the arts and crafts: an emphasis on Oregon handiwork and a liberal definition of what should be considered broadly within the Arts and Crafts aesthetic. His expansive approach became apparent several years later when he assembled the contents of the Art Room in the Oregon Building for the Panama-Pacific International Exposition in San Francisco in 1915.

A 1907 letterhead from Eaton's Eugene book and stationery store indicated that he sold art goods, Japanese ware, pottery, picture frames, Pendleton Indian-style blankets, and Navajo rugs. A full description of the store appeared in an article in the *Sunday Oregonian* on May 24, 1908. Written by Miriam Van Waters of Eugene, the article—"Reviving Individuality Among Hand Workers: Influence on Portland of the Arts and Crafts Movement which is Getting a Foothold Here; What the City of Eugene has Done in a Practical Way to Develop Hand and Brain"—was long, informative, and provocative. It started with a summary overview of the history and philosophy of the Arts and Crafts movement. Then she laid out her concern about relying too much on supporters of the movement who were not serious workers or apprentices, or, as she called them, "faddists." The faddists, she wrote, are primarily "worthy women, and lend social position to the movement, which, of course, counts for a good deal. Through these channels craftsman ideals have spread rapidly throughout the country."

Van Waters' article threw cold water on Portland's new Society of Arts and Crafts. She wrote that while she appreciated the fact that "active exertion with hammer and file" was a more useful expenditure of time than "bridge-playing and pink teas," and that she understood that "it is a firm principle of Arts and Crafts that the aesthetic impulse can and should be cultivated everywhere, even in high society," the squandering of opportunities for developing arts and crafts skills by any group not intending to become serious workers went against the ideal of the movement. The conditions in Portland, she wrote, were "due no doubt to the newness of Arts and Crafts in the West. But the time is ripe for the advent of workers of the true William Morris type."

Championing Eugene over Portland, Van Waters asserted that Portland did not hold the honor of starting the first Northwest association in support of the Arts and Crafts movement. She noted that Eugene had taken the lead in the western Arts and Crafts movement with a society organized a month before Portland's. She credited much of the Eugene association's progress to the indefatigable efforts of its president, Allen Eaton: "He owns one of the most beautiful art stores in the country, is interested in politics . . . and yet finds time personally to oversee the practical details of Eugene handicrafts." She exclaimed that Eaton's store had been called by eminent men the most beautiful art room in the West. Eaton designed and executed the store interior finished entirely of wood from Lane County, of which Eugene was the county seat. The lights were enclosed in copper lanterns and shades made and designed by Eaton. The store, she wrote, was like a beautiful room, harmonious and individualized.

The commercial element of the store, she wrote, was successfully subordinated. By displaying examples of the best craft handwork in America, Eaton sought to stimulate the local Arts and Crafts workers. Eaton assembled for show and sale a collection of art pottery from potteries such as Rookwood, Van Briggle, Grueby, Newcomb, Teco, and Pewabic. His store featured Jarvie lanterns and candlesticks from Chicago; samples of the best bookbinding from England and America; hand-tooled leather; metalwork; and Craftsman jewelry. A special feature of Eaton's store was the children's room, to be repeated in concept in the 1915 Panama-Pacific International Exposition's Oregon Building's Art Room, which featured child-sized tables, chairs, and bookracks. To this corner children at all times had free and delighted access.

Van Waters touted the success of Eaton's store on several fronts:

This Rookwood showroom ceramic plaque designed by Sarah Toohey after 1908 was probably from Allen Eaton's shop in Eugene. M. & M. Krenk Collection. Photography by Hermon Joyner.

Chief among these is Mr. Eaton's book bindery, where good work is being turned out. Here Miss Ruth Parkhurst, of Boston, served as an apprentice, mastering the craft in its popular aspects. Miss Parkhurst intends to enter artistic book binding as a profession in which there is a large Western field almost untouched. . . .

In addition to the bindery, a decided success has been made of leather and basketry, rug weaving, cabinetmaking, metal and wood work, and to a lesser extent the weaving of fabrics. These are strong indications that the seeds of an industrial colony are being sown.[49]

Van Waters' lofty praise of Eugene's arts and crafts association over that of Portland's may have been a little premature, as not even Eaton's enthusiasm could sustain its efforts. An *Oregonian* article in 1914 stated that over 5,000 people had visited an exhibit of paintings by American artists in the Eugene Commercial Club. On a Sunday afternoon in three hours, 975 people viewed the exhibit. That interest encouraged art lovers in Eugene to plan for a permanent club, making reference to the earlier formation of an arts and crafts society that "languished after a time." Among those listed who were interested in the older organization and anxious to revive it was Allen Eaton.[50]

Eaton continued to be involved with the Arts and Crafts Society of Portland, apparently staying out of any rivalries between Eugene and the state's largest city to the north. In 1910 he was chair of the society's Committee for Leather & Bookbinding as items were being sought for the annual arts and crafts exhibition in Portland.[51] Eaton exhibited a table of "books bound in linen, pretty rugs and other attractive articles."[52] At the close of the exhibit, the *Spectator* listed Eaton among those whose work was especially meritorious in design and execution, and gave him awards of merit for rugs, baskets, and books bound by him.[53]

The year 1915 was a busy one for Allen Eaton. He was appointed to the faculty of the University of Oregon as that school's first instructor of Art Appreciation, and was placed in charge of the planning, design, and installation of an Art Room for the Oregon Building at the Panama-Pacific International Exposition in San Francisco.

A three-page printed prospectus explained Eaton's concepts for the Art Room. He stated that the endeavor was to have a room artistic in design and arrangement, containing exhibits and objects of merit, but that the fundamental motive behind the room was educational: "The room in its structure, its furniture and furnishings, and all the exhibits, will aim to bring together in an attractive unity the work of the Oregon manufacturer, the Oregon artist and the Oregon craftsman, and there will be nothing in this room done by anyone else."[54] Furniture, for example, was to be made from Coos Bay myrtle, and chairs made by the Willow Furniture Company of Hillsboro, Oregon, from willows in the Willamette Valley.

Wall coverings were to be of Oregon wool by Oregon woolen mills; tiles and pottery would be made from Oregon clay; and leatherwork and bookbinding would utilize the leather taken from hides of Oregon domestic and wild animals. Eaton also promised to exhibit metalwork in lead, iron, and copper, all native to Oregon, and some examples of jewelry made from the state's gold and silver, in which would be set some semiprecious stones and agates from Oregon's coast, rivers, and deserts. Obviously, Eaton had a theme in mind. The Art Room would, the prospectus claimed, also include a careful selection of paintings, photographs, books, verse, and musical compositions, all by Oregon artists.

Eaton proclaimed that the exhibit would not be extensive but good, the selections being made largely for decorative purposes. The intent was to include something from most of the Arts and Crafts modes being practiced in America. He also intended to have indigenous Oregon flowers in the room at all times. He was already planning ahead as he wrote that he just had planted some Mount Hood lily bulbs in clay pots manufactured by the Pacific Stoneware Company, which, he wrote, would make beautiful and consistent decorations for the room. As a clincher, Eaton ended his prospectus with these words: "When the room is finished we will print a catalogue on paper manufactured in Oregon from type cast here and use inks made in Portland."

Eaton lived up to his promises. The finished room was constructed of Northwest red cedar with exposed beams in keeping with the Arts and Crafts style and was lit by electric lanterns made by a stained glass designer from Portland out of cedar frames and transparent paper enclosures with silhouettes of Oregon scenes. The Art Room contained an Arts and Crafts dining table and eight matching armchairs of myrtle wood, designed by Portland architect Wade Pipes and lent by the North Bend Manufacturing Company in North Bend, Oregon. Oregon artists and craftspeople also exhibited handmade baskets, including several from the Grand Ronde Indians of Oregon, examples of wood carving, bookplate designs, furniture, furnishings, leaded glass, metalwork, paintings, photography, pottery, sculpture, weaving, and children's toys. In addition, books, printing and illumination, and music were a part of this "Made in Oregon" display in San Francisco.[55]

While certainly different from California's exhibit of Arts and Crafts work from the Golden State shown at the Seattle Alaska-Yukon-Pacific Exposition in 1909, the Art Room in the Oregon Building of the Panama-Pacific International Exposition (1915) clearly helped set the stage for Eaton's lifework with American crafts.

As an instructor at the University of Ore-

[top] The Art Room in the Oregon Building at the Panama-Pacific International Exposition (San Francisco, 1915) was designed by Allen Eaton and featured Oregon-made furnishings, including a table and chairs designed by Wade Pipes and lighting designed and fabricated by Edward Bruns Company. Mason Collection.

[above] Mission furniture was made by Oregon Agricultural College Industrial Arts Shop students for the Oregon Building at the Panama-Pacific International Exposition in San Francisco (1915). University Archives, Oregon State University (Corvallis), HC 601.

Embracing the Arts and Crafts Movement ◆ 79

gon, Allen Eaton lectured on art history and the role of art in society, and also organized art exhibitions on campus. He spent the summers of 1916 and 1917 teaching in a summer school for art in Wyoming, New York. In addition to his work with art and the university, he maintained his book and art store, and still had time to serve several terms in the Oregon Legislature beginning in 1906.

Caught up in a controversy over his attending a Socialist antiwar rally in Chicago in 1917 that became associated with the Industrial Workers of the World (IWW), Eaton found himself a victim of wartime hysteria. Oregon media branded him as unpatriotic, anti-American, and a pro-German pacifist. He reluctantly submitted to immense pressure and resigned from his teaching position at the university. In 1918, Eaton decided to seek reelection to the state legislature. Since 1906 he had been one of Lane County's most popular delegates, but, because of the controversy still broiling around him, he finished last among six candidates. Later that year, he closed the store that had been the center of Arts and Crafts endeavors in Eugene for almost a dozen years and moved with his family to New York.[56]

Eaton's departure from the Arts and Crafts scene in Oregon was a great loss to the Northwest. He later became known as the "Dean of American Handicrafts" for his work on American folk art and craft. His books *Handicrafts of New England* and *Handicrafts of the Southern Highlands* are still considered authoritative works on pre-1930s crafts in those regions. One can only speculate what his interests and scholarship might have produced if he had stayed in Oregon.

SEATTLE

In Seattle, local interest in Arts and Crafts ideals preceded the Alaska-Yukon-Pacific Exposition of 1909 by at least six years. Ongoing coverage of women's club activities throughout the region appeared frequently in the *Seattle Mail and Herald*. The articles offer a glimpse of how one local club set itself on a path to producing yearly Arts and Crafts exhibitions that, in affiliation with the Washington State Arts and Crafts Society, showed the efforts of artists and craftspeople from the entire state of Washington, in every discipline—even pyrography, the burning of designs in wood and leather. In September 1903, the Women's Century Club of Seattle, founded in 1891, stimulated its members with a study topic, "The Arts and Crafts Movement." Three papers delivered by club members were presented about the ideas and work of Ruskin, Morris, and Hubbard.[57] The following January plans were initiated to hold an exposition of allied arts and crafts. Besides displays of fine art, the club intended to include china painting, pyrography, leatherwork, hand carving, needlework and other handicrafts. It also wanted to show the best work being done in the manual training departments of the public schools.[58]

The Women's Century Club achieved its goal of gathering a wide array of handicrafts to show along with the fine art. The *Seattle Mail and Herald* commented that, "Taken together, the Exhibit was a decided revelation of the talent in various artistic lines which Seattle shelters and of which she has reason to be proud."[59]

Delighted with the success of this initial effort, the club forged ahead after a summer hiatus to plan for an even larger display the following spring. By October it had garnered the support of the popular Tacoma artist Abby Williams Hill, who consented to espouse the movement and interests of Tacoma art. Harriet Foster Beecher, of Port Townsend, one of the mainstays of Washington's art community since the 1880s, also assured the Women's Century Club of her support and cooperation.[60]

The club's second Arts and Crafts exposition opened on May 29, 1905, with a first-day crowd of over 600 people. China, needlework, and paintings were artistically arranged, and the press was complimentary, calling it the most successful art exhibit ever given in the Northwest. The *Seattle Mail and Herald* proclaimed that, "The result far surpassed the wildest imaginations of the most optimistic member of the Women's Century Club, under whose auspices the exhibition was held, and the verdict of the public at large was that the artists of this part of the world need not fear to enter competition anywhere."[61]

These pivotal exhibits assured the Women's Century Club that it was providing a valuable service by offering an outlet to regional artists, whether they were professionals or working out of their homes. There was also value in promoting the importance of continuing manual and design arts in the public schools to stimulate talent in local communities. Finally, by giving the public an opportunity to witness current ideas about art and craft, it was creating a more sophisticated clientele for objects that were beautiful and useful in the many new homes being built.

Encouraged by its early successes, the club continued to produce yearly exhibits that attracted more and more submissions. In the press coverage for the 1906 Arts and Crafts exhibition, mention was made of Mission-style chairs and a table made by manual training students in the local school. In the following year, for the first time the exhibitor list and coverage seemed to imply a larger participation by serious craftspeople earning a living in creating handmade items, including beaten copper by Jessie Fisken and Mrs. John Ballard and photographs by Adelaide Hanscom. The exhibition also included work by the nationally known ceramic artist Franz A. Bischoff, who had been in Seattle teaching china painting.[62]

The 1908 exhibition appears to have been the club's most ambitious undertaking, preparing the group for taking charge of the handicraft exhibits at the A-Y-P Exposition the following year. An undated news clipping noted that the fifth annual exhibit of the Washington State Arts and Crafts Society was the best of its kind "ever held in size and quality." It contained nearly 500 works of art shown in seven large rooms. On display were oil paintings, watercolors, and designs from various craft disciplines: "One of the most attractive features of the exhibition is the display of chinaware and needlework for which one room is reserved. Here are seen a number of beautiful specimens of the potters' art and a collection of extremely valuable articles of needlework, among the latter being delicately worked hangings and ornamental pieces, as well as many articles of domestic use. In the same room is exhibited ornamental leather."[63]

In the same year another local organization, the Society of Seattle Artists, became the Seattle Fine Arts Society, pledging to cultivate an interest in and a taste for fine art and artistic handicraft among residents of Seattle. Although the phrase "artistic handicraft" was used, for the most part the society's subsequent exhibitions and educational efforts were more focused on the fine arts. This organization was the forerunner to the development of the Seattle Art Museum several decades later.[64]

The Western Academy of the Beaux Arts also was incorporated in 1908. Based on values encouraged by the Arts and Crafts movement, the academy's mission was:

> To make art practical, and to turn out here in Seattle good workmen in the lines of illustrating, painting, sculpture, wood carving, cabinet making, metal working, architecture, and kindred lines of art.
>
> It is not the idea of the school to strive solely for the ideals in art which are obtainable only by the genius, but rather to turn out finished workmen in all lines of art who will do real art work, which will find its way into Seattle homes and beautify the surroundings and lives of Seattle people.[65]

The small group of artists who formed the Beaux Arts Workshop shared workspace in a University of Washington–owned downtown building. Their objective was to establish a community where Arts and Crafts ideals could be lived out. They selected their Beaux Arts Village site along the wooded shoreline of Lake Washington, a ferry ride away from Seattle. Although the concept and layout of the first homes of the village, designed to blend in harmony with nature, were certainly a mentally and visually appealing part of the Arts and Crafts movement in the Northwest, there is little evidence of arts and crafts objects being created there.[66]

In the meantime, in 1908, the Women's Century Club was already preparing itself to take charge of the sixth annual exhibit of the Washington State Arts and Crafts Society to be held at the A-Y-P Exposition the following year under the leadership of Mrs. W. A. Foster, chair of the society, and Mrs. H. B. Fish, the club president. The exhibit space was to be in the rotunda of the Manufacturers Building, where there was a "well-lighted section, with floor dimensions of 90 × 100 feet and accompanying wall space." There, the club members hoped to show much of the best Arts and Craft work from around the state.[67]

Their exhibition space had been referred to as the Women's Court. It, along with an Inventor's Court, Architectural Court, Indian Court, and Court of History, featured specialized exhibits that showcased creative output in Washington: "The court will contain all work that is the handiwork of women of Seattle and the state of Washington. It will be the center for embroidery, sewing, fancy and plain, weaving, ceramic art, pyrographic work, and in fact, for all the pursuits that women enter for profit or pleasure."[68] The media and visiting public were pleased. The positive news coverage of the exhibit continued throughout the duration of the A-Y-P Exposition. Not as well documented was the exhibition of applied arts by men. Even in the published newspaper lists of award and medal winners, the entries of regional male craftsmen were seldom mentioned.

Along with this important exhibit, women's work was displayed in great quantity at the State Federation of Women's Clubs Building under the watchful eye of Mrs. H. W. Allen of Spokane, president of the federation. A September 6, 1909, article in the *Seattle Post-Intelligencer* series on the A-Y-P Exposition mentioned the extensive exhibit of the creations of Washington women in Arts and

On the second floor of the Women's Building, A-Y-P Exposition (Seattle, 1909), the Washington State Women's Exhibit was the most extensive display of art and handicraft done by women throughout the state. Paintings and textiles predominated, but ceramics can be seen on display cases. Alaska-Yukon-Pacific Exposition Commission Report. Courtesy of Wessel & Lieberman.

Crafts work on the second floor of the Women's Building. Along with a showing of paintings and other fine arts, the article also mentioned ceramics, hammered brass, tooled and burnt leather, carved and burnt wood, and needlework of every description. An interesting component of this exhibit was the inclusion of basketry and beadwork of the Indian women of the state.

With over 1,000 items featured, the article claimed that the exhibit was the largest of women's work in any exposition. In collecting the exhibited items, no attempt was made to seek studio or professional work. Instead, the organizers accepted voluntary contributions representing the work of Washington women as found in homes throughout the state. Not a single item of women's handiwork that was sent was refused space in the show. It can only be imagined the wide assortment of talent and would-be talent represented in an exhibition with no discrimination in selection.

Nationally known companies and artisans creating items in recognized Arts and Crafts styles had a visible presence at the Seattle exposition. Major awards were given to displays by Rookwood Pottery Company; Frost's Arts and Crafts Shop of Dayton, Ohio; and Mildred Watkins, the metalworker from Cleveland, Ohio, who had conducted the summer workshop in Portland.

While the fine arts exhibit warranted a catalog listing all the paintings and sculpture, there was no documentation of the applied and decorative arts in either the Women's Building or the Manufacturers Building. By contrast, the state of California issued a catalog of the fine and applied arts exhibited in its building. Included in the publication were lists of work submitted by some of today's most recognized Arts and Crafts artisans from California, including leatherwork and a variety of Arts and Crafts items from

At Mrs. Bush's studio in the Boston Block, Seattle, women painted from a model, March 12, 1907. Washington State Historical Society (Tacoma), Curtis 2782. Photograph by Asahel Curtis.

Charles Frederick Eaton and his daughter, Elizabeth Burton; leather from the Compañeros; jewelry from G. Kellogg Claxton and Mrs. R. P. Jennings; metalwork from Dirk Van Erp; bookbinding from Rosa G. Taussig; and pictorialist photographs from Oscar Maurer, Laura Adams Armer, Anna Brigman, Louis Fleckenstein, and W. E. Dassonville. The San Francisco Keramic Club, the Los Angeles Keramic Club, and individual artists displayed pieces of hand-painted china. There also was an exhibit of items from craftspeople involved with the College of Fine Arts in Los Angeles, including copper, brass, pottery, and tile work.[69]

The A-Y-P Exposition in Seattle heightened the city's interest in the Arts and Crafts movement for the next several years. An undated *Seattle Times* newspaper article, c. 1911–1912, reported that the Arts and Crafts vision was well nourished in Seattle life. As proof of the firm footing of the movement, the article referenced an exhibition of more than 2,000 pieces of pottery held in the commercial studios of W. W. Kellogg, Seattle's premier tile

distributor. More than 2,500 people attended that display. In addition, the two schools of instruction—Ella Bush's art school in the Boston Block and the Beaux Arts School for instruction in arts and crafts—were cited as contributors to a greater public interest, as demonstrated by increased enrollment. The growth of manual training in the public schools also was given credit for the surge in interest in craftsmanship in Seattle. The making of Mission furniture, metalworking, stenciling, block printing, tooled leatherwork, and bookbinding were given as examples of work being created by youth in the schools.

Seattle was initially inspired by the exhibits organized by the Women's Century Club, by the Beaux Arts Society artist workshops and its planned community, and by the progressive approach of businesses such as W. W. Kellogg's. The Alaska-Yukon-Pacific Exposition brought nationally recognized Arts and Crafts products and craftspeople to Seattle in 1909, focusing attention on items already being marketed in local stores and shops. Manual and domestic arts programs introduced school-age children to handiwork skills they could employ to produce beautiful objects for their homes.

Unfortunately, there was no continuity in

Students in a class in the art department of Oregon Agricultural College (1915) produced these hand-built clay pots and pounded metal objects. University Archives, Oregon State University (Corvallis), HC 604.

this brief interest in the Arts and Crafts movement. No one organization or dedicated individual in Seattle, with the interest and determination to sustain the movement's ideals in people's minds, stepped forward to lead the effort. National and regional attention began to refocus elsewhere as World War I became an ever-increasing distraction. Seattle's leading art school of the period, the Cornish School of Art, focused most of its attention on music, drama, painting, and sculpture rather than the applied arts. As the Northwest busied itself with war preparations, Seattle's interest in the Arts and Crafts movement waned dramatically. There were a few notable exceptions, such as Albert Berry's metalwork; regional fine artists and printmakers; and a group of photographers, predominantly Japanese American, who eventually organized the Seattle Camera Club.

Higher Education

Corvallis, Oregon, a short distance north of Eugene, was home to the Oregon Agricultural College (later renamed Oregon State University). Nicely laid out in a design by the Olmsted Brothers of Brookline, Massachusetts, the campus was the center of activity in the Corvallis region. In the early years of that institution, it was primarily known as a men's school because of the emphasis on agriculture, forestry, mining, engineering, pharmacy, and commerce. In an effort to attract more women students, OAC initiated a School of Home Economics. A 1915 catalog described the usefulness of instruction in domestic arts. Photo illustrations showed women making baskets, sewing, and cooking. Although some courses might lead to a livelihood, such as dressmaking and millinery work, they were generally home-oriented. On the last page of that catalog, however, there was an intriguing series of photo illustrations with the title "Art and Architecture," which portrayed student handiwork in pottery, metalwork, jewelry, and needlework, all done in Arts and Crafts designs and styles. Even the borders around the photographs on the page presented stylized, repeated design motifs common to Arts and Crafts texts.[70]

Another OAC publication from just a bit later in that time period, *The College Girl at O.A.C.*, indicated that the courses for young women were widely expanded, and suggested

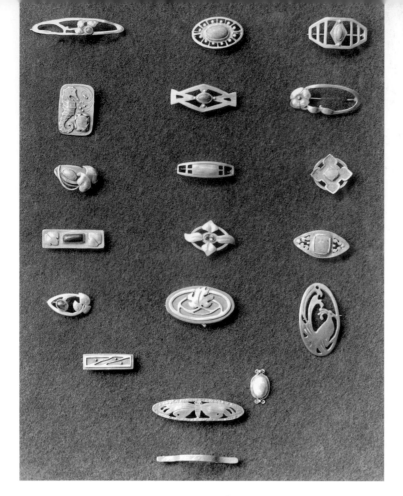

Women studying applied arts at Oregon Agricultural College, c. 1915, created these metal brooches. University Archives, Oregon State University (Corvallis), HC 604.

that there might be careers for women beyond the traditional discipline of home economics. Programs cited as being of interest included agriculture, pharmacy, commerce, vocational education, and engineering, "for no course in the College is denied to qualified women." Included in this promotional booklet was a page devoted to the basic arts:

> Beautifully modeled vases and bowls and hand-made jewelry of intricate design are a delight to the owner. But how much more so when these vases, bowls, and jewelry are our own craftsmanship, or that of some friend? In connection with the Applied Art work, the courses in Color and Design, in Clay Modeling and Pottery, and in Jewelry Making present attractive opportunities for original expression to girls in the various

schools of the institution. Original designs are worked out and applied in the laboratories. Copper, silver, and gold are used as media for carrying out pierced, carved and filigree designs with various stones used as insets. To students interested in photography or kodakry, the Physics department presents an attractive opportunity, with its courses in pictorial and commercial photography.[71]

Photographs in the Oregon State University archives show examples of manual and applied artwork created by students during the first three decades of the twentieth century. Mission-style furniture made by students in the OAC woodshops was shipped to San Francisco for seating in the Oregon Building at the Panama-Pacific exposition. Arts and Crafts design–inspired pottery, jewelry, metalwork, and textiles also were featured in many of the photographs.

Based on activities at Oregon Agricultural College in the period, it would not be surprising to find that most schools of higher education in Oregon and Washington had some instruction in coursework related to the Arts and Crafts movement. Most normal schools or teachers' colleges probably offered classes in basic design. Arthur Wesley Dow's classic explanations of good Arts and Crafts design in his book, *Composition*, and the Prang series of design booklets for young children were standard teaching aids for instructing students in the basic elements of art and design during the first two decades of the twentieth century.

In the 1920s, at the end of the Arts and Crafts movement's period of primary impact, it is interesting to note that several Pacific Northwest college teachers were fre-

quent contributors to *Design: Keramic Studio* (and its precursor titles), including Nowland B. Zane, on the art faculty at the University of Oregon; Helen Rhodes, an art instructor at the University of Washington; and Margaret B. Lawsing, of the Oregon Agricultural College. Many of those articles were illustrated with the authors' own work or that of their students. One of Zane's articles was classic Arts and Crafts design prose, modified to specifically relate to a student's interest in artistically capturing the essence of the Cascade Range of Oregon and Washington: "Taking the hint from Nature, we find the compositional factors of mountain landscapes to be the mountains themselves for necessary character, plus the secondary features of 'snow caps,' water falls, glaciers, tall trees and flowers. Reduce these factors to simple, geometric shapes and compose them interestingly and our design will express the spirit of the highlands." [72]

The Role of the Manual Arts

An important factor in the growing awareness and appreciation of the applied arts in the Pacific Northwest and throughout the nation was the expansion of manual arts pro-

[top] Display of student pottery at Oregon Agricultural College, c. 1922. University Archives, Oregon State University (Corvallis), HC 604.

[above] This ceramic pot with blue matte glaze by a student at Oregon Agricultural College may be the one pictured in the c. 1922 historic photograph. Mason Collection. Photograph by Hermon Joyner.

Students in a Monmouth, Oregon, primary school class made baskets (c. 1910). Oregon Historical Society (Portland), CN 010321.

grams in public schools. Manual training, often confused with trade schools and vocational training, had as its premise the notion that the coordination of head and hand was essential to creating a well-rounded individual with heightened sensitivities to beauty, aesthetics, and work ethics that would serve in everyday life.

Arts and Crafts proponents, such as Elbert Hubbard, saw a direct parallel between the movement and manual training in schools. They believed that young people working with their hands as well as their heads would achieve a sense of self-reliance and usefulness. Hubbard, in his own writings, quoted Friedrich Froebel, who had established the first kindergarten in Blankenberg, Germany, in 1836. Froebel believed that art and play were natural parts of the development of children. "The hand does nothing save as it is directed by the brain. And in order to develop your brain you must use both hands."[73]

An Educational Congress was held in conjunction with Portland's Lewis and Clark Centennial Exposition in 1905. The discussion leader on the topic of manual training was B. W. Johnson, superintendent of manual training in the Seattle Public Schools. Excerpts from the paper he delivered covered key values:

Children do not go to school merely to learn facts, but to be trained how to learn, how to think, how to help themselves. . . . Things and nature, as well as books and words, should form part of our educational curriculum. . . . The school curriculum should be related to life, and not merely to examinations. . . . The eye and the hand are such important aids in intellectual development that the training of these important members should form part of every natural system of education.

The advocates of manual instruction believe thoroughly in the value of literary instruction, but advocate that in a complete and harmonious education, art and industry must, too, be recognized.[74]

Oregon and Washington colleges and normal schools involved in teacher training began to introduce instruction in manual arts as early as 1899 when the State Normal School at Monmouth, Oregon, announced a new department of manual training. By 1905 the Ashland Normal School in southern Oregon offered manual training, including sewing, basket weaving, cardboard work, and woodwork. Other colleges were adding similar classes to keep up with this well-received regional and national trend.

In manual training instruction, the ability to express a student's ideas in a graphic form was considered as important as the item's construction. This fit as a logical extension of the *sløyd* method of teaching being used in the United States at the time. Developed in Germany and Sweden, the concept of *sløyd* involved learning though a series of graded exercises, each a complete project in itself, ending with the use of tools in the construction of items from wood, cardboard, or paper.

Manual arts followed manual training, a change that included the concept of beauty and design in construction. This concept worked in harmony with the introduction of drawing and art classes as an essential part of a school curriculum. A 1909 *Sunday Oregonian* article pointed out that the purpose of drawing classes in schools was not to develop professional artists, but "rather the development and completing of mind. . . . Its primal idea is to cultivate the entire circle of necessary ideas to make artistic minds, along with the exercise of their powers. Only through practical experience in drawing and painting can the pupil acquire discriminating and intelligent eyes."[75]

The 1909 A-Y-P Exposition in Seattle show-

[top] Students studied color in preparation for designing and assembling books in an applied arts class at Longfellow School, Seattle, c. 1914. Washington State Historical Society (Tacoma), Curtis 29925. Photograph by Asahel Curtis.

[above] The first floor of the Education Building, A-Y-P Exposition (Seattle, 1909), showed quality handiwork of students throughout Washington. The (foreground, left) Mission settee, table, lamp, and hanging lighting fixtures demonstrate the emphasis of the Arts and Crafts in local schools. Alaska-Yukon-Pacific Exposition Commission Report. Courtesy of Wessel & Lieberman.

cased manual arts displays from schools throughout the state of Washington and from Portland, Oregon. For the first time in the history of expositions, an education department had its own building. Mission furniture and Arts and Crafts handiwork in the Washington Education Building were the pride of school districts throughout the state.

In a Seattle newspaper, R. D. Bailey described a model schoolroom and a demonstration room for cookery and manual training. The upper floor was divided into fifteen booths, each occupied by a school display from one or more Washington counties. Many of the booths were furnished with chairs, reading tables, writing desks, and settees made by boys in manual training classes. Two booths were occupied by the three normal schools, Bellingham, Cheney, and Ellensburg. "Many handsome pieces of furniture and much of the sewing from the Seattle high schools" were located on the building's south balcony, "one of the most comfortable and attractive spots on the entire grounds."[76]

Of special note in the Washington Education Building was the live exhibit where in one room a class of boys from Olympia High School was busy with hammers and saws, creating their idea of a model kitchen and dining room. The boys also were charged with making a complete set of dining room furniture during the course of the summer. The state capital city of Olympia had good reason to be proud of its youth: "Many cities sent school representatives to inspect Olympia's departments for ideas and methods. Olympia's preeminence in this direction is further evidenced from the fact that the Olympia High School was the only one having a separate building and display at the AYP Exposition,

where the daily demonstrations of the manual training and domestic science departments, conducted by Olympia students themselves, are attracting great attention and interest."[77]

Throughout Washington, school districts worked long and hard to assemble exhibits to display in the Education Building. Articles in many newspapers carried headlines such as "Tacoma Public Schools and a Walla Walla Display" and "Benton Schools Show Handiwork; Arts & Crafts by Children to be Exhibited at AYPE." Typical was this notice from Prosser, Washington:

> Having collected exhibits from practically every school in Benton County, including displays of arts and crafts work, as well as relief and outline maps, Miss Annie Goff, county superintendent of schools, is now mounting the entire display for a showing at the Alaska-Yukon-Pacific exposition. The exhibit is one of the most complete ever arranged by any county schools in Central Washington, and when fully arranged will give any observer an accurate idea of every school district and its character, both as to school work and as to general conditions.
>
>   Manual training work is shown to some extent, principally the work of boys and girls of the fifth, sixth, and seventh grades. The boys turned their hands to woodwork and have a creditable display of furniture. The needle and fancy work done by the girls would be the envy of many who spend hours each day doing such work.[78]

The A-Y-P Exposition was also the showcase for work done by the manual training students in Portland's public schools under the direction of William J. Standley. The community thought so highly of the student work that the Portland Art Museum hosted an exhibition of

The works of manual arts students were proudly displayed at one of Spokane's public schools in 1910. Northwest Museum of Arts & Culture, Eastern Washington State Historical Society (Spokane), MS 154. Folder 2.7.

the items that would be sent to the Seattle exhibition. Completed by boys ranging in age from twelve to seventeen years, the work included furniture, such as library tables, grandfather clocks, and desks; carved and inlaid woodwork; and beaten copper work, including candle sconces, paper cutters, blotter pads, and trays of various designs.[79]

William J. Standley (1864–1939), an English cabinetmaker and woodcarver, came to Portland in 1889. A decade later he started the first manual training school in Portland. Within two years, more than 100 students were enrolled. In 1901, the YMCA took over the school, and Standley served as its director until 1903 when he became the first superintendent of manual training for the Portland public school system. He resigned that position around 1910, returning to private work as a wood craftsman. Practicing what he preached, Standley exhibited his own work in many exhibitions, including those of the Arts and Crafts Society of Portland, the Portland Architectural Club, and the Panama-Pacific Exposition in San Francisco.

Regional newspapers continued to recognize good work produced by students throughout both states even after the excitement generated over the exhibits at the A-Y-P Exposition waned. The *Sunday Oregonian* of March 29, 1914, featured an illustrated article about manual training classes in Hood River High School under the direction of N. E. Fertig. The classes were conducted before and after regular school hours and during lunch period. One of the tests for the students was the drafting of plans for a five-room hip-roof bungalow. Local hardware stores in Hood River proudly displayed the Mission-style furniture and other work of the classes in their show windows. The merchants declared that the displays attracted more attention than any exhibits of their own wares, and they offered the students their cooperation toward securing additional displays in the future.[80]

In 1915 the Portland Art Museum mounted

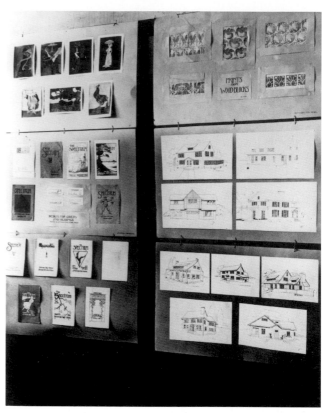

an exhibition of design and craftwork from the city's elementary and high schools. A newspaper article describing the quality of the work shown attributed it to the fact that the art and domestic art departments had worked together: "Interesting applied designs are exhibited in weaving, bookbinding, metal work, jewelry, textiles and leather. Another section of the exhibition features the development of the block print design from preliminary drawings from naturalistic flowers to the final application of the block print to the material. A number of clever posters are exhibited and several pieces of commercial work give evidence of originality."[81]

Manual training and domestic arts items probably make up the majority of the unsigned Arts and Crafts furniture, metalwork, tiles, textiles, and leatherwork that is now found in Oregon and Washington. Photographs of school displays show Mission chairs, pierced copper lampshades, jewelry, and other articles made by students. Often constructed with fir, and decorated with

mountain, tree, and animal designs easily recognized as Northwest inspired, these objects are reminders of the Arts and Crafts ideology expressed in the public schools during the first two decades of the twentieth century. By the end of World War I, manual arts training was giving way to industrial or vocational training, where the emphasis was on making a living through learning a trade rather than on developing a student's ability to think and work holistically through an appreciation for and application of the coordination of head and hand throughout his or her life.

Architecture and Allied Arts Exhibits, Organizations, and Schools

Architecture clubs in Portland and Seattle were formed early in the twentieth century to network, exhibit works, and offer competitions. The exhibitions of these early professional organizations, sometimes developed in association with their colleagues in the larger Architectural League of the Pacific Coast, served as venues for both regional and national Arts and Crafts expressions in architecture and the allied arts. Annual exhibition catalogs and yearbooks were heavily illustrated with the design work of local artisans and architects.

The Portland Architectural Club sponsored its first exhibition in 1908, following that with annual exhibits. The first exhibit, held at the Portland Art Museum, included several exhibitors who gave Portlanders a glimpse of some of the latest work in the field of Arts and Crafts—inspired design and products, including the poster-like frontispiece in the catalog designed by Morris Homans Whitehouse, a Portland architect. Local art glass designer Edward Bruns exhibited designs for stained

[clockwise from top left] The Lewis and Clark High School's booth at the Spokane Interstate Fair in 1914 displayed lamps, textiles, metal accessories, and other work by the students. The Mission light fixtures spell out the school name. Steve Franks Collection.

Students' architectural drawings, woodcuts, and book cover designs were displayed at Jefferson High School in Portland, c. 1916. Oregon Historical Society (Portland), CN 008116.

This blue vase was made by a student at Ballard High School, Seattle, 1916. Stephen and Cathy McLain Collection. Photograph by Barry Wong.

This hammered copper dish with fir tree and mountain design was typical of unsigned student work of the period. Mason Collection. Photograph by Hermon Joyner.

Portland Architectural Club poster, 1909. Mason Collection.
Photograph by Hermon Joyner.

glass windows for the Glenwood Inn in Riverside, California. The Povey Brothers Glass Company of Portland submitted nineteen entries for stained glass. William W. Kellogg, the tile distributor from Seattle, had twelve exhibits, including a cabinet of plain and decorated tiles from the Rookwood Pottery; a mosaic panel by Henry C. Mercer of Philadelphia; and mantels and tile arrangement sketches from Kellogg's own firm. Kellogg's regional competitor, Fred W. Wagner of Portland, also exhibited art tiles.[82]

The following year's exhibit was held in conjunction with the Architectural League of the Pacific Coast, which was organized in 1909 under the leadership of Ellis Lawrence, a highly regarded Portland architect. Collaboration with an organization that represented three Pacific states allowed for the inclusion of the architectural drawings and designs by the Greene brothers, architects in southern California, for their work on the Theodore Irwin house in Pasadena and the Mrs. A. Tichenor house in Long Beach. The Arts and Crafts Society of Portland's Shop of Fine Art and Industries and the Arts and Crafts Shop, owned and operated by Roma J. McKnight of Portland, exhibited Dedham and Marblehead pottery. Moore & Company of Portland showed eight pieces of Teco pottery, a large Teco pottery garden jardinière, and five pieces of Grueby. Several works related to William J. Standley were shown, including a carved oak seat done by manual arts students under his direction, as well as an oak bookrack carved by Standley and his drawings for a carved beam and other ornamentations in a Portland residence. The Pacific Art Glass Works of Portland, the Povey Brothers, and Edward Bruns presented art glass. Kellogg again exhibited Rookwood tile.[83]

Simultaneous with the exhibitions in Portland, Seattle was also exhibiting the best of regional architecture and design. A 1908 trade journal reported on the first annual exhibition of the Washington State Chapter of the American Institute of Architects in the gallery of the Seattle Public Library under the auspices of the Washington State Art Association. Applied arts were well represented in that exhibit, especially woodcarving and tiles, the latter exhibited by Kellogg.[84]

The Seattle Architectural Club published

This stained glass window triptych in the style of Arthur Wesley Dow was shown in the 1910 *Seattle Architectural Club Year Book* on the occasion of the First Annual Exhibition in Seattle of the Architectural League of the Pacific Coast. Dennis Andersen Collection.

a yearbook in connection with the first annual exhibition in Seattle of the Architectural League of the Pacific Coast in 1910, held in the gallery of the Washington State Art Association at the Seattle Public Library. Exhibitors similar to those in Portland were the mainstays in Seattle's exhibitions.

In subsequent years, Arts and Crafts—inspired architecture and applied arts items were either exhibited or included in the advertisements or illustrations of exhibition catalogs or annual yearbooks for Portland and Seattle's architectural clubs. This annual exposure to some of the best regional and national work was important to fostering Arts and Crafts ideals in Oregon and Washington.

In 1914, the University of Oregon established the state's first School of Architecture and Allied Arts, under the direction of Ellis Lawrence. That same year in Seattle, at the request of University of Washington president Henry Suzzallo, local architect Carl Gould helped to establish the University's Department of Architecture. These schools produced architects that would take the waning interest in the Arts and Crafts movement and adapt it to what would eventually become known as a Northwest regional style of architecture. While embracing modern trends in the design world, a number of Northwest architects acknowledged and were sympathetic to their natural surroundings, the particular topography, local materials, and quality of light that distinguished their environment as they planned buildings for the second half of the twentieth century.

PART II Architecture, Public and Private

·MT. BAKER LODGE·
EARL W. MORRISON·ARCHITECT·

THE INLAND EMPIRE ARCHITECT

PUBLISHED QUARTERLY BY
HYSLOP AND WESTCOTT
ARCHITECTS SPOKANE WN.

Vol. 1   1912   No. 4

FOUR
The Arts and Crafts Movement Goes Public

ELBERT HUBBARD'S SEPTEMBER 1909 trip to the Pacific Northwest included a lecture at Seattle's Arcade Hall in the Arcade Block on Thursday evening, September 30. He was there to attend the Alaska-Yukon-Pacific Exposition during its final weeks, and this gave him an opportunity to write about it in the *Fra* later that year. Unlike the substantial press he received in Spokane, neither the *Seattle Times* nor the *Seattle Post-Intelligencer* took notice of his visit, as it was inconveniently timed during the arrival of President William Howard Taft for Taft Day at the exposition. Every reporter in town was called on to follow Taft's movements, from his arrival to his dinners, his hotel accommodations, and the bee that stung him on the way to the fair.

In his report in the *Fra*, instead of describing in detail the layout, the buildings, and the exhibits, Hubbard decided to discuss the broader issues of growth and trade that were the keynotes of many of the fair's exhibits. In acknowledging the growing

[opposite, clockwise from top]
The cover of the 1916 deluxe edition of the *Craftsman Bungalows* catalog evoked the romantic relationship of house to garden. Dodge/Kreisman Collection.

Spokane architects Hyslop and Westcott promoted their projects with several handsome booklets produced during 1911 and 1912. Northwest Museum of Arts & Culture, Eastern Washington State Historical Society (Spokane).

Earl W. Morrison's 1927 design for Mount Baker Lodge referenced national parks architecture but adopted an English cottage style for the principal façade's curved roofline. The lodge's two-story bay and multipaned windows seemed more like an English manor house than a mountain retreat. Whatcom Museum of History and Art (Bellingham), x4956.

importance of Alaska's resources, he reminded his readers, "Alaska looks to the State of Washington as an entrance to the markets of America." He went on to make other astute remarks:

The sources of wealth are four. These are the farm, the forest, the mine and the sea. The factory follows, using the raw stock from one or all of the sources just named. But in securing this wealth from its natural source three necessary factors enter.

These factors are labor, capital, and enterprise. Labor alone, undirected by intelligence, is nil, and capital comes in and grubstakes both. The State of Washington has about one-fourth more square miles than the State of New York. Its line of sea-coast, however, is much greater than is that of New York. Columbia River, compared with the Hudson, traverses double the distance.

In mineral wealth, Washington is immensely rich. In coal-deposits, her bituminous supply is untouched and almost limitless in quantity. Washington has the farm, the forest, the mine and the sea.

But Washington lacks the labor, the enterprise and the capital needed to make her wealth fully available. She has tapped only a tithe of her resources. Her population is barely a million inhabitants, against New York's eight millions.

In order to give her wealth to the world, Washington must have men—the capital she can, in great measure, create. Conservative estimates show that she could support a population of ten million people.

Washington affords a natural trading-place where America and the Orient meet. Five transcontinental railroad-lines now have their Western termini at Seattle, against two for any other city.[1]

Hubbard needn't have concerned himself with growing manpower in the Northwest. It was already happening. The attention of the nation on Seattle during the exposition certainly improved business networking, communications, and trade, as well as encouraging people, who had only vague ideas about the Pacific Northwest, to visit and eventually relocate. That had certainly been true for Portland and its 1905 exposition. Population grew in both cities in the first decade of the century: Portland's increased from approximately 90,000 in 1900 to 250,000 by 1910, and Seattle's population increased from approximately 80,000 in 1900 to nearly 240,000 in 1910.

The Oregon and Washington expositions had an equally powerful impact on local politicians, businessmen, developers, and architects who visited the fair grounds. After experiencing these grand fairs—the spectacular promenades, planned vistas and fountains, handsome exposition buildings, comfortable lounges and meeting rooms, and fascinating exhibits—it was only a matter of time before City Beautiful ideas gleaned from the fair entered the mainstream.

The regional architectural community responded with building permanent buildings in the central business districts that reflected current thinking about the role of Classical architecture and the value of scale, proportion, harmony, and integrity of structure and materials. In the expert hands of such firms as Portland's Whidden and Lewis, and Albert E. Doyle, and Seattle's Bebb and Gould, A. H. Albertson, Harlan Thomas, and Somervell and Coté, as well as Kirtland Cutter in Spokane and Frederick Heath and Ambrose Russell in Tacoma, the clubs, hotels, and commercial and civic buildings that rose in Washington and Oregon business districts during this period compared favorably with their eastern and midwestern peers.

On occasion, these buildings, which could have been mistaken for buildings in any of America's large cities, also made reference to regional or local customs and heritage. The terra-cotta Indian heads along the upper façade of the 1909 Cobb Building in Seattle were allegedly inspired by the face of Chief Sealth. The terra-cotta walrus heads adorning the façade of the 1916 Arctic Club tied that Seattle building to the club members' connections to the Klondike gold rush.

Despite the assertive Classicism with which they greeted the public, the interiors of many of these buildings were designed and outfitted with Arts and Crafts furnishings. This was particularly true of clubs, hotels, and libraries, and may reflect the efforts of owners and club members to evoke a cozy, home-away-from-home environment for visitors in much the same way as the Hoo Hoo or the Arctic Brotherhood buildings had at the Alaska-Yukon-Pacific Exposition. And the style extended to churches and commercial buildings as well.

The placement of Mission oak furniture in the temple-like spaces of the Washington and New York Buildings at the exposition may have also legitimatized its use in the everyday world downtown. One can also speculate that since cost was always a factor in interior decoration and furnishing, Mission oak furniture may have been chosen because it was significantly less expensive than mahogany carved pieces. Traditional mahogany furniture might be used for the private dining room or reception room. But public lounges, libraries, and billiard and card rooms, which generally re-

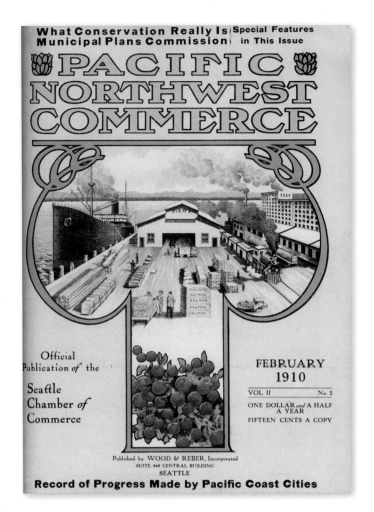

On its colorful Art Nouveau–inspired cover, *Pacific Northwest Commerce* (February 1910), a local trade journal published by the Seattle Chamber of Commerce, depicted the region's bounty being shipped and rail-freighted worldwide. Seattle Public Library.

quired numerous chairs, settees, desks, tables, and lamps, might best be furnished with affordable pieces that could handle heavy use and even abuse with hardly a nick or scratch.

Another underlying factor of furnishing choices at the time may have been class-consciousness. West Coast city dwellers, unlike their counterparts in the cities of the long-established East Coast, may have been expressing their independence from old money and long-held traditions through favoring the informality of the Mission style and feeling free to "mix and match" in architecture, interior design, and decoration.

The Cobb Building, Seattle.

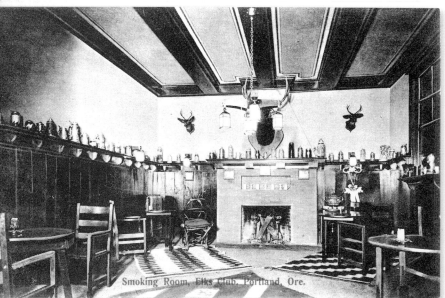

Smoking Room, Elks Club, Portland, Ore.

[left] The Cobb Building (Seattle, 1909), by Howells & Stokes for the Metropolitan Building Company, featured terra-cotta Indian heads on its cornice. Dodge/Kreisman Collection.

[bottom left] The wood paneled smoking room of the Elks Club in Portland had a Mission lighting fixture and furniture and Navajo rugs underfoot. Mason Collection.

Civic and Commercial Buildings

From the most important civic buildings to the most humble, Beaux Arts and Arts and Crafts ideals often shared turf. The formal, domed Pacific County Courthouse, designed in the Classic Revival style by C. Lewis Wilson and completed in 1911 in South Bend, Washington, had interior art glass that incorporated Classical decoration with unmistakable Art Nouveau flair. Its lobbies and courtrooms were furnished in the Mission style. The Grays Harbor County Courthouse of 1910 by Watson Vernon in Montesano, Washington, also Beaux Arts in form and execution, was similarly furnished. Its murals on the themes of power, justice, truth, science, thought, and art were appropriate Beaux Arts embellishments; and in their use of purposeful art, these murals also expressed Arts and Crafts values.

The Postal Telegraph Building at First Avenue and Columbia Street in Seattle furnished its entire third floor with Mission desks and chairs. Writing in *Pacific Northwest Commerce* on June 6, 1911, about the dedication of Seattle's King Street Station for the Oregon Washington Railroad & Navigation Company, the author noted the $1.3 million cost, "making it the most pretentious structure of its kind in the Pacific Northwest."[2] By con-

trast, there was unadorned Mission furniture in the women's waiting room.

In developing urban residential neighborhoods, real estate offices were typically designed in bungalow style to promote the Arts and Crafts lifestyle. The September 1913 issue of *Bungalow Magazine* featured an illustrated article on a bungalow office building located on California Avenue S.W. in West Seattle designed by architect W. R. Kelley. It served as office and salesroom for the Fairmount real estate addition to Seattle and was "a proper clubhouse," distinguished by battered buttresses and a heavy cornice. Brick gateway pillars with globe electric fixtures led potential purchasers along a brick and tile approach described as harmonious. The paneled reception room had an oak floor in a checkerboard pattern and the room was equipped with Mission and Craftsman furniture. Moravian tile in the fireplace mantel was arranged in square and diamond motifs.[3]

Police and fire stations in residential neighborhoods were often designed in the prevailing styles of houses nearby. Portland's Fire Station No. 18 was a Craftsman bungalow that could easily have been mistaken for an Irving-

[top right] King Street Station's women's waiting room, Seattle (c. 1906). PEMCO Webster & Stevens Collection, Museum of History and Industry (Seattle), 83.107537.1.

[center] The Herrick Improvement Company built a buttressed bungalow as its real estate office for the Fairmount Development in West Seattle. *Bungalow Magazine* (1913). Seattle Public Library.

[right] The main room of the office, with its Moravian tile hearth, was comfortably furnished in Mission objects. *Bungalow Magazine* (1913). Seattle Public Library.

ton residence. Daniel Huntington's 1912–1913 design of Seattle's Wallingford neighborhood fire and police station embraced the unequal gables of a chalet with a shingled exterior and trellising in response to that neighborhood's rapidly expanding bungalow culture. In Tacoma, Engine House No. 8 combined Neoclassical architectural features in its window headers and quoins with wide overhangs and brackets common to Craftsman buildings.

The Mission Revival style gained popularity in public architecture, as evidenced dramatically in the 1910 rebuilding of the fire-damaged Romanesque Revival–style Snohomish County Courthouse in Everett by architects Carl Siebrand and August Heide. The 1914 city hall and fire station in Montesano, Washington, the high school in Ashland, Oregon, the entrance to the Oregon State Fairgrounds in Salem, and Northern Pacific rail depots in Yakima, Washington, and elsewhere in the Northwest showed the widespread appreciation of Mission Revival architecture which continued to heighten during the 1920s. In 1920–1921, City Architect Daniel Huntington claimed that an Italian farmhouse inspired his design of Seattle's Fremont Public Library. But its stucco façade and red tile roofs were probably assumed by the public to be an

[top left] Bungalow-style Firehouse No. 18 (1913) on N.E. 24th near Tillamook in Portland fit seamlessly into the Irvington neighborhood. Mason Collection.

[center] The Snohomish County Courthouse (1897) in downtown Everett was reconstructed in the Mission Revival style in 1910. Photograph by Lawrence Kreisman.

[left] By 1924, Ashland's Mission Revival high school had acquired the ivy-covered patina that evoked history and permanency. Oregon Historical Society (Portland), CN 000 228.

interpretation of the popular Mission Revival style. The building deviated from the formal symmetry of Carnegie libraries with a less formal off-center entrance pavilion. During this period, other Washington cities, including Snohomish and Centralia, chose Mission Revival style for their city halls.

While the Prairie style was not common in public building construction in the Pacific Northwest, it appeared in the Hoquiam Carnegie Library of 1911 because the architects, Cland and Stark, hailed from Madison, Wisconsin, and had gained a reputation for their Prairie-style Carnegie libraries in that region. The building's exterior ornament was based on the design vocabulary of Louis Sullivan. A warm, wood-paneled interior with fireplaces provided a home-like environment for enjoying browsing and reading. The firm of Bigger & Warner designed a Prairie-style library in Snohomish, Washington, that seemed to have been influenced also by German and Austrian Secessionist design in its controlled use of ornament to embellish the cement stucco façade. Inside these heavily used public institutions, the durability of Mission furniture served for many years.

Clubs and Clubhouses

On December 4, 1909, *Pacific Builder and Engineer* published photographs of the new quarters of the Seattle Commercial Club, showing the general reception room with Mission rockers, and the dining room, lobby, and billiard hall with Brunswick-Balke-Collendar Company lighting fixtures. The reporter's tone of faint praise indicated his dislike of Mission furniture, and he clearly interpreted the choice of Mission furnishings as a commercial one rather than an aesthetically

Stylized floral ornament in the manner developed by Louis Sullivan was used by Wisconsin architects for their Carnegie Public Library (1911) in Hoquiam. Courtesy of Timberland Regional Library.

sophisticated one: "In accord with the principles of the club the execution of work and materials used were, as far as possible, entrusted to and furnished by Seattle firms. The trim is Douglas fir, and the general scheme of decorative treatment may be termed mission for the lack of a more pronounced type. The woodwork throughout is stained a dark brown. All ceilings are finished a light cream. The billiard room with its mission type of tables finished dark and dull is a good representation of this style. The decorations carry out the ideas of attractiveness and utility, and the simplicity of it all is characteristic of the commercial spirit behind it."[4]

On February 26, 1910, the same periodical portrayed a portion of the billiard and card

The main lounge of the YWCA in Portland (1909) was furnished with Mission furniture. *Pacific Builder and Engineer*. Seattle Public Library.

room of Seattle's 320-member Metropolitan Club, which was located on the fifth floor of the brick- and terra-cotta–clad Henry Building in the recently completed Metropolitan Building Company development designed by New York architects Howells and Stokes. The reporter described the interior with no apparent bias: "From the hall the entrance leads into the lounging and reading room, which has been fitted up elaborately with mission furniture and Turkish rugs. Just back of this room is the office of the secretary, the billiard tables and the card room. All of the rooms are finished in brown and green tints and the window casings and window seats are finished in fumed oak."[5]

Plymouth Congregational Church, a stately Classical Revival edifice of brick with Ionic terra-cotta columns designed by Seattle architect John Graham, seemed as though it had been moved to Seattle from a New England green. But the men's club, photographed in a May 11, 1912, issue of *Pacific Builder and Engineer*, was furnished in informal Mission.

A *Pacific Northwest Journal* article "Prac-

tical Work in Various lines" of January 1911 about downtown Seattle's Young Men's Christian Association showed Mission furnishings in the parlor living room. The Young Women's Christian Association quarters were also outfitted, in part, with Arts and Crafts furniture. In March 1906, the Seattle society journal, *Weekend*, reported: "[A number of] prominent women in the city have furnished the apartments with a liberal expenditure of money and thought. The reception hall, a delightfully roomy one with a huge fireplace in one end is supplied with easy chairs, tables, soft rugs, and appropriate pictures and ornaments, the gift of Mrs. F. S. Stimson. The reading room, in wall hangings of a rich warm hue, is fitted up elegantly with tables, chairs, and bookcases in mission style, and its whole atmosphere is peculiarly inviting and restful. Its appointments were contributed by Mr. M. F. Backus."[6]

The YWCA in Portland, designed by McNaughton, Raymond & Lawrence, outshone its Seattle peers. The handsome building of red pressed brick was completed in 1909. Photographic views of the appealing inglenook in the parlor and the library filled with Mission furniture accompanied a *Pacific Builder and Engineer* article in 1910: "Entering the building near the corner of Taylor on Seventh Street, one is pleased by the cheery and homelike appearance of the lobby, with its hospitable seats on either side of the big hallway. Crossing the lobby, she enters the living room, like the library, furnished in brown and Flemish oak. Enticed to the cozy inglenook in one end of the room, she drops down into a comfortable davenport and looks about at the beautiful features which accord so perfectly with the brown tone of the room. The chief

Daughters and Sons of Norway Hall,
Seattle, Wash.

In this color postcard, the Sons and Daughters of Norway Hall (1915) in downtown Seattle was depicted romantically surrounded by vegetation. Dodge/Kreisman Collection.

attraction on the second floor is the beautiful art glass in the hall. This was given by Mrs. Cyrus A. Dolph who, as state chairman, organized the association."[7]

While Renaissance Revival and Georgian Revival townhouses and skyscrapers housed these cities' club members, vernacular building types were often more comfortable choices outside the central business district. They reflected immigrant roots, a designer's experience from European travels, and the ongoing popularity of the Arts and Crafts. One unique example that represented the rise of romantic nationalism in northern Europe was the design of the Sons and Daughters of Norway Hall in Seattle. The hall was built in 1915 to house the cultural and fraternal societies organized by immigrants on the Pacific Coast between 1903 and 1906. Architect Sonke Englehart Sonnichsen (1879–1961), who had practiced in Norway during a nationalistic Romantic Revival movement, based the building on medieval structural forms of stave churches and vernacular farmsteads. The ornament also reflected Scandi-

In the Sons and Daughters of Norway Hall (1915), Seattle, one of a series of murals by Yngvar Sonnichsen and Sverre Mack (1916) depicted American Indians watching as Norwegian explorers approach the North American coast. Photograph by Luci Baker Johnson.

[top] The Tacoma Hotel remodel (1907) by Kirtland Cutter exploited the metaphor of the sea in Nordic imagery in the refurbished public rooms. Mermaids inhabit the capitals of the lobby columns. Northwest Museum of Arts & Culture, Eastern Washington State Historical Society (Spokane), L84-207.4-81.

[above] One of the Rookwood Pottery Company's major Seattle commissions was the Totem Lounge of the New Washington Hotel (1908), dominated by ceramic totems and Haida mask corbels. Washington State Historical Society (Tacoma), Curtis 11905. Photograph by Asahel Curtis.

Grande, Oregon, designed by Portland architect Delos D. Neer, was featured in the January 18, 1913, issue of *Pacific Builder and Engineer*. A postcard from Baker, Oregon, depicted a modest clubhouse that could easily be mistaken for a single-family home.

Urban Hotels

A visitor's first impressions of a city were often formed as he or she settled into a downtown hotel for a short or extended stay. Apart from providing efficient services and comfortable guest rooms, these hotels offered architects rare opportunities to explore a great variety of historic eclectic styles or aesthetics coming from emerging Continental and American design movements. Spokane architect Kirtland Cutter's transformation of the Pennington Hotel into a California Mission for Louis Davenport certainly raised expectations for hoteliers throughout the Northwest. No one came close to Cutter in imaginative reworkings of older hotel buildings.

The urge to design buildings that would be memorable to visitors stimulated Kirtland Cutter when he was commissioned in 1905 to remodel the Tacoma Hotel, originally designed by the New York firm of McKim, Mead and White in 1883. With its view overlooking Commencement Bay, a sea theme was quickly chosen. The public rooms reopened in 1907, incorporating Art Nouveau mermaid- and seahorse-decorated column capitals and a sunken ship frieze in the lobby, Viking friezes in the dining room, and a Viking frieze by Walter Crane in the ladies' reception room. Cutter had engaged local artisans for the work: the Wheeler Osgood Company for millwork and carvings, Lindstrom and Berg for seating, and Tacoma Ornamental Iron and

Wire Works for lighting fixtures and metal-work embellishments for doors.[10]

Seattle's leading downtown hotel, the New Washington, was completed in 1908 to replace its namesake, razed during the city's regrading of Denny Hill. In their designs, St. Louis architects Eames and Young utilized Classical Revival elements popular in that period in a stately two-story balconied lobby and the adjacent dining room. But the hotel's most remarkable feature was the Totem Lounge, with a specially commissioned fireplace mantel of tile by the Rookwood Company, designed by decorators Marx and Joines, which depicted Mount Rainier with stylized trees at either side extending from floor to ceiling. The fireplace was framed by two polychrome tile totem poles modeled from a totem pole publicized at Ye Olde Curiosity Shop on the city's waterfront. The nearby writing room was furnished with Mission desks and lamps.

The Sorrento Hotel on Seattle's First Hill, designed by local architect Harlan Thomas (1870–1953) in the Italian Renaissance style for clothier Samuel Rosenberg and constructed in 1908 to attract visitors attending the A-Y-P Exposition, prided itself on the mahogany main lounge with a commissioned Rookwood fireplace depicting an Italian garden. The lounge was furnished quite simply with Mission oak rockers. Guests to the beautiful top floor restaurant sat on Mission chairs, and ladies taking tea in the adjacent tearoom sat on wicker. By contrast, the hotel's guest rooms were furnished with Colonial Revival furniture, which the management explained was to evoke a home-like atmosphere. Why, one might ask, did the management feel the Colonial Revival style was cozier than the Arts and Crafts style? It may be that Rosen-

The main lounge of the Sorrento Hotel was paneled in mahogany and had a handsome Rookwood fireplace with an Italian garden scenic frieze. It was furnished with Mission oak rockers. PEMCO Webster & Stevens Collections, Museum of History and Industry (Seattle), 83.10.2195.2.

berg was targeting East Coast visitors and thought they would find more comfort in familiar New England Colonial surroundings. For Rosenberg, the design choices were probably simply business decisions—styles to follow rather than ideals to realize.

In a publicity brochure developed in the 1920s, the Sorrento Hotel management emphasized the home like character of the hotel: "It radiates quiet refinement and that wholesome, 'homey' feeling that charms and holds one and draws one back again when one is gone. When after a good dinner, groups of guests assemble in the charming lobby, around the glowing fireplace, it seems just like a great big happy family. This is a real hotel home."[11]

One of the most unusual hotels of the period rose in Portland in 1908–1909, the Seward Hotel. Designed by architect William C. Knighton, the five-story hotel had a façade of beige brick and elaborate terra-cotta. Its bold geometric ornamentation derived from Austrian Secession prototypes, though some

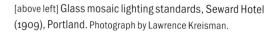

[above left] Glass mosaic lighting standards, Seward Hotel (1909), Portland. Photograph by Lawrence Kreisman.

[above] Stained glass skylit dome attributed to Edward Bruns, Seward Hotel (1909), Portland. Photograph by Lawrence Kreisman.

[left] The uncluttered brick walls, terrazzo floors, and geometric glass skylights in the entrance court of Portland's Nortonia Hotel (1907), now the Mark Spencer Hotel, placed it at the leading edge of Modern design in its time. Steve Dotterer Collection.

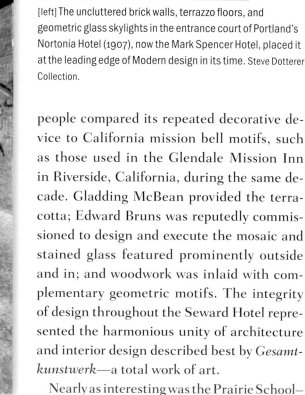

people compared its repeated decorative device to California mission bell motifs, such as those used in the Glendale Mission Inn in Riverside, California, during the same decade. Gladding McBean provided the terracotta; Edward Bruns was reputedly commissioned to design and execute the mosaic and stained glass featured prominently outside and in; and woodwork was inlaid with complementary geometric motifs. The integrity of design throughout the Seward Hotel represented the harmonious unity of architecture and interior design described best by *Gesamtkunstwerk*—a total work of art.

Nearly as interesting was the Prairie School–

[above] The richly stenciled Leopold Hotel lobby (1913), with leaded glass skylights and fixtures, was furnished with solid Mission pieces. This photograph was touched up with white paint and wood-grain highlights for its use in printed materials. Whatcom Museum of History and Art (Bellingham), 2000.37.234.

[right] Full-color design board for the stained glass tulip ceiling which was installed in the Leopold Hotel addition (1923). Raymond Nyson Collection, Special Collections Division, University of Washington Libraries (Seattle), UW 26457z.

inspired entrance court of architect Joseph Jacobberger's Nortonia Hotel several blocks away. It filled an enclosed light court between the two unadorned brick wings of the building. A simple, suspended brass lighting fixture was a prominent feature, and the space was capped by a geometric leaded glass skylight.

The Leopold Hotel in Bellingham, Washington, was built by German brewer Leopold F. Schmidt, owner of Capital Brewery (which became Olympia Brewery) and Bellingham Bay Brewery in 1902. He entered the hotel business in 1910, and his namesake hotel was completed in 1913, designed by Seattle architect C. Alfred Breitung (1868–?). The lobby was referred to by the local press as "German" in style, but its lighting fixtures and sub-

The three-story Pilot Butte Inn (1916) in Bend had a rough-cut stone base and vertical fir façade. Mason Collection.

stantial furniture were more akin to Mission. The Tulip Room, an addition to the building designed by Bellingham architect F. Stanley Piper and completed in April 1923, took its theme from the annual tulip festivals in the area. Its decor was more Art Nouveau than Modern, recalling the styles popular a decade earlier. The room's stained glass skylight, fabricated by Raymond Nyson for Belknap Glass Company of Seattle, was edged in stylized tulips. All the chairs were of bentwood, similar in style to those from Thonet or Kohn manufacturers in Austria.

Throughout the region, hotels arose to accommodate an increasing number of residents and tourists. Each promoted itself as being sophisticated and up-to-date, and interiors were designed with familiar Arts and Crafts furnishings by some of the region's most respected firms. These establishments included the Hotel Puget (c. 1910) at Port Gamble, Washington, by Seattle architects Saunders & Lawton, and, in 1916, the Pilot Butte Inn in Bend, Oregon, by J. E. Tourtellotte, the Boise architect who designed the Idaho State Capitol.

Apartment Buildings

While the impact of the Arts and Crafts movement was felt most strongly in single-family residential construction, the increasing demand for multifamily housing spurred by the rapid growth of cities meant that apartment buildings also followed current trends and took advantage of the local availability and efficiencies of Arts and Crafts furnishings.

Several popular examples were offered in *Pacific Builder and Engineer*. A May 11, 1912, issue featured photographs of a unit in the Broadway Apartments at Broadway and Third in Aberdeen, Washington, designed by Watson Vernon. The main entrance and reception hall led to a dining room that could be converted to a bedroom with a built-in wall unit. The magazine reported that each of the thirty-four suites contained a living room, a dining room that was convertible to a bedroom, a toilet, bath, and dressing room, and a model kitchen and pantry. There was a great deal of local civic pride in the fact that, with the exception of the Oregon Chair Company, all the contractors and suppliers, including the furniture installer J. J. Kaufman Company, were from Aberdeen.[12]

In Tacoma, the Lewis and Clark Apartments,

with brick lower floors, stucco and half-timbered top floors, and wide overhanging cornices supported by brackets, reflected the impact of the Arts and Crafts movement in multifamily housing. Nearby, an apartment developer was so taken by the varieties of art tile being produced that he collected hundreds of examples of Claycraft, Batchelder, Mercer, Rookwood, Grueby, and others and incorporated them into the entrance lobby and hallways of his building.

More unusual were the Tokyo Apartments and a companion project in Spokane that, one could speculate, were inspired by the developer's visit to the Alaska-Yukon-Pacific Exposition in 1909. On December 23, 1911, *Pacific Builder and Engineer* included a rendering of the Tokyo Apartments and suggested: "The Japanese style of architecture is growing in favor in Spokane, especially among those who are constructing apartment houses here. The Tokyo apartments, recently completed, are now followed with another design along different lines, but still following the Japanese style. The new apartments, shown in the illustration, are after plans by Jones and Levesque, architects, in the Mohawk block. The new apartments were erected this fall by E. L. Rice at the corner of Fifth avenue and Lincoln street, at an approximate cost of $35,000. The building is three stories in height and has a roof garden. Balconies run clear around two sides of the building."[13]

The allure of California affected Northwestern apartment dwellers as well. The romantic vision of missions, with cream-colored stucco and red tile roofs, may have offered a sense of escape from ubiquitous clouds and drizzle for those who were unable to spend time among the palm trees at the Hunting-

Lewis and Clark Apartments (1909–1910) in Tacoma.
Photograph by Lawrence Kreisman.

ton Hotel in San Marino or the Del Coronado Hotel on the San Diego oceanfront. By the mid-1920s, Mission Revival had been well incorporated into Seattle and Portland neighborhoods, although never to the extent of Craftsman bungalows.

On the western edge of Seattle's north Capitol Hill, L'Amourita Apartments, constructed around 1925, was hard to miss. The building's creamy stucco façade, red tile roofs, gables, and bays made passersby feel as though they had been transported to some tropical oasis. Nearby, architect Everett Beardsley attempted to capture the flavor of Mexico and the Southwest in his several apartment buildings near Lake Union and in the University District. The finest of these, built c. 1927, was El Monterey, with unique apartments featuring imported tile, hand-adzed beams, wrought iron details, arched portals, and charming courtyards.

Developer Fred Anhalt (1896–1996) also tried his hand at Mission-style architecture in the El Quinta Apartments on Capitol Hill, Seattle, as well as in several other buildings on Queen Anne Hill. He found his greatest success, however, in his Norman-style clinker brick buildings with romantic towers embellished with hammered metalwork, stained and leaded glass, and ceramic tile. These popular Capitol Hill apartment-homes were built at record speed by teams of workmen using components manufactured in quantity but, once completed, appeared to be handmade in the Arts and Crafts tradition.

Architect Daniel Huntington (1871–1962) had a long-standing interest in the Arts and Crafts movement and its products. As late as 1927, Huntington was following the handiwork and crafts movements in California. He decided to face his Piedmont Hotel addition on Seattle's First Hill with a colorful skirt of Malibu tile—one of the largest installations of this tile in the region. The arched surrounds for the lobby windows, the entrances to the lobby and restaurant, as well as the column capitals in the two-story lobby were decorated with tile geometric patterns. Other major Malibu tile installations were done in the studio building that was a part of the Paramount Theater project and, appropriately, for the façade of the tile showroom of W. Rodgers on Yale Avenue.

Restaurants

As discussed in an earlier chapter, C. R. Ashbee's wife, Janet, was quite taken by the Arts and Crafts atmosphere of some of the restaurants she frequented during her visit to Seattle in 1909. While she did not mention names, apart from the well-used club rooms

[top] The Mission-style L'Amourita Apartments (c. 1925) evoked southern California from their north Capitol Hill perch in Seattle. Photograph by Lawrence Kreisman.

[above] Malibu tile decorates the façade of the Piedmont Hotel, Seattle, 1927. Photograph by Lawrence Kreisman.

[top] Kirtland Cutter's Orange Bower Bar and lounge, Davenport Hotel, Spokane (1904). Northwest Museum of Arts & Culture, Eastern Washington State Historical Society (Spokane), L84-207.4-78.

[above] The Grill Room of Portland's Perkins Hotel expressed the solidity and tranquility of Arts and Crafts design in its furniture, the specially designed carpet, and slag glass skylights and column lighting (c. 1910). Steve Dotterer Collection.

and hotel lounges there were several restaurants in town that were decked out with "modern" interiors, beyond the use of Mission oak chairs and tables. Postcard views of the tearoom and writing room at Frederick & Nelson in Seattle and the restaurant and tearoom at the Rhodes department stores in Seattle and Tacoma show the influence of British interior design and also the Glasgow School publicized in America through photographs of Mrs. Cranston's tearooms. Certainly, Louis Davenport had taken the Glasgow School to heart in his women's retiring room adjoining his apartment in Spokane.

In 1903, Davenport purchased the building that housed his restaurant and the one adjoining it, and hired local architect Kirtland Cutter to blend the exteriors of the two. The restaurant was an older building that Cutter had already remodeled into a Mission-style stucco and red-tile-roofed building. The series of spaces in the restaurants and bars of the hotel were remarkable in their homage to modern design movements in Europe. The Orange Bower Bar, with the theme of oranges incorporated into its chandeliers, had woodwork and trim in the new German style and landscape wall friezes.

At the Oregon Hotel in Portland, the Rathskeller restaurant represented Arts and Crafts design ideas. A 1907 *Pacific Builder and Engineer* article showed a drawing of it by the San Francisco firm of Sutton and Weeks with tile columns and Art and Crafts fixtures. The chandeliers consisted of four lanterns, each of which was suspended from the center of a ceiling panel. There were bronze lanterns of square design on brass brackets of a dull iron finish. A Dutch landscape frieze decorated the upper walls.[14]

Religious Buildings

American churches frequently found a supportive framework for their architecture within the English Medieval tradition. Well-published descriptions of English country churches encouraged American congregations to seek equivalent architecture, which, regardless of the newness of the parish, would tie it to centuries-old tradition. The return to Medieval models, particularly in more modest churches and chapels, seemed fitting. Ellsworth Storey's Epiphany Chapel in Seattle's Denny Blaine neighborhood adapted the stone and half-timbered vocabulary outside and the timber-beamed interior in a pleasing fashion that was radically different from the Renaissance Revival and Beaux Arts forms of the city's Roman Catholic cathedral or the Presbyterian church. A similar aesthetic approach was expressed in the proposed half-timbered Craftsman building with a corner tower for the Park Universalist Church in Tacoma, for which Woodroofe & Constable were the architects.

The Fairmont Cemetery Chapel of 1890 by Kirtland Cutter in Spokane was one of the earliest (and possibly first) examples of Arts and Crafts design in a Pacific Northwest religious structure. It combined natural rubble lava masonry walls with heavily buttressed corners. The broad overhanging roof was topped with three cupolas. The gable of the apse end was shingled, with round art glass windows. In its fluid use of shingle sheathing and locally found rock, it echoed the East Coast estates designed by architect H. H. Richardson. In *A Guide to Architecture in Washington State*, Sally Woodbridge proclaimed, "In its setting this is surely one of the high moments of the Craftsman Style in the Northwest."[15]

[top] The firm of Woodroofe & Constable prepared drawings for the Universalist Church in Tacoma (1909) to reflect the informal vernacular of English country church buildings. The bracketed roof overhangs, dormers, and canopies would have melded well with a residential neighborhood. *Pacific Builder and Engineer*, March 13, 1909.

[above] Kirtland Cutter's design for the Fairmont Chapel in Spokane (1890) was an early instance of Arts and Crafts principles in the Pacific Northwest. Photograph by Henry Matthews.

The Arts and Crafts Movement Goes Public   ◆   117

The Mission Revival also found a natural role in church architecture, given its roots in the California missions. In Tacoma, Immanuel Presbyterian Church (1909) on North J Street was Mission Revival with Arts and Crafts leaded windows. And Kirtland Cutter's First Church of Christ, Scientist, in Spokane was also Mission inspired, deviating from the more commonly used Classical Revival form and ornament.

In the first two decades of the twentieth century, the Northwest public had access to Arts and Crafts architecture and interiors in many institutions and commercial buildings, clubs, and hostelries. Even if some did not frequent these venues, the onslaught of popular magazines available to anyone who had access to the public library made Arts and Crafts interior aesthetics something for which one could strive, regardless of one's financial successes or social position. So it is easy to understand how people might opt to bring the style into their newly built residences in Washington and Oregon.

[top left] Kirtland Cutter's First Church of Christ, Scientist, in Spokane (c. 1907) imitated the design of early nineteenth-century California missions. *Western Architect*, September 1908.

[center] Two nurses take a break from their work at the Craftsman-style Ashland Community Hospital and Club House in spring 1929. Oregon Historical Society (Portland), CN 000235.

[left] A shingled bungalow was an appropriate main office for the lumber company in Onalaska, Washington (c. 1910). Mason Collection.

FIVE
Perfect Homes
for the Time and Place

How could anyone resist the allure of the Pacific Northwest? Exquisite unspoiled scenery, open space, employment opportunities, and a new life awaited, away from known and often unhappy experiences in the congested industrial East and Midwest. In a 1904 article, M. A. Matthews summed up the virtues of living in Seattle:

> To have the advantages of a great and growing city and at the same time be in touch with nature is certainly ideal. There is nothing quite so inspiring as lofty mountain peaks and rolling ocean billows. To occupy a palatial home on an asphalt boulevard, where one's children may watch the ebb and flow of the tide, is a pleasure to be coveted. To live within a city that has within its corporate limits, a chain of beautiful lakes, and beyond its corporate boundaries, manufacturing plants, truck farms and forests is conducive to the development of the children and the happiness of the parents. Seattle has all these advantages and many more that might be mentioned. Nature and art have agreed to live together in this city in perfect peace and harmony.[1]

Seattle's hilly terrain and forested slopes, its many lakes and rivers, as well as the spectacular views of Mount Rainier, Mount Baker, and the Cascade and Olympic mountain ranges offered a challenging and exciting opportunity for the Olmsted Brothers in considering a city design for parks and boulevards (1903). Washington State Historical Society (Tacoma), Curtis 31258. Photograph by Asahel Curtis.

Matthews focused his attention on those who could afford palatial homes rather than the vast majority of people who labored long hours in the manufacturing plants, truck farms, and forests. Regardless, it was true that urban growth and settlement patterns had, in a half century, brought Seattle from infancy to maturity, making it a most satisfactory living environment with amenities that would have been the pride of older cities.

The population growth in Seattle and Portland in the early twentieth century reflected national trends. During the period from 1900 to 1920, more houses were built in the United States than had been built during its entire previous history.[2] In Seattle, growth did not come about without major engineering prow-ess that involved Herculean earth-moving and regrading in the central business district at the turn of the twentieth century. Land developers were intent on opening up new tracts to home ownership north, south, and east of downtown. So it was only a matter of time until privately financed railways, cable cars, and streetcar lines laid tracks along Yesler Way, Madison Street, and James Street to Lake Washington, north along Lake Union to Ballard and Fremont, and south to Columbia City and Renton. Portland, lacking the initiative of Seattle's city engineer R. H. Thomson and having fewer obstacles to commercial development on either side of the Willamette River, nevertheless encountered similar development strategies for opening up new tracts east and west, north and south.

Planning the City Beautiful

Nationally and regionally, there were a number of experiments in planned utopian communities of like-minded individuals who wished to shape a better world. Like Seattle's

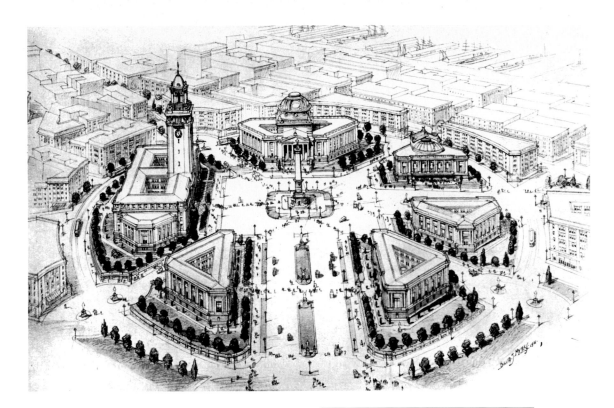

Virgil Bogue's Plan for Seattle's Civic Center (1911) espoused City Beautiful ideals in its symmetry, common architectural vocabulary, and axial boulevards terminating at significant buildings. Dodge/Kreisman Collection.

Beaux Arts Village, these communities often collapsed under the pressures of commuting to the city to make a living, feeding and educating children, and clashing opinions about the logistics of keeping the community afloat.

To some extent, architects and city planners were engaged in a similar exercise in promoting physical order, design harmony, and symmetry during the era of the City Beautiful movement. The planning of the Lewis and Clark and Alaska-Yukon-Pacific exposition sites in Portland and Seattle, as well as the site planning and buildings for the Washington state capitol in Olympia, are recognized examples, although extraordinary cases.

The true value of City Beautiful ideals was in laying the physical groundwork for attractive and workable cities. Virgil Bogue's 1911 Seattle plan and E. H. Bennett's 1912 Portland plan looked comprehensively at civic expression in architecture, at monumental avenues on axis to major government and transportation centers, and at transportation and circulation improvements that would address city growth for years to come. Bogue's 1911 plan for Tacoma's Commercial Club proposed sweeping changes to the Commencement Bay waterfront that would address industry, commerce, and tourism. While major plans of this nature were impressive on paper, they did not move the taxpaying public. Despite the lack of full support, aspects of the plans lived on in broader transportation and port recommendations in Seattle and a group of distinctive classically inspired civic, institutional, and commercial buildings in major cities.

The ideals as well as the vocabulary of the Arts and Crafts movement were present in planned development in the region on both large and small scales. Several master plans by Seattle architects Bebb & Gould—one for a logging camp (1915–1917) for the Merrill &

A hotel (c. 1915) for a large planned company town in Brookings, Oregon, was Bay Area architect Bernard Maybeck's most significant Northwest work. Mason Collection.

Ring Lumber Company on the Pysht River on the Olympic Peninsula, and the other an ambitious commission for a new army town at nearby Lake Pleasant—demonstrated how planning and Arts and Crafts principles were applied in remote areas of the state. A vocabulary was developed that incorporated landscaped curving streets following land contours and grouped civic buildings that created a sense of community. The buildings themselves, particularly the hotel at Lake Pleasant, recalled the rustic aspects of Adirondack lodges—something Carl Gould (1873–1939) would have experienced in his East Coast youth—with gables and curved dormer windows outside and heavy timber trusses supporting the roofs of the recreation hall and dining hall. Unlike rustic park architecture, Gould incorporated industrial sash windows in a manner that opened these buildings up and lightened their elevations. Unfortunately, the plan was rejected for its high cost, and was not built.[3]

Similarly, at Brookings, Oregon, a coastal town at the mouth of the Chetco River, hardly any of the master plan was developed. Had it been, it would have demonstrated that San Francisco Bay Area architect Bernard Maybeck's (1862–1957) talent for design was far broader than the art and craft of his individual buildings. Maybeck was asked by J. L. Brookings, who had acquired a timber company in southern Oregon, to design buildings for mill workers at the Brookings Lumber Company. In 1913 its deep-water facilities and a promise of the North-Western Pacific Railway to extend its tracks northward from Eureka, California, presented ideal conditions for the growth of a healthy town. Maybeck prepared drawings for temporary buildings that would serve the community until a town plan was adopted. Over two years beginning in 1913, his work included the town plan itself, along with a hotel, cottages, YMCA, and school.[4]

In Seattle, Portland, Spokane, and smaller cities, the parallel planning and actual development of parks and boulevards stimulated property development. This aspect of the City Beautiful movement was inspired regionally by expositions and plans proposed and developed by John Charles Olmsted. He prepared reports for the three major cities—Portland and Seattle in 1903 and Spokane in

1906. Where they were carried out, Olmsted's reports and recommendations embellished lakefronts, forests, and hillsides with driving routes of great beauty that encouraged the building of houses nearby. The true benefit to the cities that undertook these projects was the higher taxable value of land that adjoined such amenities. The resulting communities were distinguished and desirable. The Parks Department in Seattle immediately pursued purchase of land to allow what would become, despite some major missing links, one of the largest Olmsted-designed park and boulevard systems in the nation. In Portland, only a small number of Olmsted's proposed parks and boulevards were completed. One of these, a two-and-one-half mile forested roadway called the Southwest Hillside Parkway (now referred to as Terwilliger Parkway), was developed between 1907 and 1914.

Streetcar suburbs blossomed in Portland in the first quarter of the twentieth century. Spurred by streetcar lines and the advent of the automobile, new homes were built in established neighborhoods, such as Irvington and Portland Heights. New districts also emerged, such as Laurelhurst, Eastmoreland, Arlington Heights, Westover Terraces, and Willamette Heights. Interspersed among the various revival-style residences were the increasingly popular California bungalows.[5]

The greatest number of houses built in Seattle, Portland, and Spokane during this period were either straightforward American foursquare design or Craftsman houses or bungalows. But well-to-do enclaves often took advantage of the terrain and water and mountain views in their locations, and commissioned architect-designed houses. Many of these grander houses were constructed in

The cover of the 1911 Seattle Park Commissioners annual report, a silhouette of the city's skyline with Elliott Bay in the foreground, is framed by stylized potted plants and borders. Dodge/Kreisman Collection.

Mount Baker, Queen Anne Hill, and Capitol Hill in Seattle; Portland Heights, Laurelhurst, and Irvington in Portland; North Tacoma; Forest Avenue and South Hill in Bellingham; and Rockwood Boulevard, South Hill, and Corbin Park in Spokane. Stylistically, these houses ranged from Italian Renaissance to English Tudor, with an occasional nod to Swiss Chalet or Spanish Colonial Mission. And within these confines, some significant progressive homes were built that reached beyond the boundaries of the accepted norms of traditional historic styles.

Many of these neighborhoods were planned developments in which the owner of the tract divided or platted the property into blocks and lots for sale. Generally they were laid

Portland, Ore., Residence among the Roses

The typical American foursquare house—this one in Portland (c. 1910)—often displayed bungalow features but with abbreviated brackets for the shallow eaves. Trellises and latticework porches often enhanced outdoor spaces. Mason Collection.

out in typical rectangular grids, though in the cases where topography presented challenges, they might defer to the idiosyncrasies of the land, even using these cues to advantage. Occasionally, a development company would apply a concerted effort to work with other city agencies, and the result in those cases was neighborhoods that espoused the ideals of the City Beautiful. One such example was Seattle's Mount Baker Park.

The Mount Baker neighborhood in Seattle encompassed a number of separate land tracts. Of these, the Mount Baker Park Addition platted in 1907 by the Hunter Tract Improvement Company provided the neighborhood with its name and its identity. While not the earliest planned residential district in Seattle, it was the largest at the time and one of the first to be integrated into the city park and boulevard system proposed in 1903 by the Olmsted Brothers, and realized through the efforts of local landscape designer Edward Schwager, the city's superintendent of public parks.

The Hunter Tract Improvement Company sought to create an exclusive, upper-income residential district. In addition to its planning of the subdivision and the generous inclusion of public park land, the principal means of achieving this goal was through deed restrictions: only one dwelling was allowed per lot; houses were to be erected on established building lines; no residence could cost less than $2,000 to $5,000, depending on location within the district; every house was to contain a basement; no outhouses or stables were allowed; owners could have no animals, except domestic pets; and only one commercial building was allowed.

The company's plans evolved over an extended period of time in the areas east of Hunter Boulevard, Mount Rainier Drive, and Lake Park Drive. Other areas received

The Mount Baker development in Seattle was advertised in a promotional map (1915). Dodge/Kreisman Collection.

extensive housing improvements earlier, but tended to cater to a middle-class clientele. These areas were closer to the trolley lines that served the neighborhood. The tract was promoted: "Simply See Mount Baker Park, an Addition with Character." The neighborhood's streets followed hillside contours and afforded spectacular views of Lake Washington and the Cascade Range.[6]

From its beginnings, the polished look of the neighborhood was shaped by the Hunter Tract Improvement Company and the Mount Baker Park Improvement Club, which was organized in 1909 to "promote the physical development of Mount Baker Park, the beautification of the Park as a whole, to encourage home owners to personal effort to develop and improve their property, and to organize and aid various neighborhood clubs which may benefit the community by social, cultural, educational and charitable work." The neighborhood was to be centered around the Arts and Crafts–designed Mount Baker Club

House and a signature commercial building of similar design, which did not get built until 1930 due to a lack of funds. Consequently, the commercial building was designed in the then-popular Art Deco style by Seattle architect John Graham.

In Portland, one of the most distinctive turn-of-the-century planned neighborhoods was Ladd's Addition, named for William S. Ladd, whose timber holdings in East Portland and Tacoma, Washington, were estimated at 4,000 acres. Extending from S.E. 12th to S.E. 20th Avenues and between S.E. Hawthorne and Division Street, and originally platted in 1891, its development period coincided with the Lewis and Clark Exposition of 1905 and continued through the 1930s. It was remarkable for breaking away from the expected grid to a formal layout of streets on diagonals converging at Ladd Circle.

Another Portland neighborhood layout that

deviated from the grid was Laurelhurst, originating in property owned by the Ladd family as Hazel Fern Farm. William Mead Ladd consulted with John Olmsted on plans for a neighborhood that would appeal to upper middle-class homeowners. While Olmsted did not do the layout, that firm's penchant for gently curving streets that took cues from topography was evident in the final layout of streets in 1908 by the Laurelhurst Development Company adjoining a thirty-two-acre park. As Mount Baker and other exclusive residential developments in Northwest cities had done, there were covenants with owners governing the minimum cost of the house—$3,000, with a minimum of $10,000 in the most exclusive area. The first such restrictions were developed in the Irvington neighborhood as early as 1890. While bungalows did not meet the covenants in this area, they began to proliferate in the streets farther away from the park.[7]

Finding Appropriate Regional Architectural Expression

The debate in the architectural community about what was appropriate to build in these newly emerging residential enclaves was ongoing, particularly when it came to defining the distinguishing characteristics of a West Coast architecture. This debate was exemplified in a paper, "The Historic Precedent in Coast Architecture," delivered by Seattle architect Charles H. Alden at the second annual convention of the Architectural League of the Pacific Coast and reported in the June 15, 1912, issue of *Pacific Builder and Engineer*, illustrated with photographs of English-style housing in Seattle's Mount Baker neighborhood: "Don't assume west coast is 'Mission.'

The East coaster is not cognizant of the fact that our coast is fifteen hundred miles in extent with large areas of adjacent inland country and that the climate and natural conditions vary as they do between corresponding latitudes on the Atlantic. How to design a building for the shores of Puget Sound is quite a different problem from meeting the needs of tropical California and there is no merit in forcing a style contrary to the demands of its environment."[8]

Alden suggested that England, northern France, and parts of Germany had a geography and climate similar to the Northwest's and concluded that there was "much in their architecture that we could successfully apply, particularly that of England—'our mother country.'" Since many of the region's pioneering architects had come from England and Germany, it followed that numerous local architects embraced the timber and stucco look of medieval England or the Chalet vernacular of Switzerland and Germany in new residences. And it was not surprising that the English Arts and Crafts design aesthetic was popularized and inspired much of the interior design, furniture, and decorative accessories of these residences.

With the number of Northwest residents who had acquired their wealth either directly from the regional timber, mining, shipbuilding, and the like or through local land speculation, banking, and commerce, the architectural community found a great number of commissions and responded with extraordinary houses that reflected late nineteenth- and early twentieth-century approaches to design.

A few well-chosen examples of architectural work in various cities demonstrate the enormous range of direct and indirect influences on design professionals. They took varied approaches to the use of local versus imported materials to shape homes of grandeur and sophistication or purposeful rusticity at the requests of their clients. These architects were sometimes the same ones who had lucrative commercial and institutional practices or those whose business included selling plans, publishing pattern books for first-time homebuilders, and working with developers to plan blocks in newly platted tracts.

The distinction between architect-designed residences and common bungalows had less to do with the architect or builder's approach to a project and more to do with the social structure that distinguished between commissioned residences in certain exclusive neighborhoods and the ones built "by the book" in working-class and middle-class neighborhoods. In some cases, the latter were sturdier and more exquisite in detail because of the hands-on attention of the owner-builder than the 10,000-square-foot Arts and Crafts mansions that had many hands involved in their construction.

SEATTLE

The dawn of the twentieth century saw the introduction of a new kind of house in the Pacific Northwest. Surrounded by its older, elaborately decorated Queen Anne Victorian, English Medieval, and Italian Renaissance Revival neighbors on First Hill, the shake-and-shingle house of Josiah Collins, designed by the recently formed partnership of Charles Bebb (1856–1942) and Louis Mendel (1867–1940), stirred discussion. It was an early instance of the entry of the Arts and Crafts aesthetic into Seattle society. The "Real Estate and Building Review" of the *Seattle Times* gave the house extensive coverage on July 20, 1901:

One of the most artistic residences in Seattle is that of Josiah Collins of which one view is shown in this page. This house, which is on the corner of Boren Avenue and East Union Street, gains its chief effect from the materials used in its construction which are cedar shakes and rough posts. While it is a small house, being only 46 × 38 feet, it has the comfortable appearance of being thoroughly adequate for the needs of its occupants. From a casual glance at it one has the thought that it is the home of an artist such as one sees in Lawrence Park, that delightful little suburb of New York. Indeed the passerby would naturally take it for a studio.

The general design of the house, which is almost perfect in its detail, is greatly strengthened by its color scheme. The shingle roof is stained a moss green, while the walls are a silver gray giving the whole the appearance of an old house that had been beaten into harmony by the nature artist with the strong tools of sun and storm. A goodly porch eight feet wide which runs the full length of the house looks as if it were made to be enjoyed. The chimney of cobble stones serves to clinch the rusticity which of course is the key to the whole design.

Those who have been fortunate enough to have seen the interior say that the architects, Bebb and Mendel, have made excellent use of their space. In all there are ten rooms, and one of them the social room (for a drawing room would be rather out of harmony with the prevailing idea) had the surprising size of 18 by 30 feet. This room is finished in curly grained Flemish fir and has a beamed ceiling paneled between the beams. On the walls is a deep

The Josiah Collins residence was published in *Seattle Architecturally, 1902*. Architecture and Urban Planning Library, University of Washington (Seattle).

red burlap which brings out the beauty of the wood. An old fashioned fireplace, big enough to stand in, having a hood and swinging crane, is in thorough keeping with the general effect. . . . This house was designed after the owner's suggestion, but the architects deserve the fullest praise for the extremely artistic way in which they embodied the idea of a house which is a credit to Seattle.[9]

The Collins house was indeed "artistic" and understated. But the Arts and Crafts movement manifested itself in a wide variety of ways based on the interests of local architects and their clients. Several important houses nearby on Seattle's north Capitol Hill represented this range. The influence of the English Arts and Crafts movement was at its finest in the John and Eliza Leary residence (1904–1907), by architect Alfred Bodley, and the neighboring Pierre Ferry residence, largely the work of the same architect.

John Leary earned his first fortune in lumber manufacture and sales. The lure of the burgeoning lumber trade on Puget Sound at-

tracted him to Seattle in 1869, where he chose to take up the legal profession and was admitted to the bar in 1871. Leary also invested in coal mining, gas, water, railroading, land development, banking, and marine navigation. In 1884, he served a term as mayor of Seattle, and later was a president of the Rainier Club as well as a regent of the University of Washington. At the time of his death, Leary left an estate valued at approximately two million dollars.

Alfred Bodley (1872–?) arrived in Seattle in 1904 from Victoria, British Columbia, and formed a brief partnership with architect John Graham (1873–1955). While in Victoria, Bodley probably worked for Samuel Maclure on preliminary plans for James Dunsmuir's Hatley Park (completed in 1908). The Leary residence exhibited some external similarities with Dunsmuir's house in its massive entrance tower of stone and its half-timbered gables.

The Leary residence was Seattle's most lavish private house at the time. The focal point was the baronial great hall, two stories in height. Into this essentially Renaissance Revival setting, in which virtually every available wood surface was carved, the architects incorporated a monumental nine-light stained glass window of a peacock by Louis Comfort Tiffany, along with a smaller wisteria window by the same firm in the sun room alcove on the west side of the hall. Gustav Stickley's *Craftsman* took note of the commission in its October 1908 issue, although Stickley assumed wrongly that the window was to embellish a stairwell:

An excellent example of American stained glass is now on exhibit at the Tiffany Studios on Madison Avenue. It is a large staircase window executed in Favrile glass under the personal direction of Mr. Louis

C. Tiffany, and is intended for the home of Mrs. E. F. Leary in Seattle, Wash.

The design shows an Italian landscape—a glimpse of a garden with a vine-covered pergola with a lake just beyond and a low range of hills in the background. The foreground is a mass of gorgeous color, as it is filled with luxuriant foliage and masses of hollyhocks and azaleas in full bloom. The most noticeable figure in the composition is the peacock in the foreground, which has been treated with admirable decorative effect.

Owing to the difficulties presented by the design, the most careful use of materials was required for the execution of this work. The glass was made especially for this window and no surface paints or pigments have been used. All the gradation of color and all the effects of light and shade are obtained wholly in the glass itself, with the result that the full qualities of depth and brilliancy have been preserved.[10]

Probably on the architect's advice, the family also specially ordered an enormous carpet of animals, trees, and birds by the renowned British Arts and Crafts architect Charles Voysey. Woven in wool by the Donegal factory in Ireland, it and a smaller rug for the sunroom alcove would add color and softness in the carved wood hall. Finally, commissions went to the Rookwood Pottery Company in Cincinnati to create site-specific faience tile fireplace surrounds. John Dee Wareham, one of Rookwood's finest designers of architectural commissions (he would become head designer and manager of the company) created a scenic view of snow-capped Mount Hood as the backdrop to the Columbia River for the library and a group of swans for a guest bedroom. For Mrs. Leary's own bathroom, his tile frieze of water babies and mermaid-like

The John Leary residence (1904–1907) on Seattle's north Capitol Hill combined stone, stucco, and half timbering in an asymmetric manner that made it appear as if it had been expanded over many years. Washington State Historical Society (Tacoma), Curtis 13883. Photograph by Asahel Curtis.

children completely framed the top of the four walls.

Pierre Ferry was the brother-in-law of John Leary, and his residence was completed before the larger Leary residence. In 1903, local architect John Graham was commissioned to design both houses. Prior to the start of construction of the Leary mansion, Alfred Bodley arrived in Seattle and was given the opportunity to redesign the Leary house in 1904. Ferry then had Bodley alter his house to more closely emulate his older sister's mansion by enlarging the entrance hall to baronial proportions and relocating the kitchen to a new addition on the south. A separate staircase was designed to the basement ballroom at this time as well.

The Ferry residence was more in keeping with the Arts and Crafts philosophy regarding the harmonious integrity of outside and inside. The stucco exterior form and building materials reflected the English Arts and Crafts houses that became the signatures of

John Leary commissioned the Tiffany Company to execute a peacock window in 1908 for his Capitol Hill home (1904–1907), Seattle. Photograph by Lawrence Kreisman.

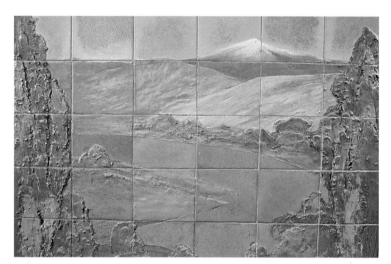

Charles Voysey and Baillie Scott, down to the arched hood over the entrance porch. Inside, the carved woodwork differed from the strict Renaissance style of Leary's mansion. It featured stylized flowers and birds, including the owl—namesake of the estate, Owl Hollow. The main hall opened to a handsome wood-paneled fireplace with mica cabinet on one end and stained glass windows on the other end credited to the Tiffany Studio.

For the Ferry dining room, Orlando Giannini, of the Chicago glass mosaic firm, Giannini & Hilgart, created an iridescent gold glass mosaic tile fireplace with a wisteria motif. The Giannini firm's work was much admired by Frank Lloyd Wright: he commissioned fireplace surrounds for the Darwin Martin House in Buffalo and the Joseph Husser House in Chicago.[11] Giannini's mosaics were known to Seattle designers: the Kellogg Tile showroom listed Giannini stock in its advertisements. Lighting fixtures and sconces were of the finest hand-wrought brass with delicate mica shades. Stylized rose plaster friezes typical of British and Continental design decorated a sitting room off the main hall. Grueby tile in plain and decorative designs surfaced the bathrooms. Bodley's involvement with the interiors and selection of the craftspeople made Ferry's house unquestionably the finest Arts and Crafts residence in the region.

[center] The Rookwood Pottery Company was commissioned to create a tiled fireplace with a colorful Columbia River theme for the library of John Leary's Capitol Hill house (1904–1907), Seattle. Photograph by Marissa Natkin.

[left] For Mrs. John Leary's bathroom, John Dee Wareham designed a wraparound tile frieze of water babies in groups of three cherub-like figures. Photograph by Marissa Natkin.

The O. D. Fisher residence designed by the Beezer Brothers firm in 1908–1909 also acknowledged the English Arts and Crafts movement. But its inspiration was less the vernacular English country house and more the lordly Medieval-style half-timbered manor. Inside were brass lighting fixtures with Quesnel shades, likely purchased from Seattle's Cascade Gas and Electric Fixture Company or Mission Fixture & Mantel Company, as well as a large number of Suess Art Glass leaded windows with different stained glass insets. While Fisher furnished most of the house in heavy mahogany pieces from the Frederick & Nelson department store, he purchased a Mission desk, chair, and tables for his study and wicker chairs for the sunroom adjoining it. Forged iron fireplace andirons that replicated Northwest Coast Indian totem poles were selected for the billiard room on the ground floor; unsigned, they were likely made in Seattle.

A block from Fisher's house on Harvard Avenue North, Lewis Peoples commissioned Cutter & Malmgren in 1908 to design a house in the Swiss Chalet style, perhaps encouraged by

[top right] The vernacular English houses of Charles Voysey and Baillie Scott were evoked in the Pierre Ferry house on Capitol Hill (1904-1907), Seattle. Photograph by Lawrence Kreisman.

[center] The main hall of the Pierre Ferry house in Seattle (1904-1907) welcomed visitors with hand-carved oak paneling, hammered lighting fixtures, and an opalescent paneled cabinet above the fireplace. Photograph by Scott Chytil.

[right] A wisteria motif glass mosaic tile fireplace by the Chicago firm of Giannini & Hilgart served as the social and aesthetic centerpiece of the family dining room in the Ferry house (1904-1907), Seattle's Capitol Hill. Photograph by Scott Chytil.

Interlakin Boulevard, Seattle, Wash.

Broad overhangs shaded the half-timbered upper story and stone main floor of the Boyer residence (1908) in the Montlake neighborhood of Seattle. Private Collection.

pictures of Cutter's own house, Chalet Hohenstein, and chalets Cutter had designed for businessmen in Spokane related to his Idaho State Building at the 1893 world's fair. The Swiss Chalet style was also chosen for the Seattle Golf Club in the Highlands, which opened in 1909. The exceptionally well-constructed Peoples' house exhibited many Arts and Crafts features, both in its emphatic use of heavy wood framing and sheathing members and in its carved and sawn decorative elements.[12]

The Boyer residence was another interesting house of the period. John Edward Boyer, son of a Walla Walla banking pioneer, came to Seattle in 1904, and in 1906 he established a law office in the Bailey Building. About that time, Boyer engaged architect Eben W. Sankey to design his Montlake residence. Sankey, originally from St. Louis, had moved to Seattle in 1901 and for some years designed residences in the prevailing eclectic styles

(particularly Colonial Revival and English Tudor) in Laurelhurst, Interlaken Park, and Queen Anne Hill. Construction began on Boyer's house in 1907 and took a year to complete. Boyer lived there with his wife, Louise, and son, John, from 1908 until 1920, during which time, as president of the Interlaken Land Company, he purchased forty acres surrounding his home and developed it for homeowners.

The *Seattle Post-Intelligencer* printed a rendering of the Boyer residence in 1907 and described it as being made of "granite cobblestones." But the granite was in fact cut in much larger chunks and appears to have been assembled without the use of mortar. The stone and brick mason who accomplished this was Norman P. Lacy, an immigrant from Ireland who moved to Seattle from Michigan in 1905 and built several houses in Seattle.

With its unique combination of English half-timbering, Richardsonian stonework, Prairie School massing, and California Craftsman features, the Boyer residence was

Bebb and Mendel designed this Mission Revival stucco and tile residence (c. 1910) for Roland Denny in Seattle. PEMCO Webster & Stevens Collection, Museum of History and Industry (Seattle), 83.10.3340.

a highly personal interpretation of American residential design. The house sat on a knoll in a large triangular lot. A driveway to the southwest led up the hill to a carriage house built of the same materials and in the same style as the house. The deep covered porches eloquently expressed the idea of integrated indoor and outdoor living spaces. Key Arts and Crafts features inside were a dining room fireplace faced with tile from Henry Chapman Mercer's Moravian Pottery and Tile Works in Doylestown, Pennsylvania, and a living room fireplace with an entire floor-to-ceiling tile face composed of birds by the Batchelder Tile Company, Los Angeles, California.

Roland Denny, the son of Seattle founder David Denny, hired Charles Bebb and Louis Mendel to design a grander house to replace his modest Craftsman house above Lake Washington in an area that would later be called Windermere. The firm's particular brand of English-style residence in brick or stone and half-timber was becoming a common sight in better neighborhoods. But for

Denny, the architects designed a Mission Revival house, and despite the formal proportions and fittings of the new house, Denny furnished it with comfortable Mission furniture and wicker, some of which may have come from (and would have been more in keeping with) the earlier, more rustic residence.

One of the city's most innovative designers, Ellsworth Storey (1879–1960), distinguished himself with his first projects: adjoining houses for himself and his parents on Dorffel Drive in the Denny Blaine neighborhood built during the years 1904–1905. His parents, who moved from Chicago to Seattle to stay close to their son, lived in the north house, while Ellsworth, his wife, Phoebe, and their daughters Eunice and Priscilla lived in the south house. The two houses were connected by a glassed-in breezeway, which integrated what were otherwise two distinct houses.

Perfect Homes for the Time and Place ◆ 133

Many homeowners in the Arts and Crafts period appreciated an eclectic mix of furnishings, including wicker furniture, Northwest Indian baskets, Southwest Indian blankets, and Japanese lanterns, as seen here in the sunroom of Roland Denny's Seattle home (c. 1910). PEMCO Webster & Stevens Collection, Museum of History and Industry (Seattle), 83.10.7892.

On his first trip to Seattle in 1896, Storey was captivated by the region's beauty and vowed to make the Northwest his home. Immediately after his college graduation in 1903, Storey returned to Seattle and purchased lots in the recently platted Denny Blaine Lake Park Addition.

In contrast to the majority of architecture schools whose Beaux Arts tradition taught a strict academic approach to composition and the use of historical European styles, Storey's alma mater, the University of Illinois Urbana-Champaign, trained students to be sensitive to historical precedents but to search for an architecture appropriate to twentieth-century America. The houses he designed in Seattle were his first opportunity to explore the possibilities.

The most striking aspect of these houses, especially his parents' house, was the exterior form. Familiar Craftsman elements were present: the rough-hewn wood shingle siding and the prominent stone foundation and chimney; the large overhanging eaves supported by heavy timbers; and the overall modesty of form and ornament. What was not so familiar were the large, two-story monolithic volume, made picturesque with the simple asymmetry of the unusual shed roof; the tapering eaves that created a dynamic sense of perspective; and the irregular composition of beautifully detailed white window frames punctuating the mass of the dark-stained siding.

Storey used illusory devices to enhance the exterior appearance of the house for his parents: stocky rafter ends alluded to heavy timber construction but the house was, in fact, of light wood-frame construction. Neither did rafter ends indicate where the true rafters lay in the roof framing system.[13] These illusions were certainly at odds with the Arts and Crafts belief in structural honesty, although they were a common approach in architectural circles regardless of the house. For example, close inspection of the wooden pegs on barge boards at Kirtland Cutter's Stimson house of 1901 would have revealed that they were not through tenons but simply glued onto the boards, in much the same way as nonsupportive brackets were placed under the eaves of thousands of bungalows in the region. Appearance frequently took precedence over Arts and Crafts ideals.

Inside, true to the aims of the Arts and Crafts movement, the floor plan opened up. Rooms were distinctly separate, but they flowed together, obviating dark hallways. Natural light, which flooded through large windows facing east, reached the deepest parts

An early view of the Ellsworth Storey family houses (1904–1905) on Dorffel Drive in Seattle. Martin Baker. Courtesy of Emory Bundy and Noel Angell.

of the house. Interior spaces had hardwood floors with white plaster walls and ample dark-stained wood trim. The interior woodwork, vertical stair rails, and trim were almost directly taken from the work of English architect C. F. A. Voysey.

Little is known about Storey's relationship with the philosophical and social aspects of the Arts and Crafts movement. Like other architects who were Storey's contemporaries, however, such as Bernard Maybeck and Julia Morgan in the San Francisco Bay Area and Samuel Maclure in British Columbia, Storey experimented with and created his own interpretation of a number of styles, nearly all of which fall within the general tendencies of the Arts and Crafts movement.[14] Storey did not make the great strides of his contemporaries, who experimented with connecting spaces vertically and with dramatically opening up floor plans—important ideas in the development of Modern architecture. However, the freedom of expression and the innovation expressed in Storey's houses were a source of inspiration for later architects.[15]

Storey's design of low-cost rental cottages in Seattle's Colman Park demonstrates his concern for modest and affordable housing that would nonetheless be comfortable and aesthetically pleasing. Four of his designs were published in *Bungalow Magazine* between 1912 and 1918, three in Seattle and one in Bothell.[16] His modest approach to Prairie School precepts was exemplified in a bungalow in Mount Baker that was showcased in a 1916 *Bungalow Magazine*. While seven of his houses could be termed Prairie style in their designs, it would take another architectural firm to fully exploit the possibilities of the Prairie School to Seattle clients.

A notice in *Pacific Builder and Engineer* on February 6, 1909, announced that the "Willatsen & Byrne partnership in effect Jan. 1 is taking over Cutter & Malmgren's work in Seattle." With this move, the Prairie School in the Midwest made its debut in Seattle. The firm's city houses for George Matzen, Langdon Henry, and J. C. Black exemplified the virtues of simplicity, honesty, and integration of

Mrs. George Hager's residence (1912) on Seattle's Queen
Anne Hill was the last house designed by the Willatsen &
Byrne partnership. Dennis Andersen Collection.

interior design finishes, built-ins, and furniture with the house style. The architects were
also given opportunities to express themselves
in more expansive country homes for Charles
H. Clarke and Albert S. Kerry in the exclusive
residential retreat, the Highlands.

According to Henry Matthews, in his book
*Kirtland Cutter: Architect in the Land of
Promise*, the Prairie house, so-named for its
aesthetic sympathies with the prairies of the
midwestern states, was in reality as much at
home in the Northwest. While in the region
of Chicago, Frank Lloyd Wright had conceived the long, low roof to echo the forms of
the gently rolling land, in the Northwest the
broad roof overhangs gave umbrella-like pro-
tection from the frequent rain.[17]

TACOMA
In 1873, Tacoma roundly rejected a plan for
the city prepared by Frederick Law Olmsted
for the Tacoma Land Company that would
have contoured the steep hillside of the downtown to follow the topography. Critics opted
for a uniform grid that made platting simpler
and more understandable to purchasers. Nevertheless, the City Beautiful movement was
shown off to good advantage in architecturally handsome civic buildings, hotels, and
commercial buildings, the development of
signature residential districts on the bluffs
overlooking Commencement Bay, and the
large amount of land set aside for public use
at Point Defiance Park.

During the first decade of the century, Tacoma also experienced planned developments
that were heavily promoted in the press. *Pacific Builder and Engineer* had a large two-
page spread on May 2, 1908, for example,
showing a birds-eye view of the Regents Park
development in that city (which later became
known as Fircrest). It included photographs
of the main entrance, with a substantial river
rock and timber pavilion. "Where six months
ago were forests, there are now about 12 miles
of streets and many miles of sidewalking,
fountains, lakes, boulevards."[18] Architect for
the project was a long-established and well-
respected one, C. A. Darmer.

A number of architects, such as Frederic J. Shaw, had studied their trade with Frederick K. Heath (1861–1953) or C. A. Darmer. Shaw's house for H. C. Green, a shingled Craftsman, was featured in a 1909 *Pacific Builder and Engineer* article.[19] A month later, the magazine mentioned the Tacoma Architectural Company organized in the Bankers Trust building in June of that year by V. Hamborg and D. D. A. Outcalt, and showed a drawing of a half-timbered Craftsman residence being designed in that office. Hamborg was Danish born and educated, and had arrived in America in 1904. He initially worked in Detroit, then with Reid Brothers in San Francisco, and finally with F. K. Heath and G. W. Bullard (1856–1935) in Tacoma. Outcalt had trained at Stevens Institute in Hoboken, New Jersey, in mechanical engineering.[20]

The versatile firm of Ambrose J. Russell (1857–1938) and Everett P. Babcock (1874–?) was responsible for a group of distinguished residences in various styles. While their 1905 work for W. R. Rust was a grandiose Colonial Revival, much of their work showed familiarity with and interest in Arts and Crafts architectural expressions. In fact, Russell's education and work experiences in Boston and Kansas City included close contact with H. H. Richardson, Bernard Maybeck, and Willis Polk.

In 1908, A. J. Russell designed a substantial Swiss Chalet house with sawn decorative balconies on N. Division Avenue. In 1909, the firm designed a house for George L. Dickson on N. Tacoma Avenue that combined aspects of British Arts and Crafts design in its irregular forms, stucco façade, and steeply pitched asymmetrical roof with Prairie School horizontality of windows accented by Moravian tile banding. The structure was a unique interpretation of modern domestic style worked in stone, stucco, and tile.

The interiors also revealed the architect's experimentation with emerging ideas about spatial relationships. The white oak foyer was framed by substantial wood pillars and partial walls, which provided visual separation of the living and dining rooms on either side but eliminated the pocket doors that would have been in earlier houses. While the tapered pillars were a common Arts and Crafts period type, the great amount of carved woodwork—from acanthus corbels and newel post caps, mirror frames, and ledges to the winged lion at the base of the stairs—reflected historic traditions, as did the heavily ornamented chandeliers and sconces. Contemporary handcrafted work, however, was offered in the large-scale fireplaces with Rookwood tile, the leaded and stained glass cabinets, and the dining room stained glass lighting fixtures by Duffner and Kimberly. Judging from photographs showing the furnishings of the house, one might conjecture that Russell and Babcock were attempting to direct their clients to modern design concepts but were stymied from completing the house as they might have wished by the clients' own wishes. In the end, the clients got the kind of house that fit their taste with a few gentle nods to the Prairie School and to Arts and Crafts design.

A cluster of Arts and Crafts houses arose in the prestigious residential neighborhood near the chateau-like Stadium High School. On N. Yakima Avenue, Charles H. Hyde commissioned a large stucco two-story house with a steep pitched roof that housed a third floor accented by large dormers. While its scale was large, the simplicity of the house was in-

Russell and Babcock's house (1909) for Tacoma businessman Frank Dickson was unusual for its stucco and tile exterior. Photograph by Lawrence Kreisman.

This Tacoma house, with its dark-stained shingles, designed for S. H. Seabury by Bullard and Hill in 1908, embodied modesty and simplicity. Photograph by Lawrence Kreisman.

tentional, as was its connection to the lawns and gardens of the estate. The architect, Edwin Wager (1866–1939), had been trained in Kirtland Cutter's Spokane office and managed the Seattle office during the design and construction of the Rainier Club before setting out on his own in 1904.[21]

Another Arts and Crafts house built in 1906 on N. Yakima Avenue, for Edwin J. Mc-Neeley, by the Tuttle brothers was dressed in stucco with Mission Revival dormers. In 1914, George Bullard and Irwin Hill (1875–1938) designed a British-based stucco and half-timbered Craftsman house for E. C. Richard, president of Hunt and Moffett Hardware Company, also on N. Yakima Avenue. And the quintessential American Arts and Crafts house—a shingled residence with open and covered porches and enclosed sunrooms—was built in 1908 for S. H. Seabury on N. 29th Street.

BELLINGHAM

Bellingham architects also embraced Arts and Crafts aesthetics on projects for local businessmen. The *Bellingham Herald* ran a regular feature on the city's beautiful housing stock, which was good promotion for leading architects and contractors, such as T. F. Doan (1866–1930) and F. Stanley Piper (1882–1950), who had a reputation for their bungalows and Craftsman homes. They were able to get several of these residences published in *Pacific Builder and Engineer*, another important step in the process of getting recognized professionally. A 1907 article in *Pacific Builder and Engineer* and reprinted in the *Bellingham Herald* fully described architect T. F. Doan's modern residence for H. Ells on stylish Eldridge Avenue. Photographs of the dining room and living room, well furnished in the Arts and Crafts mode, accompanied the article:

On entering the house one is most favorably impressed with the broad, long, home-like living room. The plate rail extended around the entire room is solid panel work to the baseboard below. The living room and dining room are practically one, with the exception of the two steps leading up from the living room to the dining room. The same panel work and plate rail is in the dining room.

Four large columns connected at the top by massive beams enclose the first landing of the stairway, and the large clinker brick fireplace, representing an isolated column, gives you the impression of absolute comfort. The windows throughout the building are all casement, supplied with polished plate glass. The woodwork of the first story is finished in weathered oak and the beautiful yellow-tinted walls betray artistic taste in the selection of colors.

The outside is finished with wide siding with the rough side out and the upper portion being finished with shingles, all stained dark brown. The roof with its projecting eaves is stained a dark green. The location of the building is unsurpassed for an elegant view, unobstructed, over a cluster of islands scattered through the waters of Bellingham bay, from which the home is separated by about 100 feet.[22]

Four years later, the same periodical covered the construction of a house for attorney W. R. Greene located in Bellingham Heights and designed by the same architect. This house had views of the bay and the Olympic Mountains. Its exterior was shingled with half-timbered second-floor gables and the first floor had five rooms finished in oak. The living room was dominated by a large cut-stone fireplace, and its open plan provided an unobstructed view of the dining room, "terminating in an elegantly finished china closet under a series of small, rather oblong-shaped windows." The second floor contained a billiard room, three chambers, sewing room, and bath. The cost of the house was $5,800.[23]

But the signature Craftsman house in the community was built for Victor Roeder, the son of Captain Henry Roeder, who, with others, established the first settlement on Bellingham Bay in 1852. Henry Roeder had established a sawmill on Whatcom Creek to contribute to rebuilding San Francisco after the catastrophic fire in 1851, and had then expanded his reach to include a coalmine, shipping company, hotel, and real estate holdings.[24]

Victor Roeder's house, located on Sunset Drive, was constructed in 1903–1908 by Alfred A. Lee (1843–1933), architect, with Roeder supervising construction. Lee had designed the administrative building "Old Main" on the Western Washington State College campus and the first City Hall of Bellingham, now the Whatcom Museum of History and Art. The stone, brick, and stucco façade and bracketed eaves of the Roeder house reflected the popular English Medieval style favored by American architects during the period. But the structure's metalwork and woodwork tied it to the American Arts and Crafts movement at its peak.

The length of time involved in building the house was a testament to Roeder's quest for a high degree of quality. He brought in rock from a local stone quarry for his front and rear entry, and he shipped in oak for his main floor, stairway, and stairway banisters.

The Victor Roeder residence (1903–1908) in Bellingham, designed by Alfred A. Lee, seemed almost overbuilt, with a great number of brackets supporting the wide eaves and shed roofs over porches and windows. Photograph by Wayne Dodge.

A painted frieze surrounded the dining room above the wood paneling. The home was ultramodern for its time, with a built-in vacuum system throughout. The vacuum pump was located in the basement, along with a wood-burning furnace made from a Great Northern railway boiler. Equipped both for electricity and gas, the elegant brass lighting fixtures shone with Steuben glass shades. The house also had five fireplaces.[25]

The *Bellingham Herald* of August 28, 1909, extolled the virtues of the house, though the article's author had some difficulty with descriptions: "The roof is Swiss Chalet in style of architecture, and the gables are on the Elizabethan order. The foundation below the ground is of concrete, and that portion above the ground of stone from a Chuckanut quarry. The first story is of clinker brick, laid in Flemish bond. The exterior of the second story will be finished in rough cast plaster, while the gables are to be made of rough-cast one-half timbers. This will give the building a massive appearance."[26]

The Roeder home became the major monument in the Broadway Park development, which was heavily promoted in the papers during the spring of 1907 with birds-eye views showing graceful curved parkways (Park Drive and Sunset Drive) framing Broadway. While houses of various styles eventually filled the lots, many were bungalows and Craftsman houses featured in the *Bellingham Herald*.

South of Bellingham off Chuckanut Drive, Cyrus Gates developed a suburban residence, Woodstock Farm, with a sprawling Craftsman house as centerpiece. The initial building had been a modest Arts and Crafts bungalow with a large, beamed entry hall. In 1912, F. Stanley Piper was commissioned to enlarge the house substantially. While the exterior façades simply adopted the siding, windows, and dormers of the original, the new living and dining rooms adhered generally to the Colonial Revival style in painted woodwork, cabinetry, and trim moldings and Renaissance Revival lighting fixtures. The sole exception was the Batchelder tile fireplace.

CENTRAL AND EASTERN WASHINGTON

Two unique Craftsman creations that set the standard for regional architecture were not in western Washington's major cities. Surprisingly, they were located in Ellensburg and Yakima, in central Washington.

Scotsman David Ramsay had arrived in Ellensburg after stints in San Francisco and Portland. His brother James had settled in Ellensburg in 1885 to deal in farm implements. The two brothers partnered in the hardware business in 1890. Ramsay admired the designs of British Columbia architect Samuel Maclure (1860–1929) during his frequent visits to Victoria with his Scottish-born wife Elizabeth. The couple became acquainted with the architect and, in 1903, Ramsay commissioned Maclure to design a six-bedroom, 6,000-square-foot shingled bungalow in Ellensburg, making it the only known example of the work of this noted architect in the United States.

A self-taught designer, Maclure was an early admirer and proponent of the work of Frank Lloyd Wright, with whom he corresponded regularly. He was heavily influenced by the Arts and Crafts designs of British designers Philip Webb and Baillie Scott in evolving his own signature style.

Decisions about the plan and appearance of the house may largely have been based on the input of Elizabeth, who spent two months in the late summer of 1903 in Victoria. By the spring of 1904, invoices from the Wheeler

Woodstock Farm in Bellingham was the home of Cyrus Gates. It was originally a bungalow, and was expanded by F. Stanley Piper in 1912 to be a large Craftsman house. Whatcom Museum of History and Art (Bellingham), 1998-74.5.

and Osgood Company in Tacoma indicated that doors, stained glass, and paneling were being ordered. In the October 12, 1904, edition of the *Ellensburg Capital*, the Ramsay house was called "the finest home in the city." It had a graceful hipped roof that appeared to float above a free-flowing first floor edged with open porches and a glazed sunroom. Locally milled heart-of-pine millwork was used throughout the interior. The central stair hall with heart-motif pierced balusters was a feature that tied this relatively modest bungalow to Maclure's grander stone and half-timbered residences in British Columbia. There were handsome built-ins with custom hardware and grape and leaf motif art glass windows.

[top] The shingled Samuel Maclure–designed bungalow in Ellensburg, Washington (1905), has a distinctive ornamental porch railing. Photograph by Lawrence Kreisman.

[above] The use of heart cut-out balusters in the David Ramsey house (1903) stairway linked architect Samuel Maclure's design to treatments popularized by Voysey and other English architects. Photograph by Lawrence Kreisman.

Maclure's talent for melding British traditional forms with floor plans and materials derived from Arts and Crafts ideals brought him success and publicity in journals as wide-ranging as *Western Architect*, *Studio*, *Craftsman*, *American Architect*, and *Pacific Coast Architect*. He has been compared to the Greene Brothers and Bernard Maybeck in terms of his unique approach to residential design and use of materials. His introduction of the English Arts and Crafts movement to British Columbia may have also encouraged its use and acceptance in Washington and Oregon.[27]

Despite its distance from a major population center, Yakima, Washington, became the location of Westhome, one of the most remarkable monuments to the Arts and Crafts movement in the Northwest. It was built over a two-year period, 1914–1916, for Chester Congdon.

Congdon was a successful attorney in Minnesota, initially in St. Paul and, beginning in 1892, in Duluth. By the 1880s and early 1890s, his business interests extended to include timber and land development as far west as Grays Harbor County in Washington Territory and to copper mining as far south as Arizona. His journey west followed the path of the newly laid Northern Pacific Railroad.

In 1887, on a homeward journey from overseeing investments in Grays Harbor, the Northern Pacific train paused in North Yakima, and Congdon decided to investigate some agricultural investments in the valley. He purchased 640 acres on the southwestern edge of North Yakima at a location known as Wide Hollow. In 1894, Congdon secured water rights, established the North Yakima Canal Company, and began digging a canal system. Between 1905 and 1912, Congdon ac-

Westhome, Chester Congdon's house in Yakima, designed by Kenyon and Maine (1914–1916). While the structure of Westhome was concrete, its stone façades appeared to be structurally honest, rising from the earth to stucco and half-timbered upper floors, topped by red tile roofs. Photograph by Lawrence Kreisman.

cumulated additional land, half planted to orchard and the remainder left for open grazing. His property then included seventeen workers' houses, a large bunkhouse, barns for stabling forty horse teams, a hop house, a carriage house, grain tanks, and a silo. In 1913, he constructed his own fruit processing and storage warehouse. To transport his delicate fruit to the railroad five miles away in North Yakima, Congdon got the Northern Pacific to extend a spur line into Wide Hollow to serve his ranch and the nearby Nob Hill and Broadway areas. The track was completed in 1915.

The architectural firm of William M. Kenyon (c. 1875–1940) and Maurice Maine (1881–1950) of Minneapolis designed the Congdon house. The Westhome country manor was quite different from Glensheen, Congdon's formal English-style city home in Duluth of 1905. Glensheen was designed with period- and style-specific rooms, its principal interiors inspired by English and Continental prototypes and its more intimate family spaces informed by the English and American Arts and Crafts movements.

By contrast, Westhome derived from both the Richardsonian Romanesque imagery of powerful, castle-like shelters and the Arts and Crafts desire to return to a simpler, more honest use of materials and building forms. One entered the grounds past a stone pergola, one of a number of stone structures that included a picturesque bridge and a waiting shelter for the rail spur. Three kinds of stone—lava rock, schist caps, and river rock—were used for construction of walls and stairs. Most of the porous and nonporous stone used in the house's construction was quarried in the Cowiche Canyon near Painted Rocks. The house seemed to rise from the earth, its stone walls lightening to stucco and half-timbered living areas beneath the many gables of its red tile roofs. In reality, the structure of the house was largely comprised of poured-in-place concrete and the stone used for the walls was a facing rather than a structural material.

[top] The untreated wood structural elements of Westhome were combined with honest joinery and hammered metal plates. From the beams hung artistic slag glass lighting fixtures. Photograph by Lawrence Kreisman.

[above] In Westhome's formal dining room, the stained glass windows were adorned with a grapevine motif within a Prairie School geometric frame. Photograph by Lawrence Kreisman.

Internally, the house was a linkage of spaces loosely grouped along the central axis of a groin-vaulted gallery defined at one end by the dining room and at the other by the lookout tower. It was at once rustic and sophisticated, with a carefully orchestrated combination of rough-hewn timbers and smoother finished woods.

The designers used a great variety of hammered and forged metal gates, grilles, hinges, hardware, and lighting fixtures for the interiors. There were leaded glass doors and windows and various sizes and colors of brick and tile by important art tile manufacturers, including Moravian tile from Henry Chapman Mercer's Doylestown Pennsylvania kilns. Furniture by Stickley and Limbert and built-in or commissioned furniture by the leading interior design firm of William A. French in Minneapolis–St. Paul made this house an extraordinary example of early twentieth-century trends in architecture and interior design.

Virtually every part of the interior of the house was designed, commissioned, made, or purchased in the East and shipped out by rail car, including lighting fixtures by Biddle and Gaumer Company of Philadelphia; screens, grilles, and doors by Flour City Ornamental Iron Works, Minneapolis; hardware by Werner Hardware Company, Minneapolis; ornamental tile by Henry Chapman Mercer, Moravian Tileworks, Doylestown, Pennsylvania, and Mueller Mosaic Company, Twin City Tile and Marble Company, and other manufacturers and suppliers; floor tile from Broseley Tile, England, ordered through Hawes & Dodd, Chicago; and major furniture from the William A. French Furniture Company.

Perhaps the most remarkable feature of the house was its lookout tower, which rose five floors above the basement swimming pool and was lit by a crown-like wrought-iron chandelier with blue glass beads. The tower's stairs were terrazzo, and the stone and tile used inside echoed the stone and tile on the outside. The tower contained a sleeping porch with a built-in rolling Mission bed hidden behind doors with large strap hinges. Below the top of the tower was a "contemplation room." The lookout had wonderful views to Mounts Rainier, Adams, and St. Helens.[28]

On a more modest scale, the Yakima sandstone residence for George Donald, reputedly designed by Spalding & Umbrecht of Seattle and built 1907–1908, was also inspired by current trends in the Arts and Crafts movement. Its interiors, in particular, took their cues from British designers in the choice of woodwork for moldings and stair balusters and in the designs of the stained glass sidelights for the front door. The custom furniture and built-ins were the subject of a major feature in the March 1909 *Pacific Builder and Engineer*.

Rockwood Boulevard, Highland Boulevard, and Grand Boulevard were components of an Olmsted parkway system for a section of Spokane south of the Spokane River. Rock-faced masonry pillars marked entrances to tree-lined neighborhoods. The men most instrumental in the development of the exclusive Rockwood and Manito Park neighborhoods were Jay P. Graves and Aubrey White, Graves through his investment in street railways and real estate development, and White as the great champion of the Spokane park system. Even areas that Graves did not market had his stamp, through the extension of street railways north of the river to Corbin

Portrait of Spokane architect Kirtland Cutter (c. 1900).

Park, with its steep slopes, basalt rock outcroppings, and curvilinear streets connecting a series of pleasing green spaces.[29]

Spokane's most talked-about architect was Kirtland Cutter, whose work on the Davenport Hotel, Spokane Club, and many important residences, including Louis Davenport's house, had made his artistic approach to design sought after by successful businessmen anxious for sophisticated homes. Cutter and Karl Malmgren billed themselves as "Architects, Decorators, & Furnishers Whose Studio and Workshops Are in the Inland Empire."

The Arts and Crafts inspiration in houses by the Cutter & Malmgren firm may have been less because of Cutter and more the result of his partnership with Karl Malmgren (1862–1921), in the period 1894 until 1917. While Cutter explored the vernacular and rustic Chalet forms in his house and in those of his clients, he generally embraced pre-1850 British and European styles in residences for Amasa Campbell, Patrick Clark, Louis Dav-

263. Entrance to R. B. Porter's Residence, Spokane, Wash.

The approach to Louis Davenport's Spokane house was through an elaborate Arts and Crafts entrance gate of local stone. This postcard view, c. 1915, was captioned with the new owner's name after the Davenports moved from the estate into the new Davenport Hotel in 1914. Mason Collection.

enport, and Jay Graves in Spokane, C. D. Stimson in Seattle, and Chester Thorne near Tacoma. Karl Malmgren brought a Craftsman focus to the work of the firm. His own house on West Sumner Avenue reflected his adaptation of Arts and Crafts principles. The liberal use of wood, basalt rock, tile chimneypieces, window seats, Grueby tile, and built-in furnishings was intended to make each room seem complete before any furniture was added.

The firm of Cutter & Malmgren was not alone in embracing the Arts and Crafts vocabulary in Spokane. In 1910, architect Alfred Jones designed a Craftsman-style house for Lawrence Weaver, a successful investor with ranching and fruit orchard interests in the Wenatchee Valley, and his wife Lydia. In 1916, Ralston "Jack" Wilbur, a partner and

salesman with Hallide Machinery Company, and his wife Sarah E. Smith, the controlling stockholder of the Hecla Mining Company, commissioned their friend architect Gustav A. Pehrson (1884–1968) to design a Craftsman house in Lincoln Heights. The plans may have been completed in partnership with Kirtland Cutter, for whom Pehrson worked at the time. Another well-established architect, Albert Held, designed a Prairie School house near Cannon Hill Park (another natural feature of the city designed from recommendations by the Olmsted Brothers) for Spokane attorney James A. Williams in 1911.

Throughout the city, the tenets of the Arts and Crafts were followed in handsome houses with basalt bases and columns, rock and brick chimneys, shingled or half-timbered façades, broad eaves, and brackets. A small group of local architects made names for themselves working within the bungalow and Craftsman idioms. Architect Wallace W. Hyslop (1867–1917) was prolific and, knowing the value of self-promotion, published an attractive catalog of his works. Other architects and builders, such as Ivan Abraham, Clayton Feltis, and Joseph Levesque, likely gained commissions by word of mouth in their close-knit community and established themselves for their distinctive applications of local building materials and, in the cases of Feltis and Levesque, their interpretations of Japanese and Chinese design forms and ornament.[30]

PORTLAND

In terms of the spread of British Arts and Crafts design ideas, no one in Portland did it better or for a longer period of time than Wade Hampton Pipes (1877–1961). Both his training and work experience solidified his standing in the community, and he gained a reputation for capturing the character of early twentieth century British vernacular housing in Portland neighborhoods.

Born in Independence, Oregon, in 1877, thirty-year-old Pipes went to London for four years of study at the famed Central School of Arts and Crafts (1907–1911) at the height of interest in the Arts and Crafts. The residential designs of Edwin Lutyens and Charles Voysey, who were inspired by the vernacular features of English country houses with combined utility and romance, were being published and appreciated. For Pipes, the experience altered his perceptions about architecture forever. During his London tenure, Pipes met W. R. Lethaby, Lutyens, Voysey, and Gertrude Jekyll, leading figures of the day. In fact, Lethaby was appointed first principal of the Central School of Arts and Crafts, whose mission was to unify all aspects of building.

Pipes returned to Portland and almost immediately began to apply what he had learned about the English vernacular. He contin-

ued to incorporate these ideas into his house plans for fifty years, even as building styles shifted into Modernism. His design vocabulary included gables, wood and cement stucco façades, casement windows, recessed doorways, and projecting bays. Pipes made an effort to have the form of each building express the uses of various spaces and to relate the spaces to the site in a way that took advantage of light and terrain. Because his buildings were constructed of local materials, they were economical and harmonious with their surroundings. He employed local craftsmen who were trained to use traditional methods of construction for authenticity. Pipes generally steered clear of ornament unless it reinforced the building and the natural setting.[31]

Wade Pipes' houses appeared in a number of newly developing Portland areas, including Westover Terraces, Riverwood, and Dunthorpe near the Willamette River. His practice was based on the idea of "total design" so evident in German, Austrian, and English work but less common in America. For him, the house and site were integrated, the house extending into landscape. When he was able, Pipes would draw the plans, all the interior appointments, choose the color scheme, and design or select furnishings. He would also select the building materials and personally supervise carpenters, masons, painters, carvers, and craftsmen.[32]

While traditional Arts and Crafts houses in Great Britain were his inspiration, none of his Portland houses were exact copies of any by the designers he valued, although several recalled those workers. For instance, there were similarities between Hollymount by C. F. A. Voysey (1905) and Pipes' Crumpacker house (1922). Common elements were a hipped roof,

[top] Architect Wade Pipes designed the Sherrard house in Portland in 1918. Oregon Historical Society (Portland), OrHi 39038.

[above] Wade Pipes designed the house (1912) for his brother, John Pipes. Oregon Historical Society (Portland), CN 023214.

cross gable, bell casting, entry pavilion with casement windows, and arched entry. Papillon Hall by Edwin Lutyens (1903) may have inspired Pipes' Sherrard house of 1918 with a modified butterfly plan, chimneys, bays, and hip and gambrel roofs.[33] The Sherrard house was featured in a lengthy article in the 1918 journal *Architect and Engineer of California*. The house he designed in 1912 for his brother John Pipes in Sellwood was also featured in March 1919 and described as "one of the five most notable examples of small house architecture in Portland." It had two stories, with a façade featuring rough cast stucco on the first floor and horizontal siding on the second floor, a curvilinear entry porch canopy, and imposing gables.

While the form and exterior features of Pipes' houses resembled those of his English mentors (he was even known for using metal casements ordered from England) his interiors tended to follow Classical traditions, with typical Classical moldings and white painted finishes reminiscent of Philip Webb's Standen, rather than Voysey's simplified vernacular approach.[34]

Joseph Jacobberger (1867–1930) successfully adapted the vocabulary of British designers to Arts and Crafts house design in Portland, in his own house and in the residences of Michael Brady, Dr. Andrew Geisy, and Alfred Smith. Emil Schacht, who practiced in Portland from 1885 until his death in 1926 and was a founding member in 1902 of the Portland Association of Architects, also helped popularize English and American Arts and Crafts ideals in Portland. Schacht designed several speculative homes for the Scottish American Investment Company along Northwest Thur-

man, Franklin, and Aspen Streets in Willamette Heights just prior to the Lewis and Clark Centennial Exposition (1905). He had turned to Gustav Stickley's *Craftsman* magazine and to the British design journal *Studio* for inspiration. Promotional possibilities were mined heavily. The Portland Street Railway Company, whose president was coincidentally an investor in the Scottish Investment Company and a landowner in Willamette Heights, arranged trolley car tours from the exposition entrance up the hill through the new neighborhood. People attending the fair might have wandered through the neighborhood to inspect the "new" style of architecture. Some new houses may even have been used as boarding houses for out-of-town attendees prior to their sale to homeowners. Schacht's work could eventually be seen in over a hundred houses throughout Portland and as far north as Winlock, Washington.[35]

Another firm with interest in the Arts and Crafts vocabulary was MacNaughton, Raymond and Lawrence. In 1906, Ellis Lawrence (1879–1946) designed a shingle house for himself. From 1910 through the 1920s, Lawrence was in demand for his attractive Tudor-style houses that, in recalling medieval and handmade houses, fit the tenets of the Arts and Crafts movement. Like the designs of his Seattle and Spokane contemporaries Bebb and Mendel and Kirtland Cutter, his houses were suitably embellished inside with Arts and Crafts features. In his 1923 house for Stanley C. E. Smith, he combined the Tudor style with simpler stucco and shingled façades common to British Arts and Crafts designers.

John Virginius Bennes (1867–1943), who

[top] Joseph Jacobberger's house (1913) for the Geisy family in Portland evoked medieval England. Photograph by Lawrence Kreisman.

[above] Emil Schacht designed this attractive bungalow (1910) with tapered porch posts and trellises for Roy Hadley on Mount Adams Drive in the Council Crest section of Portland. Steve Dotterer Collection.

[top] Architect Ellis Lawrence designed his house (1923) in Portland. Oregon Historical Society (Portland), CN 020256.

[above] The John Bennes–designed Aaron H. Maegley residence (1914) in Portland combined Prairie School horizontality with Classical ornamentation. Photograph by Lawrence Kreisman.

practiced in Portland in 1906–1943, built handsome Craftsman houses, such as the 1910 home for William Biddle Wells in Portland Heights. He also took an interest in the Prairie School, and practically at the same time as Willatzen and Byrne were executing their signature works in Seattle and the Highlands, Bennes, Hendricks and Thompson were designing Prairie-style houses for Marcus J. Delahunt (1909), for Bennes himself (1911), and for Aaron H. Maegley (1914).[36] In the Maegley residence, Bennes successfully combined Prairie geometry and overhangs with Classical brackets and ornamental embellishments.

One of the leading Midwest Prairie School designers, William Grey Purcell, left Minneapolis for Portland in 1920. While the few houses he did in Portland, including the Lillian K. Pollack and Thomas Mostyn houses, might be labeled Arts and Crafts style, they also retained many of the Prairie features he had explored in his earlier practice,

Francis A. Brown, a California architect reputed to have worked in the office of Greene and Greene, designed the 4,800-square-foot Wilbur Reid house in 1914. Portland's best example of the ultimate California bungalow, this house showed off the informality of the style with a variety of gables and dormers supported with hundreds of rafters and a magnificent covered porch supported by river rock and posts. Reid and his new wife, Evelyn, may have been won over by this type of residential design during their extended honeymoon trip to California prior to commissioning the house.

William Knighton carried the sophisticated Secession design vocabulary he had honed in

Francis A. Brown's design for the Wilbur Reid house (1914) in Portland expressed the California bungalow and also paid homage to Japanese design in its gently sweeping barge boards. Mason Collection.

the Seward Hotel into residences he designed in 1907 for Belle and Maude Ainsworth and for Charles Schnabel. These houses also illustrated the architect's ability to capture the informality of Craftsman design through the orchestration of gables and dormers.

Albert E. Doyle (1877–1928) established himself as the preeminent designer of Beaux Arts commercial buildings in downtown Portland. But when put to the task in four small cottages for friends and himself at Neah-Kah-Nie, he demonstrated full understanding of the modest and environmentally suitable vocabulary of Arts and Crafts design. These cottages are often cited as the forerunners of the Northwest Style of house design, more fully developed by Pietro Belluschi, John Yeon, and others in later years. The cottages were built for Frances Isom (1912), head librarian in Portland; the Crocker sisters (1916), one of whom was director of the Portland Art Museum; Doyle's own family cottage (1916); and the best known, the cottage designed for his friend, the Portland artist and art teacher Harry Wentz (1916).

These examples by architects in both Washington and Oregon, as well as those from the Midwest commissioned to do work in the two states, indicate the wide-ranging ideas of what constituted Arts and Crafts housing during the period. When possible, designers took advantage of liberal-minded entrepreneurial clients looking for distinctive residences in order to explore concepts derived from their architecture and design education, readings, and travel. Ultimately, it was their ingenuity in using local building materials and taking advantage of lighting, views, and topography that resulted in unique and often identifiable forms and features that set them apart as Pacific Northwest architects of reputation.

SIX
Bungalows for Everyone

In 1902, the *Seattle Daily Bulletin* made passing mention of a new style of house. The reporter could not have realized that the debut of this modest residential option—the bungalow—would irrevocably change the shape of the twentieth-century city: "During the last few years a new style of house has come into existence—new, that is, to our country. This is a plain one-storied building, with its low, overhanging hip roof. It is exceedingly interesting for summerhouses, and makes an agreeable change from the old-fashioned sheathed cottage, with its trimmings of wooden Hamburg edging with which we are familiar at seaside resorts. This new style is called the Bungalow and it should be carried out in straight lines with no ornamentation whatsoever. It is made rambling and low, and this is not practical where land is at a premium."[1]

Resources Build the Bungalow

Fortunately for developers and builders, cities in Washington and Oregon were ripe for development, with inexpensive land available for purchase and platting. A ready supply of inexpensive lumber made the region ideal for clapboard and shingle bungalow sales for the next quarter of the century.

In a 1924 brochure *The Land of Opportunity Now: The Great Pacific Northwest*, which promoted the Chicago, Burlington & Quincy Railroad, Northern Pacific Railway, and Great Northern Railway, the facts were impressive: "The annual cut of the Pacific Northwest lumber industry now amounts to 9 billion board feet. Production of shingles in Washington and Oregon totals 6 billion annually. One hundred and fifty thousand persons are employed in the logging camps and saw mills, and the annual value of the lumber produced is approximately $400,000,000. Washington alone, which for thirteen years, with one exception, has led all other states in the production of lumber and shingles, is credited with half the lumber cut of the Northwest—4 billion feet. In that state 800 sawmills and 300 logging camps are operating. There the largest shingle mills in the world are turning out two-thirds of all the shingles produced in the United States."[2]

With such abundant wood resources, there was value in promoting houses built of local Douglas fir and demonstrating that this hardy softwood, properly finished and stained, could become an acceptable interior finish. People liked the grain of the wood, whether stained or not. Some lumber mills began to produce their own catalogs for house plans, or offered precut houses in an attempt to eliminate some middleman expenses. The abundant availability of local timber may have been a factor in prolonging the bungalow-building boom up to a decade longer in Washington and Oregon than in other regions of the United States.

Along with wood products, indigenous building materials played an important role in defining Northwest regional differences in bungalow architecture and also exemplified the Arts and Crafts philosophy of blending in with nature. River rock might be a common element in Northwest bungalows, but the local prevalent basalt used in house construction and landscape features in the Spokane area made these buildings even more distinctive. Smooth river rock chimneys, fireplaces, foundations, and porch columns were used where there was an abundance of such rock. Local brick, timber, and stone were also used in tourist-oriented lodges and exhibit buildings, as well as in major public works projects, such as the construction and improvements along the Columbia Highway on the Oregon side of the Columbia River and on Chuckanut Drive along the coast south of Bellingham.

The Value of Home Ownership

The period from 1905 to the start of World War I was a growth period for Oregon and Washington, both in terms of local industry and newly arriving populations. These two factors created great demand for moderately priced houses for the working middle class. Growth picked up again after the end of the war, slowed again in the 1920s, and was severely impacted by the Stock Market Crash of 1929 and the ensuing Great Depression. There was a large community of new workers earning minimum wages for which the bungalow

[top] A promotional postcard from Seattle's Cole Bungalow Company stated: "From every aspect the time is ripe for the improvement of vacant property that has borne its toll of taxes without adequate income." Special Collections Division, University of Washington Libraries (Seattle), UW 23562.

[above] A simple river rock bungalow (c. 1915) in the Spokane Valley epitomized the Arts and Crafts ideal of building with nature in its use of locally available stone and wood to create a thing of beauty and utility. Northwest Museum of Arts & Culture, Eastern Washington State Historical Society (Spokane), L84-327.662.

was only a fantasy, but even these struggling workers yearned for a house of their own. In his social history of Everett, Norman H. Clark speaks to the value of home ownership to newly arrived and immigrant workers at the city's many saw mills and shingle mills:

They built on the twenty-five-foot lots of the Everett Improvement Company, or on two lots if they were affluent, three or more if they were rich. Most houses were designed by the carpenters who built them. They were more often than not a thoughtless imitation of the more severely unimaginative Midwestern residential styles. Crowded together, invariably oriented toward the sidewalks and streets rather than toward the bay and mountains, they covered block after block without variety or distinction.

But if his house were crowded against others, the worker had only a mile to walk to the mill. His wife and children had no geographic barriers to neighborliness and assimilation. If his living room faced the street instead of the bay, it was because he wanted to watch people, not meditate on nature. He had come to exploit, not to contemplate, and his new life demanded associations with humanity, not wilderness. The least of these homes offered the luxury of bedrooms for the children. If they were made with scrap lumber and covered with cheap paint, they were new and clean, and a man could find pride in appearances. And most importantly, he could plan to free himself from rent and debt. Most real estate sales were to wage earners, and most of the bank accounts in Everett represented the deposits of wage earners who were saving to pay off a mortgage in five or ten years. Owning real property was probably the most easy, most desirable, and most conspicuous evidence of social mobility that the newcomer could acquire.[3]

There is a fine distinction between these purpose-built cottages and the more upscale, well designed and outfitted bungalows portrayed in magazines and catalogs. Nevertheless, the overall impact was that in growing cities, workers took it upon themselves to provide shelter for their families, and gaining simple housing of whatever form was the first step in Americanization and self-sufficiency.

Architects, Builders, and Entrepreneurs

In 1906, the *Coast*, a popular Pacific Northwest journal, expressed sentiments that paralleled those of design reformers a half century earlier, with regard to the excesses of London's Great Exposition and the Victorian architecture of the time: "We hear a great deal now-a-days about 'artistic' homes. They have towers and turrets, and spindles and spools— but the gingerbread of yesterday will not suffice for the spice of tomorrow. The style changes, and the unhappy owner realizes that what he has is not only out of date, but, now that the novelty is worn off, ugly. The truly artistic house, like everything else that is truly beautiful, does not get out of date."[4]

What followed were illustrations of attractive, charming, convenient, and practical houses that included American foursquare and Classical Revival bungalows that, presumably, would not "get out of date." The implication was that these houses could be built without the expense of custom plans by architectural professionals. An enterprising would-be homeowner could simply purchase the plans and an inventory listing all the parts

[top] First-time homeowners pose in their Sunday best on the front porch of their modest residence on 13th Avenue South in Seattle's Georgetown neighborhood (c. 1910). Their simple cottage was typical of worker housing of the period throughout Northwest communities. Mason Collection.

[above] The Tom Marks residence, an 1894 Victorian home in Snohomish, with bays and scroll ornament, got an Arts and Crafts redo in the early years of the twentieth century with the addition of clinker brick porches and pillars. Photograph by Lawrence Kreisman.

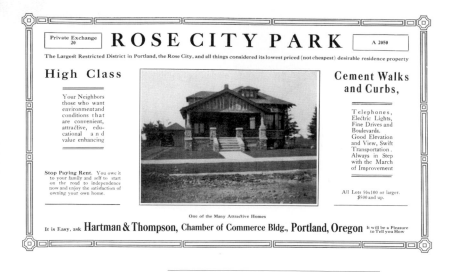

Private Exchange 20 **ROSE CITY PARK** A 2050

The Largest Restricted District in Portland, the Rose City, and all things considered its lowest priced (not cheapest) desirable residence property

High Class

Your Neighbors those who want environment and conditions that are convenient, attractive, educational and value enhancing

Stop Paying Rent. You owe it to your family and self to start on the road to independence now and enjoy the satisfaction of owning your own home.

Cement Walks and Curbs,

Telephones, Electric Lights, Fine Drives and Boulevards. Good Elevation and View, Swift Transportation. Always in Step with the March of Improvement

All Lots 50x100 or larger. $500 and up.

One of the Many Attractive Homes

It is Easy, ask **Hartman & Thompson,** Chamber of Commerce Bldg., **Portland, Oregon** It will be a Pleasure to Tell you How

Bungalow catalogs of the period routinely promoted new housing subdivisions, such as Rose City Park in Portland. Mason Collection.

needed to assemble the building, and he could build it himself or hire a capable workman.

First-time home buying and building in Washington and Oregon reflected population growth and job security of newcomers in an expanding economy. It also was tied to the domestic reforms that resulted in more women in the workplace and fewer servants in the home. The affordability of newly constructed houses was due to an increasing number of speculative developments opening up new neighborhoods. Promotional offers by competing companies enticed those with enough money for a down payment to put down their roots, with monthly costs that compared favorably with rents at the time.

In cities and towns, architects and plan and pattern book companies advertised in newspapers and magazines. The architect lucky enough to have his bungalow published in a national magazine could count on future work and recognition. While some in the architectural community would have snubbed their noses at being acknowledged as bungalow architects, others saw it as an opportunity

for job security and livelihood. For every Arts and Crafts house designed by an architectural firm with a diverse practice that usually included commercial and institutional buildings, there were many thousands of houses designed by architects whose primary market was the burgeoning number of people seeking single-family residences in established and newly opened areas of cities and towns. Some architects ran small firms catering to individualized service and custom designs. Some assembled catalogs of houses with attractive photographs of completed buildings and equally enticing renderings of suggested houses, along with floor plans and an estimate of total costs. Regardless of the practice, all of them routinely advertised in newspapers, weeklies, and monthly magazines, and promoted their wares however they could to improve their visibility.

In his 1916 edition of *Craftsman Bungalows*, Jud Yoho, the self-proclaimed "bungalow craftsman" from Seattle, made an effort to respond to criticism that questioned the status of bungalow designers in the broader architectural community. He rebuffed architects who jumped on the bandwagon of the bungalow as it increased in popularity:

> Of late other architects have taken up the subject, forced to meet the demand as best they could, whether or not they were familiar with the needs of their sections. They have gone so far in their eagerness to meet all wishes as to apply the term bungalow to many crude alterations of cottage or even more substantial types of residences.
> The designing of an artistic bungalow of the true type requires as much skill and education as does any other branch of the

architect's work. The man with the experience and training is the one to give you the best results. All of the designs in this book are bungalows pure and simple. Most of them are my own ideas. They are only a few of the many designs on hand, but they will serve to show you something of the concentrated beauty, convenience and comfort to be obtained from owning a real Craftsman Bungalow.[5]

An extraordinary promotional network provided by the regional press helped the many architects and builders who hopped on the bungalow train. Articles routinely described the virtues of the building form and its appropriateness to West Coast lifestyles. Typical of these was an April 1912 article, "Springtime is Bungalow Time: Pleasing Designs for Western Homes" in *Westerner*:

Today the ambition of man is to own and care for a home of his own. Whether it is small or large does not seem to be as important as the fact of having for his own a place where his children can look back with tender memories. In the furtherance of this idea the men of the West have evolved one of the great attractions of the Pacific Coast cities in the endless variety of bungalows to be seen along their pretty residential streets. The building of the bungalow is one of the fads of the residents of the Far West, and there have been many magnificent homes evolved on the one-floor plan. Sunny California is probably responsible for the origin of the bungalow, and the style has spread until beautiful homes of moderate costs are enjoyed by many residents of the Pacific Coast states. The mild climate of the Coast has as much to do with popularizing the modern bungalow as perhaps any other cause.

The unconventional style permits the use of a great many variety of materials and ideas. Instead of the old fashioned cottage with its steep roof, closed cornice, small porch, high windows, fancy grille work and square, box-like rooms, the bungalow of today has a low, broad roof, heavy timbers, rough siding, broad windows, open fireplace, large, airy, homelike rooms, with all kinds of built-in features, and the whole designed for pure comfort and the saving of steps for the housewife.[6]

According to the article, the cost of the bungalow depended altogether on the ideas and demands of the builder, ranging from $800 to $5,000 for a 1,000-square-foot, five-room bungalow complete with a concrete foundation, cement basement, double-wall construction, plastered walls, fireplace, cabinet kitchen, plumbing, numerous windows, and fir floors and inside trim. The variety of materials used in its construction—common or clinker brick, quarry or cobblestone, cement or terra-cotta, shingles or rough-sawn siding or shakes—would determine the cost.

The Seattle Public Library subscribed to the nation's most popular magazines—*House Beautiful*, *House and Garden*, the *Ladies' Home Journal*, and Gustav Stickley's *Craftsman*. The ease with which Stickley made plans available to people anywhere in the country is evidenced in a house built on the ridge above Frink Park in Seattle's Leschi neighborhood. The plans for house no. 78, published in the November 1909 *Craftsman*, were ordered by Mrs. Henry E. Holmes and shipped to her from New York on August 28, 1910, reputedly as a wedding gift to her daughter Ruth on the occasion of her union with at-

Seattle pharmacy owner Henry Holmes and his wife ordered house plans from Gustav Stickley as a wedding gift to their daughter. The turret of the elder Holmes's Victorian home is directly behind the newly built Craftsman house (1910). Courtesy Richard Buck and Paul Dorpat.

torney Richard Huntoon. Pharmacist Holmes and his wife, Kate, lived in a Victorian house built in 1894 and his family of four daughters and a son settled in houses on the property. The Stickley bungalow was oriented with a broad covered porch facing Lake Washington. Some differences between the design and the completed house configuration may have been a special redesign by Stickley or a redesign on site.[7]

Stickley-designed houses also appeared in Spokane, Portland, and Ashland, Oregon, and probably in other Northwest locations. For example, in 1910, Lewis and Harriet Gilliland commissioned architect Ellis Lawrence to help them modify an April 1907 design from the *Craftsman* to suit their property in Portland's Irvington neighborhood. The "H" plan home featured an ashlar foundation and trellised entrance court framed by two similar gabled wings. The interiors closely followed

Stickley's suggestions for built-ins, a stone fireplace, and fireplaces in two first-floor bedrooms, but were more lavishly handled than Stickley might, with a Honduran mahogany-paneled living room and dining room. A library housed off the balcony overlooking the living room had built-in furniture.[8]

Advertisements for the *Craftsman* ran in local periodicals, and occasionally the magazine drew the attention of editors, as in the Books and Periodicals notes of the *Coast* in 1906: "The Craftsman: This magazine does not appeal to the person who desires light reading to pass monotonous hours away, but is meant for the studious artisan who wants to learn something regarding the crafts. It is a periodical of quality, although possessing quantity as well."[9]

But people had no need to go to Stickley's *Craftsman* for building plans and interior design ideas. With a circulation of around one million, the *Ladies' Home Journal*, under progressive editor Edward Bok, influenced far more people than Stickley's journal did. Even *House Beautiful*, a high-quality shelter magazine begun by architects and aimed at a general readership, had three times the *Crafts-man*'s circulation. Not to be overlooked were the myriad house-plan books and catalogs for bungalows and other Arts and Crafts houses, as well as numerous small journals such as Will Price's *Artsman*.[10]

Bungalow Magazine Promotes and Instructs

From 1908 until 1912, Henry Wilson had published *Bungalow Magazine* in Los Angeles, and had focused on some of the newest and most interesting bungalow houses in southern California. He had even written an article in *Pacific Builder and Engineer* in 1908 on the subject—no doubt a way to stimulate interest in his new venture.

Jud Yoho, an enterprising Seattle businessman, took over the reigns of the magazine and published it in Seattle from 1912 until 1918 when it folded. During its run, the magazine attracted a nationwide audience of homebuyers, advertised the products of businesses both local and out-of-state, and showed off the newest construction of bungalow houses in Washington, Oregon, and California, as well as in the East, the Midwest, and the South. In addition to the monthly supplement, which included plans and specifications for a featured bungalow, each month there were feature articles on a variety of houses and on the technology or mechanical systems within them, as well as amateur craftsman projects in furniture design and construction, and articles on gardening and landscape.

Bungalow Magazine had nearly twice the circulation of the *Craftsman*, if one believes period circulation statistics in the Ayer & Sons' *American Newspaper Annual and Direc-tory* for 1915. It reported a circulation of 40,000 for *Bungalow Magazine* and only 22,500 for the *Craftsman*. *Bungalow Magazine* had projected a circulation of 50,000 by 1915.[11]

Yoho's entrepreneurial nature could have competed on an equal level with Elbert Hubbard. In Seattle's annual Potlatch celebration of July 1912, Yoho's Craftsman Bungalow Company entry into the industrial parade was a model bungalow, complete with river rock porch piers, drawn on a carriage down Second Avenue. The *Bungalow Magazine* float consisted of a huge reproduction of the August issue, standing on one end upon a table, with opened covers and pages, representing very accurately the appearance of the actual magazine and bearing terse inscriptions concerning the periodical and its scope. With an estimated 300,000 visitors to Potlatch that summer, Yoho's subscription booth was inundated.

In the spring of 1913, Yoho's enterprise attracted the attention of the well-established regional trade journal, *Pacific Builder and Engineer*:

> The June number of the *Bungalow Magazine*, edited by D. E. Hooker, with offices in the Leary building, Seattle, maintains the high standard set for this publication from the very start nearly a year ago. The "Supplement Bungalow," for which a complete set of working plans is included, consists of an attractive home, particularly well adapted to our wooded areas, islands, etc. The one in question is the home of B. A. Northrop, an attorney of Seattle. The publication also contains exteriors and interiors of several other moderate cost homes, with floor plans, etc. An article by Ida D. Bennett treats window and porch boxes for plants and flowers. Several other

Jud Yoho understood the value of promotion. To debut his business, he built a scale model bungalow to showcase his work in Seattle's 1912 Potlatch Parade. Courtesy of John Kelly.

features add interest to the June number. The magazine sells at 20 cents the copy, or $2.00 a year, and is well worth the price.[12]

The Craftsman Bungalow Company claimed a New York City advertising office and a representative in Los Angeles, which would account for the out-of-region advertisements that appeared frequently in its pages. Among the local advertisements that greeted readers were those of consultants and businesses who claimed to know it all when it came to design, construction, interior finishes, and furniture. For example, in the June 1913 issue, there were advertisements for bungalows by a number of Seattle companies, including those manufactured by the Nudd House and Garage Company, Ready Made or Portable Houses from the American Portable House Company, bungalow plans from W. Willard DeLong, a 92-page plan book from Frank Cruse, a 130-page book of house, cottage, and bungalow plans of buildings by Victor Voorhees, a book

of plans from Distinctive Homes Company that included "detailed elevations of interior woodwork, brick terraces, fireplaces, built-in bookcases and cupboards, also suggestions for decorations, furnishings, stenciling, electric light fixtures," and the 1912 plan book of Elmer E. Green, an architect who divided his time between Seattle and Victoria, British Columbia, and had a prolific bungalow practice. The O. B. Williams Company Sash and Doors offered sixteen Craftsman bungalow door designs.

Of course, as one would expect, the Craftsman Bungalow Company advertised its services whenever and wherever it could. In a typical month, January 1917, there were at least three references to its various enterprises. These included one for *Bungalow Magazine*, stating, "Progressive architects throughout the United States and in practically every foreign country buy Bungalow Magazine, the national bungalow monthly." Another promoted the second edition, revised and enlarged, of *Bungalows, Camp and Mountain Houses*, compiled by William Phillips Comstock, saying, "The designs are varied to such an extent that many of them are suitable only for summer use, while others are adapted for occupancy the entire year. The subject matter is treated in three parts; the first deals with what is considered the 'true bungalow,' the second with the bungalow showing a second story and the third considers lodges and log cabins suitable for mountains, lakeside and seashore." A third advertisement showed off the 1916 deluxe edition of Jud Yoho's *Bungalow Book* from the Bungalow Craftsman, its building design department.

During its lengthy run, *Bungalow Magazine* provided readers with a wealth of information on a whole range of topics regarding bungalow culture, from the actual construction of houses to the tiniest details of interior finishes, furniture, and accessories. It carried regular features on gardening and a "how to" for amateur woodworkers wishing to build their own furniture. It featured buildings in nearly every residential neighborhood in Seattle, but also bungalows and Craftsman houses in rural and vacation areas and in small cities and towns throughout Washington, Oregon, and California, with occasional guest articles on other parts of the country, including the East and the Midwest. It is no wonder that bungalow housing tracts still make up a significant number of this region's neighborhoods. They can be found everywhere. An examination of these articles reveals the extraordinary range of the magazine in promoting work in the region.

In the September 1912 issue, for example, there were several features relating to bungalows, including an illustrated article on the house of Hon. George W. Trimble, designed by Ellsworth Storey in Denny Blaine Park, with a full description of Storey's efforts to

The Singer bungalow on Lake Crescent in the Olympic Peninsula was featured on the cover of *Bungalow Magazine*, July 1914. The house embraced the dual rustic and sophisticated aspects of bungalows and their comfortable fit within the context of the Northwest forest and waterways. Dodge/Kreisman Collection.

unify the interiors through attention to detail in materials and finishes:

> The hall, dining room and living room are finished in mission oak and the beamed ceilings are likewise ceiled with narrow V'd oak ceiling. The light fixtures and furniture are hand made to match the woodwork. The fireplace is in an alcove of the living room with built-in seats along each side. In a panel of the brick mantel is a carved oak slab bearing the motto "Live, Laugh and Love—There'll Come a Time When You Can't." The walls of the living room are papered with a rich, soft mottled orange color; the wainscot panels in the dining room with a tapestry pat-

tern; and the border above, with a bluish mottled slate colored paper. The breakfast room opening off the dining room, also the sunroom are finished in fir stained a light brown, with paneled walls papered to match the adjacent rooms.[13]

Another article in *Bungalow Magazine*, "A Bungalow with Unique Conveniences," discussed a Ravenna house built and designed by the owner, Mr. F. H. Pratt, and constructed for $2,500: "Much mention is made of the enormous fireplace nook (16 ft. wide and 4 ft. deep) and its substantial cobblestone mantel. The ingenuity of the designer is evidenced on every hand by artistic and convenient fixtures and accessories. All the furniture in the living room was constructed by the owner, and is built in keeping with the mission design of the house."[14]

In December 1913, *Bungalow Magazine* featured a row of five bungalows north of Woodland Park by Hudson Brothers Designers and Builders. Though the bungalows were small, "the setting upon the embankment with pretty gardens have the appearance and effect of substantial homes; each has its own clever design, well groomed, with pebble stone steps and rockery walk."[15]

[top] The Trimble residence (1912) by Ellsworth Storey shows the architect's interest both in Prairie School design and in creating unique window treatments. Seattle Public Library.

[center] A clapboard and shingle bungalow built for F. H. Pratt in Seattle's Ravenna neighborhood was published in the September 1912 *Bungalow Magazine*. Seattle Public Library.

[left] With its leaded windows, wainscoting, stenciled tree frieze, lighting, and hand-built furniture, the Pratt bungalow (1912) offered a true Arts and Crafts environment. Seattle Public Library.

Speculative bungalows (1913) near Woodland Park, each with a different appearance, lured new homebuyers to this north Seattle neighborhood.

The January 1914 issue featured a country bungalow by Ellsworth Storey for businessman Hon. Gerhardt Erickson. In April, a rustic summer cottage for Laurence and Ida Colman by Daniel Huntington in Fauntleroy was featured. In July, the magazine appropriately focused attention on a lovely vacation bungalow for Mr. and Mrs. Al Singer designed by R. L. Robertson, on Lake Crescent, with views of the Olympic range. Farther afield, there were reports of a stucco and half-timbered bungalow in Klamath Falls, Oregon, designed by Veghte Knapp for R. M. Johnson. In September, a bungalow by the Harris and Coles firm at Wing Point, Bainbridge Island, Washington, was shown, along with two handsome Craftsman houses for Frank Hanford, a partner in the firm of Hanford and Sutthoff, mining brokers, on fashionable Federal Avenue. In October, the magazine featured the Japanese-inspired P. E. Wentworth bungalow in the Phinney Ridge neighborhood by Craftsman Bungalow Company, with its prominent river rock foundation and chimney. The December issue showed a Prairie-style house by Andrew Willatsen in West Seattle.

Starting in 1915, the influence of the Colonial style in bungalow design was expressed through magazine features on the work of architect Edwin J. Ivey (1883–1940). In April

Architect Daniel Huntington's summer cottage (1914) for Laurence Colman in Fauntleroy, West Seattle, was a sophisticated interpretation of rusticity that incorporated untrimmed timbers and rough-cut boards and shingles with multipaned windows. *Bungalow Magazine*, April 1914.

1915, his Home in the Woods, designed for E. E. Harold in Fauntleroy, West Seattle, was a feature: "Set in ideal surroundings among the giant firs of the primeval forest the Harold bungalow is flanked by a picturesque ravine which leads from the foothills to Puget Sound."[16]

In August of that year, with a headline

BUNGALOW MAGAZINE

SUPPLEMENT BUNGALOW WITH COMPLETE WORKING DRAWINGS, SPECIFICATIONS AND BILL OF MATERIAL

25 CENTS

MARCH 1916

The March 1916 cover of *Bungalow Magazine* featured a bungalow by Ellsworth Storey in Seattle's Mount Baker neighborhood that had a Prairie School appearance. Seattle Public Library.

"Bungalow equipped with many electric devices attracts much notice at Big Exposition," the magazine covered one of the popular exhibits at the Palace of Manufacturers in the Panama-Pacific International Exposition in San Francisco—a gray stucco and red tile Spanish-California bungalow billed as the "Home Electrical Bungalow."[17]

In January 1916, the magazine traveled to Medford in southern Oregon to show off the work of architect R. A. Johnson. This bungalow was "built in the middle of an orchard in the fertile Medford district. This portion of the state is famous as the land of almost perpetual sunshine and the building naturally was modeled closely along the lines of the California bungalow to suit the mild climate." The author made the point that the house was purposely simple, with no beamed ceiling, paneled wainscoting, or fireplaces.[18]

In March, the cover story concerned a cement stucco Prairie bungalow by Ellsworth Storey built in the Mount Baker neighborhood, with characteristic ribbons of windows and an entrance pergola supported by simple square columns. The article pointed out the richness of color in brickwork bases, walk, and steps, the wide overhangs given the eaves, and the frieze beneath the eaves, which was repeated in the windows, and ornamental flower boxes.[19]

The same issue offered an article on a two-story bungalow in Corvallis, Oregon, by architect C. L. Heckart for J. C. Sprague, which spoke about the value of simplicity over artifice:

The long sweeping lines of the roof are retained and the second floor provided for by the addition of dormers. There are wide cornices and a pergola to create a pleasing composition. To accommodate for the warmer climate here, there are folding doors that open from the dining room in the summer time.

The interior of the house is designed to give large comfortable rooms to live in. No attempt is made at adding useless bric-a-brac or cut up moulds which only serve to catch dust and cause useless labor in keeping the rooms presentable. Another point, which deals with the housewife, and especially the timid housewife, is an arrangement in the front and rear doors whereby glass panels in the doors maybe opened without opening the entire door.

This has been found of great service when receiving calls from tramps, book agents, and others.[20]

Also featured was a Japanese-influenced five-room bungalow by Coles Construction Company for Mrs. H. W. Cullyford in Seattle's Madrona neighborhood on a hillside overlooking Lake Washington.

Periodicals Encourage Building

Yoho and his *Bungalow Magazine* had no monopoly on bungalow promotion. *Pacific Builder and Engineer* reported periodically on particularly interesting residential architecture and covered more than a few bungalows. In October 1910, an article, "Bungalow Construction in the Northwest," featured a six-room bungalow by Merritt, Hall & Merritt Architects. The house was the Leschi residence of H. Schmidt of the Packard Motor Company, and cost $3,300. While briefly mentioning the exterior as "modest," most of the article focused on the delights of the interior, where the open construction connecting the living room, den, and dining room—a distance of more than 40 feet—became reception rooms suitable for entertaining large numbers of guests: "The idea that the home is frequently made the hospitable resort for hosts of friends is too often overlooked in laying out a floor plan that might otherwise possess such commendable features."[21]

The article fully described interior features and finishes, including oak floors; living room walls plastered and tinted an olive green, with old ivory between the beams; a den paneled in brown slashed-grain fir to plate rail, tan above and a champagne-colored ceiling; a dining room with panels of burlap to plate rail, above light-brown finishes; and the sim-

The upturned barge-board ends and the porch frame show the influence of Japanese aesthetics on Mrs. H. W. Cullyford for her 1916 bungalow in the Madrona neighborhood of Seattle. Seattle Public Library.

ple hearth, very much the spiritual heart of the house. As a promoter of Northwest industry, it was not surprising that local manufacturers were given credit for their work.

The clinker and dark paver brick fireplace in the living room meted out generous hospitality to an otherwise modest home. No effort had been made to force the brick into unnatural positions or strained designs; it was a substantial, home-like fireplace in every sense. The hearth was laid with three- by nine-inch tiles, conforming in brown tones with the brick. The fireplace was built by William Rutledge.

The lighting fixtures were all of the best

F. B. Hubbard's residence (1908) in Centralia was proudly built of local and regional materials. While otherwise a typical Craftsman bungalow, the turreted corner bay was a holdover from the Victorian Queen Anne period. Seattle Public Library.

type of modern Mission style, done in brass. Lanterns were hung from the front porches and the fireplace, and with the exception of the latter, the installations were suspended from appropriate places in the ceilings. Art glass was used in all the shades, and the dining room fixture was an appropriate design. The Sargent building hardware, supplied by the Seattle Hardware Company, was in the Alby pattern, finished in brushed brass.

In Centralia, the F. B. Hubbard bungalow by Bullard & Hill, a Tacoma firm, attracted attention in a 1908 article, "The Hubbard Bungalow built of Washington Fir, Cedar, Stone, and Cement," particularly for its effort to use only materials produced in Washington state. The article says the bungalow has "not only much beyond the average value of the residences about it, but possesses some unique and attractive features which entitle it to more than local prominence. It is, in fact, quite as fine as many of its prototypes situated in Southern California amid palms

and orange groves and surrounded by estates of great value. Hubbard's idea is to have a home built entirely from local woods, clays, and stones, using selected stock from his own mills and other materials which would entitle him to speak of his home as an 'all Washington product,' and but for one exception, was made, that being a small amount of hardwood flooring."

The article offers a complete picture of the exterior, with its concrete base with sandstone trim, the lower walls sheathed in rough-sided wood laid vertically instead of horizontally and stained deep brown, the second-story walls sheathed in acid-stained shingles and the roof shingled and stained green. The woodwork was white with black sash.

Inside, there were sandstone chimneys for the library and private lounging room, which connected with the owners' private suite of rooms, including a reception room with a beamed ceiling and cream-colored panels with a plain red line border. An autumn scenic frieze was hand-painted on burlap. The hall and living room contained hand-built tables with tops of remarkably fine curly fir. The predominant colors of the living room were brown and green, and wall covering was green of conventional foliage. Panels between ceiling beams were cream, with ends of a conventional design in green. The fireplace was faced with six-inch green Grueby tiles. The library was a brown room, a trifle darker than either the hall or living room, but harmonizing with both. Wainscoted walls and ceiling were hand decorated with a design of oak leaves in autumn tones that was complemented by a brown six-inch Grueby tile fireplace. The dining room theme was Old English. Its walls were decorated with an elderberry fiber with a reddish brown paper border of hand-painted grapes and vines, and there was an Elizabethan design in the ceiling panels. The owner's suite consisted of a bedroom, sitting room, and bath, and had a fireplace faced with pale gray Rookwood tiles.

The article concludes, "The efforts that Charles Weissenborn, the Seattle decorator, has put into this bungalow have been amply rewarded by pleasing effects and a harmonious whole. This work incorporates the latest features which Mr. Weissenborn brought with him from his Eastern trip last winter. The grounds are laid out under suggestions of E. R. Roberts, the landscape architect formerly superintendent of the Tacoma Parks."[22]

During the same period, the *Coast*, a popular Seattle magazine, began a series of illustrated articles with plans and elevations called "Architecture of the Pacific Northwest." The houses were designed by Thomas L. West, billed as one of the most successful architects of the Northwest, of the Seattle firm of Knapp & West. One of the first houses to be featured was "The Bungalow—An Inexpensive Home," with comments on its virtues. The article described the summer bungalow as being suitable for mountains, country, or seaside, and it extolled the structure's simplicity and strength, and the intelligent and artistic grouping and use of inexpensive materials in a harmonious way: "Nothing is more noticeable than the increase of these quaintly rustic homes all over the land, and why not more of them in this growing Western country, where their setting is ideal? The subject of bungalows is at this time a very interesting one to many people on account of the low cost of such structures, the uniqueness and opportunity to display their artistic tastes by their own efforts, and again, others tired of much imitation desire to be more simple and sensible in their daily life, desire to get closer to nature and to their ideals. Children love the sense of space, of freedom, and a place to romp—which are truly the delightful adjuncts of a summer home like this."[23]

West's partner, I. J. Knapp, occasionally stretched the typical bungalow idea for a client who had, perhaps, been smitten by a trip to Asia or to the Japanese pavilions at the Alaska-Yukon-Pacific Exposition. A 1914 issue of *Pacific Builder and Engineer* featured a house inspired by a Japanese temple design under the title "Residence Among the Pines": "The house shown in the illustration is not a Shinto temple from the Island of Japan, but an original idea for a summer cottage among the pines of Washington. It is the George H. Long residence at Steilacoom Lake, a few miles out of Tacoma. I. J. Knapp, the architect who prepared the plans, has carried out the quaint Oriental design faithfully, even to the chimney. The roof was one of the difficult pieces of construction, but contractors, Cornell Brothers, used tin roofing, which not

The G. H. Long house (1914) at Steilacoom Lake was designed by I. J. Knapp in the Japanese style.

only carried out the architectural effect readily, but also provided a durable roof."[24]

Yoho's Competition

Yoho's Craftsman Bungalow Company was only one of many companies intent upon becoming known as *the* builder of quality housing. The Seattle Building & Investment Company published a plan book for which it provided plans and specifications sold in duplicate. Alterations were offered at a nominal cost. Plans could be purchased with "silver, American postage stamps, or by postal order." Frank Cruse, an architect in Seattle, was the manager of the company and designed most of the featured bungalow and Craftsman-style house plans. Consequently, it is no surprise that in the plan book, there is a prominent advertisement for his firm, Cruse & Martin.

The American Portable House Company also advertised, with a photo of one of their bungalow-style beach cottages: "When you want a Cosy Cottage, Bungalow, Camp House or Summer House with a Maximum of Comfort at a Minimum of Expense, Call on or write to the American Portable House Co., The Oldest and Largest Establishment on the Coast. Building Portable Houses Exclusively. All Kinds and Sizes and suitable for All Purposes and Climates. Made in Seattle—Shipped Everywhere. Catalogue, Plans, Prices and Full Information on Request. American Portable House Co., 329 Arcade Bldg., Seattle, Wash."

Craftsman Master Built Homes was a catalog produced by the Take Down Manufacturing Company, Seattle and Portland (c. 1915). The Seattle showroom, located at 700 Westlake Avenue N., was appropriately housed in a Craftsman bungalow. The factory was at the foot of Harrison Street. Their Portland office was in the Empire Building.

The introduction to *Seattle Home Builder and Home Keeper* (1915) was prepared by Seattle architect W. W. DeLong and his wife:

This modest volume is presented, with their compliments, jointly by the editors and the firms whose advertisements appear in it. It is a book of suggestions garnered from the experiences of many home-builders. Most people build a new home but once. In a sense therefore the building of a home is a lifetime event. Consequently much importance attaches to every detail. It is not enough to learn by one's own experience what to do and what to avoid. Such knowledge will come too late. For while many of the mistakes thus made might be corrected afterward, it is always costly to make alterations. Then again some errors could not be rectified at any cost and these would be a constant source of regret. How much more satisfactory to profit by the experience of others in order to avoid their mistakes and have the guidance of the suggestions which they would follow were they to build again.[25]

DeLong offered suggestions for appropriate foundations and exterior and interior materials and finishes suitable to the Northwest. Contrary to many bungalow designers, DeLong discouraged wide verandas and covered porches because the presence of such features "darkens the rooms in winter and excludes what little sun there is at the time of year when it is most appreciated. The front veranda is, therefore, of no use at all at that season, but rather a detriment, while in summer, unless the house is far from the street, or the veranda well screened, it is not much used." He did see value in the sun porch, a "cool place to sit in the warm weather, where one can be comfortable and at the same time enjoy the air; hence an outdoor sitting-room or sun porch should be included in every house."[26]

DeLong had several interior space design suggestions that responded to Pacific Northwest weather. While in California it was reasonable for the front door to open directly into the living room, he insisted that the wet and cold local climate required an entrance hall, where people could remove muddy shoes, wet coats, and umbrellas, and to stop cold air from reaching the rooms beyond. If space was at a premium, he argued at least for a back hall with a cupboard, where hats and coats could be hung and rubbers and shoes put out of sight.

DeLong disliked open stairways from the living room despite their aesthetic effects, insisting that the inconvenience of having to traverse the living room to go upstairs negated its value. He encouraged a separate stair hall if possible.[27] He also encouraged windows. He insisted that there should be enough windows in each room to make it light on a dull day: "Since about three-fourths of the days on the Coast are dull, if not rainy, it is important to bear this in mind when providing a room with light. A dark room on a dull day is depressing to the spirits, but with plenty of window space to let in all the light there is outside we have the first essential for a cheerful room. It seems strange that in California, where sunshine is a daily blessing, the houses are nearly all glass, but in Seattle, where we have cloudy weather for several months in the year, we seem to be afraid of sunshine."[28]

Roberts Home Builder, a comparable plan book published in Portland by architects Roberts & Roberts (c. 1909), carries a similar dual message of education and self-promotion:

There was a time in the early history of our country, when people were satisfied with almost anything in the shape of a house, and did not attach much importance to the value of having that house artistic in appearance and conveniently arranged. The main idea of those days was to have a roof overhead while the fortunes were being hewed out of the wilderness.

Now, with the rapid advance of our American civilization, and its consequential demand for something better, has come the bungalow architecture of today, wherein an artistic treatment of both inside and out is used to secure a dwelling which will harmonize, be in proportion, and adapted to the comfort and purposes of those who are to dwell in it. These results can be easily secured in a building of any price.

Our objective in publishing the "Roberts Home Builder" has been to place in the hands of home builders the opportunity to secure at prices within the reach of all, the design of an artistic, well-planned residence, executed under the direction of a competent architect. (The designs in this book are especially fitted for any country where climatic conditions make basements and furnaces a necessity; in a warmer climate these features can be omitted if desired.)[29]

Another leader in the Seattle-area bungalow industry was Long Building Company. Their Horace McClure residence in the Montlake neighborhood, built complete for $3,200, featured brickwork on the porch and chimney "laid up in a rustic design with the roughest clinkers obtainable. The arch over the front porch and posts are cement plaster over lath. A well-arranged pergola off the dining room adds an attractive feature to the side of the house. The roof is pitched in graceful lines, giving the general California bungalow effect."

The interior arrangement was large, roomy, and commodious, but peculiar in that it was designed for a family of two. The living room, den, music room, and dining room were really one, being separated only by paneled partitions. The den was cozy, arranged with bookcases on either side of the fireplace and seats at either end of the room. Beams eight by twelve inches separated these rooms, while beams four by eight inches were placed in the living room and dining room proper. A half-beam extended around the den and music room. The buffet was placed in the center of the wall immediately adjoining the kitchen.

One of the more unusual features of the interior was a pivoted serving table, one of many innovations to make bungalow life more convenient and efficient for the lady of the house. "A carefully arranged pivoted serving table with false door next to the dining room is attractive, practical, and at the same time one of the new features which the house contains. This makes it possible to fill the serving table shelves with viands from the kitchen, and by simply opening the false panel door the food is immediately ready to serve in the dining room."[30]

Plans were available from many companies trying to find a niche in the new market. The *Westerner: An Interpretation of the West*, edited by Edgar L. Hampton and published in Seattle, was a leading advertising medium for such companies. In fall 1907, the magazine began a series, "Modern Homes: Conducted for readers who contemplate building of homes," by Thomas L. West, that included some Craftsman examples.

In November 1912, it featured "An Attractive Bungalow Plan, No. 2, by the Bungalowcraft Company, 405 Chamber of Commerce Building, Los Angeles, CA, Plan #624." Just as Jud Yoho had taken money from advertisers in different parts of the country, so too did other local publishers. In fact, in January 1913, the *Westerner* announced it had "made arrangements so that the plans for any the houses illustrated in this series will be furnished either as shown or reversed for $10. If you are thinking of building a home send one dollar to *The Westerner* for a copy of California Bungalow Homes, a modern, practical, and comprehensive book of the bungalow. It contains 128 richly illustrated folio pages of bungalows, inside and outside, in their latest development."

In the March 1913 issue, a feature, "Spring-

The Craftsman house (1907) of Frank Wright on Lummi Island was large enough to provide bedrooms for family, friends, and business associates who came to the island during the salmon canning season. Buswell Collection, Center for Pacific Northwest Studies, Western Washington University (Bellingham), 1173.

time is Bungalow Time," pictured examples by V. W. Voorhees and Hewitt-Lee-Funck Company, with this preface: "An up to date bungalow is a composite of all the best features of the log cabin, the cottage, and the more pretentious house. The bungalow is fast becoming the most popular style of small house, not being merely a fad of the mild-climated states of the Pacific Coast, but as well of the North, East, and South."[31]

Voorhees reached beyond Washington for his clientele. In the March 2, 1907, *Oregon Daily Journal*, published in Portland, he advertised his seventy three-page book of house plans.

Bungalows by the Thousands in Washington and Oregon

With such universal exposure, bungalows and more substantial two-story Craftsman houses proliferated in every community in Washington and Oregon. For example, Frank Wright, manager of the Carlisle Canning and Packing Company, one of three major salmon processing facilities on Lummi Island northwest of Bellingham, embraced the Craftsman style in his 1909 house at Village Point. From humble beginnings as a fisherman, Wright moved through the ranks, learning all aspects of the

industry, eventually becoming the president of Pacific Fisheries. From its roots as a major Indian fishing ground, Lummi Island grew in importance from the 1890s as the location for canneries on Legoe Bay, at Village Point, and at Point Migley.

The Carlisle Company had been an English investment and, by 1901, was headquartered in Fairhaven. In 1903, Charles Wright was president, and his brother, Frank Wright, was the manager. By 1907, a complex of buildings, including a wharf and several hundred acres of housing for a labor force of over 200 was being developed, including a Chinese house and dining hall. Because the cannery business was seasonal, generally from early summer until November or December, Wright probably maintained a permanent home in Seattle. The *Bellingham Herald* noted, "Mrs. Frank Wright of Seattle visits at the 'cottage' at the cannery," in June 1907. The large house he built served as a hunting lodge and gathering place for himself and his friends.[32]

The Modern Bungalow was published by the Ballard Plannery in Spokane in 1910. Northwest Museum of Arts & Culture, Eastern Washington State Historical Society (Spokane), Eph 728.64 B212m 1910.

East of the Cascade Range, in Wenatchee, in the 1300 block of Fifth Avenue, William T. Clark's Craftsman house was embellished with fine pyramidal river boulder porch supports and an improbable castellated round corner tower of the same material.

With its mineral wealth and growing business community, and with a well-trained cadre of local architects, Spokane's residential neighborhoods filled with large numbers of exemplary bungalows and Craftsman houses distinguished by their gray-black basalt foundations, pillars, and chimneys. They also showed off the great variety of influences on designers. The more typical California vocabulary shared streetscape with the Swiss Chalet, British half-timbered and thatched, and Japanese and Chinese uplifts, latticework, and even dragon's heads. Larger lot sizes than were common in Seattle's platted neighborhoods gave each house more room for landscape and street trees. Architects such as W. W. Hyslop did self-promotion, publish-ing handsome profiles of their work. Commercial companies such as the Ballard Plannery offered plans and expertise to would-be homebuilders. Individuals with skill and talent working with local and imported woods produced sturdy, beautifully finished buildings and interiors.

One particularly handsome example, built in 1912, was the house for Spokane attorney Mansfield Mack in Rockwood, a tree-lined neighborhood whose street plan was designed by the nationally renowned Olmsted Brothers. Ivan Abraham, an accomplished Spokane builder, designed and constructed this and several other houses in the Rockwood district. The house featured four front-facing intersecting gables supported by large beams and triangular braces. The low-pitched roof with wide overhanging eaves covered a deep front porch that was supported by tapered columns anchored by clinker brick piers. The overhanging eaves were faced with decorative verge boards accented by diamond-shape cutouts and sawtooth ends. The diamond pattern was repeated in window treatments on the exterior, and in cupboards and glass on the interior. The living room featured a corner inglenook with a fireplace, built-in bookcases, window seat, and tiger-sawn oak woodwork. The "artistic" interior woodwork, green tile fireplace surround, and built-in sideboard were of the highest quality. The garage echoed the materials and architectural elements of the house.[33]

Built in 1913 by Spokane contractor Walter L. Weld as a "spec" home, a Cannon Hill property was given to Joseph Albi and his wife, Mazie, as a wedding gift from Albi's parents. The house featured an oak-paneled library complete with built-in desk and equally handsome oak built-in buffet in the dining room.

One of Spokane's most interesting bungalow designers was Clayton Feltis, known for his personal artistic interpretation and purist approach to the Craftsman style. Feltis manifested his skills as an accomplished artisan in the design and construction of a number of houses in finer residential districts. He built a residence for Harry Stimmel in 1914 that exemplified his abilities in combining stone, brick, and wood to form harmonious compositions and well-considered interior spaces.

While Kirtland Cutter's interest in the Swiss Chalet style was evidenced in both Spokane and Seattle, a number of designers were also attracted to that style. In Lincoln Heights, a house was built in 1912 for Carl Koerner, a successful Spokane accountant, and his wife, Mathilda. Koerner worked on the plans himself, probably with the aid of Peter Moe, a draftsman for prominent Spokane architect Carl Jabelonsky, who may also have contributed to the design. With its low-pitched front-gabled roof with broad overhanging eaves, scalloped verge boards, massive decorative brackets, rough-cut wood siding, and second floor balconies and gallery porches, the house must have appeared magically transplanted from the European Alpine region to eastern Washington. Koerner designed the central fireplace in the living room, around which he built the house, with its box beam ceilings and quarter-sawn maple floors.

In Portland, the plan for Laurelhurst included various classes of housing in distinct districts controlled by building restrictions. One such neighborhood, Fernhaven Court, housed a block of bungalows that adhered to

[top] The residence of Mansfield Mack (1912) in Spokane was designed by Ivan Abraham. Photograph by Lawrence Kreisman.

[above] The Joseph Albi house in Spokane's Cannon Hill was built by Walter L. Weld in 1913. Photograph by Lawrence Kreisman.

specific design guidelines regarding size and amenities:

> Excluding the thirty-one acres comprising Laurelhurst Park, there are one hundred and seventeen large blocks in Laurelhurst. From this large area the Laurelhurst Co. selected block numbered one hundred and two as being exceptionally attractive for typical high-class California bungalows.... It is located just one block east of Laurelhurst Park, being four short blocks to the present street car line and seven short blocks to the new Laurelhurst school site.
>
> This block was redesigned to include a twenty-foot paved serpentine court running through the center of the block east and west, so that garages and the rear entrances to the dwellings would face on this court—avoiding the necessity of cutting up and ruining the lawns with runways.
>
> It was the intention of the Laurelhurst Co. to make of this block a real bungalow fairyland.

[top] The Koerner family built a Swiss Chalet style house in 1912 in the Lincoln Park neighborhood of Spokane. Photograph by Lawrence Kreisman.

[center] L. MacLean's shingled Otis Orchards house (c. 1910) outside Spokane incorporated a river rock foundation. The abundance of local stone allowed the material to be used for the outbuilding to the left. Northwest Museum of Arts & Culture, Eastern Washington State Historical Society (Spokane), L94-9.192.

[left] The living room of the MacLean house was two stories high with a timber balcony supported by substantial wall brackets. The furniture—perhaps heirlooms—represented several periods. The Arts and Crafts desk, with its handsome metal pulls, may have been a new purchase. Northwest Museum of Arts & Culture, Eastern Washington State Historical Society (Spokane), L94-24.9.

At a great expense the Laurelhurst Co. procured plans and photos of all the different attractive bungalows they could find on the Pacific Coast, offering the use of these plans gratis to home-builders to erect homes at this point.

Bungalows should be located in a block by themselves. Their style of architecture is such that they require sympathetic surroundings and they should not be placed in close proximity with other types of houses that would spoil the most attractive features in bungalow lines.

When one considers that this plan of building development can be made so much more beautiful and attractive than an ordinary two-story house, without any additional cost, one is forced to conclude that the plan is thoroughly practical from every standpoint.

The result of this development is a superb creation of both architects' and landscape gardeners' genius. Here you will find an aristocracy among bungalows that stimulates the desire for a real home. Every feature in each home is in tune with the expression of this magnificent nest of homes.

Nowhere else are the physical conditions so well-nigh perfect. The paved court running through the block is a bower of beauty. No other section of the city has ever attempted to accomplish this result on such a perfect scale, and it is to be hoped that the efforts of the Laurelhurst Co. in this connection will encourage others to adopt such a meritorious plan of development.[34]

The bungalow craze stimulated businesses in Oregon. Bungalow Book Publishing Company of Portland provided plans in their *Craftsman Book of Bungalows*. Also in Portland, H. M. Fancher offered mail-order plans. *Northwest Bungalow Book* was produced by

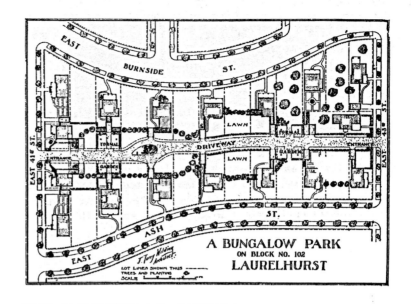

Plan for Laurelhurst Fernhaven Court, Portland (1916).

D. L. Harden in Eugene, as was a catalog by John Hunsicker. There were locally owned precut house companies, such as Ready-Built House Company and the Rice-Penne Company of Portland and the Ainslie-Boyd Company of Seattle, Washington. Aladdin Homes of Bay City, Michigan, whose precut houses were sold nationwide through its catalogs, established a Northwest branch in Portland in 1919. By 1921 the Portland plant could produce sixty houses a day. One Portland firm, Fenner Manufacturing Company, produced factory-cut houses from 1912 to 1929. Owned by lumberman J. Harvey Fenner, the company also advertised that unassembled houses, complete with instructions for amateurs, could be mail-ordered and shipped as far away as Iowa in one boxcar.

For every company that promoted plan books, there was a company encouraging first-time homebuyers to build custom-designed houses. Polk's 1913 edition of the *Portland City Directory* lists the firm of Butterworth-Stephenson Company at 705-6-7 Couch Building. An advertisement of the firm was placed on page 1398 with a photo illustration of a bungalow-style house:

He is the happiest, be he king or peasant, who finds peace in his home. Every family should own its own home. Why Not? Don't Buy It Ready Built! It is one thing to buy a home and it is another to be satisfied with it after you get it.

Have a house built for you, to your order, just as you like it, with strong lines of individuality about it. You take pride in it—your friends admire it. Satisfactory! What's the answer? A happy family. And remember that it costs no more. Butterworth-Stephenson Company.

Eugene showed the typical population growth in Northwest communities early in the century, from 3,200 in 1900 to 5,400 in 1905 and reaching 11,000 by 1910, according to *Anybody's Magazine.* The result of this rapid growth was a city with a substantial number of bungalows, particularly in its Westside neighborhood. There, a unique adaptation of the bungalow form was built in 1916 on Pearl Street near downtown; it was an L-shaped duplex built for the Soults and Westfall families. The house's corner location lent itself naturally to the inclusion of two gabled entrance porches sharing a vocabulary of dark-stained shingles, multiple gables, deep eaves, decorative brackets, and paired porch posts.

Anybody's Magazine, published in Eugene,

[top] In Eugene, architect D. L. Harden produced the *Northwest Bungalow Book* (n.d.). Mason Collection.

[left] The Portland real estate development Healy Heights was portrayed (1912) in picturesque graphic images incorporating stylized trees, winding roadways, and Swiss Chalet style houses with Mount Hood as a backdrop. Mason Collection.

took a special interest in the bungalow culture emerging in Eugene in the spring of 1911. The periodical even suggested opportunities that would appeal to various income levels and touted the favorable cost of labor and materials in the Pacific Northwest:

> While the University Center has its stylish bungalows and fashionable mansions in the $10,000 and $15,000 class, outrivaled by none in other parts of the state, and far more attractive than in many cities of equal size in the Eastern states, yet the "comfy," idealized small bungalows on city lots or suburban plats of half an acre to two or three acres, or more, is fully realized here. With from $500 to $1,000 and prudent judgment and taste, a man can build a stylish, comfortable and even attractive four to six room bungalow and enjoy practically every convenience.
>
> With his modest sum for a starter, one may add as much as cash and ingenuity permit and requirements demand. The man of small means can house his family very comfortably in a ceiled four-room cottage and figure on a cost of about $150 per room. He will find the equable, mild climate makes it possible to get along very well without plastered walls. These may be added when he gets ready for them. If one wishes to exercise discriminating taste and have the bungalow finished in polished natural woods, the beauty of the famous Oregon fir, selected for its wonderful and fanciful grain, one may go as far as one likes. It is truly astonishing to an Eastern man and woman what splendid effects in paneled walls, wainscoting, beamed ceilings, plate racks, etc., may be worked out in these designs. The "rakish" little bungalow typical of the far West and of California are very popular with all classes,

The Soults-Westfall bungalow duplex built near downtown Eugene in 1916 was richly decked out with a rhythmic combination of pitched gables, brackets, and rafters. Photograph by Lawrence Kreisman.

> irrespective of cost, and with the introduction of your own ideas and tastes and the addition of a large fireplace, which nearly all modern houses have in Eugene, the low-priced bungalow seems to idealize the home nest. Another fact about it is that the small, one-floor bungalow is inexpensive to furnish and reduces the housework for the home keeper.
>
> As far as labor is concerned, there is little difference between Eugene and a Middle Western state. Carpenters on bungalow work may be hired for $3.50 per day. The price of hardware is about the same, and the difference in this item on a six-room house, for example, would not be $10 one way or another. When it comes to lumber, lath, shingles, and the amount of lumber necessary to make the house comfortable, Eugene has the great advantage in price of materials. Lumber is one-half to one-third cheaper here than in Wisconsin, Kansas,

Anybody's Magazine (spring 1911) focused attention on bungalow developments in Eugene.

Illinois, or other states. In Kansas, one has to pay $50 to $60 for first-class flooring, for instance, while here it can be had for $30 to $35 per thousand.

The foundation is a considerable item where you have to build a stone or cement wall from 16 to 24 inches in thickness to keep out frost. The cement foundation does not cost nearly so much here, as it need only be strong enough to support the house built upon it. The frost does not enter into the question at all. With careful management, and experience, in buying and managing your work and materials, you can realize a roomy little six-room bungalow for $1,000. Several who have started humble homes, found they did better.[35]

McMinnville, Oregon, was typical of Northwest towns that embraced the bungalow. In her 1981 study *The Bungalow Aesthetic*, Janice Rutherford identified a number of local publishers who encouraged bungalows, including *Anybody's Magazine*. The *McMinnville News Reporter* ran advertisements with headlines such as "Buy a Bungalow." She also noted builders who focused on the "affordable and popular" bungalow style between 1909 and 1922. They included James Bickford, whose bungalow-style houses averaged in price around $1,200; John Cook and Albert Arthur (listed in the 1912 Yamhill directory as general contractors); Vernon Derby; and one of the busiest, Dwight Miller (who worked there c. 1908–1960s), who began his career building small, unpretentious bungalows.

Speculative building was being done on a small scale in McMinnville. In 1911 the McMinnville Land Company advertised that a bungalow could be purchased for $1,600. Portland's Henry J. Fancher, realtor turned architect, sold plans for several "Fancher" houses.[36] A former flour mill operator, F. C. Barnekoff, returned to McMinnville in 1921 and established a ready-cut house business. He advertised that he furnished everything complete, "except brick, plumbing, and concrete."[37]

James H. Gibson, owner of the Yamhill County Abstract Company, built a large, sprawling, multigabled horizontal house in 1922. He ordered the house plan from the National Builder's Bureau, a Spokane company that was in business from 1919 to 1926. The house had a rough-cut stone foundation and porch piers and a clinker brick exterior chimney. River rock aggregate lent texture to the area under the broad gable that sheltered the entrance.[38] Another McMinnville resident, Delmer E. Wheeler, built his 1911 house from plans in *Artistic Bungalows*, a 1908 Radford publication.

Outside of major cities, the bungalow became a major feature of company towns developed around the local mill. In Bend, Oregon, owners and managers of the Brooks-Scanlon and Sheylin-Hixon Lumber Companies, constructed in 1915, believed that home ownership made workers more stable and less vulnerable to radical ideas such as Socialism. So the companies bought lots in conveniently located neighborhoods and resold them to workers with good terms.[39] Seventy-five percent of the houses in the Old Mill Neighborhood are Craftsman and bungalows, the majority built in the 1910s and 1920s, while Bend's population rapidly grew from 500 in 1910 to 5,500 in 1920.

Although bungalows were slipping out of favor in other areas of the country by the 1920s, the form was still well suited for the working class because of its affordability and size. Siding, windows, doors, and built-in cabinets were all made in the Bend mills for use throughout the nation.[40] Managers and tradesmen lived in the larger one-and-one-half story bungalows on Delaware and Florida Streets. Workers lived in single-story bungalows; some built their own "mill cottages" on lots bought from the lumber companies.[41]

There was a major difference between the inexpensive worker bungalows and those of more affluent managers and local businessmen. As an example of regional use of local materials, the 1920 bungalow of Ralph and Nina Bartlett, owners of three local hotels, showed off the use of tuff, a volcanic stone quarried locally and used for many commercial buildings and some residences in Bend.[42] Herbert Engle Allen, an assistant general manager of the Brooks-Scanlon, occupied a handsome 1908 Craftsman house in the north end of the town.[43]

With its abundance of inexpensive building materials, the Pacific Northwest was able to accommodate the great number of new families that chose to relocate to the region to take advantage of the growing economy and the natural beauty of the region. And for the majority of these newcomers, whether they were at the lowest end of the salary chain or moving ahead into the expanding middle classes, the ease with which they could move into a bungalow of their own made the bungalow business a thriving industry in large cities and small towns in Washington and Oregon.

The word "bungalow" became a mainstay of American life. Whether retail businesses occupied bungalows or not, they used the word to create an image in the buying public's mind. Portland had its Bungalow Theater, Bungalow Saloon, and Bungalow Home Baking Company. Bungalow Krafts Company sold art goods. There was even a Bungalow Billiard Parlor in Pendleton.

The bungalow reflected wholesome American values at a core level—home, family, economic sustainability, support for locally produced products, and commitment to one's community. In April 1917, *Bungalow Magazine* quoted Mr. T. Lestonkirk of Bremerton, who had built his $1,800 bungalow (with some modification) from plans originally prepared by the Craftsman Bungalow Company. In his statement, one sees the linking of patriotic ideals and those of the Arts and Crafts movement, where the front porch becomes the viewing stand: "Sentiment entered

Mount Vernon, Washington, the town noted for peace and prosperity. good homes and good citizenship

in the new Residence District, Medford, Oregon.

Bungalows for Everyone

[opposite, top to bottom] For this Corvallis bungalow, builder R. E. Hall installed lighting with slag glass in the sturdy stucco porch columns. Steve Dotterer Collection.

No doubt C. L. Rose was as proud of his new automobile as he was of his tidy Salem bungalow, depicted in this May 1912 photograph. Oregon Historical Society (Portland), 0081G040.

The Marcella Court Apartments in Seattle (c. 1915) were comprised of two groups of shingled bungalows with front entries off central courts. Special Collections Division, University of Washington Libraries (Seattle), Todd PH 12174.

Craftsman Houses for Everyone

[this page, top to bottom] A Mount Vernon, Washington, promotional postcard dated 1912 sent the message, "The town noted for peace and prosperity, good homes and good citizenship." Mason Collection.

"The new Residence District, Medford, Oregon," revealed a harmonious streetscape of Craftsman houses with the beginnings of abundant rose gardens. Mason Collection.

largely into our choice of location, we choosing a site overlooking the Puget Sound Navy Yard. Nothing can be more thrilling and inspiring of patriotism than to sit on our porch and hear the bands playing the Star Spangled Banner at morn and eve with every enlisted man standing at attention facing the flag and giving the salute as it is lowered for the day; and again at 9 p.m. when taps are sounded, one's thoughts are irresistibly drawn to a contemplation of our national ideals."[44]

The remarkable prominence of the bungalow as an icon of the building industry in the region is perhaps best reflected in a proposed project atop a major office building in downtown Seattle noted in a 1915 *Pacific Builder and Engineer* article:

A four-room frame bungalow will occupy one wing of the Henry Building. The bungalow will be built of Washington lumber and shingles and will be completely furnished with Washington products. The West Coast Lumber Manufacturers' Association will furnish the lumber, including interior finish and doors, and other firms approached are enthusiastic about the idea. A city home list will be prepared showing the names of the firms who have helped to furnish the home. This list will be handed out to all visitors to the roof and will be of value to all contributors from an advertising standpoint. The bungalow will not be a cheap affair. There will be lots of room in it. We expect to have a lawn to beautify it, and the garage has already been offered us. The idea is to have it remain permanently on the roof of the Henry Building, where it will be open to all visitors.[45]

[top] A panoramic view of Ashland from the rock-pillared porch and bountiful gardens of the Baslough-Claycomb Craftsman residence in 1925 shows the Lythia Springs Hotel nearing completion. Oregon Historical Society (Portland), CN 002918.

[above] The Arts and Crafts porch shaped the way Americans experienced their neighborhood. River rock foundations and sturdy fir posts sheltered this dreamy-eyed Oregon City child. Mason Collection.

SEVEN
Retreating to Nature

IN OCTOBER 1914, *Oregon Country*, published in Portland, carried a review of a new promotional pamphlet: "The Union Pacific System has just issued a most beautiful folder entitled *The Scenic Columbia River Route to the Great Pacific Northwest*, and consists of 64 pages of beautifully illustrated matter in colors regarding the various cities and scenery covered from Omaha to Portland and Seattle. The illustrations are of unusually attractive character and the subject matter splendidly worded."[1]

Two years later, in October 1916, *Oregon Country* reviewed another pamphlet: "*Along the Columbia River to the Sea* is the title of a very artistic pamphlet recently published by the Spokane, Portland & Seattle Railroad. It is a collection of sepia prints of the immense scenery from Portland to the Sea, along the Snake River, the Columbia Gorge, etc. The extreme pains taken in this publication make it one of the most artistic and striking advertisements for Oregon and its world-famed scenery."[2]

Hundreds of such printed pieces were published regionally. They were created for a variety of reasons ranging from civic

Seaview Hall (1904), an early summer resort on Alki Point in Seattle, was built of vertical logs and decorative shingled dormers with trimmed log posts supporting a second-floor balcony. PEMCO Webster & Stevens Collection, Museum of History and Industry (Seattle), 83.10.7366.2.

Japanese aesthetics may have inspired this graphic artist for Puget Sound Navigation Company's *Puget Sound Summer Resorts* guide (n.d.). Mason Collection.

boosterism and tourism to the financial rewards to be reaped by railroads and hotels along the scenic byways. They stimulated interest in the beauties of Washington and Oregon for vacationers and for those looking to change their lives and livelihood by looking west. The natural landscape lauded in these pamphlets would also serve as artistic inspiration for writers, architects, and artists.[3]

The geographical diversity of Oregon and Washington lent itself to a variety of outdoor recreational and leisure time activities. The great outdoors also provided a healthy environment away from the polluted city air for those recovering from tuberculosis and other diseases. To answer a growing need, mountain and lakeside lodges were built, sanatoriums and health resorts were established, and small bungalows or cottages were constructed in forests and along the beaches and coastline.

Regional plan books included designs for ocean and summer cottages. Photos of hunting camps often showed simple structures with rustic Craftsman or bungalow influences. These retreats from urban life ran the gamut from rustic to highly sophisticated in form and amenities, based on the socioeconomic levels of owners and users. Some retreats accommodated large crowds, as did national park structures such as Paradise Inn and Crater Lake Lodge. Other retreats were privately owned hunting, fishing, and recreational lodges. Many of these properties, designed, built, and furnished at the same time with appropriate furniture in a Mission or a rustic Arts and Crafts manner, epitomized the "total art" qualities that Gustav Stickley and Elbert Hubbard appreciated.

Lodges and Preserving Open Space

The emphasis on harmonious built design that would have low impact on the national forests had its roots in the public park movement of the mid-nineteenth century. During the Industrial Revolution and its aftermath, social thinkers became concerned about overcrowded and unsanitary cities and the average citizen's loss of connection with the natural world. That led to efforts to set aside or create natural areas in urban settings, such as New York's Central Park (1853) and the metropolitan park system for Minneapolis–St. Paul (1872–1895). At the same time, there was a burgeoning national interest in conserving the dramatic landscapes of the West for tourism. As a result, large natural areas such as Yellowstone, Yosemite Valley, and the Adirondack Forest Preserve were reserved as "public parks or pleasuring grounds for the benefit and enjoyment of the people."

Old Faithful Inn is often credited with having influenced early national parks buildings and causing them to have a shared vocabulary. And the architect of that inn, Robert Chambers Reamer (1873–1938), thereby gained the distinction of being known as the father of a national parks style. He had the good fortune to have his talents recognized by Harry W. Child, the cofounder of the Yellowstone Park Transportation Company, who invited him to become the architect for Yellowstone National Park. This opportunity marked the beginning of a productive period for Reamer: he designed hotels, stables, barns, residences, a railroad station, and a studio. Of these, Old Faithful Inn, completed in 1903, is probably his most famous surviving work, and one that undoubtedly influenced national park architecture for many years. Rooted in the Amer-

A promotional brochure for Lake Quinalt Lodge (1926) on the Olympic Peninsula, which was designed by Robert Chambers Reamer, used Indian imagery to set the tone. Mason Collection.

ican Arts and Crafts tradition, Old Faithful Inn was constructed with regional stone foundations and chimneys, and the rafters, posts, and beams were made of exposed local logs and timbers.

Many years later, having settled in Seattle in a lucrative position as the architect for the Metropolitan Building Company, Reamer's experience with mountain lodges in Yellowstone surfaced again in resort designs on the Olympic Peninsula, including Lake Crescent Lodge and a number of other vacation retreats. For his Lake Quinault Lodge of 1926, the guest wings were set at angles to the central lobby, the focus of which was, appropriately, a substantial stone fireplace. The orientation of the lobby and the dining room allowed for views over the lawn to the lake.

The U.S. Forest Service began to allow construction of summer cabins, resorts, lodges, and boathouses in national forest lands in the early twentieth century. The Forest Service constructed its own ranger stations, roads, and trails for administrative purposes, while private interests designed and built recreation facilities under Forest Service permits and regulations. Most of these early facilities were designed to fit harmoniously into the landscape.

Public recreation facilities in a national forest were first truly planned and developed in 1916. The first occurrence took place in the Columbia Gorge Park division of the Oregon National Forest (later Mount Hood National Forest and now within the Columbia River Gorge National Scenic Area). The campground and ranger station at Eagle Creek included an entrance station, restrooms, tables, and fireplaces designed in an Arts and Crafts manner.

It was a perfect fit. The Arts and Crafts movement favored the beauty and honesty of traditional hand craftsmanship, the use of natural building materials, and emphasis on simplicity in form, line, and function. This influence was clearly visible at Eagle Creek and was a major influence in the evolving "rustic" style of architecture in natural areas.[4]

Perhaps the first resort in the area to espouse the virtues of the Arts and Crafts and the rustic style was Mineral Lake Lodge, built in 1906 by Scandinavians for the Tacoma vacation trade. But the peak of Arts and Crafts ideals was reached in the building of Paradise Inn on Mount Rainier a decade later. Mount Rainier National Park, established in 1899, was an immediate tourist mecca, though it lacked suitable accommodations for many years. Various buildings and structures were developed in the rustic style log and shingle treatments that became associated with the National Park Service, and the style continued to be used throughout the 1920s and 1930s.

The Tacoma firm of Heath & Gove was responsible for a plan for Paradise Inn. It featured a two-and-one-half-story, 100-room hotel, the focal point of which was a great hall and dining room, with wings housing guest rooms. It was built of Alaska cedar, cedar shingles, and rock masonry, and opened in July 1917. While not as dramatic as Robert Reamer's treatment of dormers and roof in his signature Old Faithful Inn, Paradise Inn displayed rhythmic rows of dormers against the steep gables that dominated the exterior of the inn's multiple intersecting wings.

The interior revealed a cathedral-like lobby and dining hall of log framing and truss work. Early photographs show the inn furnished with Arts and Crafts pieces, apparently salvaged from the Stratford Hotel in Tacoma on the eve of its demolition.[5] But the lobby quickly filled with Alaska cedar furniture handmade by Hans Fraechnke, a German woodcrafter who lived at the inn during 1916–1917 and returned each March for seven seasons. When not on site, he built furniture in a workshop in Fife, some of it for local residents. He crafted two massive throne chairs for the inn, a cedar table, piano, grandfather clock, and the log veneer of the registration desk. The inn also had hickory chairs, tables, and settees manufactured by the Old Hickory Chair Company, the largest dealer of rustic furniture at the time and suppliers to state and national parks throughout the country.[6]

In Oregon, the prototype for rustic lodges

RAINIER NATIONAL PARK

4543   DINING ROOM PARADISE INN   59-30

[top] Paradise Inn on Mount Rainier, designed and built by Heath & Gove (1916–1917), welcomed hoards of tourists from the time of its completion. This caravan of auto stages waited to depart for Tacoma and Seattle, c. 1925. Special Collections Division, University of Washington Libraries (Seattle), UW 1576.

[above] The cathedral-like dining room at Paradise Inn (1916–1917), Mount Rainier National Park. Mason Collection.

may have been the log and stone Cloud Cap Inn, designed by William Whidden and constructed on Mount Hood in 1889. Crater Lake Lodge, dramatically sited to take advantage of spectacular lake views, was constructed between 1911 and 1914 to designs attributed to R. N. Hockenberry and Company. It also embraced the vocabulary of stone base and unpainted shingles with a multigabled roof.

A late entry into the realm of rustic lodges was Mount Baker Lodge, completed in 1927 and short-lived due to a fire that completely destroyed the building in 1931. Mount Baker Lodge was designed by a Seattle architect, Earl W. Morrison. Unlike R. C. Reamer, whose early experience at Yellowstone made him a natural for this building type, Earl Morrison (?–1955) was a surprising choice. He was best known for commercial buildings in the Art Deco style, such as the brick- and terra-cotta–clad Textile Tower. Most of his work in the late 1920s and 1930s consisted of unadorned high-rise apartment blocks. Perhaps his work experience accounted for the odd skyscraper-style log lookout tower at one end of what otherwise was a typical mountain lodge with steeply pitched roofs, multiple

[top left] Crater Lake Lodge (1911–1914), designed by Hockenberry and Company, was expanded on numerous occasions after its initial opening. Mason Collection.

[center] The lobby of Mount Baker Lodge (1927) was decorated with Native American handicraft. Navajo rugs were laid on the floor, and lampshades incorporated Northwest Coast Indian motifs. Buswell Collection, Center for Pacific Northwest Studies, Western Washington University (Bellingham), 2072.

[left] The great covered porch at Gearhart-by-the-Sea Hotel in Gearhart, Oregon, was a popular gathering spot. Postcard, c. 1920. Mason Collection.

dormers, and stone chimneys. Hints of the building's modernity were its large expanse of multipaned windows to let light into the enormous timber post-and-beam main lounge and dining room. The Indian-influenced decoration of the lounge was stunning, particularly the geometric capitals of timber columns and the ornamentation of the shades for chandeliers and standing lamps.

The tourist industry was served by promotional packages that encouraged a rail trip to Bellingham, overnight accommodations at the Leopold Hotel—not surprisingly the headquarters of the Mount Baker Lodge Company—and twice-daily bus service to the lodge. The Mount Baker Lodge was seen as the lynchpin of a plan modeled after Mount Rainier National Park by Bellingham civic leaders that would have designated a national park around Mount Baker. But as World War I unfolded, these plans failed to come about.

Less grand, perhaps, but ultimately the lifeblood of Oregon and Washington rural communities were the countless Arts and Crafts–style hotels, inns, and guesthouses that pro-

[top right] Agate Beach Inn was a handsome shingled lodge with dormered rooms on the third floor and a large covered balcony taking advantage of ocean views. Not long after opening, the porch was enclosed with a band of windows so that guests could enjoy the view during inclement weather. Postcard, c. 1920. Mason Collection.

[center] Warren Hotel in Cannon Beach was constructed with a log base punctured by an unusually broad expanse of windows facing the beach from the main lounge, a shingled upper floor, and a substantial stone chimney. Postcard, c. 1920. Mason Collection.

[right] Saltair was a small resort town on Rockaway Beach, Oregon. Postcard, postmarked April 1915. Mason Collection.

liferated along the seacoast catering to visitors from every part of the United States. With evocative names like Pacific Beach Hotel, Gearhart-by-the-Sea, Agate Beach Inn, and Sea Crest Apartments, these retreats from the busy commercial world offered restful surroundings, hearty food, and social opportunities.

Country Homes

In some ways, it seems strange that a city such as Seattle, which in 1903 was only fifty-two years old, would be questioning the values of urban life and a goal of growth, expansion, and promotion. But that year, an article in the *Seattle Mail and Herald* proposed "An Interurban Colony" adjacent to the newly developing electric commuter line. The article was prophetic about the challenges that urban life had brought and how they were impacting family life:

A movement is on foot to establish a colony of country dwellers from the city somewhere along the line of the interurban electric car line between this city and Everett. It is thought by those initiating the movement that there will be no difficulty experienced about getting people to join in such an enterprise.

The desire for country residence is getting stronger in the minds of city people each year. The possibilities for a pleasant home life are far greater in the country than in the city. In fact, the home life gets very little consideration at the hands of the average businessman. From morning until evening he is at the office or store. In the evening it is either the club, or the lodge, or the theatre, or some business or political conference that takes him downtown again. The city man who can get his home located far enough out in the country will spend more of his evenings at home. Then too, the opportunity to have larger grounds gives more freedom and room for beautifying by means of flowers and shrubs and orchards.

This colony project is a good idea. Along the line of such transportation a person can get to and from their homes in as short a time as can be made by those who live in the suburbs and have to ride on those slow going trolley cars. With the possibilities of such transportation through the country it is only a question of time when the better class of the population of the cities will all live in the country and only the ultra poor and the criminal classes will live in the city. There is so much more of health and beauty and freedom and good living in the country, it surely is the place to enjoy life.[7]

Bungalows gained visibility and marketability in the newly emerging streetcar suburbs of cities, but they also were heavily promoted as the ideal solution for people wishing to escape the increasing pressures of urban life. Zoe Kincaid of the *Seattle Mail and Herald* was quick to point out their virtues in an article in summer 1905 with the headline "The West Outdoors: How the People of Puget Sound Spend their Summer Time":

They build inns in the mountains, and on the bays and inlets of the Sound; and erect bungalows on islands and lakes. The businessman has his cottage across the Sound, where he returns after office hours. The owners of fine city mansions vacate them for canvas homes in the wildwood.

Now the wealthiest inhabitants are building summer castles on overlooking promontories, on cliff-sides, or in the wooded paradises of the islands. With every facility of nature close at hand, these

The boathouse and store at Lake Ballinger (c. 1915) north of Seattle had untrimmed log posts and clapboard siding. Close-in resort areas such as this one attracted seasonal residents, who built modest cabins and formed community. PEMCO Webster & Stevens Collection, Museum of History and Industry (Seattle), 83.10.4003.5.

summer mansions have pointed the way to the possibilities of homes on the Sound.

But it does not take a palace to enjoy the woods or the water. People of moderate means build bungalows half hidden by the firs, and but a short distance from the salt water. Some of these homes are of logs and built upon a mountain slope that commands a sweeping view of the water— others are nestled among the shrubbery close down to the tide. To own five acres of woodland and a bungalow is to live a luxurious and independent life. Year after year the owners of the bungalows return to their homes in the woods. Their children grow straight as pines, learned in water, craft and wood lore. Brought up in the shadows of the mountains, they are taught to be true Westerners, men and women of right-living and thinking.[8]

In Seattle, summer castles were beginning to take shape in 1909 in a pristine forested residential area, the Highlands, several miles north of the city limits. Kirtland Cutter's Chalet-style golf club set the stage for the building of a variety of impressive country retreats ranging from modest Arts and Crafts cottages, such as the first residence on the bluff property owned by lumberman C. D. Stimson, to more substantial mansions for year-round use.

As the Alaska-Yukon-Pacific Exposition (1909) was putting Seattle on the world map, one of its guiding lights, Albert S. Kerry, also stretched Seattle's understanding of traditional housing by commissioning two young architects to design a summerhouse for him and his family north of Seattle in the Highlands. This building, along with the C. H. Clarke residence nearby, brought Frank Lloyd Wright's progressive philosophy about housing to a region where residential architecture was generally conservative.

Kerry was an ambitious lumberman, mill owner, and businessman. He made his fortune

Willatsen and Byrne learned from Frank Lloyd Wright how to prepare evocative presentation drawings, such as this one for Albert Kerry's country house (1910–1911) in the Highlands in Seattle's north end. Architecture and Urban Planning Library, University of Washington (Seattle).

in the Yukon during the gold rush and established a sawmill in Seattle. Undaunted when it burned down, he salvaged what equipment he could, shipped it to Skagway and then over the steep Chilkoot Pass to Lake Bennett, built the steamboat *Olive May*, and began logging and freight operations. His Seattle home, designed by Charles Bebb and Louis Mendel about 1903, was a substantial English-style manor house with a granite base and clapboard upper exterior. For his summerhouse, he wanted something different. He rejected a Swiss Chalet design by Spokane architect Kirtland Cutter, whose firm was applying finishing touches to the grand chalet for the nearby Seattle Golf and Country Club.

Instead, Kerry opted for a refined and contemporary approach by Andrew Willatsen (1876–1974) and partner Barry Byrne (1883–1967) that reflected these architects' experience as part of Frank Lloyd Wright's Oak Park Studio during its progressive period designing "Prairie" houses. Willatsen worked periodically for Wright from 1902 or 1903 until 1907. He came west to Spokane in 1907 and worked for Cutter & Malmgren, arriving in Seattle in 1908 to supervise construction of the coun-

try club. Willatsen took over responsibilities as chief draftsperson in Cutter's Seattle office for a short time. But in 1909, he formed a partnership with Byrne, with whom he had worked in Wright's office.

Kerry's house, built 1910–1911, bore all the signatures of Wright's Prairie designs: long, low-pitched roofs with cross gables; broad overhangs; stucco walls with horizontal bands of wood trim; and bands of grouped windows. The vertical and horizontal geometry of the house was emphasized and repeated in specially designed stained glass lighting fixtures, gateposts, and window mullions. The Kerry family spent entire summers there, although Kerry himself continued to work in town and came out only on weekends during 1911 and 1912. The main house was completed in an abbreviated form, possibly as a result of a downturn in finances. Kerry was forced to move his family to Oregon for two years to revitalize his timber interests there after a disastrous fire destroyed acres of forestland.

In 1928, Willatsen was invited back to develop plans to finish the house much as he had suggested in 1910. The expanded home would have a covered entrance porch, entrance hall, and lounge aligned on an axis perpendicular to the living and dining rooms. It would have a large dining room and a living room with French doors on three sides leading to terraces overlooking the lawn and northwest forest. Once again, the project stalled, possibly because of the financial crash the following year.[9]

As the population of Seattle increased, putting increasing pressure on the existing American Indian tribes that inhabited Puget Sound, some Northwest residents began to have a nostalgic view of the regional Native peoples. Judge Burke and his wife filled their rustic Lake Washington retreat Ilahee, with baskets, blankets, and Edward Curtis photographs of Native Americans. Mrs. Burke would dress up in Native costume, entertain her society friends and invited guests from Native tribes, glide through the waters of the lake in her dugout canoe, and display the family's collection of Indian rugs, baskets, and utensils within the highly eclectic interior of their home. Their collection of Native objects outgrew space in their First Hill home as well, leading them to hire Kirtland Cutter to provide plans for a two-story addition with a hearth in the shape of a tepee.

For some local entrepreneurs, the idea of a log retreat away from the congestion of the city was an appealing option. Soup manufacturer William J. Bernard had Fir Lodge, a spacious house near Alki Point in West Seattle, built for himself and his wife in 1903 (by an unknown architect). It was equipped with a great stone fireplace and wraparound porches so they could take in the air and enjoy the Puget Sound view. Only four years afterward, they moved, and the Automobile Club took it over. It was the ideal spot for rest and relaxation for the club members who enjoyed the new recreational sport of cruising in that sensational vehicle, the motorcar.

Interest in the Arts and Crafts ideals extended outside of Seattle into King County,

[top] The living room at Ilahee (n.d.), the Burkes' rustic house on Lake Washington (architect unknown), rose to a balconied mezzanine. In addition to an enormous collection of Native baskets and rugs, there was wall space devoted to Edward Curtis's photographic portraits of America's Indians. This photograph was probably "styled" by Mrs. Burke to show off her Native American dress laid out on the chair next to the table. Special Collections, Washington State Historical Society (Tacoma), Curtis 6929. Photograph by Asahel Curtis.

[above] The living room at Fir Lodge (1903), Bernard's spacious West Seattle house, was rustic only to a point. The river rock fireplace was carefully laid out with graded stones. Oriental rugs carpet the fir floor and cushioned chairs were chosen for comfort. Washington State Historical Society (Tacoma), Curtis 1678. Photograph by Asahel Curtis.

[top] The billiard room of the Clise house, Willowmoor (1904–1907), featured Stickley Craftsman Workshop fixtures, art tile inserts in the wood mantel above the fireplace, and Mission style chairs with curved profiles that may have been locally commissioned. Eastside Heritage Center (Bellevue), Or.L79.79.319.

[above] The living room at Willowmoor had a hand-hammered copper hearth with a tree motif and a hand-painted woodland frieze, The enormous library table with true tenon construction was locally built. The carpet may have been specially commissioned as well, its pattern reflecting designs promoted by Gustav Stickley. Eastside Heritage Center (Bellevue), Or.L79.79.326.

particularly in the hands of major businessmen turned country gentlemen farmers. Erick Gustave Sanders developed a twelve-gabled Craftsman house at his country estate in the fertile Kent Valley about 1912. Swedish-born settlers had begun to arrive to the valley as early as 1904. Sanders, president of Standard Investment Company, and several partners founded the Standard Dairy and the Standard Mill. Lumber for his house came from his own mill. He obtained stained glass from the Alaska-Yukon-Pacific Exposition of 1909 when it ended, and bricks for the house came from construction of the new highway.[10]

The 350-acre Clise estate, called Willowmoor (1904–1907), was located in Redmond, near Seattle. James W. Clise of the Clise Investment Company originally intended Willowmoor to be a hunting preserve, but he instead developed it into a model farm. He eventually added an art gallery, a narrow-gauge railroad, a boathouse, a dove house, and greenhouses, as well as farm buildings and a picturesque windmill. The half-timbered English-style main house was an expansion of a modest hunting lodge into a twenty-eight-room mansion by Seattle architect Max Umbrecht, who shared an office with Clise Investment Company. The house featured a number of substantially scaled Arts and Crafts tables, settees, chairs, a hammered copper fireplace hood, and a billiard room light fixture custom built locally for the house. Such large pieces as the hood ornament with its tree imagery or the three-cylinder copper billiard table light were specially commissioned. But suspended lights were stock items from Gustav Stickley's Craftsman Workshop.

In 1904, Bebb and Mendel had designed a gracious English manor for Frederick Stimson on the south slope of Seattle's Queen Anne Hill. The William French Company of St. Paul was largely responsible for the interiors, which included William Morris papers in upstairs bedrooms, white painted moldings and hearths reminiscent of the work of Baillie Scott, and a reception room frieze attributed to Arthur and Lucia Mathews of Oakland.[11]

Only a few years after the house was occupied, Frederick and his wife began searching for property in the country for a summerhouse and weekend retreat. They found acreage in the Sammamish Valley near the farming community of Woodinville, a few miles north of the Clise estate in Redmond and near brother C. D. Stimson's own rustic hunting retreat, the Willows. The couple commissioned an estate house for that location in c. 1910, possibly by local architect Fred Sexton. Sexton had worked in Tacoma in the 1880s and 1890s and had done a substantial amount of institutional work in Ballard, where the Stimson shingle mill was located. Among his projects had been two log and river rock chalets in the Craftsman style for Annie and Homer Russell in 1904 located in northeast Seattle. These houses took full advantage of "rustic" features, with logs crossing at the corners and knotty porch posts and chimneys built up of neatly stacked river boulders.

Stimson's house was oriented toward a formally planted garden. It was a handsome oversized bungalow with a broad central gabled roof, overhanging eaves supported by decorative open brackets, and two symmetrically placed cantilevered gabled bays. Three sets of French doors fronted on a trellised veranda, permitting easy flow of traffic to and from the main living room, which was dominated by an enormous river rock fireplace. Many bedrooms and sleeping porches on the second floor accommodated the extended family during weekend visits and summer retreats.

The house became the showpiece of Stimson's Hollywood Farm. Other buildings included a four-vehicle carriage house, a superintendent's house, and numerous agricultural buildings. Here Stimson introduced many innovations, including a modern laboratory for scientific testing of milk production, a powerhouse, an ammonia plant to produce ice, trout ponds, and extensive greenhouses where his wife raised roses for sale. From the nearby main line of the Northern Pacific Railroad running through the Sammamish Valley, a siding was built that terminated in front of an ice cream parlor on the farm.

On October 10, 1914, the *Town Crier* carried a detailed description of the property in an article entitled "A Little Journey to Hollywood." Perhaps Elbert Hubbard's popular "Little Journeys" publications inspired *Town Crier* to try its own spin on portraying the course of locally important figures. It took readers by car from Seattle "to the edge of a great valley," and described the first glimpse of "a great low manor house, burnished gold beneath its wide roof, with other picturesque attendant buildings clustered around about":

There were spacious terraced gardens, in which even from the heights we could distinguish the glow of many colored flowers and the wink of tumbling water. Descending the steep hill with cautious brakes, the car came to a great iron gateway and passing this, swept up a fine boulevard beneath slender concrete lamp posts, each surmounted by a single great globe, to the courtyard of Hollywood Farm, the famous estate of Fred S. Stimson, capitalist, lum-

Frederick Stimson's Hollywood Farm house (c. 1910) was an enormous bungalow that had numerous bedrooms on the second floor to accommodate a constant flow of family and friends. Washington State Historical Society (Tacoma), Curtis 27557. Photograph by Asahel Curtis.

berman, country squire, and owner of one of the finest herds of Holstein-Friesians in the United States. Four years ago, this great homestead, comprising nearly a section of land in the rich black valley of the Sammamish Slough, was an unpromising jungle of logs and tangled second growth. Today it is as perfect an estate as the West can show.[12]

Seattle's successful entrepreneurs ventured farther afield than the county limits in their search for sylvan retreats. Robert Moran, whose wealth came from shipbuilding in Seattle, developed an estate on Orcas Island dominated by a large stone and shingle house of his own design, begun in 1906. He reputedly was not satisfied with the plans drawn by Seattle architects Spaulding and Umbrecht, and chose to design the house himself and

have it built by fifty or sixty workers, most of them trained shipwrights and carpenters at the Moran Brothers Yards. Moran incorporated shipbuilding imagery in the building, from porthole windows to cabin-like interiors in Indian teak and Honduran mahogany to specially made hardware. A teak clock with a beaten copper face was built for the mansion and located on the main staircase landing. Another case clock built in 1913 by Herschel Clock Company of Cincinnati also was ordered for the house. Furniture in the geometric Mission style was built by his carpenters to his own designs, including banquet tables, chairs for the billiard room on the lower level, conversation chairs (a Mission interpretation of the traditional two seats attached and facing each other), and dressers. Ernest Miller was in charge of the woodworking.

Moran had communicated with Louis Comfort Tiffany about the design for a hexagonal glass lighting fixture depicting the seven liberal arts for the music room. On the eighth panel was etched a poem called "Opportunity." A painted and etched glass clere-

Robert Moran's enormous Craftsman estate (begun 1906) on Orcas Island was designed for entertaining his many guests arriving by boat for extended periods. PEMCO Webster & Stevens Collection, Museum of History and Industry (Seattle), 83.10.4844.

[above] Metal light fixtures were like practical ship's lighting at the Robert Moran house, Orcas Island. Whatcom Museum of History and Art (Bellingham), 1980.75.601.001.

[right] The focus of the living room at Moran's Orcas Island house was its pipe organ and Tiffany chandelier. Whatcom Museum of History and Art (Bellingham), 1980.75.331.

Orre Nobles created this woodblock print incorporating his name with a Hood Canal landscape. He may have used it as a bookplate. Erna S. Tilley Collection, Box folder 1/25 Special Collections Division, University of Washington Libraries (Seattle), UW26462 7z.

story window depicted the harbor of Antwerp, showing steamers and sailing ships. The work, signed L. de Contini, Brussels, Belgium, was commissioned for the mansion.

Other distinctive Arts and Crafts features included a fireplace faced with green Grueby ceramic tile, trimmed with copper, and inset with blue and white tiles of sailing ships. Marine lanterns accented each side of the hearth. The fireplace mantels in the living and dining rooms were unique, composed of molded concrete inlaid with polished marble chips from Seattle's old Union depot.

Moran included living quarters for staff on the estate: two rustic Craftsman bungalows with peeled log porch posts—a larger cottage for the maids and a smaller one for the cook. Two of Robert's brothers, Frank and Sherman, built identical three-story Craftsman houses next to each other on the slope above the lagoon.[13]

Other Seattleites anxious for country retreats found them a boat ride away at Restoration Point on Bainbridge Island or at Three Tree Point overlooking Puget Sound to the south and along the shores of Lake Ballinger and in the evergreens of Lake Forest Park to the north. In June 1903, the *Westerner* carried an advertisement for "Three Tree Point, A Summer Resort. Three Tree Point Company, 625 First Avenue. C. B. Livermore, manager, 267 acres with beaches extending five miles. Dock, natural park. Selling lots." Not coincidentally, a later issue in May 1905 carried an enticing story about "Three Tree Point: A Place of Summer Homes Close to the Throbbing Heart of the Great Northwest Metropolis."[14]

In the 1920s, Orre Nobles had his Olympus Manor built on Hood Canal with various Asian fittings, including a tori gate entrance and outbuildings. The retreat accommodated a steady flow of literary and visual artists and musicians who routinely visited the place. The interior design was eclectic, combining architectural salvage and Asian and western European furnishings with Arts and Crafts elements. Essentially, he created a welcoming environment for artists, writers, and Pacific Northwest bohemians—a place where they would feel comfortable and creative.

"Bungalow Man" Jud Yoho's vision extended far beyond individual buildings in the city, though his motivation was surely the more practical one of investment income. In the

Renfro's Swiss Chalet-inspired Beaux Arts Village house (1909), which had served as the model for the emblem of the Beaux Arts Society, was suggested as an appropriate design for Jud Yoho's bungalow colony to be built on Hood Canal. Seattle Public Library.

July 1915 issue of his *Bungalow Magazine*, he announced plans for a "purely bungalow summer resort at Beachmont, Washington, where the exquisite litoral of Hood Canal gently slopes through a scenic paradise to the foothills of the far-famed Olympic Mountains. Interest in the project has been intensified by the fact that the services of the best available experts in landscape design have been enlisted to assure that the resort will be laid out to harmonize with the matchless beauties of the ideal locality. This end is always to be kept in view."

He wrote of "building bungalows by the thousand, placed to take advantage of the land, water, and mountains," and described the "hundreds of acres on which this bungalow township is being laid out."

Naturally, Yoho used his magazine as the promotional arm of his new venture: "Any one may easily secure a location at Beachmont and also the working drawings for a bungalow in keeping with the general idea. Many of these bungalows will be direct reproductions of homes already in existence, which have been illustrated in *Bungalow Magazine* and which have been commended by experts for their aesthetic features." [15]

The featured bungalow that month was Alfred Renfro's house at Beaux Arts Village on Lake Washington, which had already been documented in an earlier issue. In future issues, Yoho promoted additional bungalows that were said to be appropriate models for his bungalow villa township. Given the disappearance of these magazine features, it is likely that this development never proceeded beyond a few buildings and that Yoho was forced to sell the property if, in fact, he ever owned it.

Less elaborate plans for bungalow colonies were featured periodically in *Bungalow Magazine*. One article concerned four summer bungalows "built by the Distinctive Homes Company of Seattle for Mr. Colin O. Radford at Yeomalt, a sylvan settlement on the shores of Bainbridge Island. Their closeness to the city makes it possible even for the busy man, to go back and forth in the morning and at night, as well as allowing him to spend his Saturday afternoon and Sunday with the primeval forest and the eternal sea as a setting for his family surroundings. These four are among a dozen recently built at Yeomalt for Mr. Radford. All have large verandas or sleeping porches." [16]

In February 1917, *Bungalow Magazine* mentioned a $4,600 bungalow in Lake Forest Park, north of Seattle. It explained that the linking of the lakes had created "scores of miles of shore lands on Lake Washington with completion of the canal responsible for opening up of Lake Forest Park, a new suburban residential section. Dozens of beautiful bungalows were built there by enterprising owners while the work of digging the great

The entrance hall of Louis Simpson's Shore Acres estate (1906) near Coos Bay showed off the beauty of Oregon wood in paneling and furniture. Courtesy of Stephen Dow Beckham.

canal was in progress." The focus of the article was the house of Mr. A. H. Reid designed by architect W. C. Jackson: "Not only is this fine home accessible direct by water craft, but it may also be reached by a fine state highway and by an electric interurban street railway line."

The lure of the country was equally strong in Oregon. Ainsworth lumberman Louis J. Simpson developed Shore Acres, a 1,600-acre estate extending along the ocean cliffs near Coos Bay. While the shingled house that was constructed in 1906 owed more to Dutch Colonial forms than to Art and Crafts design, its interiors were strongly influenced by the Arts and Crafts movement and by the use of local materials. Oregon myrtle wood was chosen for paneling and furniture in the entrance hall.[17]

On the Oregon coast, the Nehalem Bay Land Company advertised Necarney City, Seabright, and Nehalem Bay Park: "Situated on Nehalem Peninsula and bordered by the Pacific Ocean and Nehalem Bay, and but two and one-half hours ride over the new P.R. & N. Railway, from Portland. . . . Select a

lot and plans for a cottage from this excellent sketch book, and build you a summer home in the most interesting place in Oregon. Nehalem Bay Land Company, 274 Oak Street, Portland, Oregon." The 1926 plan book *Portland Homes*, in which the advertisement was placed, showed several different plans for beach cottages in the bungalow style.

On May 9, 1909, the *Sunday Oregonian* offered a full-page illustrated article on houses in the Ashland and Medford areas, "Beautiful Homes in Rogue River Valley: Some of the Handsome Residences in the Garden Spot of Southern Oregon":

Rogue River Valley is rapidly becoming a land of beautiful homes, homes where exteriors with costly interiors well adorn the matchless orchards surrounding them. [The article promotes the wealthy orchardists coming into] the Rogue River Valley, where conditions and climate, in their opinion surpass those of California.

In nearly all cases the structures are placed so as to command a sweeping view of the valley, famous for its beautiful landscapes. With the completion of the proposed state highway to Crater Lake, Rogue River Valley will be seen annually by thousands of money-spending tourists, the class that made California famous for its beautiful homes, and it is evident that within a few years, when the charms of Southern Oregon become familiar to the Nation, countless numbers of the wealthy class will choose this region to spend their leisure, for it offers more advantages than even Southern California.

Among the beautiful manors recently constructed is the palatial bungalow erected by J. Stillwell Vilas, a Wisconsin capitalist and nephew of the late ex-Postmaster-General. The bungalow cost in the

The Clancey Lewis house in Beaux Arts Village, built in 1910, took its design from vernacular housing the owner experienced during his years in China. Seattle Public Library.

neighborhood of $30,000, and is located on an eminence giving a sweep of almost the entire valley, including historical Table Rock. The porch of this attractive bungalow is built of rough agates of all sizes gathered from a near-by plain called the desert, at a cost of more than $2,500.

The interior is most artistic. The furniture is in colors to harmonize with the walls and ceilings, which are of wood in the natural grain and highly polished. Costly works of art, bric-a-brac and famous paintings adorn the walls. In the center is an open court over which trailing grape vines grow. Screened sleeping-rooms open upon this court.[18]

Retreats to Stimulate Creativity and Good Health

In its issue of July 1913, *Bungalow Magazine* had major coverage of the idealized Northwest art colony, Beaux Arts Village, in which ten acres were set aside for community enterprises—art studios, workshops for woodworking, sculpture, typography, photography, engraving, wrought iron design, and any other art activities the members followed for either profit or pleasure. The writer described in this article and in the August issue some of the most significant Craftsman houses being built, particularly those of Frank Calvert, Clancey Lewis, and Alfred Renfro.

The Frank and Laura Calvert home was a "fine example of Swiss chalet type but without elaborate ornamentation which is too often copied without regard to merit or proper association." It was constructed of cedar with fir framework. Beams were an integral part of the framework, and there was no false work in framing or finishing. Large brackets in the front elevation were held in place by bolts and lag screws.[19]

The other and more unusual house featured was a Chinese-inspired bungalow owned by Clancey Lewis, editor of *Pacific Builder and Engineer*, and his wife Aurelia. William Sayward, of Willcox and Sayward, helped design this house, which recalled architecture familiar to Lewis during his residence in China.[20]

The August 1913 issue of *Bungalow Magazine* described the A. T. Renfro house, built of rough selected fir, weathered and finished with creosote and oil, with a shingle roof and porch posts of solid timbers fourteen inches square. The verge boards were mortised together at the top, with the ends protruding in a crisscrossing "Norske fashion"—the symbol adopted by the Beaux Arts Society as its official mark. Inside, there were cedar ceilings, vertical paneled boards with battens below the picture rail, and large wood panels placed horizontally above. A clinker brick fireplace was the focal point of the living room. The author wrote, "Mr. Renfro has designed, and is constructing, Beaux Arts furniture for all the rooms. This furniture is to be of golden cedar, the 'Totem Wood,' which has a fine grain, takes a highly polished finish and stands hard wear. The upper floor is Mr. Renfro's atelier. In the dormer is a studio with a beautiful out-

The covered porch of Renfro's Beaux Arts Village house (1909) was large enough to encourage connections with the natural world, which he espoused in his commentary about living at Beaux Arts Village. Seattle Public Library.

look across the lake. In another portion of the attic is a work-shop, containing all manner of tools for the Craftsman."

The interviewer quoted the owner's reason for adopting the unusual type of construction, offering rare insight into the passion of the Beaux Arts Society founders for working and living in harmony with nature:

> Sometimes I am asked, "Why the heavy construction?" If one of the towering firs, which surround and guard us from the wind and rain of winter, should be swept over in defeat while battling with the elements, and fall crashing on our little home, then the heavy timbers would do their part in breaking the fall. Besides, we like the look and feel of heavy, massive timber, and believe it has a good influence on the children. Simple, substantial, honest construction—nothing to come unglued or fall off; no gingerbread work to weary of. You can lean against it, or sit on it, without fear of scratching or breaking it. In designing this home we had in mind one we could use and live in.
>
> The birds, squirrels and chipmunks are all welcome inside the house or outside. We feed them and they can help themselves to anything we have. They were here first. They come into the house and build their nests around it and we are all friends. We have tried to live on peaceful terms with Nature, as her guests and disciples, rather than masters or innovators. We try hard not to molest her plans in any way, or mar her work by cutting down, digging up, or attempting to re-create artificially after our own ideas. The trees, shrubs and ferns grow just about as she placed them, and we only help as servants. Our motto, "Sine Cera," has been used out of doors as well as in the construction of the house. We believe a person should think at least twice before cutting down some towering tree which nature has taken years to make. The penalty of breaking Nature's laws is severe, and many people in many localities are now paying it heavily.[21]

While the vision of artists working and living together inspired Calvert and Renfro, it was naturopathic healing that led Louis Dechmann, a self-proclaimed physician and biologist in Seattle, to establish a resort on the Olympic Peninsula on the shores of Lake Crescent, named Qui Si Sana, referring to a place of good health. His guests and patients were treated to hydrotherapy, diet, and exercise while enjoying the restful nature of the surroundings, complete with gardens, statues, a bathhouse, and a spring of "radioactive" water. Accommodations were in cabins, but the true sense of a community was formed in the lounge and dining room of the rustic Craftsman lodge, which was dubbed the Great Pavilion.

Dechman took great pride in the lodge and its interior. In a 1913 Christmas album of photographs, guests are seen lounging in rockers on the wide covered porch admiring the views of Mount Storm King and Eagle Falls. Dechman described this charming spot in the forests of the Olympics:

> Qui Si Sana has been for me a work of real love, and its accomplishments a real joy.
>
> You may imagine that architecture of this kind cost us some little thought. The rustic walls are of native cedar. The panels are oil paintings and there are many of them; there is allegory in their design, for with these paintings life is typified—they are all nature scenes, and beginning with the birth in the first panel each succeeding painting tells some lesson of life and nature thereafter. The elk horn chandeliers and the hickory furniture are unique features.
>
> At the opposite end of the pavilion, the massive fireplace is the gathering place for all kinds of social amusement or study. . . . The homelike character of the pavilion, its raftered ceiling, and rustic beams and walls, makes all feel at home.[22]

In this period, whether it was the lure of the countryside for one's health, for solitude and retreat, or to experience the vast American wilderness and its beauties, the architecture and interior design elements of the American Arts and Crafts movement were perfectly suited to time and place. And the Pacific Northwest, with its many natural attractions and its mystique of being remote, was just beginning to spread outside its city borders to exploit its own virtues—mountains, forests, lakes, and seashore—to residents and to an increasingly curious and travel-oriented American public.

[top] Louis Dechmann's natural healing lodge, Qui Si Sana (pictured here in 1913), was perched on the edge of misty Lake Crescent on the Olympic Peninsula. Special Collections Division, University of Washington Libraries (Seattle), UW8850.

[above] Guests at Qui Si Sana lodge on Lake Crescent in 1913 shared time together as a community in the great hall with its welcoming fireplace. Special Collections Division, University of Washington Libraries (Seattle), UW26463z.

PART III Applied Arts and the Designed Interior

EIGHT
The Artful Interior at Home and at Work

IN THE FIRST DECADE of the twentieth century, the proliferation of Arts and Crafts housing in the Northwest for families of all economic means, including architect-designed houses for the more affluent, offered national and regional manufacturers, local retail stores and suppliers, specialty shops, craftspeople, and artisans the opportunity to sell their wares. Numerous magazines and journals championed aesthetically pleasing yet practical artistic interiors. Nearly every issue of Gustav Stickley's *Craftsman*, as well as *House Beautiful*, *Woman's Home Companion*, *Ladies Home Journal*, and other national publications, contained illustrated articles on interior furnishings and household hints to complement the Arts and Crafts house.

The September 14, 1907, issue of *Pacific Builder and Engineer* published a long article on modern house furnishings. The shift away from late Victorian aesthetics at the close of the nineteenth century was addressed in the opening paragraph: "A very marked

A page from Pendleton Woolen Mills' 1910 catalog demonstrates how to decorate your home with Pendleton blankets. Courtesy of Pendleton Woolen Mills.

The interior of a bungalow or Craftsman house, like this one in Portland c. 1916–1920, may have had a mixture of several generations of furniture and decorative arts, but often featured a fireplace, a few pieces of Mission furniture, some pottery or hand-painted china, an item or two of copper, photographs on the wall, and period textiles. Mason Collection. Photograph by Hale & Redmond.

change in the general character of interior decoration has occurred during the past few years. The present school of architects, painters, decorators, and designers is aiming at artistic effects in which simplicity is the dominant note. Results are sought through symmetry and grace of outline, and broad, even surfaces with effective chromatic harmonies, and the mass of minor accessories and elaborate detail, which have hitherto characterized the treatment of interiors and the art of the upholsterer, are being discarded."[1]

For the do-it-yourselfer, national periodicals offered suggestions on every imaginable household topic. Public libraries stocked the latest "how-to" books, along with publications extolling the latest in popular taste. Local sources of advice were available through weekly columns in newspapers, in the Seattle-based *Bungalow Magazine*, and in books written especially for the Northwest regional market. For locals, no single book matched the completeness of the *Seattle Home Builder and Home Keeper*, written and published in Seattle by architect W. W. DeLong and his wife in 1915.

The DeLongs' book contained sections on everything from selecting a building site, choosing house plans, constructing a house, creating interior finishes, and adding decorative features, to guidance on exterior lawn and garden care and food recipes. They claimed that the book with its advertisements would give the homeowner access to "expert advice on the countless points that arise for decision in the choice or this or that in the construction, decorating, furnishing and keeping of the 'Home Beautiful.'"[2]

The DeLongs' advice at the beginning of the interior decoration section was to consider, first of all, the style of the house, the exterior and interior architectural features, and related requirements for the walls, ceilings, woodwork, furniture, draperies, stained glass, and electric fixtures. They urged the homeowner to consider all details as part of the whole, including the furnishings required to make a complete home, regardless of whether the house was a simple bungalow or a mansion. Each house, they claimed, required its own unique interior furnishings treatment: "A bungalow requires very simple furnishings to be in good taste; the wood work should be plain and simple in lines, with dull wax finish, and the furnishings, such as rugs and draperies, of suitable qualities and finish in soft harmonious colors. On the other hand, the more pretentious homes require more elaboration in treatment to harmonize with the period the house is supposed to represent."[3]

There were probably very few Oregon and Washington homes in this period with Arts and Crafts furnishings and interiors throughout. Family heirlooms and the reality of economics encouraged mixing styles. Most historical photographs of middle-class bungalow interiors reveal a combination of furnishings representing several generations and individual tastes. And many show interest in simple Mission furniture, built-ins, light fixtures, brick or tile fireplaces, and artistic treatments of walls and floors.

Built-In Furniture

For many homeowners, furnishing a bungalow or Craftsman house with appropriate Mission furniture would have been too costly. Built-in furniture as a part of a house's construction increasingly became an appealing option. The house could be equipped with hidden or fold-up storage, seating, tables, desks, and beds that could be put away when not in use, allowing maximum use of space. Other types of built-ins, such as bookcases, fireplace alcove seating, and china cabinets, eliminated the need for expensive pieces of furniture. In a 1911 *Pacific Builder and Engineer* article, Okey J. Gregg, wrote:

> Built-in furniture has followed closely the development of the bungalow idea. . . . The lady of the home has been so often thrown upon her own resources of help that she has anticipated this by having every con-

The plans and specifications for a built-in buffet could be ordered for one dollar from the *Roberts Home Builder* plan book (Portland, 1909). Mason Collection.

venience possible built into her home. . . . To the one who has the care of the furniture, the built-in product appeals because it requires less work to keep clean and in its place. It is usually more sanitary, being entirely enclosed there is no open space beneath for the accumulation of dust, hairpins and collar buttons.

> Built-in furniture appeals to one because of its fitness. The architect has the designing of it and it therefore harmonizes with its surroundings, occupying beyond question the very place it should have in a room. It is then finished after the manner of the rest of the room and the sense of harmony in color treatment is not rudely interrupted by a store piece that is continually swearing at its neighbors.[4]

In a 1915 *Bungalow Magazine* article, Seattle entrepreneur Jud Yoho argued that one of the reasons for the growing popularity of the bungalow was the option of built-in conveniences that could be incorporated into the interior arrangements of a one-story plan. His ideal was a carefully designed house of ample space with no waste: "Some housewives are willing to live in a house where work is hard and useless steps are many, but the thoughtful woman of today wants a real home with all the little conveniences that make a home what it should be."[5] Yoho explained the value of built-in closets, cupboards, bedroom wardrobes, buffets and kitchen cabinets, disappearing ironing boards, medicine cabinets, and a Pullman breakfast nook. The latter, he proclaimed, was "one of the cutest little built-in-affairs for bungalows."[6] His magazine provided design plans for an array of built-in furniture.

Gregg, in his 1911 article, wrote that with all the assortment of built-ins available through the coordination of the architect and cabinetmaker, "there isn't much left for the dealer but a few chairs and a table or two."[7]

Furniture

Those "few chairs and a table or two" in all price ranges, styles, and degrees of quality could be purchased in nearly every large community in Oregon and Washington. The furniture of choice for many owners of bungalows and Craftsman houses was the Mission style. At its best, Mission furniture emphasized beauty in the simplicity of its lines, balanced proportions, and a high degree of craftsmanship in its detailing.

A 1907 Portland newspaper article applauded the general "revolt against the ugliness and fussiness" of Victorian furniture and the adoption of the Mission style. The writer, Helen Hawthorne, extolled the virtues of the simpler Mission style, but was blunt in her criticism of cheaply produced knockoffs that took advantage of the style's popularity but failed in execution and disappointed the purchaser:

> The emphasizing of the beauty of simplicity in lines and construction was a much

needed renaissance. In its original, or one might say, its craftsman made pieces, such work was immediately recognized as desirable, and it is highly esteemed in its place by those who take delight in what is genuine and sincere, either in furniture or in character.

> The only thing against the revived Mission style, and it is hardly fair to criticize a good thing because of its attempted imitation, is the cheap, clumsy class of articles which have been paraded to view under that name. It is like the sort made by Johnnie, who "Tired of his cozy corner and then, He decided to build his Mission den. So with a few knocks he's Split up some old boxes, And nailed 'em together again."

> Too much which goes under the name is of this sort, and instead of being beautiful it is ugly because it is clumsy. It is too heavy, and makes the labor of caring for it burdensome. It is a relief after too much of this sort to turn to the contemplation of the smoothly hand-polished surface of a well designed table, which, instead of a coat of black stain, reflects the soft natural tones of fine woods, and which, because of the care and skill used in its construction and the labor required to bring about the beautiful polish of the surface, satisfies with its form, its color, and its brightness. . . .

> When we get into our home some degree of restfulness for mind and body, and make our living places express individuality instead of a blind following of "style," we shall achieve some of the results for which homes exist. We want more restful homes, but we cannot have them until we give time and thought to the selection of each piece of furniture, and have in mind the harmony of the whole.[8]

Gustav Stickley's Craftsman furniture, considered some of the best of the Mission style, was readily available in Washington and Oregon after 1910. With several mainline railroads crossing the northern part of the United States from the Midwest and East Coast directly into Spokane, Portland, and Seattle, furniture shipments were easily accommodated. Although Gustav Stickley's published list of distributors in 1909 did not include any retailers in the Pacific Northwest, in fact, the Crescent Department Store in Spokane ran an illustrated ad in the *Spokesman-Review* in September of that year for Craftsman Furniture "made by Gustav Stickley, the originator of the famous Craftsman idea and publisher of *Craftsman* magazine."[9]

The Crescent was one of a number of Northwest retailers competing to represent major national Mission-style furniture companies. A survey of Spokane newspapers from 1904 through 1912 indicates that the Grote-Rankin Company advertised Stickley Brothers "Arts and Crafts" furniture as early as 1907 and the "Quaint" line by 1909. Limbert Mission rockers and chairs were sold at Goble, Pratt & Robbins furniture store. The Crescent handled Gustav Stickley, while Tull & Gibbs carried L. & J. G. Stickley Handcraft furniture. Another store, Cohn Brothers, in 1913 offered adjustable reclining back "Stickley" rockers.

The distribution of national brands to competing furniture stores in Portland and Seattle mirrored the activity in Spokane. By 1912, the L. & J. G. Stickley catalog listed Meier & Frank in Portland and the Grote-Rankin Company in Seattle as joining Grote-Rankin in Spokane to sell their furniture line. The Tull & Gibbs store in Portland also sold Quaint Furniture of 'craftsman' designs. Portland's Henry Jenning & Sons advertised Limbert's Dutch Arts and Crafts furniture in 1914.

Tull & Gibbs, a home-furnishing store in Spokane, featured the L. & J. G. Stickley national logo on the cover (lower left corner) of their 1914 catalog. Northwest Museum of Arts & Culture, Eastern Washington State Historical Society (Spokane), Eph 658 T822c.

The Standard Furniture Company in Seattle handled a number of lines, and its Home Fair, exhibited in its two-story atrium each year, was a popular showplace for Arts and Crafts furniture. In 1913, as a celebration of its twenty-fifth year in business, the Standard Furniture Company constructed a river rock and shingle bungalow on its main floor as the centerpiece for a display of carpets and Mission and wicker furniture.

The April 25, 1909, *Sunday Oregonian* contained ads for at least three different furniture stores in Portland selling Mission furni-

THE GROTE-RANKIN CO'S MAIN FLOOR, PIKE ST. AND FIFTH AVE

[top] The main-floor showroom of the Grote-Rankin store in Seattle featured a variety of Mission-style furniture, including what appears to be both Limbert and L. & J. G. Stickley pieces (c. 1915). Grote-Rankin had additional stores in Portland and Spokane. Michael Voris Collection.

[above] A river rock and shingle bungalow was the centerpiece of the 1913 Seattle Home Show in the two-story-high main floor of Standard Furniture, where the company exhibited their Mission and wicker lines. PEMCO Webster & Stevens Collection, Museum of History & Industry (Seattle), 83.10.9755.

ture. Edwards Company, House Furnishers, offered three rockers in two finishes; William Gadsby & Sons' illustrated ad showed thirty-two pieces of Mission furniture at 20 percent off; and Powers Furniture was selling a Mission hall clock of solid oak for $17.65. The next week, J. G. Mack & Company, also of Portland, announced that it had just received beautiful and inexpensive draperies for bungalows, plus "a carload of the celebrated Quaint Furniture."[10]

The abundance of wood in Oregon and Washington, coupled with the availability of easy transportation routes to markets both within the region and out, helped foster the growth of a large furniture-making industry. A 1917 promotional pamphlet stated that the growth of the furniture manufacturing business in Portland had been phenomenal over the past ten years, estimating that four million dollars worth of furniture was sold from that city's factories during 1916.[11] Recognizing the public's interest in Mission-style furniture, many regional companies were formed to produce "look-alike" furniture that could compete in the marketplace against the national brands. Among those local manufacturers were the Century Furniture Company and Empire Furniture Company in Seattle; Tacoma Chair Company and F. S. Harmon Manufacturing Company of Tacoma; and Heywood Brothers & Wakefield Company and the Oregon Chair Company in Portland. One major furniture company, the Carman Manufacturing Company, had branches in the Northwest's four largest communities: Tacoma, Seattle, Spokane, and Portland. The company's massive illustrated catalog for 1911–1912 contained many images of "quartered oak Mission furniture."[12] Their catalog issued seven years later still featured Mission furniture, but not to the same extent.[13]

The Empire Furniture Company, when announcing the construction of their plant in 1910 near Lake Union in Seattle, proclaimed that anything made in the East could be "made in Seattle." They advertised themselves as an exclusive high-grade furniture manufacturing company.[14] The c. 1910 catalog issued by the Oregon Furniture Manufacturing Company of Portland contained photo illus-

OREGON FURNITURE MANUFACTURING COMPANY.

No. 17 M. Desk.

No. 7 M. Book Case.

No. 8 M. Clock; 6 feet high; weathered Oregon oak.

Some of our Mission Furniture made of Oregon Oak, weathered finish.

[top] The F. S. Harmon Manufacturing Company's rocking chair, Model 4931-2, was sturdy and affordable. Scott and Mary Withers Collection. Photograph by Hermon Joyner.

[right] Mission furniture made of Oregon oak with a weathered finish was the claim to fame of the Oregon Furniture Manufacturing Company. A 1910 catalog boasted that the firm's new plant was the largest furniture factory in the West, covering ten acres not far from downtown Portland. Washington State Historical Society (Tacoma), Eph-A.645.4.Or 140.1910.

trations of a chair, rocker, table, desk, bookcase, and standing hall clock all made in the Mission style from "weathered Oregon oak." Another page illustrated a bed and dresser set advertised as an "Old Mission Suite" of Oregon pine, more commonly known as Douglas fir.[15]

In 1907 the Covell Furniture Company in Portland advertised a magazine stand "made from Oregon fir; finished weathered and shellacked. Made on stout Mission lines."[16] In this case, quarter-sawn oak was being replaced by less expensive, omnipresent regional softwoods. Fir, so common in Oregon and Washington, was frequently used for inexpensive furniture, both manufactured as well as in home projects and manual training classes.

For the most part, locally produced furniture lines were cheaply made and not always aesthetically pleasing in design or proportion. Although such furniture was cheaper, the manufacturers of higher quality furniture were sure that when compared side by side, quality would win out over a matter of a dollar or two. In 1909 the Edwards Company, House Furnishers, of Portland ran the following ad in the *Sunday Oregonian*: "We have chairs from twenty factories. It does not worry us if the Oregon Chair Company puts a retail price on their goods or not. Oregon chairs are worth every cent you pay for them. They are equal to any, and better than many, and let us say that the fixed factory price is such that their chairs will sell in competition with any on the market."[17]

The Oregon Chair Company was one of the few exceptions to the lower quality, inexpensive Mission chairs commonly made in Oregon and Washington. Organized in 1906, the company had been in business several years before newspaper ads illustrated Mission-style dining chairs and other furniture made by this firm. Their oak chairs were well proportioned, with pleasant lines and good joinery, rivaling the Mission products of many of the Grand Rapids, Michigan, furniture companies.

By 1914 the Oregon Chair Company was producing a line of high-quality Mission chairs and other pieces of furniture that were either branded or labeled King Craft. In mid-February an *Oregonian* ad proclaimed: "All values are relative. You can buy an ordinary chair and it seems attractive. Place it beside a King Craft Chair and it immediately sinks in our estimation. You see instantly that it lacks . . . strength and individuality."[18]

A week later an illustrated ad of a child sitting on a Mission chair that looked similar to a L. & J. G. Stickley chair, announced: "King Craft Chairs are the achievement of a lifetime of experience in design, material and workmanship. They are sold by King Craft dealers in Portland, and in every town where superiority is sought. If you don't know him, write us direct. Oregon Chair Company, Portland, Oregon."[19]

The weekly advertisements in the *Oregonian* continued, and on April 13, 1914, the ad queried: "If quality, style and price were equal, would you give preference to home industry? You have a chance to do so when you buy chairs, by asking for King Craft Chairs."

The popularity of the furniture manufactured by the Oregon Chair Company extended beyond the Portland metropolitan area. In 1912 it was reported that the Mission chairs used to furnish the Broadway Apartments in Aberdeen, Washington, were made by the Oregon Chair Company.[20]

The Coos Historical & Maritime Museum

The stacks of chair parts in the furniture assembly area are indicative of the popularity of the Mission line from Oregon Chair Company, Portland (c. 1914). Oregon Historical Society (Portland), OrHi 64977.

Construction quality and a strong sense of design and proportion made King Craft the top name among all the widely produced regional furniture during the second decade of the twentieth century. Mark Humpal Collection. Photograph by Hermon Joyner.

The Oregon Chair Company, Portland, manufactured other pieces in the King Craft line besides chairs, including this oak writing desk. Mark Humpal Collection. Photograph by Hermon Joyner.

Mission rockers made of Oregon coast myrtle wood were manufactured by the Myrtle Furniture Company in Myrtle Point around 1907. Coos Historical & Maritime Museum (North Bend, Oregon), 959.63.

in North Bend, Oregon, has a well-made Mission-style rocking chair in its collection that may have been made by a short-lived furniture company in Myrtle Point.[21] The 1907–1908 R. L. Polk & Company directory for Coos Bay contains an advertisement for the Myrtle Furniture Company, which claimed to be the exclusive manufacturer of furniture made of the beautiful myrtle wood of Coos County. The company had exhibited its myrtle wood chairs in the Coos County Building at the Lewis and Clark Centennial Exposition in Portland in 1905. Their specialty line included Mission chairs, rockers, roll-top desks, tables, cellarettes, and china closets. Although heavy, the rocker in the museum's collection is of fine construction, showing off the distinctive myrtle wood grain to full advantage. There was no mention of the Myrtle Furniture Company in the 1909–1910 Polk directory.

The native characteristics of myrtle wood attracted the attention of Portland architect Wade Pipes. With that wood in mind, he designed an Arts and Crafts dining set, consisting of a large table and eight armchairs, for San Francisco's Panama-Pacific International Exposition in 1915. The set was made by the North Bend Manufacturing Company in North Bend, Oregon, from full-sized drawings Pipes had submitted to "ensure fidelity to design and construction details."[22] The current whereabouts of this magnificent dining set is unknown.

The Art Room in the Oregon Building at that exposition also featured a grouping of wicker furniture exhibited by John Boeker of Hillsboro, Oregon.[23] In his printed prospectus, Art Room organizer Allen Eaton mentioned that an attractive lot of chairs would be furnished for the exhibition by the Willow Furniture Company of Hillsboro. He noted that, "The willows grown in the Willamette Valley by these people for their furniture are the finest in the world."[24] It is assumed that Boeker represented the Willow Furniture Company.

Wicker furniture during the Arts and Crafts period became a popular complement to heavier, darker Mission oak furniture. The promoters of wicker were quick to point out how much lighter it was than the massive oak when the lady of the house wanted to rearrange furniture. Popular in restaurant tearooms and as verandah and porch furniture, wicker was used in lamps, chairs, tables, and stands placed in the midst of Mission oak furniture, as shown in period interior photographs. In the Northwest, the Portland Wicker Furniture Manufacturing Com-

[top] The myrtle wood dining room set exhibited in the Oregon Art Room at the Panama-Pacific International Exposition (San Francisco, 1915) was designed by Portland architect Wade Pipes and made by the North Bend Manufacturing Company. Toenniessen-Lundberg Collection.

[above] Wicker was the bungalow owner's popular choice for sunrooms, porches, and pergolas, according to the 1913 showroom at the Standard Furniture Company in Seattle. PEMCO Webster & Stevens Collection, Museum of History & Industry (Seattle), 83.10.9756.

Wicker chairs mingled compatibly with Mission furniture, a Prairie-style lighting fixture, built-ins, and a copper hooded fireplace in this Portland living room (c. 1915). Doug Magedanz Collection.

pany offered potential buyers the option of saving money by buying from their factory on Northeast Broadway in Portland.

Another Portland firm, Peters Manufacturing Company, also avoided the middleman of the retail store by selling its wares direct to the customer. Their c. 1915 catalog cover stated their identity: "Makers of Genuine Solid Oak Mission Furniture, Sold Direct, Factory to Home." They sold their furniture for cash only for the exact cost of production "plus a fair factory profit."[25]

The Peters catalog warned the prospective customer of the pitfalls of buying Mission furniture based solely on appearance. It also criticized imported furniture from the East, further encouraging buyers to purchase from local and regional companies that could do equal or better work at a more reasonable cost:

There are two kinds of Mission furniture—the cheap muckrake kind and the genuine reproductions. We are proud of the fact that our line is of the latter class. The words "Mission furniture" do not mean any old piece of furniture so long as it has a Mission color stain on it. The lines and designs of the piece itself stand for the Mission effect, not the stain. There are thousands of dollars worth of so-called "Mission furniture" dumped out here on this coast by Eastern manufacturers and resold to the people for "Mission" furniture, when, in fact, they are no more Mission designs than an empty piano box.

We would not have you to understand us as trying to lead you to believe that there is no genuine Mission furniture in the stores out here. There is abundance of it, fine, elegant pieces; but look at the prices at which it is sold to the people.

We are not spending barrels of money in advertising our business. We are laying our proposition before the people as plainly and as economically as possible. We regard each piece of furniture we place in the homes of the people as the greatest and most effective advertising we could have.[26]

The furniture illustrated in the Peters catalog included settees, chairs, tables, and accessories. While furniture was shipped ready to use for an additional 10 percent covering greater packing costs, the company designed its furniture in sectional and setup modules that one usually thinks of as a recent innovation. The Peters Manufacturing Company claimed: "It requires only a few moments to set up and finish any of our designs. We furnish any color stain, glue, brush, and all necessary articles so that anyone can complete the furniture without any trouble."[27] The Peters catalog quoted freight rates to thirty-three towns in Oregon, fifteen in Washington, and four in Idaho. Residents of Portland were given the option of either purchasing the furniture in sections or assembled at the same cost.[28]

Wade Pipes' furniture designs for the North Bend Manufacturing Company's myrtle wood dining room set were not an unusual departure for Northwest architects during the Arts and Crafts era. Many affluent clients insisted on specially designed pieces for their architect-designed houses. Well-established architects and artists were regarded as arbiters of taste. They were frequently commissioned to design not only the building but its contents as well, because of their understanding of up-to-date trends in design and interior decoration.

Architects often relished the opportunity to design furniture and fittings for a house of their design. Kirtland Cutter had many such opportunities, as did Ellsworth Storey and Andrew Willatsen of Seattle. Storey turned

[top] According to the Peters Manufacturing Company's catalog, it took only about thirty minutes to assemble any of their pieces of furniture that were shipped or delivered in sections. Mason Collection.

[above] Langdon C. Henry commissioned Seattle architects Andrew Willatsen and Barry Byrne to design the furniture and lighting for his house (c. 1912). Dennis Andersen Collection.

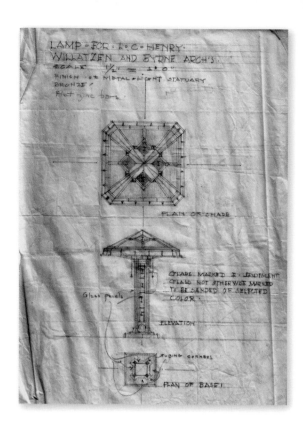

[top left] Willatsen and Byrne's working sketch for a lamp designed for L. C. Henry of Seattle (c. 1912). Willatsen Collection G0159. Special Collections Division, University of Washington Libraries (Seattle), UW 2646oz.

[top right] Willatsen designed his office furniture, lighting, and windows (1915) in the Prairie School style, reflecting the influence of his training under Frank Lloyd Wright. Willatsen Collection PH Coll 340. Special Collections Division, University of Washington Libraries (Seattle), UW 14762.

[above] A built-in sideboard (1908) designed for the George Donald residence in Yakima was built locally by the Cascade Lumber Company. *Pacific Builder and Engineer*, March 27, 1909.

his designs over to Seattle Turning & Scroll Works for execution when he designed the Hoo Hoo House furniture made of native fir for the 1909 Alaska-Yukon-Pacific Exposition. Willatsen, who trained under Frank Lloyd Wright, was a versatile artist who designed Prairie-style chairs, tables, and lamps for Seattle clients Landgon C. Henry and George Matzen. For his own office, Willatsen designed furniture, stained glass windows, and bookcases. Carl Gould, known for his formal residential designs, nevertheless chose to build a Mission-style settee for Topsfield, his Bainbridge Island cottage, in 1915.

Yakima, Washington, businessman George Donald commissioned the Seattle firm of Spalding and Umbrecht to design some of the furnishings in his new home, including a hand-carved built-in sideboard, glass cabinet, hall tree, and table, which were constructed by the Cascade Lumber Company of Yakima. The designs, while referred to as Mission in an article in the *Pacific Builder and Engineer*, also reflected the influence of the German Secession in their geometry and the selective placement of conventional carved ornament. The materials used were quarter-sawn white oak, South African mahogany, and art glass. The house, for which Donald spent $25,000, was noted for its carved woodwork and stained glass windows derived from British Arts and Crafts stylized design prototypes.[29]

The local individual cabinetmakers, woodworkers, and carvers who did furniture work and interior detailing in the Arts and Crafts style are not well known. Many had emigrated from central and northern Europe or the United Kingdom, where they had learned their craft. Generally one comes across references to these regional craftsmen only by reading through newspapers and periodicals of the era, such as the following example in a 1908 *Pacific Builder and Engineer*: "Down in South Bend, Washington, there is a German benchman, a master workman in about all woods known to the cabinetmaker, and an artist when it comes to exclusive handmade furniture. Henry Schenk, for that is his name, learned his trade at Frankfurt-on-Main, and for 30 years he followed it in the United States."[30]

The article also mentioned that Schenk had built furniture for the Dr. Cole residence in Portland, and was in the process of making a library table and an eight-foot extension table of myrtle wood for a ship captain in South Bend, plus a duplicate of that same order for the captain of the *Daisy Mitchell*. He also had a commission to make two library tables for a client in Victoria, British Columbia.

William J. Standley, the man who had overseen the development of the manual training programs in Portland, continued his work as a cabinetmaker after leaving his job in the school system. His craftsmanship was displayed in various exhibitions, including the 1915 Panama-Pacific International Exposition in San Francisco, where he showed an Arts and Crafts carved wood bookcase.[31] In 1913 Standley had exhibited a child's table and chair in the First Annual Exhibition of Artists of the Pacific Coast at the Portland Art Museum.[32]

The 1908 exhibition of the Arts and Crafts Society of Portland featured carved furniture by James R. Forden of Portland; two tables, a desk, and a chair designed by G. A. Walker and executed by the Art Furniture Company of Portland; and two library tables and a Morris chair exhibited by C. W. Johnson.[33] The society's 1910 exhibit catalog listed a chair and bookrack made by Rev. W. S. Gilbert of Astoria.[34]

The collection of the Coos Historical & Maritime Museum includes another regional piece of Arts and Crafts myrtle wood furniture—a buffet or sideboard that was handcrafted by George Humphrey, the stepfather of Stanley Henderson. It was made as a wedding present for Henderson and his bride Esther Johnson in November 1914.[35]

Interior Decoration

Interior decorators, usually people with a background in design and art or architecture, began to promote their talents in Northwest newspapers and periodicals shortly after the turn of the twentieth century. They either had their own studio and business, or worked out of furniture or department stores. Their services were aimed at creating a unified look throughout a home.

The Frederick & Nelson department store in Seattle advertised in *Bungalow Magazine* that they "specialized in bungalow furniture, draperies, floor coverings and wall hangings." The store urged readers to call upon their interior decorating department for suggestions and estimates. They were available for tinting, painting, and decorations of all sorts and could accommodate out-of-town clients.[36]

The interior decor of the Hoo Hoo House at the A-Y-P Exposition was an opportunity for another Seattle company to show off its artistic design work. The draperies were of a "green bungalow lattice effect" with black cats, the Hoo Hoo symbol, done in appliqué. The smoking room featured a hand-decorated frieze of Washington forests. "The entire decorative scheme, as executed by Weissenborn

& Company, is a demonstration of what may be done on a small appropriation."[37]

Frieze and fresco work, whether done by hand or replicated by wallpaper designs, adorned the interior walls of many Northwest homes, businesses, and club halls. Stylized regional motifs, such as mountains, lake and ocean scenes, and trees were common themes. The interior decorating and painting firm in Portland, J. A. Graef & Company, displayed examples of its fresco work in both the 1908 and 1909 Portland Architectural Club exhibitions. In 1908 Graef exhibited twelve room sketches for various houses, along with designs for the Heilig Theater and the Elks Club. His ad for that same year indicated that he was a fresco artist who decorated public and private buildings with special designs.[38] The following year Graef exhibited three entries of frieze, panel, and interior work.[39]

In 1906 John W. Graham & Company in Spokane proclaimed in a newspaper ad: "We Know We Can Do Your Decorating Satisfactorily, for We Have Fine Wall Papers and Skilled Mechanics to Hang Them. Nothing Is Impossible for Us in the Decorative Line: Designing, Frescoing, Tinting, Paper Hanging, Interior Painting and Finishing. Our wall papers were carefully selected for a purpose, not with an idea of having every paper fit any room in the house. Our hangings are classed as hall designs, library patterns, Mission room papers, etc., all following distinct periods and having distinct character. These papers, with their variety of textures and finishes, their harmonious and restful colorings, readily recommend themselves to all persons seeking artistic results."[40] Illustrated ads in the Spokane newspapers, depicting Arts and Crafts motifs, continued to promote the inte-

[above] This watercolor display board (c. 1910) illustrated a fresco design of stylized Northwest evergreen trees that matched the proposed tile work. Kirtland K. Cutter Collection, Ms. 49. Northwest Museum of Arts & Culture, Eastern Washington State Historical Society (Spokane).

[right] John W. Graham's ad in the March 26, 1911, issue of the Spokane *Spokesman-Review* newspaper featured period wallpaper and friezes.

rior design capabilities of John W. Graham & Company as late as 1914.

Architects, like Spokane's Kirtland Cutter, sometimes conducted secondary businesses as interior decorators and furnishers. Included in the Cutter architectural collection at the Eastern Washington State Historical Society in Spokane are clippings from local newspapers, c. 1909–1910, advertising the services of Cutter & Plummer.[41] Two years later, Plummer was no longer associated with the studio name. A full-page ad in the *Spokesman-Review* of April 23, 1911, stated that the facilities and equipment of Cutter Studios were such that no undertaking was consid-

DECORATION

Mural work in its various branches in conformity with the style of architecture and in harmony with the furnishings for residences and public buildings △ △ △ △ △

ELECTRICFIXTURES

Decorative and architecturally correct in design and finish △ △

FURNITURE △

Consistent comfortable upholstered and cabinet of all kinds.

RUGS Carefully selected Oriental △ also hand tufted made from special design

DRAPERIES

For all purposes △ appropriate in design and fabric △ △ △

CUTTER&RUMMER INC.

Studio of interior decoration and furnishing 719–6ᵗʰ Ave. at head of Wall street △ △ △ △ △

For a brief period, Spokane architect Kirtland K. Cutter was involved in an interior design business, as announced by this ad in the November 1, 1909, *Spokesman-Review*.

ered too large or too small. The studio embraced all classes of private homes and other buildings. Coinciding with the arrival of summer, the ad promised that they had a large shipment of wicker furniture on the way to Spokane. Their art novelties section included well-established national accessories such as Hampshire pottery and candlesticks in brass, carved wood, and silver.

Another Spokane architect, C. Ferris White, received major publicity for his interior design studio from a photo-illustrated article "A Decorator and His Art" in a 1909 issue of *Pacific Builder and Engineer*:

Right in the heart of Spokane . . . stands as artistic a studio as one could find in old Boston or Philadelphia. From the fantastic dragon chair in the vestibule, to the immense old-fashioned fireplace with copper hood, set in pale green tiles, there is an air of unique adaptability which makes the heart of any connoisseur glad. An ordinary office room has been transformed in a delicately tinted exhibition salon. Light green is the prevailing color unless the push of a button sets the many parti-colored lights aglow. Two huge beams cross the ceiling. A pronounced cornice and tapestried panel overtops a plate rail on which are placed several utensils of copper. Over the fireplace a mantel supported on huge brackets of fir, displays specimens of hand-wrought work from an art craft shop. Cozy cabinets with large iron hinges line the fireplace and the walls opposite; while a provisional balcony window discloses two high-backed settles between a serving table . . . Such is the Studio of Decorative Art which must be visited in order to be appreciated.[42]

White had opened the studio in July 1908, after twelve years in practice designing many fine residences. He had also served as the architect for the Potlatch Lumber Company, for which he designed over 300 houses for the town of Potlatch, Idaho. Turning his attention to interior decoration, C. Ferris White had the "exclusive agency of many high-class wallpapers, special tiling, furniture and lighting fixtures, hand-wrought hardware. And so forth."[43]

Commercial businesses, eager to present themselves as up-to-date and modern in their marketing approach and salesroom appearance, used the services of regional firms to create the right ambience for their customers. The King Brothers in Seattle, when outfitting

The Studio of Decorative Art, a business owned by architect and interior designer C. Ferris White in Spokane, advertised on the back of this 1909 postcard that they had in stock "high grade wall papers and interior decorations," including wall fabrics, special lighting fixtures, and draperies. Arts and Crafts accessories, such as table runners and metal ware, are visible in the salesroom. Maslan Collection.

their new clothing store in 1906, had the interior fittings, including all the showcases, manufactured in the Mission style by a local firm, E. L. Gomoll & Company. Gomoll was credited with furnishing several other Seattle businesses during that same period, including the Stone-Fisher Company and the Shaw Drug Store in the American Savings and Trust Company's building. *Pacific Builder and Engineer* carried photographs of the store interiors in March 1906, and wrote positively about the firm's other work: "Another specimen of the art which may be shown in interior decoration and finish is that of the Joe Schlumpe cigar store. . . . Here again, the Mission style worked out beautifully and the expensive show cases, finishings, etc., are a source of constant satisfaction to Mr. Schlumpe and his patrons."[44]

A 1912 advertisement for the Mission Furniture Works of Grants Pass, Oregon, offered their services as "Up-to-Date Cabinet Makers" who could provide store and office furniture, fixtures, and showcases. Clearly, most towns of any size in Oregon and Washington had companies that could appropriately furnish business showrooms in the popular Arts and Crafts style.[45]

The Hearth and Fireplace

The domestic artistic interior, so often illustrated in the *Craftsman* and numerous national books and magazines, was not defined by its solid oak furniture alone but also by several fundamental components. The foremost interior feature of a bungalow or Craftsman home was the presence of a fireplace, often with art tile surrounds and mantels awaiting the perfect piece of art pottery, glass vase, or Indian basket. Whether made from native basalt, smooth river rock, or clinker or standard brick, the fireplace became an important artistic statement coinciding with the importance the Arts and Crafts movement placed on the hearth as the heart of a home.

Regional promoters of current trends and good taste, such as Seattle's *Town Crier*, proselytized the importance of a fireplace in the Northwest. In her article "Artistic Fireplaces," Barbara Dunn wrote:

Spokane architect Kirtland Cutter's living room (c. 1906) embodied the Arts and Crafts sentiment that the fireplace, here with Moravian tile from the Mercer Tileworks, was the heart of a home. Craftsman Workshop fixtures hang from the ceiling. Northwest Museum of Arts & Culture, Eastern Washington State Historical Society (Spokane), L84-487.61.

From the earliest times the hearth has always typified the home. All along the line, from the days of ancient Greece . . . to the present era of the bungalow, everything connected with domesticity has centered around the fireside. Some one has aptly defined home as "four feet on a fender" and an alleged humorist has declared that a home without a fireplace is like ham and eggs with the ham left out. All of which makes a not inappropriate introduction to what I am about to say.

In the Puget Sound country, where much of the time a furnace fire is unnecessary and where an open fire is much appreciated in cloudy weather, the fireplace is an essential feature of every household. Most of the more pretentious homes have so many fireplaces that they may be described as being composed of rooms grouped about a number of chimneys. With its increasing

popularity the fireplace has acquired a new dignity so that for the last few years the matter of its decoration has become an art itself.

In artistic rooms the fireplace is the keynote of the decorative scheme and its treatment determines the charm of the room. Tiles are especially to be recommended as facing in that they lend themselves to an almost infinite variety of designs and coloring.[46]

Many reports in regional newspapers of new bungalows carried descriptions of interior spaces of the more notable houses, often mentioning the fireplace as a focal point in the living room. *Pacific Builder and Engineer* also carried articles about new house construction. In describing the interior of the H. E. Schmidt house in Seattle, designed by Hall & Merritt, the trade journal reported: "The clinker and dark paver brick fireplace in the living room metes out a generous hospitality to an otherwise modest home. No effort has been made to force the brick into unnatural positions or strained designs; it is a substantial, homelike fireplace in every sense of the word. The hearth is laid with 3 × 9 tiles, conforming in brown tones with the brick. The fireplace was built by William Rutledge."[47]

Tile

The key national companies producing high-quality tile found their way into Oregon and Washington during the Arts and Crafts period, including Grueby Faience in Boston, Rookwood in Cincinnati, Henry Mercer's tile works in Doyletown, Pennsylvania, and Ernest Batchelder in Los Angeles. Other companies, particularly those in California, including Muresque, made major inroads into the Northwest market toward the end of the period. The presence of these tiles in major Oregon and Washington cities was due to the entrepreneurial nature of several local distributors. Prominent in the print media and Arts and Crafts trade exhibits, several companies stood out: William W. Kellogg in Seattle, Fred W. Wagner of Portland, and Empire Tile and Mantel Company in Spokane.

William W. Kellogg exhibited in the 1908 Portland Architectural Club's First Annual Exhibition, showing twelve exhibits, including a "Cabinet of Examples of Plain and Decorated Tiles," a "Framed Panel of Decorated Tiles" from the Rookwood Pottery Company, a mosaic panel by Henry C. Mercer of Philadelphia, and some of his own miscellaneous sketches of mantel and tile arrangements. As the general Northwestern agent for Rookwood tiles, his ad in the same catalog featured the Rookwood Pottery mark and indicated that the Kellogg Studios specialized in mantels and tiles, but for architects and "special designs only." He listed offices in Portland, Seattle, and Tacoma.[48] That same year Kellogg exhibited Rookwood tile in the first

The Kellogg Studio of Seattle submitted this grape and leaf tile design to architect Kirtland Cutter in Spokane, c. 1910. Kirtland K. Cutter Collection, Ms. 49. Northwest Museum of Arts & Culture, Eastern Washington State Historical Society (Spokane).

annual exhibition of the Washington State Chapter of the American Institute of Architects in Seattle's public library.[49]

For the 1909 Portland Architectural Club exhibition, Kellogg submitted many entries, including two sketches for a "Faience Show Window" for the Harrington Company, florists in Seattle, and an "American Indian—Glass Mosaic Panel" from the Rookwood Pottery Company.[50] Recording a significant regional Kellogg fireplace tile design, the *Portland Architectural Club Year Book* for 1910 included a photo illustration of his design for the fireplace at the Hotel Oregon in Portland. Above the fireplace, Rookwood tiles comprised a scene of Mount Hood. The name "Oregon" appeared within a shield in the lower center portion of that design. Mottos and ornamental tile along both vertical

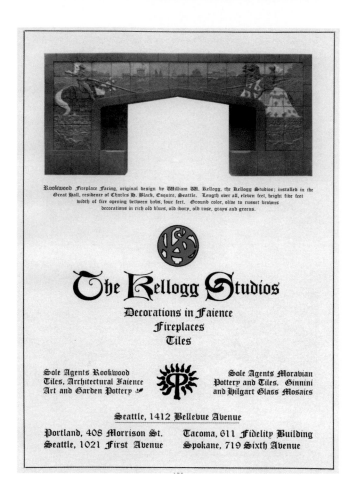

Rookwood Fireplace Facing, original design by William W. Kellogg, the Kellogg Studios; installed in the Great Hall, residence of Charles H. Black, Esquire, Seattle. Length over all, eleven feet, height five feet width of fire opening between hobs, four feet. Ground color, olive to russet browns decorations in rich old blues, old ivory, old rose, grays and greens.

The Kellogg Studios

Decorations in Faience
Fireplaces
Tiles

Sole Agents Rookwood
Tiles, Architectural Faience
Art and Garden Pottery ✿

Sole Agents Moravian
Pottery and Tiles. Ginnini
and Hilgart Glass Mosaics

Seattle, 1412 Bellevue Avenue

Portland, 408 Morrison St.　　Tacoma, 611 Fidelity Building
Seattle, 1021 First Avenue　　Spokane, 719 Sixth Avenue

sides of the fireplace made up the rest of the design.[51]

A major exhibit at the W. W. Kellogg main Seattle showroom in January 1911 warranted a trade journal article that was a thinly disguised advertisement for Kellogg's wares. The exhibit included Rookwood tiles and faience, Moravian tiles and mosaics, and Giannini glass mosaics. Kellogg was the exclusive agent for all three of those firms. The exhibit included only a few examples of regular commercial work, but the article stated that the company carried in its warehouse the largest commercial stock in the city, specializing in the highest quality of this class of work.[52]

The article mentioned that although the company was a comparatively new one, Kellogg himself had been studying and working with the decorative use of tile and faience and the laying out of fireplaces and other tile work to "conform to architectural details and to harmonize in style and color with specified schemes." Some of his downtown Seattle installations included the Sorrento Hotel, Frederick & Nelson, and Bauer's Chocolate Shop. The article stated that Kellogg's "studios and salesrooms . . . [in the] . . . Moore Theatre building, are easily the finest and most ar-

[top left] By 1909, the Kellogg Studio had representatives in the four major cities of Washington and Oregon. Kellogg designed fireplace facings such as this Rookwood installation with a medieval theme for Charles Black, Seattle. *Portland Architectural Club Year Book* (1909).

[left] Kellogg's main Seattle showroom exhibited a wide range of ceramic tiles and faience, mosaics, terra-cotta, pottery, and decorative arts from Gothic and Classical styles to the Arts and Crafts mode. A Rookwood retail store plaque is displayed at the lower right of the platform. *Pacific Builder and Engineer* (January 28, 1911).

tistic of their kind in the United States, and among the finest in the world."[53]

A month later, the Kellogg studios hosted an exhibition of fine pottery from Seattle area collectors. Of course, Kellogg had a "few souvenirs for select distribution, and among them were Rookwood pieces of Poe's raven in suitable size for paper weights."[54] Kellogg hosted other exhibits at his Moore Theater building studios and was a prominent figure in the Seattle arts scene of the time.

Kellogg's work as a tile designer and supplier frequently kept him in the public's consciousness as descriptions of new houses were published in local newspapers and *Bungalow Magazine*. In the May 1913 issue of the magazine, for example, reference to the new house of J. M. Tracy of Seattle featured a fireplace mantel and hearth of Rookwood tile from the Kellogg studios.[55]

An earlier unattributed newspaper clipping dating sometime after mid-1910 offers a little more insight into Kellogg's business:

> W. W. Kellogg has a salesroom in the Moore Theater building where he carries on a business in the design and manufacture of tile and pottery. Mr. Kellogg is the agent for the Northwest of the renowned Rookwood and Moravian wares, and his windows and tables are never without attraction to those who wish to study these forms of work.
>
> His studios are most tasteful in their scheme of color and arrangement and visitors are interested in the interior decorations worked out after Mr. Kellogg's own designs. This shop was opened as recently as July, 1910, although its proprietor has been connected with the arts and crafts side of Seattle for ten years.[56]

As more competitors entered the market, Kellogg stepped up his advertising. He signed this design for an ad in the *Seattle Home Builder and Home Keeper* book, published in 1915. Mason Collection.

Competition from other Seattle area tile dealers, primarily the Charles W. Rodgers Company, prompted Kellogg to advertise his wares and services in many different publications. Kellogg's 1915 ad in the DeLongs' *Seattle Home Builder and Home Keeper* was done in poster style, giving the impression of a tile installation featuring two peacocks. The type used was consistent with Arts and Crafts printing designs of the time—bold and easy to read, while at the same time aesthetically pleasing.[57]

Kellogg's counterpart in Portland was Fred W. Wagner. The *Spectator* claimed, in 1909, that Wagner was the best-known tile man in

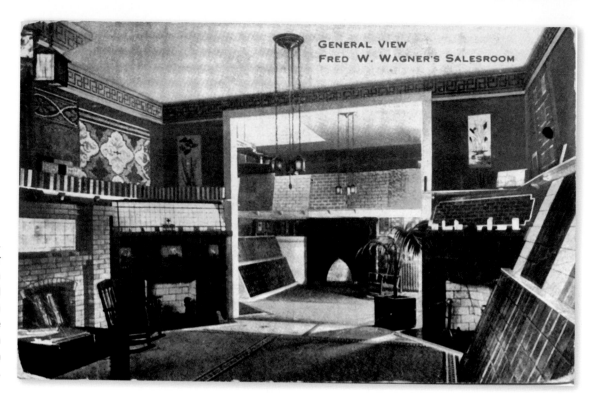

GENERAL VIEW
FRED W. WAGNER'S SALESROOM

Fred Wagner issued a promotional postcard in 1912 for his tile showroom in Portland. Mason Collection.

Northwest Architect (June 1910) featured an illustration of the tile fireplace in Fred Wagner's home near Portland. A year earlier, the *Spectator* claimed that the tile installation in Wagner's residence was unequalled anywhere.

Portland. His specialties were tile, mantels, and grates. The article indicated that Wagner had learned his trade in New York, and had moved to Portland and opened up his tile business in approximately 1904. Out of hundreds of installations to his credit, the weekly selected these buildings as representative of his Portland commercial work: the Corbett Building, Board of Trade Building, Nortonia Hotel, Danmoore Hotel, Worcester Block, Couch Building, Jaeger Brothers' jewelry store, Clark Brothers' florist, Feldenheimer's jewelry store, and the U.S. National Bank. It also claimed that Wagner's installation of a mosaic floor in Dr. Coffey's office in Portland was the "handsomest west of Chicago." The listed examples of his residential work for Portland society families were equally impressive. The article concluded by saying that the tile work in Wagner's own residence was unequaled anywhere.[58]

An interior photograph of Wagner's Portland area bungalow, showing a grouping of Mission furniture in front of a fireplace adorned with a variety of tiles, was featured in the June 1910 issue of *Northwest Architect*. As seen in the illustration, Wagner apparently was combining different types and manufacturers of tile in a single artistic design.[59]

Wagner exhibited art tiles in the Portland Architectural Club's show in 1908. In a direct challenge to Kellogg's Seattle studio, Wagner's ad in the Portland Architectural Club's 1909 exhibit catalog stated that his artistic tile company had the "most complete exclusive tile showroom in the Pacific Northwest." One of Wagner's advertising postcards, mailed in December 1912, shows a view of his studio spaces and tile exhibit. The printed message on the back reads: "We are now in position with our Beautiful Tile Exhibit and enormous stock of the latest creations in Tile for the Home and Public Buildings to give you a correct idea by a visit to our store, how your work will look when installed."

Fred Wagner also may have executed or sold regional designs similar to Kellogg's Mount Hood Rookwood tile design for the Hotel Oregon. A private collection contains a tile candle sconce, probably produced by Claycraft of Los Angeles, with an image that resembles Mount Hood and has "Fred Wagner, Portland" impressed on the back. Although it may have been just a generic mountain scene made up for a special order from Wagner, the image certainly would have appealed to his Portland-based clientele, since Mount Hood dominates the city's eastern horizon.

By 1913, Wagner had several competitors in Portland. In a 1912 newspaper ad, M. J. Walsh on Stark Street, Portland, only a block away from Wagner's business address, announced that his business was "the Portland headquarters for faience, Rookwood and Grueby

tile mantels, as well as for all other tiles of high merit."[60] A year later, the Oregon Art Tile Company promoted themselves as "distributors for Batchelder, Mueller, Moravian, Rookwood and Grueby tiles."[61] In the same publication, Wagner advertised that he provided tile for the artistic architect, including Mueller handmade Flemish tile and faience for interior and exterior decorations.[62]

Architects, contractors, and residents in Spokane did not need to order their tile from Seattle, Portland, or the East. The Empire Tile and Mantel Company, advertising in the 1911 Spokane City Directory, claimed to be able to provide almost everything anyone would want or need in tile. They listed the company as dealers in all kinds of tiles, including Welsh Quarries, Moravian, encaustic, Grueby faience, Strobel faience, Cambridge faience, imported Holland, Mueller Mosaic art tiles, and Ludowici Promenade tiles. In addition, they could provide a variety of fireplace accessories, including andirons, screens, fire sets, and copper and brass fireplace hoods.[63]

One of the few Northwest businesses that actually produced tiles as part of their commercial ventures was the Washington Brick, Lime & Sewer Pipe Company, with headquarters in Spokane. Originally founded in the 1880s as a company supplying utilitarian drainage and sewer products for the building trade, it developed several artistic lines after the turn of the twentieth century and became well known for ornamental terra-cotta work throughout the Northwest. Spokane's Davenport Hotel, built in 1914, featured the firm's terra-cotta rams' heads on its façade. In Clayton, Washington, home of the company's factory and its clay deposits, the Washington

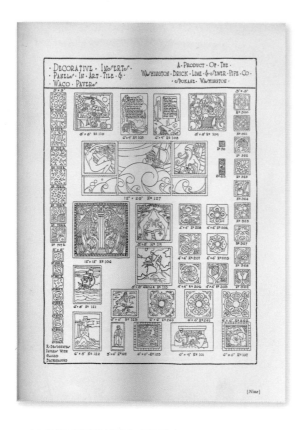

[top] The catalog (c. 1925) of Washington Brick, Lime & Sewer Pipe Company, Spokane, for WACO tile and pavers illustrates products similar to those of their established, primarily California-based, competitors. Northwest Museum of Arts & Culture, Eastern Washington State Historical Society (Spokane), Eph 693.3 W279c 1925.

[above] WACO tile no. 103, 6 × 6 inches (c. 1925). Thomas H. Wake Collection. Photograph by Barry Wong.

Brick and Lime Company (as they became popularly known) built a Moose Lodge hall that featured almost every imaginable type of ornamental terra-cotta, including a figure of a moose and a clock.[64]

By the 1920s, the company, which used WACO as a trade name, had already introduced their WACO tiles and soon began to promote a new line of products: decorative inserts and panels in art tile and pavers. A 1925 illustrated catalog presented this "comparatively new WACO product, adapted to the embellishment and service of our modern homes and public buildings." The company made four classes of tile: WACO art tile, WACO faience tile, WACO pavers, and WACO quarry tile. Even though these products were introduced toward the end of design prominence of the Arts and Crafts period, the tiles continued to embody the movement's ideals of handwork, beauty, and harmony of color and texture.

WACO art tiles, recognized for their universal beauty, were crafted through a special hand-finishing technique and were fired at a very high temperature. The term *notan*, a Japanese word meaning "dark-light," best describes the unusual appearance of the tiles' glazed surface, and refers to the quality of light reflected from the tiles, which resulted in a unique harmony of dark and light spaces. The *notan* tile surface was available in eleven art tile colors, making possible a large variation in hue and intensity.[65]

In describing how complete satisfaction in the use of tile can only come from the careful selection and proper installation, the company's 1925 catalog went on to say, "Consideration must be given to utility as well as beauty of the tile selected. Lighting arrangements as

well as other interior appointments require color and texture treatment of proper values. Line and form play an important part in the design where there is an appreciation of clay molded by the hands of men and fired to an imperishable state of beauty. Consult your architect or seek guidance from the men who manufacture and install WACO art tile."[66]

The catalog recommended WACO art tile for both interior and exterior installations: "On interior work a unique effect, thru color, texture and character of line, is obtained when considering surrounding furnishings. Satisfaction in floor and wall work of domestic architecture is guaranteed by the use of WACO Art Tile because of their durability and mechanical strength. On exterior work, superior and lasting color effects thru strength and harmony are obtained with WACO Art Tile."[67]

Easily mistaken for Batchelder tiles, many ornamental tiles in Northwest homes may well be the work of this Spokane firm. The WACO catalog of available tile and paver designs illustrates design similarities with tiles of Batchelder and other California companies of the period.

An interesting footnote to the Washington Brick, Lime & Sewer Company's work is the production of a series of Christmas tiles created for the A. B. Fosseen family, owners of

[top] Muresque Tiles of Oakland, California, produced several decorative tiles of Northwest scenes in the 1920s, including two from along the Columbia River highway and this one of Crater Lake. Collection of Ron Endlich, Tile Antiques (Seattle). Photograph by Barry Wong.

[above] WACO tile no. 205, 4 × 4 inches (c. 1925). The pinecone motif was a popular standard in the Northwest because of the pine forests in parts of Oregon and Washington. Collection of Ron Endlich, Tile Antiques (Seattle). Photograph by Barry Wong.

[top] The designer and maker of the Portland Fire Department's fireplace over-mantel tile installation have not yet been identified. Collection of the Portland Fire Department (Portland). Photograph by Hermon Joyner.

[above] The Portland Fire Department's bungalow fire station featured a firefighting tile installation above the fireplace that coordinated perfectly with the station's Mission furnishings. Postcard, c. 1918. Mason Collection.

the company, as well as several regional tiles not illustrated in their catalog. On one such tile, a northern Idaho mining scene appears to be the design inspiration. The National Recovery Act was the theme for an Art Deco tile from the 1930s. More than likely, these special tiles were designed and created by Leno Prestini, who had begun working for the company in 1925.[68]

Northwest scenery, so inspirational to local artists and craftspeople, was also incorporated into the tile designs of nonregional tile companies. Claycraft Potteries in Los Angeles probably manufactured the Mount Hood wall sconce for Fred W. Wagner in Portland. A fireplace in a Craftsman home in southeast Portland features three tiles with Northwest scenes manufactured by Muresque Tiles of Oakland, California: Multnomah Falls and the Oneonta Gorge, spectacular geographic features along the Oregon side of the Columbia River east of Portland, and Crater Lake in southern Oregon.

An unknown tile maker produced a mural originally installed above the fireplace in Portland's Fire Station #18. Now relocated to the fire department headquarters building, the multicolored tile composition portrays three running white horses pulling a steam fire engine with a uniformed fireman at the reins. The work may have been commissioned specifically for Portland.

Metalwork and Hardware

While the fireplace, with its tile surrounds, may have been the focal point of a Craftsman-style living room, it was often the hand-hammered light fixtures, sconces, and fireplace hardware that best expressed the hand-wrought ideals of Arts and Crafts enthusiasts. The color and look of well-designed metalwork were considered consistent with an appealing, artistic interior.

Hammered copper fireplace hoods, often with Arts and Crafts designs worked into them, appeared in private residences and public buildings throughout Oregon and Washington during the period. Kirtland Cutter incorporated an ornamental copper fireplace hood and surround into Louis Davenport's apartment in Spokane, prompting Elbert Hubbard to proclaim the room as one of the best examples of Arts and Crafts design in America. The attached copper floral designs on the copper surround matched the motif on the room's paneling and doors.

A 1911 newspaper article addressing the Frederick Wilson residence in Spokane, designed by Keith & Whitehouse, described a number of key Arts and Crafts features. The living room had beamed ceilings and a massive Grueby tile fireplace and mantel. The den was finished in fir, with an arched ceiling and a mantelpiece, also in Grueby tile. Above the mantel was "a hammered copper hood to match the hardware." [69]

The Walter Link home in McMinnville, Oregon, which had been remodeled into a

The hammered copper fireplace hood and stylized rose design surrounds installed in Louis Davenport's suite at the Davenport Hotel (1904) in Spokane prompted the Roycroft founder Elbert Hubbard to proclaim the room as one of the best examples of Arts and Crafts design in America. Hanging lights were from Gustav Stickley's Craftsman Workshop. Mason Collection.

Craftsman-style house in c. 1915, featured a full-length tiled fireplace with a hammered copper hood bearing the verse, "Stay, stay at home my heart/And rest./Homekeeping hearts are happiest./For those that wander they know not where/Are full of trouble and full of care./To stay at home is best." [70]

Several regional companies offered "bungalow" hardware, such as strap hinges and door handles, mailboxes, house numbers, and other items for building use. Ware Brothers Company in Spokane promoted Art-Craft Builders' Bungalow Hardware as extremely important in decorating the front door of a house: "It is at the Front Door that you welcome your friends and bid them adieu. It is that which attracts their attention while awaiting the answer to their summons, and unconsciously makes an impression as to the

...FOR...

BUNGALOWS AND KRAFTSMAN COTTAGES

KRAFT HARDWARE will give your home an air of elegance and refinement not otherwise secured.

ANTIQUE, COLONIAL and MODERN designs, in brass, copper or bronze metal. Plain or hand-hammered, elaborate or inexpensive.

For interior or exterior use.

MADE IN SEATTLE

For Sale by
HARDWARE DEALERS

Made by
ART HARDWARE & MFG. CO.

SPOKANE ORNAMENTAL IRON & WIRE WORKS.

SPOKANE ORNAMENTAL IRON & WIRE WORKS.

The following pages are devoted to a few designs of the most favorite antique fixtures and trimmings for Mission style homes. Workmanship and finish are of the most artistic, and can be made entirely of wrought iron, brass, burned or hammered copper finish. Special designs submitted upon request.

No. 830. Nine light chandelier, 30 inches in diameter, 4 by 8 inch lanterns, all iron and copper combination, $100.00 each.

No. 831. Lantern, 8 to 15 inches, with opalescent glass, from $8.00 up, according to sizes and number desired.

No. 832. Twelve-light candle chandelier, $30.00 each.

No. 833. Same lantern as No. 831, with bracket and chain, $3.00 extra.

No. 830

No. 831

No. 832

No. 833

Length in feet	Dimensions of Cross-Sections in Ins. Safe load in tons of 2000 lbs.						
	12x6	12x7	12x8	12x9	12x10	12x11	12x12
12	21.0	24.5	28.0	31.5	35.0	38.5	42.0
13	19.9	23.2	26.4	29.8	33.2	36.4	39.7
14	18.8	21.9	25.0	28.1	31.4	34.4	37.6
15	17.9	20.9	23.8	26.8	29.8	32.8	35.8
16	17.1	20.0	22.8	25.7	28.6	31.4	34.2
17	16.4	19.1	21.8	24.6	27.4	30.0	32.7
18	15.7	18.3	21.0	23.6	26.2	28.8	31.4
19	15.1	17.6	20.2	22.7	25.2	27.7	30.2
20	14.6	17.0	19.4	21.9	24.4	26.7	29.2
21	14.1	16.5	18.8	21.2	23.6	25.8	28.2
22	13.6	15.9	18.2	20.5	22.8	25.0	27.2
23	13.1	15.3	17.4	19.6	21.8	24.0	26.2
24	12.6	14.7	16.8	18.9	21.0	23.1	25.2

STRENGTH OF WHITE PINE STRUTS OR PILLARS. Continued.

120

121

[top] The Art Hardware & Manufacturing Company advertised that their Kraft-Hardware line for bungalows and Craftsman houses, whether plain or hammered, was made in Seattle. *Seattle Home Builder and Home Keeper* (1915).

[above] A Spokane Ornamental Iron & Wire Works catalog from the 1910s featured a variety of metalwork, including lighting fixtures in the Mission style. Rejuvenation Collection (Portland), courtesy of Bo Sullivan.

---

character and taste of the man within. In fine, the Front Door Hardware is one of the most prominent features in the exterior decoration of a house, and on account of its prominence should lend tone and dignity to the whole."[71]

The DeLongs, in their book *Seattle Home Builder and Home Keeper* (1915), also talked about how home hardware details were a crucial field for displaying artistic feeling: "One does not have to look beyond our own city for the best there is in modern Art Hardware for we have a local factory whose sole product is bungalow hardware and their wares are to be had through any dealer either in stock patterns or in original designs to order if preferred at prices within the reach of the ordinary home builder."[72]

The facing page of the DeLongs' book offered an illustrated advertisement for hardware made in Seattle by Art Hardware and Manufacturing Company, whose Kraft-Hardware was specifically designed for "bungalows and kraftsman cottages." The ad stated that Kraft-Hardware gave a home an air of elegance and refinement not otherwise secured, and provided the option of antique, Colonial, or modern designs in brass, copper, or bronze metal. "Plain or hammered, elaborate or inexpensive. For interior or exterior use."[73]

The owner of Portland Art Metal Works, I. K. Tuerck, had offered ornamental work in iron, brass, and steel since the 1890s. His display of artistic metalwork won a gold medal at the 1905 Lewis and Clark Centennial Exposition. A newspaper reported that the award was no surprise, because for years Tuerck had been the regional leader in the manufacture of metal goods that provided an attractive combination of art with utility. His work included elevator enclosures, grills, bank and office railings, fireplace fittings, and chandeliers. Portland Art Metal Works also produced mausoleum and monumental work, as well as statues, signs, gates, and fences. He provided the fountain chandeliers that adorned the terraces and boulevards of the Lewis and Clark exposition grounds.[74] Tuerck consistently showed his work in the annual exhibits of the Arts and Crafts Society of Portland and the Portland Architectural Club.

Spokane Ornamental Iron & Wire Works issued a major catalog, probably dating from the 1910s, of the metalwork it designed. The items, which could be fabricated for builders and contractors, included ornamental railings and grillwork as well as copper lighting fixtures. The company did its own work, claiming, "Workmanship and finish are of the most artistic, and can be made entirely of wrought iron, brass, burned or hammered copper finish. Special designs submitted upon request."[75]

In the Seattle area, Michael Uttendorfer, known as "Iron Mike," gained a reputation for his ornamental ironwork, particularly during the later part of the Arts and Crafts movement. Trained through a formal guild apprenticeship program in his home country of Germany, Uttendorfer produced works now recognized as some of the finest regional examples of this craft. Maria Pascualy, who curated the *Handwrought in Washington* exhibit at the Washington State Historical Society in 2000, said that the key to appreciating Uttendorfer's skill is that he worked iron the way artisans today work silver. "The iron was sinuous and smooth."[76]

Uttendorfer's fellow countryman Oscar Bruno Bach, who emigrated to New York in 1913, became one of America's premier metalworkers and designers. Bach did one commission in Oregon, just outside of Portland, for Lloyd Frank's Fir Acres estate in 1925. Bach designed much of the metalwork ornamentation and carvings incorporated into Frank's English-style manor house and grounds (now a part of Lewis and Clark College), including bronze weathervanes, exterior lighting fixtures, grill and window work, and four bronze dolphin-shape pool ladders.[77]

Lighting

Thousands of lighting fixtures were sold to Northwest homeowners who needed to bring electric light into their bungalows and Craftsman houses. For the most part, during this period the fixtures they chose were not the Neoclassical chandeliers that fit into more formal interiors, but were instead the geometric or curvilinear hand-wrought fixtures with iridescent or slag glass shades inspired by the prevalent Arts and Crafts and Art Nouveau designs.

The DeLongs recommended to their Northwest readers that the fixtures should be in keeping with the rest of the interior design to achieve a visually pleasing effect. They noted that because light fixtures are usually the last things to be installed during the construction of a new house, they tended to be the first thing sacrificed if money was running short. They suggested keeping aside a fixed amount for the installation of appropriate electrical fixtures. The DeLongs advised that homebuilders should obtain designs and estimates on fixtures from local firms, noting that the Seattle area had "a number of manufacturing concerns turning out fixtures equal to any made in the East." They reinforced the notion of creating a harmonious interior deco-

YOUR HOME
IS MADE COMPLETE BY OUR
BUNGALOW CRAFT
PORCH LANTERN

$4·85

YE WARDER SHOPPE
WE HAVE THE UNUSUAL

228 MADISON ST
SEATTLE WASH

CALL OR
WRITE
FOR
FULL
INFORMATION

[top] A hand-hammered copper sign of a ship in full sail hung from above the Warder Shop studio door in Seattle, and became the business's logo for advertising purposes. Following the popular design edict of the period, the owners believed that if you lived in a bungalow, you needed lighting fixtures in keeping with that style. They used that philosophy to market their wares in Seattle's *Bungalow Magazine* (June 1913).

[above] The Homecraft Shop, operated by Otis Sargent of West Seattle, designed and fabricated the Mission-style hanging lanterns for the Hoo Hoo House at the Alaska-Yukon-Pacific Exposition, Seattle, 1909. Ellsworth Storey Collection, PH Coll 336. Special Collections Division, University of Washington Libraries (Seattle), UW 1948. Photograph by Frank H. Nowell.

rating scheme, and pointed out that electrical fixtures are so prominent they are the "first thing to attract the approval or disapproval of the visitor or guest."[78]

Toward the end of her article in the *Town Crier*, Barbara Dunn mentioned a leading lighting fixture shop in Seattle. Emphasizing that lighting fixtures should be of a design consistent with house furnishings, Dunn described the attractive, artistic lamps shown at the Warder Shop on Madison Street: "Some of the lamps looked like candlesticks from an ancient monastery and had the advantage of being fitted with modern electric lights. Mr. Warder, who has studied designing in some of the leading art schools of Berlin and Paris, is rapidly becoming well known in Seattle as a designer and executor of artistic fixtures. Some of his finer work is in tooled brass. Fixtures of this material recently made for the bedrooms of a pretentious dwelling were in the form of wall sconces with delicately wrought shades in the shape of poppies. The effect was most artistic and dainty."[79]

The Warder Shop was most likely a popular venue for metalwork. In the same undated but probably c. 1910 newspaper clipping "Arts and Crafts Well Nourished in Seattle Life," which described William W. Kellogg's tile showroom and studios, a reference was made to the Warder Shop as a creative center for artistic metalwork. The business name came from the senior partner, Carroll Warder, who was associated with Irving Weltzlen, a Norwegian with "a thorough training in workmanship and design." The two men had opened their shop on Madison Street in Seattle in 1910 and hung out the sign of a ship, hammered out of copper, over their studio door. They specialized in the "craft of metals, copper, brass, lead and silver, and their originality in design and execution . . . made their unique atelier a center of interest."[80]

The scope and production quantity of the work of the Warder Shop is unknown. The brief description of their business suggests work other than architectural metalwork, but research has not turned up identified, marked pieces of copper or silver work such as bowls, vases, compotes, trays, jewelry, or other work usually associated during this period with fine craftspeople in the medium. A *Bungalow Magazine* ad in the June 1913 issue for metalwork from Ye Warder Shoppe in Seattle stated: "Your home is made complete by our bungalow craft porch lantern." Beyond that, little is known.

Equally of interest, and certainly worthy of further investigation, is the work of Otis Sargent of West Seattle, who operated a business called the Homecraft Shop. He created the Arts and Crafts fixtures for the Hoo Hoo House at the Alaska-Yukon-Pacific Exposition of 1909, but little else is known about him or his products. The description of Sargent's lighting is intriguing: "The lanterns express originality, coupled with uniqueness and the emblem of the order; they are of the mission type with a truncated trapezoid cross section, wood corners, panels of soft green glass and a black cat with red or green eyes in each of the four panels of the lantern."[81]

Throughout most of the first decade of the twentieth century in Seattle, the Mission Fixture & Mantel Company garnered a good share of the trade in lighting fixtures. A 1907 notice of the company's relocation to the newly completed Flatiron Building at the

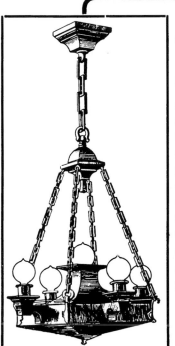

When in need of Lighting Fixtures, Mantels, Tiling and Grates see us. We carry the largest line of artistic fixtures in the Northwest as well as everything for lighting purposes. If you want something special, something out of the ordinary, we will be glad to have our artist draw up designs in accordance with your ideas without extra charge. Come in and see us; we will be glad to show you our large assortment.

Mission Fixture & Mantel Co.
"FLATIRON BUILDING"
Pike St., Fourth Ave. and Westlake Boulevard
Sunset Main 2414; Ind. 3949

The Mission Fixture & Mantel Company of Seattle advertised the "largest line of artistic fixtures in the Northwest as well as everything for lighting purposes." *Pacific Builder and Engineer* (July 1907).

corners of Westlake Boulevard, Fourth Avenue, and Pike Street described the showroom and some of their products. The notice mentioned a line of electric and gas lighting and heating fixtures, both in the Mission style as well as other "modern styles," that was said to be the largest and most complete in Seattle. The company fitted up several dark showrooms where their own make of mantels and lighting fixtures could be seen to the best advantage, "as daylight may be entirely excluded and the fixtures under inspection illuminated at will."[82]

Leaded and Stained Glass

Northwest glass companies were producing handsome and well-designed traditional glass for churches, fraternal organizations, hotels, and clubs in the Pacific Northwest in the nineteenth century. Because of the wide range of buildings being constructed from 1900 until the Great Depression, glass manufacturers were called on to create everything from simple beveled transoms and sidelights, and built-in bookcases and china cabinets for cozy bungalows, to large narrative stained glass windows in stair halls and on landings for larger houses of the affluent.

Oregon sustained several glass companies, the best known being the Povey Brothers Glass Company. The three Povey brothers, George, John, and David, came to Portland in c. 1888, most likely to work on the commission for stained glass windows for the First Presbyterian Church. Setting up a permanent business in Portland shortly after, Povey Brothers became synonymous with art, leaded, and stained glass throughout the Pacific Northwest.[83]

David Povey, who had trained at New York's Cooper Institute (later Cooper Union), was the principal artisan and designer of the company's window work until his death in 1924. Brother John most often supervised the installation crews. Povey Brothers was a widely known producer of church and memorial windows; large glass installations for hotels, businesses, and fraternal organizations; and fine residential work. They completed regional church commissions, for example, in Albany, Corvallis, Astoria, Portland, and Walla Walla. A great many of the Povey Brothers' ecclesiastic and memorial church window installations are still intact, including a fair number in downtown Portland churches.

The May 2, 1908, issue of *Pacific Builder and Engineer* credited Povey Brothers with conducting the largest complete glass establishment in the United States: "This is not gauged by the number of employees, nor the amount or value of work turned out, but upon the many different lines of glass handled by one management."

While many of the Povey Brothers' nonresidential installations were designed in Classical style, in its domestic glass the company seemed to embrace Arts and Crafts and Art Nouveau design conventions. Windows showing grape clusters, birds, dogwood (which was used so often it became a Povey Brothers design signature), water lilies, and the stylized rose were designed and installed in Portland residences from the 1890s through the first two decades of the twentieth century. Such windows often featured a variety of glass, including Kokomo, opalescent, crackle, rippled, granite-textured, and machine-rolled. Faceted jewels also were commonly used. Char-

[top left] The Povey Brothers Glass Company of Portland used their illustrated 1903 catalog to promote the practical as well as the artistic value of using glass to decorate homes. Doug Magendanz Collection.

[top right] This stair landing window installation in a Portland home is an example of the domestic art glasswork of the Povey Brothers. Photograph courtesy of Michael McCary, McCary Art Glass (Portland).

[bottom] An interior view of the Povey Brothers Glass Company workroom (c. 1908) shows a group of hanging stained glass light shades on the floor with other art glass, primarily windows, around the perimeter. Courtesy of Tom Robinson. Photograph by Clyde McMonague.

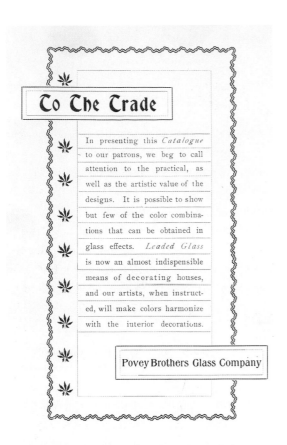

To The Trade

In presenting this *Catalogue* to our patrons, we beg to call attention to the practical, as well as the artistic value of the designs. It is possible to show but few of the color combinations that can be obtained in glass effects. *Leaded Glass* is now an almost indispensible means of decorating houses, and our artists, when instructed, will make colors harmonize with the interior decorations.

Povey Brothers Glass Company

The Povey Brothers designed and fabricated this Prairie School–style stained glass light shade with stylized roses around 1908. It appears to have been designed to hang from the ceiling. Rejuvenation Collection (Portland), courtesy of Bret Hodgert. Photograph by Steve Hohenboken.

acteristic of Povey's Northwest designs, glass installations sometimes had clear glass in the background to allow light to pass through on gray, rainy days.

Povey Brothers also made other glass products, such as lighting fixtures. Several extant examples of the Povey Brothers' Arts and Crafts–style stained glass lampshades demonstrate some influence from the longer, horizontal features of the Prairie School of design.

Upon the death of the last of the three brothers, David, in 1924, the firm continued under the Povey Brothers' name until W. P. Fuller bought the company in 1930. The W. P. Fuller company was a paint, sash and door, and glass enterprise with operations in several Northwest cities. Fuller's post-1930 catalogs continued to offer Povey, or Povey-like, window designs years after its acquisition of Povey Brothers.

The art glass designer and artist who perhaps best represented the Arts and Crafts style of work, comparable to that of his southern California counterparts, was Portland's Edward Bruns. While a smaller firm than Povey Brothers, the Edward Bruns Company seems to have specialized in modern

rather than traditional art glass, and most of the published work by his firm (c. 1908–1915) shows strong Arts and Crafts influence.

Little is known about Bruns's pre-Portland years. He may have worked in California under another name before appearing in the 1909 Portland City Directory as an art glass designer and maker. His leaded glass design entries in the 1908 Portland Architectural Club's exhibit have a California theme running through the titles. He exhibited twenty-one sketches, drawings, and designs, including leaded glass designs for the Glenwood Inn in Riverside, California; a leaded glass design of the Santa Barbara Mission; and a drawing for a leaded glass landscape titled *Pasadena*. Two of his entries are illustrated: a three-panel landscape that might be the *Pasadena* piece, and a design for an art glass window for the Glenwood Inn. Edward Bruns's ad in the exhibit catalog presented him as a designer and maker of art glass, including glass mosaic work, and gas and electric domes and shades, with his studio and workshop on N. 10th Street, Portland.[84]

Bruns had fourteen entries in the Portland Architectural Club's 1909 exhibition, including designs titled *Dragon Shade*, *Arctic Night*, and *Call of the Wild*. The last two designs suggest a shift in focus to the Northwest. One of Bruns's art glass designs was chosen for the catalog's frontispiece. His ad noted that he had relocated to an address on First Street.[85] Stained glass designs by Bruns also were illustrated in the Portland Architectural Club's 1910 yearbook.[86] His illustrated ad in that same organization's 1913 yearbook indicated that he was a member of the Portland Architectural Club, Arts and Crafts Society of Portland, and Builder's Exchange.[87] Bruns

exhibited nine leaded glass designs in the Art Room of the Oregon Building at the 1915 Panama-Pacific International Exposition, each titled in the catalog. He also fabricated the four hanging electric lanterns, made out of cedar frames and wood pulp transparent paper enclosures with silhouettes of Oregon scenes, which illuminated the Art Room.[88] Bruns's art and mosaic glass also may have embellished Portland's Seward Hotel, built in 1909.

The C. C. Belknap Glass Company was a leading glass firm in Seattle during the Arts and Crafts period. Their handsome 1920s promotional brochure for leaded art glass featured a watercolor-tinted cover depicting *The Crusader*, with illustrations of *The Sea Demon* and *The Siren* on the inside cover. The text reads: "The beautiful and original leaded art glass panels shown here were designed and executed in our art glass department. The lead is hand carved and the workmanship is true, sincere, and good. The glass is American opalescent, with colors carefully selected to obtain rich and pleasing harmony. The leaded art glass is the treasure of all of us and the aim of our creations is to introduce art in glass in your church and home."[89]

Raymond Nyson, who was a designer for Belknap in 1915, became foreman in 1916, salesman in 1921, and department manager in 1925. By 1929, he had established his own Nyson Glass Company. Three of the major works produced by him during his time at Belknap were the tulip stained glass ceiling at the Leopold Hotel in Bellingham, installed in 1923; the more classically inspired stained glass skylights of the Butterworth Mortuary Columbarium ceiling of the same year; and the Metropolitan National Bank in 1925.

Although a good portion of Nyson's work

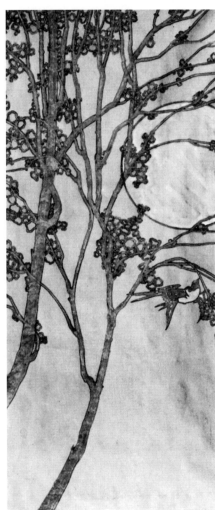

[above] Edward Bruns created some of the best regional expressions of the Arts and Crafts aesthetic in his art glass designs and installations, including this stair landing window in an Irvington, Portland, neighborhood home. Photograph courtesy of Michael McCary, McCary Art Glass (Portland).

[left] This Arts and Crafts stained glass design sketch by Edward Bruns was published in the *Portland Architectural Club Year Book* (1910).

occurred after World War I when the Arts and Crafts aesthetic was no longer in vogue with the general public, his work continued in the styles popular during the previous decade. In a collection of 182 colored presentation renderings, 25 drawings, and 150 miscellaneous sketches and cartoons related to stained glass work in the University of Washington's Special Collections, there are a number of Arts and Crafts designs reflecting Medieval, Art Nouveau, and Prairie School vocabularies in conventionalized flowers, landscape, and geometric treatments. Nyson's shop was responsible for supplying all the leaded glass and stained glass windows for a group of Norman and French-style apartment houses built by Seattle developer Fred Anhalt during the late 1920s.

[top] Raymond Nyson prepared watercolor-on-board presentation drawings, such as this stylized design for a window (c. 1925). Raymond Nyson Glass Company Collection. Special Collections Division, University of Washington Libraries (Seattle), UW 26456z.

[left] A color illustration of *The Crusader* was featured on the cover of the leaded art glass catalog of C. C. Belknap Company, Seattle. E. T. Osborne Collection. Special Collections Division, University of Washington Libraries (Seattle), UW 26458z.

Jones & Dillingham of Spokane was best known for its paints and stains. In fact, an ad for shingle stains said that the beauty of the bungalow depended largely on the stain used in its finishing: "A cheap stain gives a cheap effect. To get that rich, rustic, velvety appearance which is so much admired by Spokane architects and builders, use J & D Shingle Stains." However, they also advertised that they were manufacturers of leaded art glass.[90] One extant example of their leaded stained glass work is the Miss Spokane window designed and fabricated by the firm in 1912 for the Spokane Chamber of Commerce. It featured a Plateau Indian woman in a buckskin dress with her welcoming arms offering up the fruitful bounty of the Spokane region. The window was made in a characteristic Arts and Crafts style by John A. Scott, an employee of Jones & Dillingham.[91]

It was relatively easy to order beveled glass from catalogs by major manufacturers elsewhere in the United States and have the pieces shipped by rail in a matter of days. But there was a desire on the part of local homeowners, business managers, and civic leaders of the period to know the person doing the work, to perhaps have some input into the process, and to take pleasure in watching the work being created at a local shop.

The same was true for any of the varied applied arts, including pottery, ceramics, metalwork, and leather craft. Despite the infusion of national brands into the regional marketplace, there were still opportunities for Northwest artisans to produce fine craftwork, set up studios or shops, and attempt to find discerning clientele for their work.

The Miss Spokane window, commissioned by the Spokane Chamber of Commerce in 1912, was fabricated by the Jones & Dillingham Company. Northwest Museum of Arts & Culture, Eastern Washington State Historical Society (Spokane), 2962.24.

NINE
Handcrafted in the Pacific Northwest

"THE ARTS AND CRAFTS are more of an idea and a fad by far than they are a reality," said Frank Vincent DuMond, when choosing work for inclusion in the Fine Arts exhibit at Portland's 1905 Lewis and Clark Centennial Exposition.[1] Three years later, Miriam Van Waters, writing in the *Sunday Oregonian*, came to the same conclusion. She was narrating a history of the Arts and Crafts movement, including Gustav Stickley's efforts to establish arts and crafts organizations in rural areas where farm families could do handcrafts during the winter to supplement their income and also add beauty in their lives. Van Waters recognized that for the most part, the efforts of organizing Arts and Crafts societies in America had been concentrated in cities like Portland. These urban societies, she said, were usually composed of three classes of people: "Practical workers, men and women, who, after efficient training have entered the field of arts and crafts as a profession and really use their hands; sympathizers, who understand and appreciate the true craftsman spirit; faddists, whose perennial thirst for novelty leads them even to the unaccustomed field of work. The latter are worthy women, and lend social position to the movement, which, of course, counts for a good deal. Through these channels craftsman ideals have spread rapidly throughout the country."[2]

Except for the quality work and instruction of craft workers John Nelson Wisner and Roma J. McKnight, Van Waters did not know of anyone else in Portland at the time seriously inclined to take up handcrafts as a profession. "Pupils in general they have," she said, "but no apprentices. In the East the vitality of the movement is shown by the number of serious workers, or apprentices; when no serious workers are present, the movement is looked upon as a fad."[3] She concluded that because a great preponderance of the Arts and Crafts members were in the third class, Portland's Arts and Crafts movement should be described as faddish.

Notwithstanding the great number of quality architectural expressions of the Arts and Crafts movement and associated building trade arts, an overview of the applied arts production in the Pacific Northwest appears to support Van Waters' assessment. With a few notable exceptions, much of the metalwork, jewelry, leatherwork, china painting, textiles, and needlework was done by women of financial means. Many of the names of exhibitors and members of the Arts and Crafts Society of Portland, for example, could be found week after week in newspaper society columns: they or their spouses were usually involved in cultural and social organizations in the community. Catalogs and newspaper accounts of Arts and Crafts exhibits suggest that few exhibitors made a living from their handiwork. Many of those women produced quality work; most were given as gifts or kept within the family rather than sold. Others indirectly got involved commercially in the Arts and Crafts movement by overseeing shops that sold handicrafts. For several years the Arts and Crafts Society of Portland's retail outlet, the Shop of Fine Arts and Industries, was managed by several socially prominent women who also took metalworking and jewelry classes. Some of these Pacific Northwest artisans and craftspeople appear so frequently in exhibitions and news articles that they must have created a substantial body of work.[4]

Metalwork and Jewelry

Many people in the Northwest were exposed to handcrafted metal objects and jewelry through exhibits and demonstrations at both the Lewis and Clark Centennial Exposition in 1905 and the Alaska-Yukon-Pacific Exposition in 1909. Portland, Seattle, and Spokane either organized Arts and Crafts societies or found existing venues for hosting exhibits and workshops for those interested in trying their hand at hammering copper and silver or crafting jewelry in the new design styles sweeping America and the Northwest. Specialty crafts shops were opened, and some jewelry stores, art galleries, and major retailers began to carry hand-wrought metal goods of national and, to a lesser extent, regional artisans.

As early as 1906, John W. Graham & Company in Spokane advertised in the *Spokesman-Review* that it carried the New York firm Apollo Studio's high-quality copperware, in-

This assemblage of works in the applied arts is representative of the majority of pieces found in the Pacific Northwest. The items are not attributed and were most likely the product of interested amateurs or students, not professional artisans or craft workers. Lamp from Bill Henderson Collection; all other items from Mason Collection. Photograph by Hermon Joyner.

cluding candle stands, match stands, fern dishes, tobacco jars, and hand-beaten jardinières.[5] In 1908 Allen Eaton's store in Eugene sold Jarvie lanterns and candlesticks from Chicago.[6] From 1908 through the 1920s, Portland's Shop of Fine Arts and Industries regularly featured work from some of the most respected metal and jewelry workers in America, including Boston artisans George Gebelein, Frank Gardner Hale, Karl Leinonen, and Arthur Stone; Mildred Watkins of Cleveland; and Dirk Van Erp of San Francisco.

The first of the annual exhibitions initiated in 1907 by the Arts and Crafts Society of Portland highlighted the metalwork and jewelry of nationally recognized artisans, such as Elizabeth Copeland, Seth Ek, Mildred Watkins, Jane Carson, Gebelein, Leinonen, May S. Haydock, Adolphe C. Kunkler, L. H. Martin, Margaret Rogers, Arthur J. Stone, Maude Woodruff, Arthur Irwin Henessey, the Kalo Shop, L. B. Smith, and Florence A. Richmond.[7] That impressive lineup of participating craft workers derived from Portland's Julia Hoffman's close association with the Boston Arts and Crafts Society, and in particular her metalwork mentor and friend, George Gebelein. It had been Hoffman, following the success of the Arts and Crafts exhibition, who encouraged the Portland Art Association to bring Cleveland metalworker and jewelry artist Mildred Watkins to Portland for several months in 1907 to teach the first formal classes in metalwork in the city.

While the people of Portland may have had more opportunity to experience quality metalwork first-hand, other communities in Oregon and Washington were introduced to it through other means. Following the national interest, magazines such as *Popular Mechanics* and how-to books were quick to promote metalworking kits, enabling the interested amateur to set up a workshop in a back shed or basement. For these hobbyists, metalworking meant less investment in expensive equipment and tools. Metalwork also had the advantage of broad appeal. Women could craft wearable pieces of jewelry following instructions from their favorite women's periodical, while men hammered out their copper smoking set. Younger people, often receiving metalwork instruction at school through manual training classes, designed and handcrafted copper letter openers and desk pad sets as Christmas presents.

Despite the popularity of metalworking, there were relatively few practitioners in the Pacific Northwest who attempted to make a living from their craft, and only one, Albert Berry of Seattle, who achieved some national recognition. Because of Albert Berry's prolific output over a long period of time, as well as his unique designs, use of fossil ivory, and quality craftsmanship, many of his copper pieces have survived and are in private collections and museums as examples of some of the finest metalwork done in America during the Arts and Crafts period.

Born in England in 1878, Berry moved to the United States with his family at the age of ten. He studied at the Rhode Island School of Design in Providence and worked as a designer of gold and platinum jewelry and silverware at the Gorham Manufacturing Company in Providence, and at Tiffany's and at Frederick Keim in New York City. For health reasons, Berry moved to Fairbanks, Alaska, about 1905. There he met and married Erwina Jeanneret, a widow who had survived the loss

This repoussé copper picture frame showcases Albert Berry's metalwork talent. Thomas H. Wake Collection. Photograph by Barry Wong.

of most of her family in the 1906 San Francisco earthquake. Erwina was a needlework artist and a carver of ivory, making her a good artistic partner for Albert. She collaborated with him in some of his metalwork that incorporated fossil ivory. Her Alaska-inspired animal carvings were sold in Berry's shop along with his metalwork.[8]

The Berrys were fascinated with Northwest Coast Indian art and Alaskan fossil ivory. Inspired by his interests and experiences, he began to use his metalworking skills in Juneau in 1913 to create hand-hammered copper objects that often included Indian and Alaskan motifs and incorporated the use of fossil ivory. The bluish and earth tones of fos-

sil ivory blended well with the dark tones of Berry's hammered copper. Berry's Arts and Crafts Shop featured hammered and acid-etched copper bowls, vases, smoking sets, goblets, and lighting pieces. Many of Albert Berry's lamps featured cutout filigree scenes of Alaska landscapes, animals, or flora. His shop also featured handcrafted Alaska Native baskets and woodcarvings.

Albert and Erwina moved from Alaska to Seattle in 1918, establishing a retail shop and studio using the same name as the Juneau enterprise. It quickly became a stopping point for tourists and residents interested in handwork and Indian imagery.

In December 1921, Seattle's *Town Crier* did a profile of Berry's Arts & Crafts Shop:

> To admirers of the art of handcraft, the studio of the Berry Handcraft Shop is one of the most interesting places in the city. The shop itself, filled as it is with lamps, trays, desk sets, bowls, fire andirons, smoking sets, artistically designed jewelry and

[above left] Although this photograph of Berry was taken in his studio in Juneau prior to 1918, no doubt his workspace in Seattle would have looked much the same. The artisan is surrounded by the tools of his trade, design sketches, and in-process and finished work. Winter and Pond Photograph Collection (1893–1943). Alaska State Library Historical Collections (Juneau), ASL-P87-2435.

[center] An interior view of Berry's Arts & Crafts store in Seattle was published as an advertisement in the *Social Blue Book of Seattle, 1927–1928*. It is reported that Berry created the sketch for the curved-top stained glass installation in the background.

[left] Albert Berry's Craft Shop hallmark identifying work from his Seattle period beginning in 1918 is different from his earlier Alaska hallmarks. Thomas H. Wake Collection. Photograph by Barry Wong.

a host of other beautiful and unusual art objects, is fascinating, but the studio in the rear is even more so. Here the secrets of handcraft are made manifest—here the ideas are sketched, the designs executed.

Many of the motifs worked out in the shop's designs are inspired by the Indian legends of Alaska—an almost inexhaustible field for inspiration. How readily does fossil ivory lend itself to these legendary designs, blending perfectly with the silver, brass, copper and art glass used.

There is, at the Berry Handcraft Shop, a pervading atmosphere of artistry and good will, making one feel the truth of the old saying that "Art is the expression of a man's joy in his work."[9]

Albert Berry continued to work in Seattle in the Arts and Crafts style until his death on October 10, 1949. His wife operated the shop until her death in 1957, doing much of the ivory cutting herself. Two assistants did the copper designing originally handled by Albert Berry's brother, Wilfred Berry. Wilfred had been involved as a designer of copper pieces at the shop since shortly after the arrival of the Berrys in Seattle from Alaska. Upon the death of Erwina Berry, the business continued under the guidance of the Berry's bookkeeper, Hilda Hale, until the early 1970s.

Albert Berry's work compares favorably with that of the Roycrofters and other nationally known metalworkers of the Arts and Crafts period. His small, round hammer marks, flowing designs, and use of fossil ivory and regional motifs are executed with the highest quality workmanship. Unlike many of his colleagues on both a regional and national level, he was able to continue his work and make a living as a craftsman throughout the Great Depression, demonstrating the public's inter-

[top] This lidded, hammered copper cigarette box (post-1918) with a Northwest Coast Indian motif is typical of the work from Berry's Craft Shop in Seattle. The box lid is inlaid with semiprecious stones and fossil ivory. Thomas H. Wake Collection. Photograph by Barry Wong.

[above] This pair of copper bookends is decorated with Northwest mountain and tree motifs and inlaid with fossil ivory. Berry's Craft Shop, Seattle, post-1918. Thomas H. Wake Collection. Photograph by Barry Wong.

est in his work and willingness to buy artful objects even during tough economic times. Today, pieces of hammered copper with any of Albert Berry's several marks on them are still highly regarded and sought. The public's continuing interest in Native lore and quality items locally designed and handcrafted sustains a demand for Berry's work.

Among other Seattle area metalworkers who promoted their work were the proprietors of the studios of Ye Warder Shoppe and the Homecraft Shop, both operating c. 1909–1911. They produced lighting fixtures, but their other applied artwork in metal is unknown. Only Jessie Fisken was consistently mentioned in Seattle Arts and Crafts exhibit catalogs as showing copper and brass metalwork. She exhibited in both the 1904 and 1907 Allied Arts and Crafts shows in Seattle and was president of the Seattle Artists' Club during the 1911–1912 year. Examples of her metalwork have not been located, nor were her entries described in any detail when mentioned in media articles.

Two Seattle jewelry-related businesses have associations with Seattle's Arts and Crafts period. Albert Hansen, who advertised himself as a jeweler and silversmith in Seattle, displayed the sterling silver "Century Vase" from the Gorham Company of New York during the Alaska-Yukon-Pacific Exhibition in 1909.[10] Unfortunately, examples of Hansen's work have not been located. Joseph Mayer & Brothers (later Jos. Mayer) also was involved in jewelry and silverwork in Seattle. Their intent when they were established in 1898 was to develop the largest jewelry plant on the Pacific Coast. In addition to jewelry, the Mayer firm made several patterns of silver flatware and numerous souvenir spoons for which they were best known.[11] An exquisite four-piece silver coffee service in a hammered strap pattern, similar to that of San Francisco's Shreve and Company and the Wallace Company's Carmel pattern, bears a Mayer hallmark, along with the initials of one of the Mayer family members.

A company hallmark, the crossed pick and shovel with M and B initials on either side, relates to a long-favorite souvenir spoon and pin design referring to Alaska gold rush days and the interest in Alaska prompted by the A-Y-P Exposition a decade later. Several of their ring designs, again relating to Alaska and the Northwest, have a hammered silver look incorporated into portions of the band.[12] The company continued successfully until about 1945 when it was acquired by the E. J. Towle Manufacturing Company. Although some of the company's output was obviously done by hand, much of it was stamped. The firm's creativity in stamped work was in the design of the finished product.

Portland's Arts and Crafts Society, with its exhibits and metalworking classes, created a greater interest in hand-wrought metalwork and jewelry than was present in other Pacific Northwest communities. Prominent artisans included John Nelson Wisner, Roma J. McKnight, and Florence Knowlton. All three not only were metalworkers but also taught classes.

Julia Hoffman, one of Portland's most energetic Arts and Crafts proponents, was, herself, a skilled worker in metal, having trained under the instruction of George Gebelein in Boston. Several of her women friends of the same social standing, and a few of their daughters, including her own daughter, Margery, her daughter-in-law Caroline Couch

Burns Hoffman, and her niece Alice Robbins, also took an interest in artistic metalwork, frequently showing their work in regional Arts and Crafts exhibitions.

Two craftspeople from back East, Mildred Watkins and Frank W. Higgins, instructors associated with metalwork and jewelry classes sponsored by the Arts and Crafts Society of Portland and the Portland Art Association in the years 1907–1911, were both in Portland long enough to produce a body of work. Most of the early Arts and Crafts exhibitions in Portland included examples of their work, along with some of their students' pieces.

John Nelson Wisner was one of the most widely respected artisans working in the Arts and Crafts manner in the Portland area. A silver bowl made by Wisner and owned by a prominent Portland family, and a copper bowl made and lent by Wisner were among the few local pieces included in the loan portion of the Arts and Crafts Society of Portland's first Exhibition of Applied Art in 1907. Wisner was listed as a resident of Oregon City, a community a short distance up the Willamette River from Portland. An *Oregonian* review of the exhibit made note of Wisner's silverwork: "A hammered silver punch bowl, the property of Mrs. David Honeyman, is a beautiful piece of work which suggests the Tiffany ware from the iridescent tints. The bowl was the handiwork of Mr. J. N. Wisner of Oregon City, who is a cousin of Mrs. John McCraken." [13]

It is probable that one of the two bowls was the subject of a letter from Wisner to Henrietta H. Failing, curator of the Portland Art Museum, in response to her request for material to show in that first Arts and Crafts exhibition. Writing from Oregon City, he says:

[top] This hammered, sterling silver coffee service (c. 1915) was made by the Mayer Brothers Company of Seattle for a member of the Mayer family. Stephen and Cathy McLain Collection. Photograph by Barry Wong.

[above] This 3-inch-high pedestal-base silver bowl (c. 1910) is attributed to Caroline Couch Burns Hoffman, daughter-in-law of Arts and Crafts Society of Portland founder Julia Hoffman. Caroline Hoffman exhibited metalwork in several of the society's exhibits. Oregon College of Art & Craft (Portland). Photograph by Hermon Joyner.

The letterhead of John Nelson Wisner of Oregon City, dated September 1908. The intertwined initials may have served as his silver hallmark. Margery Smith Collection, Mss 2660. Oregon Historical Society (Portland), OrHi 105600.

As yet, by reason of the fact that my regular employment has given me little time, I have been unable to finish the bowl.

I have, however, taken action which will, I trust, give me ample time and if my plans carry I can finish the bowl in four or five days. I can at least make it presentable in that time unless I should attempt to do away with too many of the tool marks.[14]

By November 1907, Wisner had taken a studio at the former Lewis and Clark Exposition grounds and began teaching metalwork classes.[15] The preceding two months, Mildred Watkins of Cleveland had taught classes there through a joint venture between the Portland Art Association and the Society of Arts and Crafts of Portland.

In the 1908 Arts and Crafts exhibit in Portland, Wisner showed nine pieces of copper and brass work, including bowls and vases. In addition, several silver and copper pieces executed by him but owned and lent by others were exhibited. Again, the *Sunday Oregonian* singled out his work: "John Wisner, who conducted the Arts and Crafts school last Winter, in one of the buildings of the Lewis and Clark Exposition grounds, has possibly the largest collection. Notably artistic and original are his beautiful bowls of various metals, which nothing from the Eastern craft shops surpass in beauty of design or execution."[16]

Miriam Van Waters' article in that same newspaper issue cites John Nelson Wisner as one of the leading craft workers in Portland: "Mr. Wisner is an expert metal worker and many things of rare beauty have been turned out from his workshop in the Fair Grounds. His pupils have become skillful in hammering copper and silver. Most of them are socially prominent. Mr. Wisner has recently left Portland to set up a workshop in Oregon City; this is a blow to arts and crafts in Portland."[17]

Julia Hoffman, in a series of letters to her daughter, Margery, traces Wisner's work on a bowl that he was making for Margery as a wedding present for Margery's brother Lee Hawley Hoffman and his fiancée Caroline Couch Burns.[18] On March 19, 1910, Julia Hoffman writes about ordering silver from Gebelein in Boston "for the bowl the order for which I have given Mr. Wisner. This is an idea of the shape [drawing] . . . with a beautiful Greek fret carved on the straight side and the curved part fluted." In a subsequent letter dated May 9, 1910, Hoffman writes her daughter about Wisner's progress: "Wisner brought the bowl on the hill yesterday for me to see before he shaped it (he has it raised). It is larger than he & I planned but it is going to be cooking!"

Wisner must have finished the work on time, because Hawley and Caroline Hoffman's wedding gift registry contains the notation that Margery Hoffman gave them a "hand beaten" silver punch bowl.[19]

The exhibition review in the *Sunday Oregonian* of the 1910 Arts and Crafts exhibition exclaimed: "The most pretentious piece exhibited was a large silver bowl, exquisitely wrought, and a handsome tea service, creamer and sugar, the work of J. Nelson Wisner of Oregon City."[20]

The review of the next year's exhibition also highlighted work by Wisner: "Foremost of the metal workers is J. Nelson Wisner, whose work compares with that of the best silversmiths in Boston or New York. He is represented by a silver fluted bowl with a Greek repouse and a plain bowl striking in its simplicity of line and finish."[21]

Other than these few references, little else is known about Wisner and none of his work has surfaced to date.[22] By 1912 Wisner may have left the region. In a letter from George Gebelein to Julia Hoffman dated March 7, 1912, Gebelein expressed his regret that Wisner was no longer in the Portland area: "Mr. Wisner, having gone away, I hope some one else has developed into his work, so that you may have an ardent worker there continually."[23] Gebelein's reference to Wisner more than likely means that Wisner was known to the Boston metalworker, or at least that Julia Hoffman had often talked or wrote about Wisner when writing or visiting Gebelein. In any case, the correspondence reveals that both parties had great respect for John Nelson Wisner's talent.

With Wisner's absence, Florence Knowlton was the remaining Portland metalworker gainfully employed in the execution and teaching of her craft, and supplementing her income from her Arts and Crafts sales shop. Knowlton was born in 1872 in Freeport, Illinois. As a young woman she had the basement of her family home fixed up for a social club for boys ranging in ages from ten to fourteen. In an interview recorded in 1916, Knowlton said that since the boys were interested in woodcarving, she took up the craft. She explained that she had always been fond of handwork and had done needlework before that time: "When I came to Portland and decided to do something for myself I naturally turned to handiwork and my little shop is the outcome."[24]

The newspaper article went on to say: "The Fad for arts and crafts and handiwork of all kinds which sprang into popularity a few years ago is now successfully commercialized by a few artistic and enterprising women. Portland's representative in this very interesting line of endeavor is Miss Florence Knowlton, whose studio on 10th Street is the center of the arts and crafts work of Portland as well as the exhibit shop for specimens done by some of the leading arts and crafts artists of this and foreign countries."

Knowlton may have arrived in Portland from Illinois just before the 1907 Arts and Crafts exhibition. She had two pieces in that show, a silver bowl and a frame made of walnut and copper. A year later she showed several pieces of her handcrafted jewelry. Knowlton's pair of pierced silver candle shades and her fine jewelry were among the most notable pieces in the 1911 Arts and Crafts exhibition in Portland.[25]

For two years prior to her starting an Arts and Crafts sales shop in 1912, Florence Knowlton had a studio in Portland; she was listed in the city directories as an art metal worker. The *Spectator* mentioned Knowlton

Florence Knowlton was an accomplished metalworker and jewelry maker in Portland. She also taught classes and maintained a sales shop for art and craftwork until her death in 1945. *Oregon Journal* Collection, Oregon Historical Society (Portland), OrHi 105598. Photograph by Bushnell.

in a 1912 article, "Handicraft Work in Portland," which implied that she was a leader in the growth of the Arts and Crafts movement in Portland: "Miss Florence Knowlton, who for the past two years has had a workshop for hand wrought metal work, and has been conducting classes in this craft, is chairman of the circle of craftsmen. Under her direction and in connection with her shop, in the Marquam building tower, there has been opened a small salesroom, where the work of the handicrafts can be exhibited, and where those interested in having special designs worked out may be directed to the proper worker."[26]

Her realistic appreciation for the hard work that went into creating something by hand was apparent in her 1916 interview in the *Oregon Daily Journal*. The article demonstrated her multiple roles as a philosopher, a practitioner of handicraft, and an instructor:

"Fascinating, perfectly fascinating," is so often said by enthusiastic visitors [to her shop], after looking over a few fine pieces of handiwork. "I would love to do it," is a conclusive remark that often follows. It is fascinating, truly, but I often wonder if it is realized where the fascination lies. Surely nine out of ten of these enthusiasts would change their minds if they followed any good piece of handiwork from start to finish.

If it is a fine bit of jewelry being made up of many small parts, there are times when every single piece seems animated with a devilish imp of its own, that keeps it from staying in its place, or sends it hopping from the pliers into some corner of the work bench, so that every tool and tray has to be carefully moved in the effort not to lose it hopelessly. Or a tiny diamond will just disappear from under your very eyes and manage to avoid the generous apron that is swung underneath the bench for the express purpose of catching it.

Then, instead of proudly finishing a beautiful ring at the appointed hour, you are humbly sweeping your floor over and over again or even descending to all fours in an effort to catch the least gleam of encouragement, until you wonder why you care about such a small piece of carbon anyway, or why people ever wear rings.

There are parallel stages in all kinds of handiwork whether it is large or small, and there must be much more than the actual making of it to feel the real fascination or charm.

At least, in my own experience, it is only

after going back and realizing the part that handicraft has played in history, and the various and skillful ways the different peoples have used it to express their peculiar characteristics and ideas that it can take a strong enough hold to make one want to plod through the laborious processes of achievement.

At the same time, in becoming acquainted with the earlier work comes the realization of the inadequacy and superficiality of the greater part of the modern movement to revive the handicrafts. There are, however, a few master craftsmen who are also artists, and who, with the substantial undercurrent that is gradually deepening, will keep alive the processes and the interest until a generation or two hence, when there may be an age of less pressure and more time for artistic development.

Whether the present tendency to include so many of the handicrafts in every school curriculum is worth while, is hard to say. It is, in so far as it develops an intelligent appreciation of good work, or helps a boy or girl to decide whether their head or their hand is to be their greatest resource, or even provides what may be a recreation.

The average, or even superior worker who wishes to earn a living by his craft alone, must be prepared to take special training, to do a good deal of experimenting on his own responsibility, to be as patient as Job and withal to be content with a modest income.[27]

During the 1910s, Florence Knowlton's Arts and Crafts shop, later known as the Florence Knowlton Gift Shop, became an outlet for members of the Arts and Crafts Society of Portland. Several of her reports on the sales activity of the society's members are included in the School of Arts and Crafts Collection at the Oregon Historical Society. She continued

her business for thirty-three years until her death in 1945 at the age of seventy-three.

Roma J. McKnight, daughter of an early Oregon pioneer family, was prominent for a few years in the early days of Arts and Crafts endeavors in Portland as both an artisan and an instructor. She first exhibited some of her silver and copper items at the Arts and Crafts Society of Portland's 1908 exhibition. McKnight must have been teaching handicrafts by late 1906, however, since the correspondence between Julia Hoffman and Henrietta Failing of the Portland Art Association in early 1907, concerning bringing in an artisan in residence to teach metalworking classes in Portland, makes reference to her. Failing had tried to get McKnight to consider administering the proposed two-month summer workshop. It was noted that there might be an interest in such a class because "Miss McKnight has more pupils than she can accommodate in her little place."[28] Three days later, Failing wrote Hoffman again to tell her that Roma McKnight declined to undertake the organization of the class, citing McKnight's interest in going East. McKnight told Miss Failing that if she did not go East as planned, and Mildred Watkins came to Portland to teach, she would want to study with Watkins and "would not want to give any of that time to practical details."[29]

In her *Sunday Oregonian* article of May 1908, Van Waters named Roma McKnight as the other leading craft worker in Portland, besides John Nelson Wisner. After Wisner's departure to Oregon City, McKnight, Van Waters claimed, "rightfully occupies first place."[30] Trained in New York, McKnight specialized in design and jewelry making, though it was noted that she had a level of knowledge of the crafts in general. Her Arts and Crafts shop was mentioned as the one place in Portland where a person might get a glimpse of true art as the craftsman conceives it.

The *Spectator* chronicles Roma J. McKnight's Arts and Crafts shop activities from September through December 1908. Among the courses she taught at her school of Arts and Crafts associated with the shop was metalwork. Thereafter her business was referred to as the School of Art and Handicrafts. In September the article reported: "The business women who can spare Saturday afternoons are turning their attentions from matinees to the study of metal and leather work. Miss Roma McKnight, director of the School of Art and Handicrafts . . . has quite a large class of business women each Saturday afternoon who are busy in the making of Christmas gifts both in the metal and the tooled leather."[31]

After December 1908, McKnight no longer advertised in the weekly, and there were no further references to her shop. She may have curtailed her retail business because of competition from the Arts and Crafts Society of Portland's new salesroom, the Shop of Fine Arts and Industries, which opened in November of 1908 and offered many of the same types of merchandise. In the *Sunday Oregonian* of May 9, 1909, it was announced that Roma McKnight was closing her Arts and Crafts shop in order to spend the summer in the Orient. She planned to reopen the shop in October of that same year.

The Portland city directories list McKnight in an importers and craft-workers business with Mrs. R. R. Bartlett in 1910 and 1911. From 1913 through 1915, Roma McKnight was listed as a teacher. By 1916, none of the McKnight family members were listed in the Portland directory.

Mildred Watkins and Frank W. Higgins were skilled craft workers who came to Portland as short-term instructors in metalworking and jewelry. Their classes were popular and well attended. Watkins, from Cleveland, was the better known of the two. A year after her two-month metalworking workshop in 1907, the *Spectator* mentioned her visit to Portland as she prepared to return to Cleveland after a several-month stay with one of the community's Arts and Crafts supporters, Mrs. M. A. M. Ashley:

> It is her intention, however, to return next spring, bringing with her other members of her family, and to make her home permanently in this city. Miss Watkins is one of the best known craft-workers in the country, and is an artist of rare ability. Some of her beautiful work is at the Shop of Fine Arts and Industries. . . .
>
> Miss Watkins' work was first made known to the Portland public through the Arts and Crafts exhibition at the Art Museum. The charm of her designing and the excellence of the workmanship made many friends, who have followed her course with interest. It will be a decided acquisition to the craft fellowship of Portland to have Miss Watkins as a permanent resident.[32]

Watkins did not relocate to Portland, but continued to send work to the annual exhibitions and to sell in the Arts and Crafts Society's retail shop. She also exhibited at the Alaska-Yukon-Pacific Exposition in Seattle in 1909, winning a major medal for the excellence of her jewelry and metalwork. Probably upon her return trip from the exposition, she again took time to visit Mrs. Ashley. Once more the *Spectator* sang her praises: "Miss Mildred Watkins is the clever girl who did so much toward making arts and crafts work popular in Portland, and in doing so became very popular herself. She left Oregon with much reluctance, and promises to return in the near future."[33]

Frank W. Higgins, another craftsperson from the East Coast, was present in Portland from time to time probably due to his acquaintance with Julia Hoffman and her connections in Boston and with Mildred Watkins, under whom he had studied. Hoffman mentioned Higgins several times in her correspondence with her daughter in 1908 and 1909. While visiting Boston in January 1909, Hoffman wrote that Frank Higgins was going to take a bench in the shop that George Gebelein was going to open. In that same letter, she mentioned that Higgins went to Salem to help Mr. Little in a boys' class in metalwork at the YMCA.[34] A month later she wrote her daughter again from home, saying that Frank Higgins wanted to come to Portland for a summer school and was making plans accordingly.[35]

As his planned arrival drew nearer, Julia Hoffman expressed concerns: "This morning I remained in town and am busy trying to get things arranged for Frank Higgins. We are to have the rooms at the Fair Building—I said we—I meant he—but we are all working for him & people here said they want to study or work with him but you can never tell. I don't want him to expect too much."[36]

Late that summer, the Arts and Crafts Society of Portland announced the Arts and Crafts School of Metal Work, under the instruction of Frank W. Higgins, to be held on

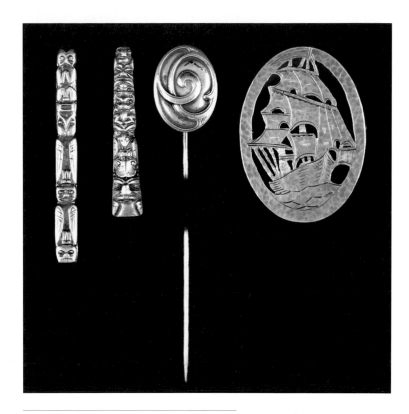

Most of the vintage sterling silver jewelry found in the Northwest is not marked; it was probably made by students or accomplished amateurs. Many pieces are done in universal, stylized designs, but the two totem pins (c. 1920) are distinctively Northwest Coast Indian in style, similar to stamp work produced by Mayer Brothers, later Joseph Mayer Company, in Seattle. Mason Collection. Photograph by Hermon Joyner.

the former Lewis and Clark Centennial Exposition fairgrounds. The notice claimed that Higgins was a former member of Amy Sacker's class in design and a pupil of Mildred Watkins, Mrs. Jane Carson Barron, and George C. Gebelein. The fall term was to open on November 1, 1909. The metalwork shop was to be open from 8 a.m. until 6 p.m. and instruction was to be given three half days of the week on Monday, Wednesday, and Friday. The tuition was set at $10 a month or $1 a lesson; bench room was $5 a month.[37]

In 1910, the *Spectator* noted that Higgins's School of Metal Work class was well represented in an Arts and Crafts exhibit with a variety of interesting work, among which was a gold ring set with a diamond and rubies made by Ida Scoggin.[38] Two weeks later it was reported that, "The school of metal work under Frank L. [sic] Higgins is rapidly increasing in numbers and interest."[39] Jewelry was one of the most popular expressions of Arts and Crafts design, and the work exhibited by Higgins's students, most of whom were women, was no exception. Of the sixty-five objects exhibited by fourteen of his students, more than half were rings, brooches, pins, or buckles.[40]

Unfortunately, like so many of his Portland contemporaries, no examples of Frank Higgins' regional metalwork or jewelry output have been located bearing his mark or with provenance strong enough to attribute the work to him.

Very little evidence of professional-level metalwork from the period has been found in Pacific Northwest communities outside of Seattle and Portland. Spokane, one of the few exceptions, evidently had some classes being taught, as Julia Hoffman's sister, Deenie Robbins, and her niece, Alice, were involved in metalwork there. Both sold pieces of their work, although neither was doing handcrafts full-time.

The letters that Margery Hoffman Smith saved from her mother's frequent correspondence to her while in college are some of the best primary sources relating to regional Arts and Crafts work. While visiting her sister and niece in Spokane in 1908, Julia Hoffman wrote about her observations of the metalwork being done in that eastern Washington city: "You never saw anything more backhanded than the way in which they were doing their hammering. . . . Alice has made a dear little pin (silver). She seems to do that

very well, but she doesn't apply herself. They do seem helpless."[41]

Hoffman's professional training and aesthetics got the best of her, and a week later she wrote: "I simply had to stay & get these people started. We are in the shop every day. It's good fun, too. . . . I have taught Aunt Deenie all I knew about metal."[42]

Alice Robbins came to stay for a while in Portland with her aunt Julia to take metalwork lessons from Frank Higgins. She must have been a good student: one of her pieces, a bonbon dish, "beautiful and rich in appearance," was illustrated in the 1910 Arts and Crafts exhibition review article in the *Sunday Oregonian* as one of the pieces that "excited favorable attention."[43] The article also mentioned a copper fernery entered by Alice Robbins.

An undated letter from Alice Robbins, probably from Spokane, c. 1910, to her cousin Margery Hoffman gives considerable insight into the realities of economics and effort of producing handcrafted items for sale. From the letter, one can assume that Margery was acting as an agent for Alice by taking orders from her college classmates at Bryn Mawr in Pennsylvania:

> I am sending you the extra candy spoon that you wanted right away. I will have the bowl and spoon ready to send off either tomorrow or next day. I couldn't get it ready any sooner as I guess you know I have to send away for all my silver and it takes from 5-6 days to get an order back here. The spoon to the bowl is finished but I thought I would send them together. I will have your pin and probably a belt buckle ready by the end of the week.

Marge, [I] will make [you] a bargain: all the orders you get for me you are to take a percent say 20% as that is what I have to give to the guilds; at least I think its so. Please don't get any ring orders as I've had beastly luck with the four that I have made and anyway there is more money in pins, spoons (all silverware), buckles, etc. I don't think I'll tackle another bowl as the silver cost me $10 and I couldn't ask more than $15 for it, and talk about working. Your Mother said I should get $5 a day for my work and it has taken me over a day already and it's not finished yet. The silver is heavy and hard to hammer up.

The silver in the spoon cost me $1.10 a piece and as it took me a good half of the day to make each one I think they ought to be worth $2.50 or $2, don't you? All the candy spoons that I have priced here in the jewelry stores are . . . generally $3 to $4.50, and very lightweight bonbon dishes $15 & up.[44]

Julia Hoffman, herself a trained and accomplished metalworker of the period, frequently exhibited her own work and pieces from her collection of handicrafts by other craftspeople she admired. There is no indication that she sold her work, so Miriam Van Waters would have put her in the second and third classes of those supporting the Arts and Crafts. However, more of Hoffman's work has survived than that of any other Portland metalworker of that time. If the quality of work of her contemporaries compares at all to her surviving pieces, then Portland's output must have been quite impressive.

Passages from Julia Hoffman's letters between 1907 and 1911 provide valuable first-hand insights into working in metal, even if only on a recreational level:

This footed silver bowl, 2½ × 9 inches, is attributed to Julia Hoffman (c. 1910). Oregon College of Art & Craft (Portland). Photograph by Hermon Joyner.

Have had an interesting morning re metal work. Some bowls in process—3 stages that may be used by Mr. Wisner in an illustrated talk to Arts & Crafts.[45]

This morning . . . I worked in my shop . . . polishing Hawley's brass box that I gave him for Xmas & the silver bowl that I intended for the Taylors but it has been so much work & we have no large piece for ourselves, so I thought I would keep it until I have something made. That polishing is the dirtiest work possible. I look like Stokes after it.[46]

I am trying to get the little silver pitcher finished that I have been working at so long.[47]

I'm in my shop every day. Did I tell you I had to finally give up the silver pitcher that I labored with after the acid ate it too thin to stand the flame? So it goes into the scraps.[48]

One other metalworker with connections to the region was Clara P. Barck, founder of the Kalo Shop in Chicago. Barck was born in Oregon in 1868, but relocated to Chicago in

Family tradition attributes this silver compote with red carnelians to Julia Hoffman, c. 1910. But "Douglas Donaldson, 1927" is inscribed in the foot. Donaldson came to Portland from California several times to teach design and metalworking. Perhaps Hoffman and Donaldson collaborated on the piece. Oregon College of Art & Craft (Portland). Photograph by Hermon Joyner.

the 1890s to study at the Chicago Art Institute. Originally focusing on leatherwork and weaving, the Kalo Shop began to move toward metalwork after Barck's marriage in 1905 to George Welles. Within a year the Kalo Shop was already well known for its quality silver, copper, and jewelry work.

Clara Barck Welles's family ties to Oregon may have accounted in part for her willingness to lend Kalo art metal to Portland's first Arts and Crafts exhibition in 1907. Prominent families in the Northwest, such as the Louis Davenports of Spokane, acquired hammered Kalo silver for its aesthetic beauty and functional household use. In the Davenport collection, there were several beautifully handwrought silver items, with a raised stylized "D" on each piece. The family story is that Davenport gave his wife a piece of Kalo sil-

ver each year for several years after their marriage in 1906.

Pottery and Tile Work

By 1910 many people in Oregon and Washington had been exposed to some of the finest art pottery being produced in America. Examples from the Newcomb Art Pottery, J. B. Owens Pottery Company, and from S. A. Weller had been shown at the Lewis and Clark Centennial Exposition in 1905. The Women's Century Club's Arts and Crafts exhibit in Seattle in 1906 included examples of Teco and Van Briggle pottery. The 1907 Arts and Crafts exhibition of the Portland Art Association featured examples of Marblehead, Dedham, Rookwood, Volkmar, Newcomb, Van Briggle, Teco, and Grueby—many lent from Portland families. A year later, at the first annual exhibition of the newly formed Arts and Crafts Society of Portland, more Grueby, Van Briggle, Dedham, and Marblehead pottery pieces were on loan for public view.

Porcelain vases, mainstays of Victorian decorative arts that filled most every curio cabinet in parlors throughout America in the nineteenth century, began to decline in favor of the newer Arts and Crafts design and craftsmanship ideals at the turn of the century. Porcelain, fragile and often overly decorated with flowers or sentimental scenes, gave way to art pottery (pottery being a generic term encompassing earthenware and stoneware) that was hand-shaped and crafted. Designs for individual pots and vases produced during the Arts and Crafts period in America were often simple, unadorned forms, or were based on nature-inspired motifs. Stylized renderings of animals and birds, landscapes, river and seascapes, lotus and other flowers, were typically used, whether incised, painted, or otherwise shaped by hand in the pottery-making process. Although some potteries and potters still produced hand-painted pottery, many more created incised, molded, or otherwise shaped pieces.

As with other artistic creations from this period, art pottery and, later, tile, most often contained colors found in nature: browns, greens, yellows (particularly ochres), the orange reds of clay, and blues. Surface glazes varied from matte to glossy, and retained the sense of the handwork. Each piece was individually crafted and was as distinctive as any other work of fine or applied art. Most often pieces were signed by the artist as well as identified as from a particular pottery or tile company. It was the philosophy of the individual artisans, working on a pot all the way through the creative process from molding the clay to pulling the pot from a kiln, that defined art pottery, rather than particular styles or techniques. Work was deliberately produced to be artistic, not necessarily commercial. Ironically, the popularity of art pottery resulted in companies commercially creating similar looking pieces using molds, rather than each being individually shaped by the artist, in order to satisfy demands of the market.

The popular appeal of art pottery and tile, which reflected the characteristics of other decorative arts during the period in approach to design, color, shape, and motif, was evident by their inclusion in exhibits and expositions as well as their increasing availability in shops and galleries, even in the Pacific Northwest.

A newspaper ad in 1907 for John W. Graham & Company in Spokane informed the public: "More Teco pottery just in. . . . This is the only store in the city where this ware is sold. Look for the name engraved on the bottom of each piece. All others are imitations. When you select a piece of real Teco pottery as a gift you can feel positively certain that your selection will be accepted with most hearty approval by the recipient; and should you buy for your own home use it will be a worthy purchase and one that you will never regret. That pale, flower-stem green color of Teco ware is so pleasing to the eye and harmonizes so beautifully with all flowers and decorations in a home that one never tires of it."[49]

Allen Eaton's store in Eugene by 1908 also was carrying Teco, along with Grueby, Newcomb, Rookwood, Van Briggle, and Pewabic art pottery lines.[50] As early as 1903, the Washington Fixture & Mantel Company in Seattle was selling Grueby pottery and Rookwood pottery table lamps as well as tiles from those same companies. William W. Kellogg later offered Rookwood pottery for sale in his display rooms in the Moore Theatre building. The major department stores in Seattle, like Frederick & Nelson, carried art pottery in their high-quality decorative arts and gift departments.

Despite the public's exposure and interest in art pottery, few craftspersons in the region worked with clay during the first fifteen years of the twentieth century. And it was not for the lack of local raw materials. Utilitarian earthenware made from regional clay, primarily crocks, jars, butter churns, and jugs, had been made at various sites in Oregon and Washington since the 1860s. Places like Buena Vista, Oregon, and Mica and Clayton in eastern Washington provided the clay for sizeable productions of utilitarian pottery. Fine clay deposits stimulated the making of products of terra-cotta by the Northern

More Teco Pottery Just In...

This Is the Only Store
In the City Where This Ware Is Sold

Look for the name engraved on the bottom of each piece. All others are imitations.

When you select a piece of real Teco pottery as a gift you can feel positively certain that your selection will be accepted with most hearty approval by the recipient; and should you buy for your own home use it will be a worthy purchase and one that you will never regret.

That pale, flower-stem green color of Teco ware is so pleasing to the eye and harmonizes so beautifully with all flowers and decorations in a home that one never tires of it.

Call and inspect our interesting display. We have handsome pieces at **50¢**, **$1.00**, **$2.00**, **$5.00**, **$10.00** and upward. Clifton Pottery Tea Pots, in green and grays, **$1** to **$2.75** each. Mexican designed Tea Pots **75¢** to **$1.75** each.

**Art Store
Upper First Floor**

[top] John W. Graham & Co.'s ad for Teco pottery appeared in the December 8, 1907, issue of the *Spokesman-Review* newspaper in Spokane. Products of most of the nationally known pottery companies could be purchased in the larger towns of Oregon and Washington.

[above] Along with their more traditional utilitarian ware, the Standard Stoneware Company displayed several pieces of art pottery at a fair in Spokane, c. 1901. Northwest Museum of Arts & Culture, Eastern Washington State Historical Society (Spokane), L87-1.502.

Clay Company in Auburn, Washington. More than likely, the contributing factors for so little local Arts and Crafts pottery were the absence of experienced teachers of the craft, the expense of owning and running a kiln, and the challenge of situating a kiln so it would not pose a fire danger.

Besides the ornamental tile from Washington Brick, Lime & Sewer Pipe Company of Clayton and Spokane, two other Northwest pottery companies produced decorative pottery in familiar Arts and Crafts shapes and glazes. An early photograph of the Clayton Pottery Company's exhibit at the Spokane Interstate Fair (c. 1901) shows several artistically shaped vases designed for decorative arts purposes, not utilitarian kitchen use. The other regional business that manufactured a simple design line of art pottery in a light green glaze was the Pacific Stoneware Company of Portland.

Pacific Stoneware Company's primary product was utilitarian ware, but the company must have had some interest in work that mirrored the popular art pottery being produced elsewhere in America. The Arts and Crafts Society of Portland sent a notice to its members in 1914 about a planned visit to "the Pacific Stoneware Company, makers of pottery."[51] In 1915, Pacific Stoneware made several large jars and vases with green, blue, brown, and gray glazes, along with red and tan clay pots, designed by Florence Knowlton of Portland and Mrs. Allen H. Eaton of Eugene. These pots were part of the Art Room in the Oregon Building at the 1915 Panama-Pacific International Exposition in San Francisco. In addition, Thomas Mann, president of the stoneware company, donated a number of sconces with blue and gray glazes for use throughout the room.[52]

As the Portland Art Museum's Art School added faculty and a greater variety of programs, pottery grew in popularity. Helen Putnam, an art instructor at the school, presented a studio lecture, "Pottery: An Illustration of the Control of Design Thought Process" in 1915: "Through the courtesy of the Pacific Stoneware Company, there will be a demonstration of the use of the wheel in making pottery, and the lecture will be illustrated by pieces of pottery of various periods, from the primitive Indian forms to modern wares."[53]

In a 1917 exhibit review of work by students of the art school, the *Oregonian* noted that the pottery was particularly interesting: "One of the bowls is completed by a lively lizard modeled to hold the flower stems in the bowl. The pottery made by the children is so full of naivety and the pleasure of expression that it makes the beholder smile involuntarily."[54]

Four days later another article on the exhibit in the *Sunday Oregonian* mentioned that Leta Kennedy, Miss Halverson, and Clara Manny had designed some distinctive pottery.[55] By 1922, Leta Kennedy, a former student of the museum's art school, had joined the faculty.

The whereabouts of Arts and Crafts pottery produced by students, particularly young women, at Oregon Agricultural College in Corvallis remains a mystery. Photographs in the college's promotional materials from c. 1915 to 1925 show students molding pots by hand, with examples of finished, artistically designed and crafted pottery sitting on work tables and windowsills. The July-August 1924 issue of *Design: Keramic Studio* included an

Although Pacific Stoneware Company of Portland was known primarily for its heavy crockery ware, the firm did produce several vase forms and sizes (c. 1915–1920) with glazed finishes in various shades of green and blue that were very popular for floral arrangements. Collections of Stephen and Cathy McLain and Lawrence Kreisman. Photograph by Barry Wong.

intriguing photograph captioned "Oregon Agricultural College, Corvallis, Oregon, Pottery Exhibit—Instructor, Marjorie Blatzell." There was no accompanying text.

Among the few Arts and Crafts period potters in the region, although only here for a brief period, was Olive Newcomb (1875–1935). Her work first appeared in the Northwest when included in the *Catalogue of Fine Arts Gallery and Exhibit of Arts and Crafts, California Building, Exposition Grounds, Seattle,* for the Alaska-Yukon-Pacific Exposition, 1909. Newcomb was listed under the exhibitors from the College of Fine Arts, Los Angeles. She showed four pieces, including two

The College Girl at O.A.C., published c. 1915 by Oregon Agricultural College in Corvallis, included a photo of students making fine pottery.

ceramic vases and a tile. In a review of the December 1911 exhibit of the Arts and Crafts Society of Portland, the *Sunday Oregonian* reported, "Pottery, although in its infancy as a local craft, is of more than ordinary excellence. Miss Newcomb, Miss Hult and Miss Harmon all show pleasing articles."[56]

A reference to Olive Newcomb in a 1952 letter written by Allen Eaton, who had just visited his old hometown of Eugene, provided a clue about her time in Oregon. Writing of his nostalgic visit to his old house, Eaton says: "[I] went down to see the owners of the little board-and-batten house I built for Olive Newcomb, the potter, soon after we moved out to Fairmount [a residential district close to the University of Oregon]. And I am still making myself believe that one of the principal contributors to this house is the big brick chimney I designed and helped lay up for Olive Newcomb."[57]

Newcomb's cottage still stands. Imbedded in the fireplace hearth are three tiles done by Newcomb. Other tiles are still present in and around the house, including designs of children at play, animals, landscapes, and prose. Several tiles are polychromed and glazed. Others are not. Three large scarab paperweights with her mark of an "N" within an "O" are also on site. The current owners of the house indicated that a kiln was originally located on the lower level.

A search of Eugene city directories shows her listed for 1914, living with her mother, Katherine Newcomb, a widow. There is speculation that she may have been an instructor at, or somehow involved with, the University of Oregon. A check of the university's faculty listings for that period did not uncover her name. However, several of her smaller tiles bear the logo of the University of Oregon, perhaps designed as promotional or fundraising items. In 1915, Newcomb's work was included in Allen Eaton's installation in the Art Room of the Oregon Building at the Panama-Pacific exposition. Listed in the catalog were two tiles, one of a castle design and the other a landscape.[58]

Newcomb's influence on Eaton's wife's artistic endeavors is evidenced by Cecile Eaton's entry of a landscape tile in the Oregon Art

Room at the Panama-Pacific International Exposition, plus another reference in a letter written by Allen Eaton in 1947. In his annual Christmas letter "To the Dear Ones Whom It May Concern," Eaton writes: "I intended to tell you of a few of the things in the attic, things I love to be around . . . a beautiful blue pottery jar that Cecile made in Fairmount."[59] The neighbors, Allen and Cecile Eaton and Olive Newcomb, must have enjoyed working in clay together, using Newcomb's kiln to fire the pieces. One of the tiles in the Newcomb house bears a mark with the initials of Cecile Eaton.

By 1918 Olive Newcomb was back in southern California on the faculty of Los Angeles High School. After several years teaching art there, she joined the faculty at the Chouinard School of Art, Los Angeles, as a pottery instructor, c. 1929–1933.

Other references to regional pottery of the era include a mention of Marjorie Noble's blue vase exhibited in the joint Arts and Crafts Society of Portland and Portland Art Association exhibition in 1915. It was described as "lovely in color and . . . of good design."[60] Portland craft workers sent materials, including pottery, to an exhibition of Arts and Crafts in the rooms of the Seattle Fine Arts Society that same year.[61]

In an undated newspaper clipping (c. 1911) from Seattle, an item discusses pottery making after the installation of a kiln in Queen Anne School. Twenty-five works of pottery from the girls at the school were exhibited in William W. Kellogg's tile and pottery art rooms in downtown Seattle. The article mentioned that all of the pieces shown were entirely built by hand without using a potter's wheel.

[top] *Road to Newcomb House* (c. 1914–1916), by Olive Newcomb. Tile, 4¾ × 3⁵⁄₁₆ inches. The drive to Newcomb's Eugene house, still extant, looks like her early design. M. & M. Krenk Collection. Photograph by Hermon Joyner.

[above] *Castle* (c. 1915), by Olive Newcomb. Tile, 9 × 9 inches. One of the tiles Newcomb exhibited at the Panama-Pacific International Exposition (San Francisco, 1915) in the Oregon Art Room was listed as a castle design. M. & M. Krenk Collection. Photograph by Hermon Joyner.

The paucity of Arts and Crafts pottery workers in the Northwest in the first two decades of the twentieth century seems surprising, given the number of high-profile studio potters working in Oregon and Washington from the 1960s to the present. The absence of much pottery, however, is more than compensated for by the abundance of other types of ceramic work, such as hand-painted china.

China and China Painting

China painting was a popular artistic expression in the Pacific Northwest in the late nineteenth and early twentieth centuries. Most of the state and country fairs and art exhibitions included china painting as a category. Regional newspapers usually listed the names of prize-winning exhibitors, most often women. How-to books on china painting were common, and women's magazines often included new china painting designs. Periodicals, such as the early issues of *Keramic Studio*, were published almost as trade journals, keeping china painting enthusiasts current on modern trends. Local stores sold china blanks (ready-made fired clay pieces surfaced with a fired neutral glaze), patterns, and paints for china artists; or if the china painter lived in a rural area, supplies could be ordered by mail from a number of companies back East.

Coinciding with the arrival of the Arts and Crafts movement in Oregon and Washington, the pictorial and naturalistic designs, often floral, that were so popular in the late Victorian era, gave way to what were called conventional or stylized designs. Following Charles Locke Eastlake's philosophy that an attempt to copy nature was only a poor imitation of the real thing, china painters began to work with two-dimensional, geometric, abstracted or conventionalized designs that are now widely associated with American Arts and Crafts style. Art Nouveau and emerging modern design influences were also popular with china painters. Art Nouveau designs were based on abstractions of organic forms, often characterized by flowing lines and curves. The modern style that was later called Art Deco was even more geometric than the simplified patterns of Arts and Crafts designs. These three styles were all receiving attention around 1915, the high point of the popularity of china painting in the Northwest, prior to American entry into World War I.[62]

The new trends in china painting designs in Portland were mentioned in a 1909 issue of the *Spectator*. The brief article described what one could see in the studio of Mrs. Edwin A. Smith, including a "choice assortment of hand-painted china": "The pieces represent the realistic, the conventional, and semi-conventional styles. 'The realistic style is quietly giving away to the conventional and semi-conventional,' said Mrs. Smith, 'yet the former will always be good for the large Belleek vases, while the latter are the more appropriate for plates and bowls.'"[63]

Ironically, many of the Northwest's early china painting instructors continued working in the naturalistic style, often years after the public's taste had changed to the more popular conventional designs. The surviving work of two of the best-known teachers, Mary E. Steele of Spokane and Jeanne M. Stewart of Seattle and later Portland, often features floral designs. Steele was listed as a china artist and instructor of china painting in the Spokane city directories from 1900 through 1920. Stewart showed some of her china painting at the Alaska-Yukon-Pacific Exposition in 1909.

By 1914, she was living in Portland and teaching china painting at her studio in the Pittock Block.

Jeanne Stewart was well known to the editors of *Keramic Studio*, and she often advertised in that publication. She also sent in original designs, some of which were printed in the journal, including a naturalistic design for a plate she called "Thimble Berries." By 1922, *Keramic Studio* featured an ad for a series of one dozen monochrome studies for china painting for $1.50. Included in the list of choices were several of Stewart's designs with titles that related to the natural flora and fauna of the Pacific Northwest: "Wild Grapes and Wild Roses on Vase"; "Bowl in Blackberries"; "Fernery in Toadstools"; "Currants on Stein"; and "Sea Gulls on Pitcher." She also had her "Blackberries" design featured in the November 1923 issue of *Keramic Studio*.

Along with artistic needlework, china painting instruction was among the most frequently appearing subjects in regional newspaper ads and city directory listings for Arts and Crafts activities. In Spokane, for exam-

[top] As the Arts and Crafts aesthetic became more accepted, stylized designs replaced the floral patterns popular for late nineteenth-century hand-painted china. Many of these new patterns introduced c. 1900–1920 became a mix of Arts and Crafts, Art Nouveau, and, later, Art Deco design motifs. Mason Collection. Photograph by Hermon Joyner.

[above] China painting was one of the most widely practiced decorative art expressions of the American Arts and Crafts movement. Mason Collection.

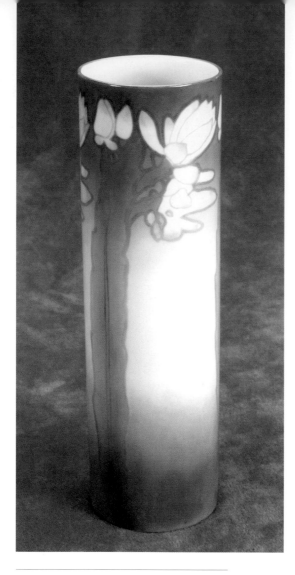

Vase by Lillian Seufert Rice (1911). Hand-painted chinaware, 10 inches high. Rice (1882–1976) was born in The Dalles and moved to Portland in 1907. She became well known for her fine ceramic painting and exhibited frequently. This vase has the appearance of some of the vellum finishes of Rookwood and other major art potteries. Mason Collection. Photograph by Hermon Joyner.

ple, Mary E. Steele was accompanied by Mary Gamble, Luella A. Russell, Lena Eddy, Mrs. A. Hobart Baker, Jones & Redfern, Florence I. Davis, Mrs. S. L. Weygant, and Olive L. Farwell as practitioners and instructors of artistic china painting during the first two decades of the twentieth century. According to Spokane city directories, Farwell also ran the School of Art and Handicraft in Spokane, c. 1908–1914, while Weygant was providing instruction in her Weygant School of Art from 1907 to 1909.

As in other communities, Spokane hand-painted china was shown at local fairs and exhibits. Awards for professional china painting exhibited in the 1901 Spokane Interstate Fair went to Mrs. George Rhodehamel, Miss Chideater, and Mrs. J. Martin, and awards for amateur china painting went to Katherine Brown, Mabel Wilson, Mr. and Mrs. George H. McConnell, Nettie S. Hanauer, Mrs. C. O. Donason, Mrs. William Nelson, Mrs. C. G. Brown, and Mrs. E. L. Kimball. Lena Eddy of Spokane exhibited china painting in the Arts and Crafts exhibit held by the Spokane Art League in 1903.

Portland's china painters, and china painting in general, received considerable attention at the Lewis and Clark Centennial Exposition in 1905. In a display of women's handiwork in the gallery of the Oriental Building, more than a dozen showcases held fine examples of decorated china and needlework. An *Oregonian* article mentioned a case full of work from members of the National League of Mineral Painters, including a large Florentine vase executed by Mrs. D. M. Campana, the author of many how-to china painting booklets of the period, and a conventional plate of a peacock design by Evelyn Beackey: "But some of the best decorative work on porcelain has been accomplished by our home artists. The case of china of the Oregon Ceramic Club is a credit to that organization. Mrs. F. A. Routledge has a vase with thistle design in bronze luster, and a stein in copper. The conventional work by Miss Minnie Parker is also excellent. . . . Mrs. Alexander Muir's Dutch stein is unique, and the coffee set by the same artist well executed."[64] The article also mentioned the work of Annabelle Parrish, who helped set up the National League of Mineral

Painters' exhibit, Mrs. Pope of Oregon City, and several other exhibiting women china painters.

The Oregon Ceramic Club, sometimes referred to as the Oregon Keramic Club or the Portland Ceramic Society, was founded c. 1904 in Portland. *Keramic Studio* quoted a 1910 letter from the club's secretary, Mary D. McGinnis: "We are making a fight for original work and find your magazine a great help in our trouble. . . . The Oregon Keramic Club is six years old with eighteen members, ten of whom are working members. Every December we hold an exhibition and sale and this year's was the most successful of all, with more visitors and press notices than heretofore." [65]

The following month, *Keramic Studio* showed a few of the original designs by the Portland Ceramic Society: "It is a creditable lot, for a first showing. . . . Another year we hope to be able to show another lot of designs by its members and are sure they will show a marked advance in every way after such a good beginning." [66]

Even though many of the women associated with china painting in Portland were also members of the Arts and Crafts Society of Portland, relatively few examples of hand-decorated china were included in the society's early Arts and Crafts exhibitions. Seattle, on the other hand, seemed to more openly embrace the work of china painters in their shows. The first exhibition of Allied Arts and Crafts held by the Women's Century Club in Seattle in 1904 featured the local china painters Sara A. Hanna, Mrs. A. G. Hastings, Miss E. R. McIntyre, Anna Beach, Bessie Louise Beach, and Susan B. Wilson.[67] The club's 1905 exhibition again contained a "keramic display," with work from Mrs. Hazelwood, Ella Shep-

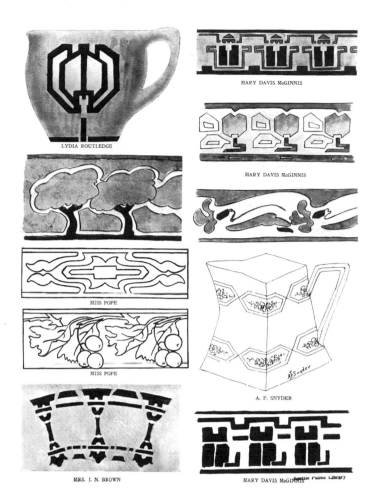

Stylized designs submitted by members of the Portland Ceramic Society were featured in the June 1910 issue of *Keramic Studio*. All the designs were by women active in regional china painting and its exhibitions. Routledge and Pope were the two best known artists.

ard Bush, Mrs. Bevans, Miss Wilson, and other exhibitors.[68]

A review of the 1906 Arts and Crafts exhibition by the Women's Century Club stated: "There is much that is really superior in the painted china and Seattle is happy to have so many artists in this line. The arrangement of Miss Nellie J. Hazelwood's work was such that it is more clearly and easily seen than most of the others, and certainly it was work before which one would linger long. The pieces displayed as the work of Franz A. Bischoff are lovely and have attracted much attention." [69]

A month earlier, an exhibit of the ceramic work of Bischoff, a nationally celebrated artist and china painter from California who was teaching classes in Seattle, had been held at the studio of Ella Shepard Bush. *Weekend* encouraged the public to attend, "to be able not only to see examples of his work, but to enjoy his own demonstration of his methods." [70] At the close of his classes, before he returned to California, *Weekend* again made mention of his time in Seattle: "His Keramics are exquisitely beautiful, painted from life in rich, limpid colors of his own manufacture, and to see him at work producing his charming effects is delightful. Seattle is particularly fortunate in having enjoyed so rare an opportunity." [71]

The 1909 Alaska-Yukon-Pacific Exposition's Women's Building exhibit of the handiwork of women of Seattle and the state of Washington included a large number of china painting entries. The *Catalogue of Fine Arts Gallery and Exhibit of Arts and Crafts* listed items exhibited in the California Building, including 143 pieces of hand-painted china submitted by members of the San Francisco Keramic Club and 15 examples from the Los Angeles Keramic Club. Eight examples of the work of Mary Leicester Wagner of Santa Barbara also were listed. [72]

The Pacific Coast China Company of Seattle won a decorative arts award at the A-Y-P Exposition for its display of hand-painted china. The company was the major regional supplier of white china blanks, paints, brushes, and all other materials needed for the china decorator. As the following nationally circulated ad indicated, the company also held classes to further encourage the use of their wares: "Wanted, A First Class Teacher of unquestionable ability to take charge of our Classes in China Painting. Must be able to do Conventional and Naturalistic Work. Write fully what experience you have had and what you can do. Pacific Coast China Co., 905 Third Avenue, Seattle, Washington." [73]

The Oregon Ceramic Club continued to hold periodic exhibitions of members' work. The *Sunday Oregonian* of May 27, 1917, contained a review of one of their shows: "In the Keramic exhibit there are several tables showing beautifully decorated china and porcelains. In the absence of French china, the Satsuma and the Beleek . . . are used by the club decorators. A gem of the collection is a bowl in Wedgwood blue with luster lining and conventional design in gold and silver outline in black, done by Mrs. Routledge." The article described a tiny vase and a fern dish in "smart design" done by Elizabeth S. Buck, and listed several of the china painters "who deserved mention," including Mrs. L. Pope of Oregon City, Nellie Lehman, Genevieve Barnes, and Mrs. T. T. Geer. Most telling, though, of the future of china painting was the phrase "in the absence of French china." [74]

By the time the United States entered World War I, the china painting craze began to decline. European imports, including whiteware blanks and supplies that American china painters used, were no longer accessible from Germany and France. That fact, along with a spreading art elitism, led to a drop in the popularity of china painting. Because so many of the practitioners of china painting were women, the issue of gender bias caused some to regard the work as inferior to some of the fine arts or more accepted handicrafts such as metalwork and pottery. In addition, women who relied on china painting for a livelihood were faced with an unavoidable reality: the time it took to produce a single piece of hand-painted china did not equate with a marketable price on the finished product.

Adelaide Alsop-Robineau, the talented potter and publisher of *Keramic Studio*, in a personal and emotional editorial in 1913, addressed her frustration at being a woman artist at that time:

And now what are we going to do about the domestic problem, those of us who have homes and children and husbands and still feel called to follow the lure of art? For four long weeks, the editor has been struggling with the mysteries of breakfast, lunch, dinner, sewing on buttons and darning, sweeping and dusting and otherwise trying to cling to some shreds of decency and order in her household while a two hundred and fifty dollar order stands, needing only a few hours to finish and suspended ideas in porcelain are fading in the dim distance and others are crying to be put in execution. This is a periodical discipline that never fails as a chastener and the periods are coming with momentarily lessening intervals. If only some good whole-souled woman with a love for art but talents only in the way of caring for a household and children would have the inspiration to take the home in charge and make it possible for the artist to devote her entire energies to doing something worth while in her art, heaven would have come upon earth, and, between you and me. The honor of the artistic achievement would belong to her almost as much as to the artist herself. It is because of the children and the home that we cannot and will not give up that the woman can never hope to become as great in any line as man. Art is a jealous mistress and allows no consideration whatever to interfere with her supremacy.[75]

Pair of candlesticks (c. 1922), by Helen M. Beecroft, Everett, Washington. Hand-painted chinaware, 4¾ inches high. Mason Collection. Photograph by Hermon Joyner.

Although there was some high-quality painted china work and instruction in Oregon and Washington in the 1920s, such as the fine conventional designs executed by Helen M. Beecroft of Everett, Washington, and the efforts of Keramic Studios and Miss Woodward's Lavergne Studio, both of Seattle, china painting became more a hobby than an accepted part of arts programs.

As part of a last-gasp effort to sustain the china painting business in the Northwest, the Cascade China Company was formed in Portland c. 1922 to produce chinaware from Oregon clay brought from the Molalla region and other districts around Portland. This effort was probably in direct response to the general unavailability of white china blanks then from post-war Europe.

A public exhibit in 1923 introduced the pub-

Vase (c. 1922) by Bess Sheperd, Portland. Hand-painted chinaware on a Cascade China Company blank, 8½ inches high. Sheperd was one of several competent china painters engaged by the Cascade China Company of Portland in the 1920s in an attempt to rekindle the interest in china painting that began to wane after World War I. Mason Collection. Photograph by Hermon Joyner.

lic to sample promotional wares of the Cascade China Company, announcing that the production had developed to the point where articles manufactured by the plant soon would be available for sale in one of Portland's department stores. The company president, H. C. Elliot, reported, "Experts have inspected the Portland product and said that it would compare favorably with some of the highest grades of china."[76] He also mentioned that pieces already produced had been hand-decorated by a group of Portland china painting artists. The company lasted in name through 1928 with art ware and semivitreous table and restaurant ware listed as their specialties.

Examples of signed, hand-decorated Cascade China Company art ware that have been found include a paperweight by Lydia (Mrs. Fred) Routledge and vases decorated by Nellie G. Lehman and Bess Sheperd. Although the company existed less than five years, the quality of its chinaware and of its artists is among the highest of the region.

Textiles and Needlework

Weaving and needlework decoration are among the oldest traditional arts. Weavers for several millennia have woven wool into clothing, blankets, rugs, and other useful necessities. Artistic needlework as a means of creative expression is a long-practiced tradition, especially among women. In America, woven coverlets, embroidered quilts, towels embellished with needlework designs, and pillows for every room and use have prominently displayed the handiwork artistry of the household's occupants.

Of the types of handwork done during the Arts and Crafts period in the first part of the twentieth century, needlework was probably the most common. Major factors in the popularity of art needlework in an Arts and Crafts style were the prolific number of women's periodicals, specialized needlework magazines and books, and the advertising of companies that produced thread, materials, patterns, and whole kits of the latest in the Arts and Crafts textiles market from 1900 on into the 1920s. Needlework, like no other handicraft, had no boundaries in appeal or practice. Patterns were inexpensive or sometimes free when issued as promotional items by periodicals, department stores, or art needlework shops. And domestic arts training classes of the period in schools across America stressed nee-

The use of Arts and Crafts textiles was a popular way to decorate bungalows and Craftsman homes of the period. Mason Collection.

dlework as an important life-long skill that all young women should learn, not only for its practicality, but as a way to creatively make their homes more beautiful places to live.[77]

Art needlework designs in the Arts and Crafts movement essentially went through the same evolution as hand-painted china, from naturalistic, floral, or scenic designs to conventional, stylized, and geometric designs, and to some degree curvilinear designs. Surviving textiles in stylized and geometric designs are widely accepted today as especially representative of the Arts and Crafts period. Many of the hand-embroidered textiles were created from kits that contained the pattern, fabric, and embroidery thread. Even though the design was already determined, the mere act of hand embroidering the stenciled pattern into something beautiful for the household was an important part of the Arts and Crafts philosophy.

Pacific Northwest imagery was most often accomplished through individual expressions of creative design rather than use of the more generic needlework kits. Commonly, needleworkers might embroider the name of a city or college on a pillow and add an image or logo associated with the subject. An embroidered pillow with a cherries design, for Salem, Oregon, a city known for its cherries, is an example. Another pillow that plays with the theme of rain in Oregon and Washington shows a frog under an umbrella. The potential designs and motifs are endless, and many regional examples have survived. One example was written up in the *Spectator* in 1908: "Mrs. E. H. White of the Original Needlecraft Shop . . . is showing a fine display of soft pillows ornamented with the 'football' emblem of the colleges and of the Multnomah Athletic Club."[78]

Since so much of embroidery work on textiles during this time was done at home for personal use, few surviving pieces are signed. Often it is only through the provenance of family history that an Arts and Crafts textile's needlework artist is known.

Yet an extensive list of women, along with

The Arts and Crafts Society of Portland began to teach loom weaving after Julia Hoffman arranged for the acquisition and shipment of the several looms in the early 1920s. Hoffman is said to have woven this textile (c. 1920s) herself on one of those first looms, which were originally sited on her property. Oregon College of Art & Craft (Portland).

Oregon's woolen mills were well known by the turn of the twentieth century. In fact, two of the five major companies competing nationally for the Indian trade blanket market were from the Northwest.[83] Oregon City Woolen Mills was established in 1864, and the Pendleton Woolen Mills was founded in Pendleton, Oregon, in 1896. Even though it was one of the latest mills in the business, Pendleton has become synonymous with American Indian trade blankets. The American Indian was the market and design inspiration for many of the blankets produced during the Arts and Crafts period. Oregon City and Pendleton made an effort to weave blankets in a variety of colorful and striking patterns to compete in both the Indian as well as the non-Indian market. Many of the designs were improvised versions of traditional Native designs. Pendleton's 1910 catalog features a full-color illustration of a woman in an Arts and Crafts interior sitting on a couch covered with a Pendleton robe: the ad is a suggestion for decorating a bungalow with this colorful American Indian woven motif. Pendleton's regional competitor, the Oregon City Woolen Mills, established retail operations in Portland, Tacoma, and Oregon City, as well as in San Francisco, Oakland, Denver, and Minneapolis, for selling their blankets during the early part of the twentieth century.

Pyrography

Pyrography, or the branding or burning of designs into soft wood or leather, was a common pursuit in the applied arts during this period. Most pyrography was done by burning through stencils with a heated iron instrument similar to a soldering iron to create designs without much individual artistic input. Like needlework kits, pyrography kits were popular and readily available.

The *Oregonian* of April 19, 1907, contained an ad from Woodard, Clarke & Company illustrating their boxed pyrography kit for sale. The Portland firm declared that burning on wood or leather was a simple art, easy to learn, referring to it as "artistic work done by beginners." Potential buyers were encouraged to watch a demonstration of pyrography in the store's window, then go inside and buy a kit for $1.50 and up. Wood, stamped ready for burning designs, could be had for as little as five cents.

Many of the pyrography kit assemblages were done up and given as gifts. Like art needlework projects, the pyrographic embellishment of boxes, plaques, frames, and other items, while often not the original design of the craftsperson, still embodied the Arts and Crafts spirit of creating beautiful things by hand. Leather kits were also available for doing burnt work. Pyrography kits could be purchased by mail order through many of the women's periodicals of the day, craft-related magazines like *Popular Mechanics*, and from most department stores and Arts and Crafts specialty stores.

Not all of the pyrography was done with kits. Some of the finest examples were obviously designed by the maker, and often included presentations or other personalized information in the design and execution of the finished project. Many were done on "found" pieces of wood or wooden cigar boxes in a kindred connection with what is considered American folk art. More and more, early twentieth-century folk art is being accepted as the creative expression of an individual seeing beauty through their own eyes, not necessarily caring about how the item may be perceived by others.

On rare occasions, examples of pyrography made their way into regional Arts and Crafts exhibits. One of those occasions, the A-Y-P Exposition, encouraged the entry of pyrographic work as representing a component of handiwork that Washington women could pursue for profit or pleasure.

Leatherwork

The hand tooling of leather was perceived to be in the applied arts hierarchy and was readily accepted into the mainstream of Arts and Crafts work. The *Spectator* made several mentions throughout the second half of 1908 of Roma McKnight teaching leather-tooling classes in her School of Art and Handicrafts in Portland. That same year Ada F. Elder included a class on leatherwork in her Pacific School of Arts and Crafts curriculum.[84]

Regional Arts and Crafts exhibitions pre-

Pyrography kits were available even in rural communities. Ella Parrett Smith, who lived on a farm in Yamhill County, Oregon, burned this small, lidded box as a Christmas present for her sister in 1909. Collection of Crystal Dawn Smith Riley Foundation (Newberg, Oregon). Photograph by Hermon Joyner.

sented the work of nationally known leatherworkers to the Northwest, and later included work of regional leather artists. In the first Arts and Crafts exhibition in Portland in 1907 that featured Boston area artists, Amy M. Sacker showed two leather mats that were tooled and colored. The following year, Roma McKnight entered six pieces of tooled leather. Eight other Portland craftspersons exhibited at least one leather item in the 1908 exhibition.

In the 1910 Arts and Crafts exhibition in Portland, leatherwork exhibitors included the Campañeros of Santa Rosa, California; Rose and Minnie Dolese of Chicago; Fanny V. Cross of Malden, Massachusetts; and Bertha and Ellen Kleinschmidt of Berkeley, California; along with local handicraft workers Lily Fox, Miss F. G. Crocker, Mrs. T. T. Geer, Florence Knowlton, and others. One reviewer was intrigued by an entry by one of the Kleinschmidt sisters: "a wallet decorated with green and purple thistle which exquisitely blends in tone with the leather."[85]

At the A-Y-P Exposition in 1909, Mrs. A.

Often created as gifts, Arts and Crafts leatherwork took the shape of book covers, portfolios, purses, wallets, desk pads, and other functional objects. These pieces, featuring stylized period designs, were created by students at Oregon Agricultural College (c. 1920s). University Archives, Oregon State University (Corvallis), P189.

H. Foote of Seattle won a grand prize for her tooled leather. Seattle craft worker Anne M. Holmes won a gold medal for her leatherwork. In addition to the Compañeros from Santa Rosa and Charles Frank Ingerson of San Francisco, who both won gold medals, exhibitors showing artistic leather goods in the California exhibit of Arts and Crafts included the Kleinschmidt sisters, O'Hara & Livermore of San Francisco, and the fine work of Elizabeth Eaton Burton of Santa Barbara.[86]

The *Spectator* announced in its November 20, 1909, issue that the salesroom of the Arts and Crafts Society of Portland was showing exquisite work in leather, done by and under the instruction of Mrs. Ripley of New York, one of the finest American artists in leatherwork.

The medium of leather was extremely popular in the Northwest during the Arts and Crafts period. The quality of the out-of-region leather artists exhibiting work in Portland and Seattle was very high. And the listing of regional leatherwork entries was frequent in various exhibitions. In addition, numerous classes in leatherwork were available, and many local stores sold tooled leather goods as gift items.

Basketry

Many families collected regional Indian baskets, appreciating them for their pureness in material, design, and fabrication, as well as their inherent aesthetic beauty. One of the most-used books in the personal library of Julia Hoffman, the inspirational leader of the Arts and Crafts Society of Portland, was a copy of George Wharton James's *Indian Basketry*. Hoffman, like many others in Oregon and Washington, appreciated Native American handmade objects that demonstrated exquisite design composition and quality craftsmanship. One room in Hoffman's Portland home was full of her collection of Indian items, including Klamath Indian baskets acquired from tribal members during her visits to the Klamath Falls area of southeastern Oregon.[87]

Craftsman magazine, Seattle's own *Bungalow Magazine*, and other popular periodicals of the early twentieth century espousing the Arts and Crafts movement commonly featured illustrations of house interiors decorated with Indian baskets, rugs, pottery, and other Native American items. To meet that market, shops selling what they described as "relics and curiosities from primitive races who are fast disappearing" became commonplace throughout the Northwest. Many Native women on Washington and Oregon reservations supplemented their income by making baskets for the tourist trade. Both the Lewis and Clark Centennial Exposition and A-Y-P Exposition featured the display and sale

[top] While not all Native American art collections were as extensive as the one in Judge Thomas Burke's Seattle home, Indian baskets were desirable decorating elements for many bungalow and Craftsman house owners. Washington State Historical Society (Tacoma), 14513. Photograph by Asahel Curtis.

[above] The eclectic wares of Paul's Curio Shop in Portland accommodated the popularity of American Indian objects in the early part of the twentieth century. Items from Northwest Indians were sold along with Native materials from elsewhere. Ashford Collection. Oregon Historical Society (Portland), OrHi 28881.

of Indian baskets and other Indian goods. In Seattle, the Washington State Federation of Women's Clubs was the enlightened organization behind the gathering of women's work of all sorts, including Native American, for inclusion in the Women's Building exhibit at the A-Y-P Exposition. A 1908 newspaper article indicated that arrangements were being made for an exhibit of the baskets and beadwork of the Indian women of Washington and that a portion of the building would be assigned to such work.[88]

As a result of public interest, basket making in both Native American and early East Coast traditions, such as Shaker and Appalachian, became extremely popular handicrafts, because baskets served both functional and decorating purposes. Basket weaving was introduced into the schools as part of domestic and manual training programs. Illustrated how-to books were popular, and many people followed easy step-by-step instructions to create their own baskets. Arts and Crafts–inspired businesswomen of the period who ran schools of instruction taught basket making.

Baskets were often exhibited in Arts and Crafts shows in Seattle, Spokane, and Portland. In Portland, the Raffia Club of basket makers was formed, and they exhibited their work as part of the 1908 Arts and Crafts exhibition: "The Raffia Club has a collection of baskets [that] receives much notice. The peculiarity of this work is the original method of the workers, who endeavor to do all their own coloring and as far as possible to use native materials."[89]

For the Art Room of the Oregon Building at the Panama-Pacific International Exposition, Allen Eaton selected a Native Grand Ronde Indian hazel wood market basket to be exhibited, along with other baskets crafted by Cecile Eaton of Eugene, Florence Knowlton, John Boeker of Hillsboro, and Mrs. Hall from Wendling, Oregon.

Julia Hoffman's sister, Deenie Robbins, wrote several letters from either Spokane or Bellingham during the period from 1922 through 1925 about her work in basketry. The correspondence reveals some idiosyncrasies of working in that medium:

Lately I am working at my basketry. Now I find I have to sort of work out the principles and rules I learned in class. Miss Druse used to tell us after we had worked at it three years we ought to turn out a good basket. I sent and got a very good book on reed basketry and I get lot of help from it. . . . Do you know of any good fast-colored raffia? It is discouraging to put a lot of work on design and then have it fade out in a year or so. . . .[90]

I want to tell you too the photograph of Margery's basket came a few days ago, and I have a basket nearly finished. But I must tell you Miss Druse said, "You can never make two baskets just alike." I am trying to get it as nearly as possible from the picture for I don't remember exactly how hers was shaped, and then I am trying to shape it somewhat by trying milk bottles in it and you said to not make the mouth too narrow.[91]

I sent another basket yesterday, a gathering. I forgot to put the price on. It should bring $5.25. The 25 [cents] pays for the shipping. Then the Arts and Crafts take the one and send me the four. Will that be right? They should get enough out of it to pay me four. But I will have to take what they can sell it for.[92]

What Rank Shall We Give It?

Miriam Van Waters, concerned that the regional Arts and Crafts movement might be little more than a fad unless some serious workers emerged, concluded a 1908 article with a positive note: "Summing up the Arts and Crafts Movement, what rank shall we give it? Is it merely a reversion to a past [expression] of culture, by sentimentalists who are ever ready to bemoan the past, or does it possess some vital modern spark that gives it a right to be called progress?"[93] In her understanding of the movement, she agreed that it represented much-needed reform and, if done carefully and with sympathy, could lead a person to the true spirit of work and happiness.

For hundreds of individuals in Oregon and Washington in the first quarter of the twentieth century, the personal experience of creating beautiful things by hand became an important part of their lives. There may have been only a few who worked in an aspect of the Arts and Crafts movement over an extended period of time and made a livable income. But countless others found, perhaps for the first time, that they had the ability to create, and received a sense of fulfillment, validation of self-worth, and a chance to express their creative selves. Those positive attributes went a long way in creating the true spirit of work and happiness to which Van Waters referred.

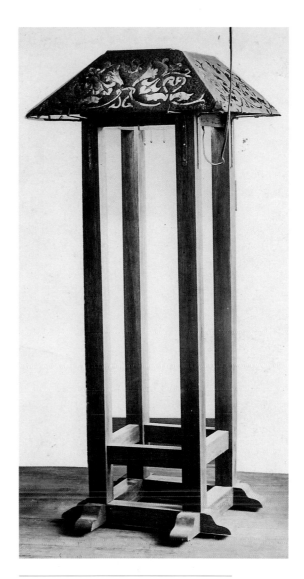

Craft workers, whether professional or amateur, were enriched by the experience of creating handiwork, a direct benefit and precept of the Arts and Crafts movement. This postcard of a Mission style floor lamp was sent as a Christmas greeting (c. 1912). On the back, the artisan proudly wrote, "One of my recent efforts." Mason Collection.

PART IV Regional Artistic Expressions

TEN
Painting and Printmaking

ALONG WITH APPLIED ARTS, during the first two decades of the twentieth century the fine arts were influenced by Arts and Crafts aesthetics. Classes in design, painting, sketching, drawing, illustration, print making, and poster art were commonplace during the period. In Washington and Oregon (perhaps because of the economic imprudence of spreading too thin an immature art community and its patrons to support many different art education schools and courses), classes in various arts and crafts were often taught side by side with fine art classes of figure drawing and painting. It was not unusual to see the signature of an early Northwest artist on both an oil painting hanging in a museum exhibition and on a hand-painted piece of china.

Paintings were exhibited in the Northwest not long after the immigration of predominantly Euro-American settlers in the 1840s and 1850s. Responding to a more family-oriented environment than many areas of the American West, early colleges in

Cedar Swamp (c. 1920), by Elizabeth Colborne. Color block print on tissue, 12 × 8¾ inches. The image evokes the mystery of the primeval Northwest forest. Dodge/Kreisman Collection.

In a Spokane studio (c. 1908), a woman works at her easel while the young girl paints chinaware. Northwest Museum of Arts & Culture, Eastern Washington State Historical Society (Spokane), L84-324.

Oregon and Washington offered classes in art and art history. Local, regional, and state fairs exhibited paintings by Northwest men and women along with needlework, fruit, animals, and oversized squash. Late nineteenth-century industrial expositions in Spokane, Tacoma, Seattle, and Portland, held in the name of progress and accomplishment, included fine arts exhibit categories. These exhibits reaffirmed the local board of trades' posturing about their cities being progressive rather than provincial backwaters. Spokane's North-Western Industrial Exposition in 1890, hosted to celebrate the rebuilding of a "modern" city in less than a year after a disastrous fire had destroyed most of the downtown, devoted most of the third floor of the exposition building to an art exhibit. The show featured over 250 oil paintings and watercolors, many by eastern Washington artists.[1]

In 1882 Seattle artist Harriet Foster Beecher was listed as faculty member of the University of Washington's art department. She offered instruction in oil and watercolor painting, crayon work, freehand drawing, and sketching from nature. In 1882 the Seattle Art Association was organized. Across the state, the Spokane Art League was formed in 1892. Walla Walla organized an art club in 1898.

Several Oregon art organizations were founded in the late nineteenth century, including the Portland Art Club (1885), Oregon Art Association (Portland, 1895–1898), and the Portland Sketch Club (1895). Willamette University in Salem had offered art classes since the 1850s.[2]

Throughout the 1890s and during the first part of the twentieth century, women's clubs and organizations were established in many Oregon and Washington communities, large and small. They encouraged, among other things, an appreciation for art and culture and championed social reform. By the time Arts and Crafts ideals reached the Northwest, fine art was an accepted element of modern community goals.

Although art was being created in the Northwest, it may have suffered from the regional remoteness of the artists. *Pacific Monthly*, published in Portland, carried an article by W. E. Rollins in 1898, "Art and its Possibilities in the Northwest." Known for his marine paintings, Rollins was a member of the Sketch Club, one of the city's active art organizations at the time. He wrote: "The condition of art at the present in the Northwest is not encouraging. The commercial, the social, and the pessimistic feeling that exists here is chilling to every effort on the part of the struggling artist. Yet to those who remain here better times are coming. A new era is about to dawn. Surrounded as we are by these eternal and beautiful truths, we shall awaken to their meaning. We shall learn in time to appreciate and love them. Then there shall be born an Art for the people,—by the people,—an Art fed, plentifully and freshly from the glorious possibilities of the great Northwest."[3]

With the arrival of the Arts and Crafts movement to the Northwest, the next decade saw a tremendous change in Rollins's observations, whether founded in fact or not. The Lewis and Clark Centennial (1905) and the Alaska-Yukon-Pacific (1909) Expositions pro-vided the impetus for artistic communities in both Oregon and Washington to organize and show off their work. Many groups that would exhibit had already developed infrastructure, exhibit schedules, and marketing strategies. By 1910 Portland had an art association with an active school and an art museum. In 1908 the Society of Seattle Artists became the Seattle Fine Arts Society, formed to show to Seattle people what their town contained of artistic value, and to bring to notice those struggling artists who were doing good work in the city. In addition, the group aspired to cultivate an interest in and taste for fine art through such programs as exhibitions and educational programs. Spokane started a museum with an emphasis on art in 1916.

In 1912 the University of Washington established its College of Fine Arts, followed in 1914 by the founding of a Department of Architecture. In Eugene, the University of Oregon had been offering art instruction in its curriculum years before it officially opened its School of Architecture and Allied Arts in 1914. Private schools and art courses were being started throughout the region in many communities, such as the Cornish School of Art in Seattle. In both states, most of the normal schools for training teachers offered art appreciation and design classes. In 1912 the Holy Names Academy and Normal School in Spokane, conducted by the Sisters of the Holy Names of Jesus and Mary, advertised, along with their accredited normal department, studio instruction in oil, watercolor, and keramic painting.[4] Other colleges in the communities of Salem, Forest Grove, Tacoma, Walla Walla, Salem, Newburg, and Ashland also offered art classes at some level.

Students interested in advanced art training and studies were encouraged to go East, and also to Europe. Visiting artists and instructors from eastern schools influenced local students to enroll at their respective institutions, such as the Art Students League of New York, the Art Institute of Chicago, and the Pennsylvania Academy of Fine Arts.

As the level of regional art instruction rose and competency grew, many young people elected to train near home at the Portland Art School associated with the Portland Art Association and its art museum. By the beginning of World War I, student enrollment was increasing in art programs at the University of Washington and the University of Oregon.

Many of the Northwest's art instructors in the early twentieth century were themselves young artists. Some were enamored with the Impressionist style of painting, which had originated in France during the final quarter of the nineteenth century. Impressionism, with its emphasis on attempting to capture light on canvas through the vibrancy of color, brush strokes, and the blurring of hard edges, fit well into the Arts and Crafts vision about the beauty of nature and natural forms and the aesthetic power of landscape. Some of Oregon and Washington's younger painters believed in a close relationship between the Impressionist style and the rich palate of the Northwest landscape. Many painters worked *en plein air* (outdoors), quickly and loosely capturing on canvas their impressions of the Oregon coastline, Cascade mountain peaks, or cityscapes. Their method was not aimed at catching a photographic image, but at capturing the color and vibrancy of the moment as it played out in nature. Even the portrait work of these local artists frequently employed soft lines and bright colors. These *plein air* painters of the Northwest, while not technically Impressionists, adopted some of the methods and artistic sensibilities of their European predecessors and California counterparts.

Painting in Oregon

Work with an Impressionist tendency began to be painted and shown in the region as early as 1904 when New York painter Childe Hassam visited Oregon. Noted for his Impressionist paintings resulting from his extensive study in France, Hassam was invited to Oregon for a painting trip by his friend Charles Erskine Scott Wood of Portland. Wood was a man with a fine appreciation for art, and was an influential and vocal arts patron in Portland. He was an extremely complex person who seemed to be able to do anything he attempted and do it well, and he was an accomplished amateur painter. After arriving in Portland in 1904, Hassam traveled with Wood throughout Oregon, to the Willamette Valley, the eastern Oregon desert, the northern Oregon coast, and into the Cascade Range of both Oregon and Washington. The two often painted landscapes side by side, in the outdoors. Hassam also painted several portraits and views in and around Portland. In 1908 Hassam returned to Oregon, intending to spend much of his time in the Harney Desert country of the eastern part of the state.[5]

Following an exhibition of his paintings in 1908, a group of art patrons pooled resources and made the first purchase of a Hassam painting for the Portland Art Museum. The piece was one of his eastern Oregon paintings, *Afternoon Sky*. A local weekly had given high praise to the Hassam exhibit: "It is the sincerity of the artist which first strikes one. These are pictures, but they are also very nature, and nature in one of her most direct moods. The dry air of the desert region is responsible for much of this feeling, and the large open spaces and clear atmosphere, giving rigidity of outline and great distinctness of vision, are most ably interpreted."[6]

The Lewis and Clark exposition in 1905 offered Northwest art lovers an opportunity to see some of the best work from America and abroad, including not only the Old Masters and French Impressionists, but also the more contemporary art of the time. The exposition may have served as a catalyst for Oregon's maturing artistic community by exposing it to new international expressions, including paintings by Impressionist painters such as Claude Monet, Mary Cassatt, and Camille Pissarro. The credit for assembling what was heralded as the greatest exhibition to date of "world class" artworks rests entirely on the curatorial efforts and personal vision of Frank Vincent DuMond.

DuMond, who was retained by the Lewis and Clark Centennial Exposition administration as head of the Fine Arts Department, had been teaching at the Art Students League of New York since 1892. He had married Helen Savier, an artist from an old Portland family, in 1895, and as a result became well-known in Portland. He involved himself in Portland's art community by agreeing to speak at or teach for various art groups when in Oregon visiting his wife's family. Julia Hoffman, a primary spokesperson for Arts and Crafts instruction in Portland, hosted DuMond in her home studio in the mid-1890s where

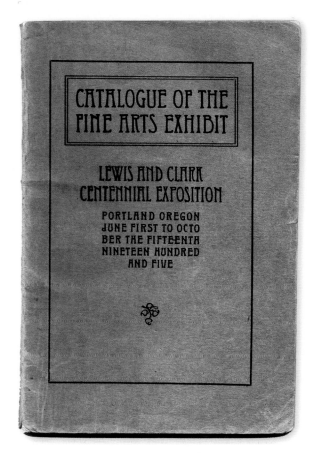

The Lewis and Clark Centennial Exposition (Portland, 1905) brought to the Northwest some of the finest American and European art ever assembled in a single exhibition. Mason Collection.

he taught classes. His presence encouraged some of Oregon's aspiring young artists to attend the Art Students League, where he became a mentor to many.

DuMond took on an ambitious curatorial mission for the Lewis and Clark exposition. He set out to provide an educational overview of the history of art over the previous 200 years, and he was very strict in his selection process. He was adamant about having complete curatorial decision-making authority. Most troublesome to DuMond was having to decide which of his fellow contemporary American artists to include. Since making curatorial decisions is often a subjective exercise, he was bound to come under criticism for his choices. DuMond's commitment to his high personal standards is clearly demonstrated in a series of letters between him, while still in New York making efforts to secure the artworks of his choice, and Henry E. Dosch, director of exhibits for the exposition, for whom DuMond officially worked:

In regard to your statement, that it is absolutely necessary to reserve quite a lot of space for local Artists, permit me to say, that this is precisely the thing which I am not going to do. While there may be amongst the local Artists, the general proportion which exist the world over doing good work, it must be obvious to you that my every source to secure as fine a show as this country has every had, would be entirely up set by the infusion of anything which I could not say and identify as possessing great merit. Furthermore, the department exhibit is already an accomplished fact and there will be no deviation from the very high standard already attained. One word more I should like to say, that unless I could promise to the foremost collectors and connoisseurs in the land, that we were to have a show in which nothing but standard of excellence was considered, they would not for a moment consent to the loan of their treasures. I should prove false to my whole attitude and promise if I did not abide strictly by this principle.

If there be any scheme which I can devise for selecting anything good from the local Artists you may count upon it that I shall leave no stone unturned to do what is right.[7]

Dosch's response to DuMond's letter is also strongly stated:

Kindly bear in mind that the Fine Arts Building belongs to this division, over which I have absolute control, and all the Chiefs of the different departments are subject to my orders. While I do not want to dictate to you what pictures should be selected, and what pictures should be hung, not being an artist myself, I do claim the right to say what districts should be represented. While there may be no pictures nor artists here, as you seem to intimate, worthy of recognition, this is a matter that will have to be decided by the local artists' committee of this city. I know of some which possess a great deal of merit, and if the local committee insists upon selecting some of these pictures, space must be provided for them. I have also referred this matter to our President, who has expressed the same opinion as myself in regard to this matter. I simply state this to you so that further and unnecessary friction may be prevented. I, therefore, request you again to reserve some space for whatever pictures may be selected from the local people of this city.[8]

DuMond's response to Dosch's demand seemed rather demure considering DuMond's adamant initial position: "You seem to have misunderstood about the local artists—I had already taken steps in their interests. I wanted you to understand that the standard of the Exhibit *must be kept very high at any cost*."[9] The step that DuMond apparently took to appease the local committee was to work "through Mr. Harry Wentz of the Portland Art Club, to secure whatever worthy work is to be had by the local Artists."[10] The choice of Henry (Harry) Wentz to act as the go-between with local artists seemed a natural. Wentz had studied under DuMond while a student at the Oregon Sketch Club and the Oregon Art Students League. He also had attended the Art Students League in New York where he had further contact with DuMond.

To have adequate space to hang artwork by local artists at the exposition, the Portland Art Association hurried along construction of the new Portland Art Museum building in downtown Portland, so that its inaugural exhibition could be an extension of DuMond's epic plan. The museum's show, called Section B of the Fine Arts Department Exhibition, consisted of almost 400 additional works beyond the over 600 paintings hung in the exposition's Fine Arts Building some distance away in northwest Portland. There were only four Oregon artists represented in the Section B exhibit and there were none in the main exhibit. The four were Helen Savier Du-Mond, Harry Wentz and Clara Jane Stephens (who had both been DuMond's students), and C. E. S. Wood.

Art lovers in the Northwest may have appreciated DuMond's curatorial achievement in exhibiting some of the best of world art over the previous two centuries. But it appears that the Impressionist-style *plein air* paintings of Oregon landscapes, similar to Childe Hassam's, continued to attract the buying public for the next ten years or so.

In Oregon, several artists best represented the *plein air* style of Northwest Impressionism connected with the Arts and Crafts period. Portland area painters who produced Impressionist-style work during the period 1904 to 1920 included Edna Cranston Breyman, Anna B. Crocker, Clyde Leon Keller, Charles C. McKim, Clara Jane Stephens, Carl Walters, Harry Wentz, Floyd Wilson,

Wentz, the Artist (c. 1905), by Myra Albert Wiggins. Photograph, 8¼ × 6¼ inches. Martin-Zambito Fine Art (Seattle).

and C. E. S. Wood. Outside Portland, artists included John Marion Crook (of Astoria), Regina Dorland Robinson (of Jacksonville), and Melville Wire (of Salem). Their artwork was akin to Arts and Crafts ideals with their choice of Oregon landscapes as subject matter, the portrayal of beauty in nature, the effects of natural light on forms and in dissolving edges of forms, and the use of bright pure colors.

Of that group, biographical sketches of Breyman, Crocker, Robinson, Stephens, and Wood were featured in the article "A Few of Our Artists" in the February 26, 1910, issue of the *Spectator*. Breyman, Crook, Keller, McKim, Stephens, and Wentz were included in the Portland Art Museum's First Annual Exhibition of Artists of Portland and Vicinity, held in 1912.[11] Crocker, Stephens, Walters, Wentz, and Wilson were represented in the Artists of the Pacific Northwest show hosted by the Seattle Fine Arts Society in 1915.[12]

Paintings by Breyman, Crocker, Keller, Stephens, Walters, Wentz, Wood, Wilson, and Wire were among those displayed by Oregon artists in the Art Room of the Oregon Building at the Panama-Pacific International Exposition in San Francisco, 1915. The majority of the paintings' titles indicated the content was Oregon landscape scenes or flowers.[13]

The Oregon landscape paintings of Charles C. McKim (1872–1939) seemed alive with vibrant color and suggested the illusion of motion through brisk brushstrokes. McKim came to Portland in 1911 from Maine via New York and remained in Oregon until his death. Although Crater Lake and the Oregon coast were among his favorite subjects, he captured many dimensions of Oregon's spectacular scenery, in most every season. He is considered to be the state's most consistent representative of regional Impressionism.

Clara Jane Stephens (1877–1952) came to Portland from England in 1894 when she was seventeen years old. She studied with Frank V. DuMond and Kenyon Cox at the Art Students League in New York, and later with New York painter William Merritt Chase in Italy. Chase painted her portrait there to honor her as his outstanding pupil. In Portland she was deeply involved in a variety of artist organizations, eventually becoming a member of the faculty at the Museum Art School in 1917. Art exhibition reviews of the period often mentioned her use of color, originality of expression, and strong artistic feeling.

The *Spectator*, in the article "A Few of Our Artists," quoted C. E. S. Wood discussing a small canvas by another Oregon artist: "This is by Regina D. Robinson, of Jacksonville, Oregon, and for originality and breadth of treatment it is wonderful and unusual."[14] Robinson (1891–1916), one of Oregon's fine unheralded artists of the period, showed such artistic talent at the age of five that her parents built her a studio in their home in the southern Oregon town of Jacksonville. She received training at the Pennsylvania Academy of Fine Arts, and continued her studies in Oregon and California. In an exhibit of regional artists at the Portland Art Museum in 1916, she exhibited five paintings. Tragically, she committed suicide in 1917 at the age of twenty-six. Her work remained relatively obscure because she lived so far away from a major art center and so few of her works found their way into the art marketplace. Fortunately, the Southern Oregon Historical Society has a good body of her work in all sorts of media in its permanent collection.[15]

A West Point graduate, C. E. S. Wood (1852–1944) had fought in the Nez Perce Indian War against Chief Joseph, with whom he

[top] *Mount Hood from a Marsh* (c. 1911), by Charles C. McKim. Oil on canvas, 22 × 40 inches. Impressionist artist McKim reportedly carved the frame for this painting. Miranda Collection. Photograph by Hermon Joyner.

[bottom] *Sunset After Rain, Willamette Valley* (c. 1919), by Clara Jane Stephens. Oil on board, 9 × 12 inches. This painting is one of two with the same title exhibited by Stephens in the Seventh Annual Exhibition of Pacific Northwest Artists in 1919. *Spectator* (February 15, 1919) referred to it as "very characteristic of our valley, and full of outdoor sweep." Mark Humpal Collection. Photograph by Hermon Joyner.

Moonlight on the Desert (c. 1908), by C. E. S. Wood. Oil on canvas, 18 × 24 inches. Livingston Collection. Photograph by Hermon Joyner.

later became friends. Resigning his commission in the army, he attended Columbia Law School. In 1884 he returned to Portland and set up his law practice. Besides being an avid art critic, patron, and artist, he was a social activist, an advocate for women's suffrage, a politician, and a poet and author. While he was referred to as an amateur, his work stood up to that of any professional artist in the region.[16]

The *Spectator* said about Wood: "His work is among the best produced in the city, and when hanging beside that of Childe Has-sam, critics have found it hard to say which were the pictures of the amateur and which those of the professional."[17] Many of Wood's Impressionistic paintings of Oregon's varied landscape were similar in style and palette to Hassam's: he often used horizontal shades of color and light to unify the composition.

Harry Wentz (1875–1965) seemed to have a particularly close connection with the Arts and Crafts scene in Portland. In a 1909 article, the *Spectator* announced: "Harry Wentz, instructor of art in the public schools, and one of the cleverest of the younger artists on the Coast, will leave in June to pursue his studies in Europe. Mr. Wentz has a fine eye for

Sand Dune, Neah-Kah-nie (1914), by Henry Wentz. Oil on canvas board, 11 × 16¼ inches. Portland Art Museum, 15.5.

composition and an exquisite color sense, and among picture gatherers has already made a name for himself. Some of his latest work may be seen at the Shop of Fine Arts and Industries."[18] (The shop was the retail store connected to the Arts and Crafts Society of Portland.) Wentz also exhibited a piece of hand-wrought metalwork in the Arts and Crafts Society's 1908 exhibition.[19]

Wentz was deeply involved in art education and became one of the first teaching faculty members at the Portland Art Association's Art School in 1910. According to a newspaper article in 1911, Wentz was also involved with the Circle A Club in Portland, whose aim was

to provide the opportunity for newspaper artists, commercial artists, and others to meet a few times every week and to work from models without an instructor, "mainly for the benefit to be gained by observing each other's work. Considerable out-of-door sketching has been done in oils and members of the club were fortunate enough to get criticism from C. C. McKim, the landscape and marine painter . . . who criticizes the work of several classes at the Art School of the Portland Art Association. Henry Wentz was one of the charter members of the club and much plea-

sure and gain were derived by the other members from working with him."[20] Wentz's *Sand Dune, Neah-Kah-nie*, which was acquired by the Portland Art Museum from his one-person show there in 1914, is a striking example of Northwest Impressionism, capturing the feeling of Oregon's wind-swept north coast dunes in both color and movement.

Proclaimed by the *Spectator* to be one of Portland's most promising young artists, Edna Breyman (1881–1918) was cited as having done "some beautiful ocean scenes as well as excellent portraiture work" which was exhibited at the Art Students League exhibit.[21] She had also studied under DuMond. Only one of her paintings is known in local collections. A scene of the Portland waterfront at dusk, with the lights of the city and the remaining light from a darkening sky, it is rich with horizontal brush strokes that render the reflection of rich color as light spreads over the water. The blues and purples of the evening water are pulled up through the boats and docks to the skyline, enhancing this noteworthy example of Oregon Impressionist painting.

Melville T. Wire (1877–1966) moved to Oregon at the age of seven with his family in 1884, and they located in Salem where his father became pastor of the First Methodist Episcopal Church. Within two years, young Melville was taking art classes from Marie Craig,

[top] *Old Boats near Steel Bridge* (n.d.), by Edna Breyman. Oil on board, 10¾ × 13 inches. Collection of Michael Parsons and Marte Lamb. Photograph by Hermon Joyner.

[bottom] *Scotch Broom* (c. 1920), by Melville T. Wire. Oil on canvas, 9 × 11 inches. Harvey and Steve's Gallery (Portland). Photograph by Hermon Joyner.

the painting instructor at Willamette University. Craig, with training from the Pennsylvania Academy of Fine Art and the Philadelphia School of Design, is credited also with developing the talents of Myra Albert Wiggins and Clyde Leon Keller.

Wire studied with Craig for eight years. Although he chose the ministry as a profession, he continued to pursue his avid interest in painting, drawing, and printmaking throughout his life. Between 1902 and 1943, Wire and his wife lived in many towns and cities across Oregon, which gave him the opportunity to paint much of the state's varied landscape.

His early oils, during the first three decades of the twentieth century, were often done in an Impressionist style, quickly painted outdoors. When art historian Henry Sayre saw Wire's eastern Oregon painting *Steens Mountain, Alvord Ranch*, completed in 1928 and featured in color in *Oregon Artist*, he commented that it was "painted with a vigor and energy almost unknown in this country at that time." Its "deeply impastoed and built-up brushstrokes," Sayres wrote, reminded him "of Claude Monet's paintings of his Japanese bridge."[22]

Although his church pastorships were usually some geographic distance from Portland and the majority of Oregon's exhibition venues, Wire still managed to stay in contact with the regional art scene. While he was serving as pastor of a church in Grants Pass, Oregon, three of his oil paintings were included in the Art Room of the Oregon Building at the Panama-Pacific International Exposition in San Francisco, 1915. The titles of these works reflected his broad interest in the natural beauty of Oregon: *Blooming Camas*

Untitled [Oregon coast] (n.d.), by John Marion Crook. Watercolor, 15½ × 19⁹⁄₁₆ inches. Coos Historical & Maritime Museum (North Bend, Oregon), 996-P44.

dent who has made good every opportunity for work that has come her way and who has made most of the opportunities for herself."[27]

Crocker brought to her new position knowledge of the Portland Art Museum's history, the training and aesthetics of a skilled artist, a talent with design, and an enthusiasm for embracing new ideas and concepts in art. She did not seem bound to any particular school or style of art. In her reflections of the early years of the museum's art school, Crocker wrote in 1946: "We wanted our students to live and work in the present—the advancing present—and to see this as resting firmly upon the past." She strove to give students knowledge of the correct use of art tools and materials so they could work "from the center of their being with all they have of intelligence and feeling; it is this that is good schooling."[28]

Crocker had the support of the applied arts community in Portland: Julia Hoffman and the Arts and Crafts Society of Portland were largely responsible for underwriting a portion of her salary the first several years of her employment. The Arts and Crafts Society also worked with Crocker to bring Kate Cameron Simmons from New York to Portland in 1909 to become the first design instructor at the museum's art school.

Crocker's own artwork took several different forms. Her paintings were exhibited in Portland and Seattle. Three were hung in the Art Room of the Oregon Building at the Panama-Pacific exhibition. Her self-portrait reflects her studies under Robert Henri. She showed some of her design and textile work, notably weaving, in exhibits of the Arts and Crafts Society of Portland. She was also known for her illustrated and hand-illuminated cards, often designed in a flowing naturalistic manner popular with Arts and Crafts enthusiasts.

Anthony Euwer (1877–1955) appeared on the regional scene toward the end of the Arts and Crafts period, but his regional work embodies much of the movement's aesthetics. Euwer came to the Hood River area of Oregon along the Columbia River to visit his brother who was living there, and decided to stay. He received his art training at the Art Students League in New York, and had already published a book of humorous poetry.[29] Although well respected today for his paintings of Oregon and Washington scenery, especially of the Columbia Gorge, Hood River, and Mount Hood regions, during the first two decades of the twentieth century he was primarily known for his illustrations, cartoons, bookplate designs, poetry, and humorous writings. He often provided the illustrations for his publications. By about 1920 Euwer began to produce paintings in several media that depicted the powerful landscape and constantly changing weather and colors along the Columbia Gorge.

Painting in Washington

In the first decade of the twentieth century, Washington did not yet have arts organizations in any of its cities that were as advanced as Portland's art museum and its Arts and Crafts Society. But there were several women who were every bit as committed to the pros-

Anna B. Crocker (1926), self portrait. Oil on panel, 19 × 13¾ inches. Portland Art Museum, 2001.65.

perity of the arts as Henrietta Failing, Julia Hoffman, and Anna Crocker in Oregon. Ella Shepard Bush and Helen Rhodes, for example, were involved in art instruction in Seattle and Spokane and made significant contributions to the advancement of the fine arts in the Northwest.

Ella Shepard Bush (1863–1948) received instruction at the Corcoran Gallery in Washington, D.C, and later at the Art Students League of New York. Like Oregon's Anna B. Crocker she studied with painters Frank Vincent DuMond and Robert Henri. She also studied with painters Kenyon Cox and J. Alden Weir. She established the Seattle Arts

School in 1894 in the Boston Block of Seattle and became a force in local art instruction. With the Seattle Arts School as the artistic cornerstone, the Boston Block became an enclave of artists' studios and early art centers.

Bush became the first president of the Society of Seattle Artists when that group formed in 1904. The new organization, which in 1908 became the Seattle Fine Arts Society, was a forerunner to the Seattle Art Museum. In 1907 Ella Shepard Bush became the art critic for the *Weekend*, writing a column called "Art and Artists." She remained an active artist and art instructor in Seattle until she moved to California in 1915.[30] During her time in Seattle, Bush's artwork was included in a number of regional exhibitions. Most often her entries were examples of her portrait work, both standard size as well as miniatures, for which she was highly acclaimed.

Helen N. Rhodes (1875–1938) arrived in Spokane in January 1904 to take over as instructor and director of the Spokane Art League, established in 1892. Rhodes received her training at the National Academy and Columbia University in New York, and the Cowles Art School in Boston. Work being taught under her direction in 1909 included advanced antique drawing (drawing from plaster casts of antique works), studies from life, work in oil and watercolors, illustrating, and modeling.[31] Under her direction, the Spokane Art League also sponsored annual exhibitions of regional artists.

Rhodes was known for design work. In 1904, when she was announced as the new director of the Spokane Art League, the Spokane community had the opportunity to see an introductory exhibit of her artwork:

Her specialty is illustrations and posters, and a number of her designs have appeared on the covers of magazines. She is also doing illustration work for a number of children's magazines and papers.

A number of proofs of designs and sketches are in the collection. Among the special samples are a number of designs for book covers and book plates. Miss Rhodes has also made a specialty of sketches of children in water colors, of which there are a number of samples.

There are also on exhibition pictures of flowers and still life in water colors, the best examples of flowers being nasturtiums and apple blossoms. Examples of still life are grapes and onions.[32]

Rhodes went on to teach design at both the University of Oregon and the University of Washington. At Washington, she became known as one of the university's most influential teachers.

Washington also claimed several noteworthy Northwest Impressionist painters. Artists concerned with Impressionism in Washington who produced a body of work throughout the first two decades of the twentieth century included John Butler, Edgar Forkner, Paul Morgan Gustin, Alonzo Victor Lewis, William T. McDermitt, Lionel Salmon, and Fokko Tadama.

Born in Fort Vancouver in southwest Washington, Paul Morgan Gustin (1886–1974) received his early training in art from German artist Jean Mannhein in Denver, Colorado, after Gustin's family moved there in 1892. The Gustin family returned to Washington, settling in Seattle in 1906. By 1913 he was exhibiting paintings at an exhibition of the Seattle Fine Arts Society. An art reviewer for the

Untitled (c. 1909), by Paul Morgan Gustin. Oil on board, 9 × 12½ inches. Martin-Zambito Fine Art (Seattle). Photograph by Ken Wagner.

Town Crier described his landscapes in terms of his treatment of atmospheric subjects, different times of day, and different qualities of light, all descriptive phrases of the Impressionist style.[33]

An undated clipping from the *Seattle Post-Intelligencer* quoted Gustin as saying, "[I try to paint] not only what I actually see with my eyes in a landscape, but what I feel in the landscape, the sense of freedom or of quiet, or of freshness." The writer of the article went on to describe a Gustin painting that contained trees: "Did you ever see trees like that? Perhaps not exactly. But if you have been out in the very early morning, you may have seen trees that made you FEEL as this painting does. 'They were trees like a beautiful dance,' said Mr. Gustin. Well, that is what he has painted. 'Many artists paint trees as if they were dead. Just beautiful designs. I am interested in them as lines of life. I want their roots firm in the soil, and every branch showing that it is growing, pushing upward and outward, moving in the wind.'"[34]

Gustin exhibited at the Panama-Pacific exposition in San Francisco and served as a juror for the Annual Exhibition of American Oil Paintings and Sculpture at the Art Institute of Chicago in 1915. In 1916 he became the first director of the Seattle Fine Arts School. Before leaving Seattle for the period 1923–1926 to study and work in Europe, Gustin continued to show his artwork to acclaim in Seattle and elsewhere in the United States. His ability earned him the honor of being one of Washington's premier artists of the first half of the twentieth century.

Before settling in Seattle in 1914, Indiana-born J. Edgar Forkner (1867–1945) had

Spokane Falls (1911), by Alonzo Victor Lewis. Oil on canvas, 30 × 42 inches. The painter has artfully captured the enormous power of the Spokane River falls as they flow through the city. Bill Henderson Collection. Photograph by Hermon Joyner.

trained at the Art Students League in New York and taught art in Chicago. He was enamored with the Northwest landscape and specialized in floral and marine subjects.[35] His harbor scenes are reminiscent of the California artist Edgar Payne.

Alonzo Victor Lewis (1886–1946), best known for his heroic public art sculptures in Washington, produced several interesting Northwest Impressionist paintings. Trained at the Art Institute of Chicago after being encouraged by painter Charles M. Russell to study art, Lewis lived in Spokane for several years before leaving for Seattle in 1912.[36] While in Spokane he painted some landscapes, including an Impressionist view of

the falls of the Spokane River as they cascade through the city. He was reported to have also painted scenic spots around Tacoma and Seattle in a similar fashion.[37]

Although few of his earlier Washington landscapes have been located, judging from extant work from the 1920s William T. Mc-Dermitt (1884–1961) exemplified the Northwest's regional adaptation of Impressionism. Closely connected with artists in southern California, McDermitt came to Pullman, in eastern Washington, as an art instructor at Washington State College in 1912. He later became the first professor and head of the Department of Fine Arts at that institution, now known as Washington State University. He was attracted to many of the precepts of Impressionism, including first-hand experience with nature and a strong interest in the way light shapes color, atmosphere,

Tatoosh Range (c. 1919), by Lionel E. Salmon. Oil on board, 10¼ × 8⅜ inches. Toenniessen-Lundberg Collection. Photograph by Hermon Joyner.

and form. McDermitt's work in the late 1920s, although more than a decade past the height of public interest in the Arts and Crafts ideals, could just as easily have been painted in 1915. Throughout his time in Washington, he was fascinated with capturing in his art the wildness of the Northwest's high desert and mountain areas.[38]

Tacoma artist Lionel E. Salmon (1885–1945) received much of his training in his native England before permanently settling in Washington in 1913 after traveling throughout British Columbia and the Northwestern states. He is known for his numerous paintings of Mount Rainier. He may have painted this great mountain of the Cascade Range as many as 2,000 times in his *plein air* Impressionist style. To do his outdoor painting, he often camped near Rainier National Park's Paradise Inn, where his work was offered for sale.[39]

John Butler (1890–1976) and Fokko Tadama (1871–1937) were frequently mentioned in the print media of the period. Butler, who graduated from Seattle's Broadway High School in 1910, won first prize at the Second North-

[top] Untitled [landscape] (c. 1915), by John Butler. Oil on board, 19 × 23 inches. Martin-Zambito Fine Art (Seattle). Photograph by Ken Wagner.

[bottom] Untitled [Nocturne] (c. 1914–1920), by Fokko Tadama. Oil on canvas, 12 × 16 inches. Martin-Zambito Fine Art (Seattle). Photograph by Ken Wagner.

west Annual exhibit in 1915 with a painting titled *Tea*, which was described as an Impressionist painting with beautiful colors. By 1916 he was teaching art at the Cornish School of Art. He became well known for his mural work. Two of his murals were purported to be in local Seattle high schools, including one in his alma mater that he may have left unfinished when he joined the Ambulance Corps during World War I and was sent to France.[40] Neither mural has been located.

Fokko Tadama's vividly colored and visually active paintings of Seattle are fine examples of how this transplanted artist of Indonesian and Dutch heritage saw his adopted city in the 1910s. Tadama taught art classes in Seattle until the Depression.[41]

Printmaking

The great impact of New York painter, photographer, and influential art educator Arthur Wesley Dow upon design and composition reached Oregon and Washington through his many students who became Northwest artists and art teachers. He encouraged translation to western art of early Japanese aesthetics and, in particular, the color block printing process; he promoted color wood block printing as an accepted medium; and he emphasized that crafts were not inferior to fine arts. Regional exhibitions included Dow's prints,

and his books and articles were widely read. In an article in the *Delineator*, Dow wrote, "The art lies in the fine choices, not in the truth, likeness to nature meaning, story-telling or finish. . . . The artist does not teach us to see facts: he teaches us to feel harmonies and to recognize supreme quality." Harmony in design, according to Dow, was based on three primary compositional elements: line, color, and the relationship of areas of light and dark.[42] The Japanese term for the third element, dark and light, was *notan*, which also became the name of the Seattle Camera Club's publication in the 1920s, recognizing the sensibilities of the group's large percentage of member photographers who were Japanese American.

Dow's influence was brought to Oregon in part through the efforts of Anna B. Crocker, who had received instruction from Dow while at the Art Students League of New York. Crocker designed a number of personal greeting and seasonal cards in Portland that followed the design principles of Dow's teaching. Crocker's influence as the curator of the Portland Art Museum and instructor of design classes at the museum's art school gave her opportunity to pass on Dow's philosophies of Arts and Crafts ideals to students and the general public. Crocker was successful in convincing Dow to come to Portland to conduct a series of classes for the Portland Art Association. Described as summer classes in fine arts, his courses ran from July 16 to August 18, 1917. He also gave five public lectures on "The Appreciation of Art" at the Portland Art Museum.[43]

Portland artist Edna Cranston Breyman studied privately under Dow in New York, and Harry Wentz, one of the most influential and best-loved art instructors in the history of art education in Oregon, was taught by Dow at the Art Students League. Dow's conviction that the applied arts were as legitimate as fine arts as long as the work exhibited a high standard of quality inspired Wentz in his first teaching experience in Portland, at Washington High School, where he taught both art and manual training. In 1910 Wentz began his thirty-one-year association with Portland's Museum Art School.[44] Throughout that period he continually interacted with the Arts and Crafts Society of Portland.

Kate Cameron Simmons, the first paid instructor at the Portland Art Museum's Art School from 1909 to 1910, was also a student of Arthur Wesley Dow during her studies at Columbia. Shortly after her arrival in Portland, Simmons was hosted at a reception by the Arts and Crafts Society in their Shop of Fine Arts and Industries.[45] Likely through Simmons and Crocker's connection with Dow and East Coast artists working under his influence, block prints and colored etchings by Maud Hunt Squire and Ethel Mars soon were shown at the Shop of Fine Arts and Industries.[46] In December 1909 the shop held another exhibit of prints and cards of Japanese life by Bertha Lum and Helen Hyde.[47] Lum and Hyde's color woodblock prints must have reinforced Dow's teachings being advanced by Simmons and Crocker at the Museum Art School.

In the 1920s and 1930s, as Northwest interest declined in Arts and Crafts ideals, several regional artists continued to use the color woodblock print as their primary medium of expression. Best-known practitioners of this art were the brothers W. Corwin Chase (1897–1988) and Waldo S. Chase (1895–1988), who specialized in Washington landscapes and seascapes. The eccentric brothers at times lived and worked out of teepees of their own design and construction, moving around Mount Rainier and the Cascade Range, Hood Canal in the south Puget Sound region, and Lake Washington in Seattle. They claimed to be largely self-taught. Corwin, in his strange but delightful memoir, *TePee Fires*, credits a textbook by the British woodcut artist Frank Morely Fletcher, *Woodblock Printing: A Description of the Crafts of Woodcutting & Colour Printing Based on the Japanese Practice*, published in 1916, as their source of instruction. Corwin Chase wrote that he and his brother began to work with color woodblock printing of works presenting Northwest scenery in summer 1924.[48]

A Boston gallery acquired a Chase print in 1992, and discovered a large paper label on the back without a date (but probably late 1920s or early 1930s) designed in an Arts and Crafts style. The long text of the label reveals many technical details about the Chase brothers' process:

The Chenuis Color Prints of Mount Rainier Done by the Chenuis Craftsmen at Their Workshop in Killarney-on-the-Lake, Bellevue, Washington.

These prints of Mount Rainier, the Great White Monarch of the Pacific Northwest, are done according to an original water-color process evolved by the Messrs. Corwin and Waldo Chase of woodblock hand printing based on ancient Japanese methods. While traveling in the Orient the Messrs. Chase were impressed by the beauty of the ancient Chinese and Japanese color prints, and on their return to America they began experimenting along similar lines, endeavoring to portray the mysterious and austere beauty of this great fourteen thousand foot Sentinel of the Cascades as the Japanese artists have portrayed the myriad aspects of Fujiyama.

While preserving the purity of color, grace of line and feeling for design so admirable in the work of the Oriental craftsmen, the Chase brothers have executed their pictures in the more realistic, Occidental manner.

In the Chenuis process carvings are made on wood from selected authentic photographs taken by Mr. Corwin Chase himself during long months spent on the various slopes of the Mountain. From these woodblocks the prints are made, hand printed, and each picture retouched by Mr. Waldo Chase and his associates, thus adding to the process the individual and personal touch of the artist.

The word "Chenuis" is the original Indian name of one of the minor peaks of Mount Rainier. . . . Many Art and Picture Shops are handling these Chenuis prints. They can be procured in most American and Canadian cities. If your dealer doesn't handle them, write us direct, giving his name, and we will be delighted to send you whichever picture you desire.

Whether the Chase brothers actually toured Asia has not been substantiated. In fact, the Seattle artist Bruce Inverarity told art historian David Martin that he had taken block printing classes with the Chase brothers in the 1920s from a Japanese artist in Seattle.[49] Nevertheless, the Japanese influence on the

Nomad (n.d.), by Waldo Chase. Color block print, 12¼ × 7¼ inches. Thomas H. Wake Collection.

Chases' color woodblock prints of the Northwest is unmistakably present. Washington's natural beauty stirred the souls of the Chase boys, and this is reflected in their life work.

Norma Bassett Hall (1889–1957) was born in the southern Willamette Valley rural community of Halsey, Oregon. Interested in art, she attended the Museum Art School in

Portland in 1910, after which she moved to the Midwest and taught and advanced her art training. Hall learned the color woodblock print process in Kansas about 1923. Although she did not live permanently in Oregon again, she made periodic trips back to her native state. Oregon's landscape, particularly the mountains and trees, prompted her creation of several striking color woodblock prints of the state. In anticipation of a proposed 1925 Atlantic-Pacific Highways & Electrical Exposition in Portland, one of Norma Bassett Hall's brightly colored images appeared on a poster stamp (resembling a large postage stamp) to help promote the exposition. Her use of an Indian motif with a great river falls in the background, done in bright red, green, gold, and black colors, resulted in a striking image characteristic of earlier Arts and Crafts designs.

Born in South Dakota, Elizabeth Aline Colborne (1887–1948) began her art studies at the age of five. She was most likely influenced and encouraged by her father, a civil engineer, whose careful drawings impressed the young artist. When she was twelve, she came to Bellingham to live with her aunt. After completing high school, Colborne went back to Brooklyn, New York, to attend Pratt Institute. She studied with Rockwell Kent and Robert Henri, and learned block printing under Allen Lewis and etching under C. W. Mielatz at the Art Students League. While living on the East Coast she primarily worked with the Decorative Designers of New York City as a delineator and illustrator for publishing companies including Harper Brothers, Reilly Lee, and A. L. Burt & Company. The illustration of children's books, especially

for the publishing firm of Platt & Monk, was her economic mainstay for many years.

Colborne moved back to Bellingham to teach art for several years at the local normal school. Throughout her artistic career, she maintained a strong connection with New York City. She found that people in the East were very interested in her artwork in a variety of media. Her color woodblock prints of regional scenery represent some of the most striking prints produced in the Northwest during the latter part of the region's interest in Arts and Crafts. Comparable to the better known work of the Gearhart sisters and their southern California imagery as well as the prints of her Washington contemporaries the Chase brothers, Colborne's block prints vividly portray the water, mountains, and the forests of the northwest corner of Washington.[50]

Roi Partridge, born in Centralia, Washington, in 1888, grew up in Seattle, where he studied art with Ella Shepard Bush at the Seattle Art School. In 1909 Partridge received instruction in drawing, design, and lithography at the National Academy of Design in New York, where he also studied painting with Emil Carlsen for a short time. Along with John Butler, another young artist from Seattle, Partridge studied, traveled, and worked all over Europe. He learned the etching process in Paris and quickly became an excellent printmaker.

Some of Partridge's friends back home arranged a one-man show of his work in the Boston Block art area in downtown Seattle in 1913; the show included thirty-three etchings and twenty-five drawings. Thirty-one pieces were sold from that show, allowing him to

The Cloud (1916), by Roi Partridge. Etching, 6 × 8⅞ inches. Partridge was fascinated with the beauty and majesty of Mount Rainier. Martin-Zambito Fine Art (Seattle).

stay in Paris another year. Photographer Imogen Cunningham, a friend of one of the promoters of Partridge's exhibit in Seattle, began to correspond with him after she reviewed the show.

Partridge returned to Seattle in 1914, and the following year he and Cunningham were married. They moved to the San Francisco Bay Area in 1917. His work had been well received while exhibited at the Panama-Pacific International Exposition in San Francisco in 1915 and he became attracted to the California landscape and art scene.

While in Washington, Partridge produced a number of etchings of the state's natural features, including several done in 1915 when the newlyweds were photographing and sketching on a camping trip on Mount Rainier. In November of that year, Roi Partridge and Imogen Cunningham, along with their friends and fellow artists John Butler and Claire Shepard, held a group show of their work at the Seattle Fine Arts Society. One of his etchings exhibited there, *The Marvelous Mountain*, was acquired in 1916 for the permanent collection of the Art Institute of Chicago after being shown at a Chicago Society of Etchers exhibition. The etching evokes the graphic qualities of a woodblock print, and in capturing the essence of the snow-covered mountain through the medium of etching, Partridge was able to achieve a visceral effect pursued by many of the Northwest Impressionists.[51]

The Seattle artist Paul Morgan Gustin also

By the Straits of Fuca (1917), by Paul Morgan Gustin. Color block print, 11⅛ × 8½ inches. Martin-Zambito Fine Art (Seattle).

created powerful imagery of Mount Rainier and the North Cascades of Washington using the etching process as his medium. Highly applauded for his oil paintings, he created etchings that were equally as popular with the buying public. Gustin also produced some of the earliest color woodblock prints executed in Washington.

The Northwest landscape dominated the subject matter of these early twentieth century artists, regardless of their medium. These Northwest artists were influenced by the European and American Impressionists, the *plein air* school of painting, and the philosophies of nationally known art instructors such as Arthur Wesley Dow. Whatever the source, though, regional artists working within the fine arts concepts of the Arts and Crafts movement were clearly affected by their natural environment. For almost two generations, the Pacific Northwest's impressive surroundings served as artistic inspiration, including the spectacular landscapes and mountain ranges, ever-changing quality of light, high desert skies, bustling cities and industries, undulating valleys and hills, wild rivers, and the Pacific coastline.

ELEVEN
Photography with a Softer Focus

PHOTOGRAPHY WAS WELL ESTABLISHED throughout Oregon and Washington before the arrival of the Arts and Crafts movement in the region. Commercial photographers had been documenting and selling their views of people, town scenes, and the local scenery since the 1850s. With the advent of the Kodak camera in the late 1800s, photographic capabilities spread quickly to the general public. By 1900, it was common for Northwest families to carry a camera with them on picnics, excursions, and trips. At home, whether in town or on the farm, children were photographed at play, while grandparents and pets were posed for the amateur photographer of the family. Scenes of parents or friends working, studying, or playing were snapped and developed. Photography instruction was widespread, with several national and regional periodicals devoted to the subject. Camera and photo supply stores and photography sections within drugstores were common in almost every community in Oregon and Washington by

Many soft-focus portraits, like this boy with an apple (c. 1905), and landscapes by Northwest pictorialist photographers are unidentified. 7⅞ × 6 inches. Mason Collection.

1910. Anyone, including children, who had an interest could take his or her own photographs and do printing and developing. This democratization of photography within the home was in keeping with the Arts and Crafts philosophy that everyone should be able to, or at least have the opportunity to, create beautiful things—in this case images and memories—by their own hand.

Art Photography and Pictorialism

Along with the thousands of Northwest shutterbugs documenting their nearby scenery and family environment were those few prac-

titioners who viewed photography as a legitimate art form equal to the creation of a painting on canvas. These art photographers, or "pictorialists" as they were called, were dedicated to using the medium to create images that demonstrated interesting and even eccentric compositions, tonal qualities, linear gestures, and aesthetic impact. Attention to light and shade were also important. A soft focus, to create atmospheric effects, was often characteristic of pictorialist images, earning the not always kind nickname "fuzzy photos." The pictorialists believed that it was acceptable to manipulate, or reposition, the subject and composition of the photograph. They also could use darkroom processing or special lenses or other equipment to achieve desired effects. This form of expressive photography acknowledged that technique, once mastered, was secondary to the end creation of an image that could evoke an emotional response from the viewer.

In a book published by Eastman Kodak and revised in 1907, a photograph by Helen Gatch of Salem was used to exemplify pictorial photography in a chapter defining the topic:

Pictorial photography may be broadly divided into two classes; landscapes and figure studies. Either line is a study of itself, yet so much depends upon the personality of the operator that we can only indicate a few of the qualities, some at least of which are necessary in every real picture, whether photograph or painting. First of all there must be a motif, a reason for making the picture. This motif may be one of the following: to preserve a record of some interesting place or occasion, to picture the beauty of some bit of landscape under certain conditions, to tell a story by means of a picture, or to produce a picture which shall appeal to the observer by its beauty of line or tone. A successful picture may combine more than one of these qualities, but one is always dominant and there should never be any question as to the principal motif which caused its being.[1]

The pictorialist movement spread quickly, championed in the 1890s by the writing, photography, and leadership of photographer Alfred Stieglitz of New York City and his cadre of Photo Secessionist photographers who shared and demonstrated Stieglitz's philosophy. The Photo-Secessionists took the stance that photography, rather than serving only as a documentation medium, could achieve equality with the fine arts by applying the same guiding principles. Stieglitz's illustrated periodical *Camera Work*, initiated in 1903, helped bring the images and philosophy of the movement to the Pacific Northwest. Other West Coast photography journals, such as *Camera Craft* out of San Francisco, were quick to take up the cause.

While nationally there was still an ongoing debate in the early twentieth century over whether photography was an art or a craft, and whether, in some cases, it should be considered fine art, apparently the two views coexisted compatibly in Oregon and Washington. The public could view exhibited photography in museums, arts and crafts galleries, and sometimes in other public venues.

Even Frank Vincent DuMond, with his adamant stance that only the finest of art should be hung in his Department of Fine Art at the 1905 Lewis and Clark Centennial Exposition, showed some artistic photographs. Photogra-

A Little Lunch (c. 1907), by Helen Gatch. Illustration from a chapter on pictorialist photography in a book published by Eastman Kodak. Mason Collection.

phy was not among the categories listed under "art" in the exposition's *Official Classification and Rules of Exhibit Department* booklet. Instead, photography was included as a category in the Liberal Arts Department.[2] Regardless, DuMond accepted one of Edward S. Curtis's photographs of Northwest Coast Indians and arranged for the exhibition of work from Alfred Stieglitz's Photo-Secessionist group.

Stieglitz wrote DuMond from New York in May 1905, apparently responding to a request for photographic prints to be included in the fine arts exhibit. Somewhat apologetic in tone, Stieglitz indicated he was submitting twenty-five photographic prints, the best he

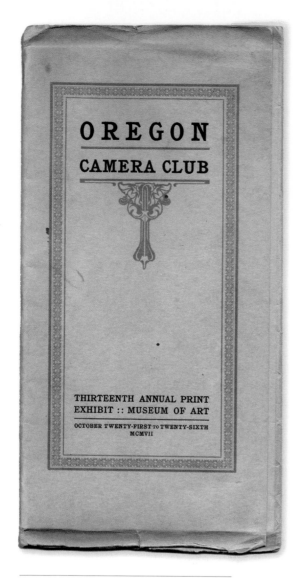

During its early years, the Oregon Camera Club exhibited at the Portland Art Museum, successfully bridging the "Is it art?" controversy. Mason Collection.

hibit listed twenty-five photographs exhibited in gallery G of the Fine Arts Building by sixteen different photographers, including one by Edward S. Curtis. The other twenty-four photographs were from those Stieglitz had sent DuMond. A virtual "who's who" of Photo-Secession photographers, the exhibitors included Stieglitz, Edward J. Steichen, Gertrude Kasebier, Alvin Langdon Coburn, William B. Post, William B. Dyer, and Clarence H. White.[4]

Many of the exhibited photographers at the 1909 Alaska-Yukon-Pacific Exposition in Seattle would be classified as pictorialists. California's exhibit of Arts and Crafts in the California Building included photographic works by Anne Brigman, W. E. Dassonville, Oscar Maurer, Arnold Genthe, Louis Fleckenstein, Laura Adams Armer, and Emily Pitchford. Pitchford won a bronze medal for her exhibited photographs.[5]

Following a popular exhibition of photographs by Alice Boughton of New York, the Portland Art Museum in 1908 chose to exhibit some of the personal collection of William B. Dyer, another early member of the Photo-Secessionist movement who at the time was living in Oregon. The *Spectator* reported:

could do in the comparatively short notice he was given, and hoped that DuMond would not regret having asked the Photo-Secessionists to participate. His letter suggests that the two knew each other as part of the art scene in New York, because Stieglitz laments that he has not visited the DuMonds recently due to illness and his busy schedule and gives his regards to Mrs. DuMond.[3]

The official *Catalogue of the Fine Arts Ex-*

At the Art Museum may be seen a collection of interesting works in the new photography, or the photo-secession art, which has been attracting much attention in the past few years. W. B. Dyer, one of the secessionists who did much to advance the art in Chicago, has come to make his home in Hood River. Many of his delightful photographs are shown in this collection, and the distinctive place which the art has made for itself challenges attention.

Mr. Dyer's work has a masterly style, and is especially strong in portraiture, where the handling of curves, of flesh and of mass is so striking that it is difficult to perceive what so insensate an article as a camera has had to do with the product. Other fine examples of the movement are shown by S. L. Willard, Clarence White, T. M. Edmiston, Edward Steichen, Gertrude Kasebier, Mr. Stieglitz, Mr. Annan of Glasgow, and other artists.[6]

William B. Dyer, born in Racine, Wisconsin, in 1860, was a well-known photographer in the Chicago area by the turn of the century. Winning high praise for his strong images, in spite of his commercial work (which some thought interfered with his artistic photography), Dyer was featured in a joint exhibition with Alice Boughton and C. Yarnell Abbott at the Photo-Secession Gallery, New York, in 1905. That same year, two of his images were published in *Camera Work*.[7]

The photographs shown in 1908 at the Portland Art Museum were from his own collection. In a letter to museum curator Henrietta Failing, Dyer made clear that the collection was not one of selected prints sent out by the Photo-Secessionist group as representative of their philosophy and work. Rather, it was "purely my own private collection of work by Secessionists and their friends." He stressed to Failing that the exhibit should not proclaim him the leader of the Secessionists, "for Mr. Stieglitz is such, but I have been one of the most active. Although working hard at portraiture in Chicago for a number of years, and in fact the first to bring out the newer work there, I always found time to be active in pictorial work."[8]

Deeply involved in the establishment of a ranch, Calamus Lodge, in the fruit-growing area of Hood River from 1908 to 1915, Dyer was taking time to do a limited amount of portraits and illustrative work. He also expressed an interest in securing some Portland patronage for photographic work during the winter months when his agricultural pursuits were put on hold because of the weather.[9]

While in Oregon, Dyer apparently created a body of work depicting regional scenes. Eleven of his images were exhibited in the Art Room in the Oregon Building at the Panama-Pacific International Exposition (1915) in San Francisco. At least two of his titles listed in the *Catalogue of the Art Room in the Oregon Building* related specifically to regional sites: *Benson Point* and *Columbia Highway Bridge*.[10]

William L. Finley, H. L. Bohlman, George F. Holman, Henry Berger Jr., Sarah Ladd, and C. Ford Richardson, all Portland photographers, also exhibited in the Art Room in the Oregon Building at the Panama-Pacific exposition. So, too, did photographers Maude Stinson of Eugene and Allen J. Stover of Corvallis.[11]

Oregon Camera Club

Henry Berger Jr. and George F. Holman were among the mainstays of the Oregon Camera Club, an active organization established around 1894. Although headquartered in Portland, its membership was open to all enthusiasts photographically inclined. In the introduction to the club's catalog for its *Thirteenth Annual Print Exhibit* at the Portland Art Museum in 1907, the positive progression of work shown was compared to that of

Untitled (c. 1910), by William L. Finley. 7½ × 12 inches.
William L. Finley, an Oregon naturalist, was well known for his
photos of wildlife and their habitats. Doug Magedanz Collection.
Photograph by Hermon Joyner.

past exhibits: "But a few years ago they [the club's members] were content, and its patrons pleased, with the exhibition of contact prints, small in size and not altogether in accordance with the principles of art; now the difficult processes of Carbon, Gum-bichromate and Platinums, in monochrome and colors, are the principal mediums of showing the beautiful in nature. They are always on the alert to experiment with any new medium flashed by wire from Eastern art centers and Europe, with the ever cardinal principle before them that 'True Art is to Conceal Art.'" [12] The Arts and Crafts ideals about beauty in nature and the creative process, expressed in photographic terms, were clearly evident in the words and work of the club's members.

Throughout a good part of the first two decades of the twentieth century, awards presented at the Oregon Camera Club's exhibits seemed to be dominated by Berger, Holman, Harry G. Smith, James A. Haran, Clarence Ford Richardson, and Albert G. Meyers, none of whom were practicing professional photographers at the time. Berger, who later opened a photo studio, was a vice president in his father's wallpaper company; Richardson was a clerk in the Portland Railway, Light & Power Company; and Haran was a salesman.

Descriptions of the photographs shown in those early exhibitions, of which few survive, indicate that many of the club members were practicing their art in a manner like that of other photographers during the Arts and Crafts period in America. In 1909 Albert G. Meyers showed *Rising Mist*, "a beautiful landscape, excellent in composition." [13] A year later, one of Henry Berger's photographs,

Still Waters, was reviewed as "a pin-hole study [that] has an unusual attraction of misty atmosphere and distances."[14] Berger's prints often were described as being noteworthy because of their softness and beauty.

Henry Berger Jr. (1877–1939), Portland's most prominent art photographer from 1900 to 1915, consistently won awards whenever he exhibited his photographs. Besides his active involvement with the Oregon Camera Club, Berger exhibited in Germany and won medals in Budapest (1910) and Dresden (1911). With international acclaim validating his photographic work, Berger opened a portrait studio in Portland c. 1912. One of his photographic entries in the Panama-Pacific International Exposition, *The City*, won a gold medal for first place in landscape. Following his success at that exhibition, he moved to New York to work in color photography, and then returned to Portland in 1918 to reopen his studio. He was as successful a portrait photographer as he was a pictorialist. The *Oregonian* reported on September 9, 1923, that Berger had won first prizes in both the men and children's portraiture classes in an exhibit held in conjunction with the annual convention of the Photographer's Association of the Pacific Northwest in Victoria, British Columbia.[15]

The work of Berger and his Oregon Camera Club colleagues was appreciated as much outside the region as it was at home. In 1909 the *Spectator* reported: "Encouraged by the success of their last exhibit, members have sent examples of their work abroad, where their pictures received many honors. Out of 18 prints for the Dresden exhibition, 16 passed the examining critics of New York, who examine all work before it is permitted to enter,

A Leaden Sky, An Unusual Scene in Portland (c. 1910), by George F. Holman. 9½ × 7¾ inches. Doug Magedanz Collection. Photograph by Hermon Joyner.

and eight or twelve of the club's photographs are in the Royal Exhibition at Birmingham, England, attracting much favorable comment from artists."[16] The article went on to say that the Oregon Camera Club was the largest of its kind west of the Mississippi, with the single exception of the San Francisco photography club, and that those two organizations represented the West in all the eastern exhibitions.

The Portland Art Museum's willingness to host photographic exhibitions was testimony to its enlightened attitude. The institution refused to get caught up in the "Is it art?"

Oregon Camera Club members Frank J. Jones and Henry Berger Jr. were frequent exhibitors in photography shows. Oregon Historical Society (Portland), OrHi 105597.

of entries and accepted only 350. Among those accepted were six photographs from Oregon photographers: Helen P. Gatch of Salem; and Ormsby M. Ash, Bertha Breyman, and George F. Holman, all of Portland; plus a photograph by a Portland husband and wife team, Cora T. and Will H. Walker. A Gatch entry, *The Usurper*, was illustrated in the catalog for the exhibition.[17]

Women Behind the Camera

The regionally focused Oregon Camera Club seemed to be male dominated as indicated by the number of awards garnered by men. However, the photographic production by Oregon and Washington women working in the pictorialist style was impressive and received national acclaim. Among the Northwest photographers recognized for their work on a national level were Gatch and Myra Albert Wiggins of Salem; Sarah H. Ladd, Maud Ainsworth, and Lilly E. White of Portland; and Imogen Cunningham, Ella E. McBride, and Adelaide Hanscom of Seattle. Wiggins, Ladd, and White were associate members of the elite Photo-Secession group in New York. Helen Gatch was a member of Rudolph Eickemeyer's Philadelphia Salon. Adelaide Hanscom, already well known in California before she moved to Seattle in 1906, and Imogen Cunningham have become icons in the history of West Coast photography. Far from the epicenters of photographic work, each of these women photographers helped redefine photography and its creation in alignment with the ideals of Arts and Crafts reform and contributed to the recognition of photography as an art form. Their pictorialist and artistic imagery in and of the Northwest influenced

debate. In 1905 the museum played host to a traveling exhibition called The First American Photographic Salon that was sponsored by the Metropolitan Camera Club of New York. The Portland Society of Photographic Art was instrumental in securing this prestigious exhibit, as it traveled to only six other locations throughout the United States and Canada: New York, Washington, D.C., Chicago, Boston, Toronto, and San Francisco. The selection committee reviewed thousands both amateur and commercial photography within the region.

Adelaide Hanscom, born in 1875 in Empire City, near Coos Bay, Oregon, moved from the Northwest to California as a young girl in 1881. She studied at the Mark Hopkins Institute of Art, and by 1897 was exhibiting and teaching art and learning photographic processes. She began her photographic work in earnest in San Francisco in 1902. Within a year she had been featured in regional photographic exhibitions. By 1905 Hanscom had exhibited in both the First and Second American Photographic Salons and had her work illustrated in several prestigious publications, including *Photograms of the Year, 1904*. She became an immediate celebrity with the highly acclaimed publication of her photographically illustrated 1905 edition of the *Rubaiyat of Omar Khayyam*. After losing her studio in the great San Francisco earthquake and fire of 1906, she moved to Seattle that September.

During the time Hanscom was in the Seattle area from 1906 to 1911, she did commercial portrait work and weddings for Seattle's prominent families. Her photographs often appeared in Seattle newspaper society pages. Hanscom still had time to enter her artistic work in major photographic exhibitions, such as the Royal Photographic Exhibit in London (1906), Liverpool Exposition (1907), the 1907 exhibit at the Photo-Secession Gallery in New York, and the Second Exhibition of the Berkeley Art Association (1908). Adelaide Hanscom joined the Photo-Secessionist group in 1908 and was mentioned in *Camera Work* and *Photograms* of 1908. She continued to work on her photographic illustrations for various editions of the *Rubaiyat* and began a similar body of art photos to illustrate a new edition of Elizabeth Barrett Browning's *Sonnets from the Portuguese*. She also entered photographs in the 1907 Arts and Crafts Exhibit sponsored in Seattle under the auspices of the Women's Century Club.[18] Although she lived in the Pacific Northwest for only five years, her aesthetic sensibilities and artistic abilities seemed to have influenced other photographers in the Seattle area, including Wayne Albee, a proponent of the Seattle Camera Club in the 1920s, who published his own photographic illustrations for an edition of the *Rubaiyat*.[19]

Adelaide Hanscom's most lasting legacy in the Northwest may not have been her photographic work but her winning design for the official emblem of the Alaska-Yukon-Pacific Exposition (1909). By unanimous vote of the publicity committee, she won the competition against hundreds of leading artists and designers in America. Her submittal more than the rest of the entries "filled all requirements, significance, comprehensiveness, and accuracy of line, harmony of color and suitability to the occasion." *Pacific Builder and Engineer* reported in its May 15, 1909, issue: "Three figures, right Pacific Slope holding train of cars representing commerce by land; left figure represents Orient, and the ship in her hands commerce by sea; the central figure in white is that of Alaska, the white representing the North and the nuggets in her hand representing her vast mineral resources. Across the sky in background is seen the Aurora Borealis. Purple background with many colors. At the side of the figure on right are tall trees—the forests."[20]

Adelaide Hanscom's design chosen for the official A-Y-P Exposition logo (1909) was used on a variety of souvenirs, including this plate issued by Seattle's Bon Marché department store. Mason Collection. Photograph by Hermon Joyner.

Myra Albert Wiggins (1869–1956), another native Oregon photographer, became nationally known as an artist who created aesthetically strong photographic work. After three years of study at the Art Students League of New York, Myra Albert returned to Oregon in 1894 and married Fred Wiggins in Salem. Her photography in the late nineteenth and early twentieth centuries is well recognized as related stylistically to the Arts and Crafts movement. Researcher and author Carole Glauber's book and article about Wiggins put forth persuasive arguments that a close association between Wiggins' creative photographic methodology and her personal connection to nature, along with her appreciation for the "Arts and Crafts emphasis on simplicity, the picturesque beauty of idealized rural life, and attachments to the rhythms of nature contributed to Wiggins's style and expression."[21]

To exemplify a simple, hearty lifestyle (in reality a somewhat romanticized one) in her photographs, Wiggins often used Native American models or dressed her children and friends as Dutch peasants. She also was intent on artistically capturing the spirit of the Oregon landscape and the essence of various portrait sitters. Glauber stressed Wiggins' skill in manipulating light and dark, along with her use of soft focusing, to obtain soulful photographs that evoked a powerful response in the viewer.

Myra Wiggins' images were featured in the most respected national and international photographic exhibitions and her photographs could regularly be seen in journals and articles from 1893 into the 1930s. She corresponded frequently with Alfred Stieglitz and others and, along with Oregon photographers Sarah Ladd and Lily White, was elected an associate of the Photo-Secession in 1903. But national attention did not detract from her connection to the Northwest. She received an award for her photography at the Oregon State Fair in Salem in 1886, the first of ninety-five state fair awards she won between 1886 and 1907.

The Wiggins family moved from Oregon to the Yakima-Toppenish area of Washington in 1907. Wiggins continued her photographic work in her new environment, but began to turn more of her creative energy to painting. At the A-Y-P Exposition of 1909 in Seattle, she was awarded a bronze medal for her watercolors and photographs. Because of her talent, training, and aesthetic eye, Myra Wiggins became as well known in her later years for her paintings as she had been for her photographs in the first half of her life.

Helen Plummer Gatch (1861–1942), who moved with her husband to Salem, Oregon, in the mid-1880s, was also a well-known pictorialist art photographer. Gatch was a founding member of Philadelphia's Salon Club Committee, which at times was at odds with the Photo-Secession to which Myra Wiggins belonged. Nevertheless, the two Salem women, from all indications, were friends and colleagues. Between 1895 and 1905, Gatch's photography was exhibited internationally; she often won prizes and was featured in publications. Two of Gatch's photographs traveled with the First American Photographic Salon Exhibition (1904–1905), which was featured as the first show in Portland's new art museum in April 1905. Her work also was included in the next two Photographic Salon Exhibitions. She moved to Berkeley, California, in 1912 and apparently discontinued her active involvement in photography.[22]

Not to be outdone by Salem's claim to Myra Wiggins and Helen Gatch, Portland could boast of two members of Stieglitz's Photo-Secession, Sarah H. Ladd (1857–1927) and Lily White (c. 1868–1931). While there survives only sketchy information about these two women and their friend and fellow pho-

[top] *The Edge of the Cliff* (1903), by Myra Albert Wiggins. Platinum print, 8 × 6 inches. This photograph was included in Photo-Secession exhibits in 1904 at the Corcoran Art Galleries, Washington, D.C., and the Carnegie Art Institute, Pittsburgh. Courtesy of Richard D. Rhoda.

[right] *Hollyhocks* [also titled *June Idyll*] (c. 1909), by Myra Albert Wiggins. Platinum print, 8¼ × 6¼ inches. Martin-Zambito Fine Art (Seattle).

Untitled (c. 1905), by Maud Ainsworth. 4⅞ × 3⅛ inches. This image of young Jane Friedlander under a fruit tree in bloom is representative of this Portland photographer's pictorial portrait work. Doug Magedanz Collection.

tographer Maud Ainsworth (1874–1962), their surviving photographic images demonstrate a tremendous artistic sensitivity.[23] Ainsworth's pictorialist figure and portrait work are masterful examples of artistic photography, and White made several finely composed figure studies of Northwest Indian women.

Ladd and White both captured the vastness of the landscape, the beauty and power of the mighty Columbia River, and the various moods of the great Columbia Gorge from a unique perspective—the deck of a houseboat. Several photographs by Ladd and White were published as part of a 1906 article about houseboat living in the Pacific Northwest. Without naming the women, except in the photo credits, the author described in detail the photographers' floating studio:

> An up-to-date dark room with complete photographic outfit, including running water and every necessary detail, further show that a photographer of no mean talent was a "charter member" of the gallant crew of *Raysark*. . . . That this ark of exploration might be able to carry back to stay-at-home friends some of the inspiration of her summer of life upon the Columbia, the Captain of the craft, an expert amateur photographer, was prepared at all time to photograph everything in sight, which the dark room and all necessary photographic paraphernalia at hand made it possible to turn out at any time a finished picture. The success or failure of this part of the project is left to the reader, for all the Columbia River scenery shown herewith, and many of the other illustrations, are the work of the artistic and energetic Captain, ably seconded by two clever assistants, the Hostess and First Mate.[24]

Here were women experiencing first-hand the essence of the Arts and Crafts movement's connection to the natural world, while at the same time being able to capture the spirit of the Northwest through their photographic endeavors.

When Imogen Cunningham's photographs were featured in an exhibit at the Portland Art Museum in 1914, a local newspaper article proclaimed, "Miss Cunningham is a young artist who uses her camera with much temperament and expressive force."[25] Two years earlier, Seattle's art weekly *Town Crier* announced an exhibition of photographs at the studio of Imogen Cunningham, saying that she was "a Seattle young woman who has achieved distinction as an artistic photographer. After completing her college course at the University of Washington in 1907 she worked for two years in the Curtis studios where her work at portraiture attracted no little attention. . . . While Miss Cunningham does excellent work in landscape photography, portraits are her specialty and her exhibition will largely consist of photographs of this type."[26]

Born in Oregon in 1883, Cunningham grew up in Seattle and attended the University of Washington. After her graduation in 1907, she spent two years working in the studio of photographer Edward S. Curtis. She specialized in portraits, and her early photographs in the pictorialist soft-focus mode may have been influenced by her appreciation of the photographic work of Gertrude Kasebier. Cunningham won a gold medal at the Alaska-Yukon-Pacific Exposition in 1909. That same year she received a $500 fellowship from the national organization of Pi Beta Phi, her sorority at the University of Washington, which allowed her to study photography in Germany.[27]

Returning from her studies in Europe, Cunningham opened her first studio in Seattle in a little farmhouse on First Hill. She appears to have interacted easily with the Seattle and entire West Coast art communities, both with fine artists and photographers. She was the only photographer to be a charter member

On Mount Rainier #5 (1915), by Imogen Cunningham. Imogen Cunningham Trust.

of the Seattle Fine Arts Society in 1908 and was the only photographer to join the Society of Seattle Artists. Her studio in Seattle became known as an artistic gathering place, and many of her earlier, well-known portraits are of regional artists of the period, including Paul Morgan Gustin, Maude Kerns, John Butler, and Roi Partridge.[28]

One of Cunningham's first exhibitions of photographs took place in 1911 at her studio on First Hill, and included portraits of Seattle people and photographs taken while she had been in Europe.[29] Her first solo show on a national level was mounted in 1912 at the Brooklyn Institute of Arts and Sciences in New York. Her photograph *The Shipbuilders* was reproduced in the annual publication of the

Photographers Association of America and also on the cover of the *Christian Herald*. By the time of her exhibition at the Portland Art Museum in 1914, Imogen Cunningham was a well-known photographer.

In early 1915, Cunningham and Roi Partridge married in Seattle. That summer the couple spent several weeks on Mount Rainier, Cunningham shooting photographs and Partridge making drypoint etchings. Among the pictorialist images that came from that excursion was a series of nudes of her husband.[30] Later that same year, Cunningham was chastised in the *Argus*, a local Seattle publication, for having two nude studies published in the *Town Crier*. The *Argus*, attacking both its rival newspaper and Cunningham, was outraged that such a "bestial portrayal of shame would be flaunted in the face of the public, even in this far-off corner of the world."[31]

Two years later, Partridge and Cunningham relocated to the San Francisco Bay Area in California. The controversy over her nude images and Partridge's successful showing of artwork at the 1915 Panama-Pacific International Exposition as well as his growing fondness for California may have been contributing factors in the couple's decision to leave Seattle.

By the early 1920s, Cunningham began to depart from her pictorialist work to a style with a sharper focus, concentrating on natural forms, while still creating magnificent portrait work. During Cunningham's time in Seattle, the images she created were some of the best of the region's pictorialist output. Unfortunately, she destroyed most of her glass plate negatives from the Seattle period in 1917 because they were too heavy to move to California.[32]

Northwest Indians, the Grandeur of Nature, and Studio Work

Seattle photographer Edward S. Curtis (1868–1952) was probably the best known Northwest photographer associated with imagery in keeping with the Arts and Crafts ideals. His monumental twenty-volume set of photogravure prints, *The North American Indian*, was the result of a twenty-eight-year self-directed mission to photograph all of the Indian tribes that still held on to a considerable degree of their precontact customs and traditions. Curtis's work and subject matter embodied some of the precepts of pictorialist photography. He sought out or created scenes that implied a simpler life in an idealized, romanticized past, and, in doing so, through artistic composition and technical processes, emotionally pulled the viewer into his finished work.

In response to Curtis's efforts to raise financial support in Portland in 1909 through prepublication subscriptions to his massive undertaking, an article appeared in the *Spectator* that eloquently suggested the emotional response of the writer to Curtis's work:

> Portland, like other places, is prone to forget to do honor to its prophet—in this case, artist. However, it is not so blameworthy in the particular case I have in mind, as the artist happens not to be of this country but of our sister city, Seattle. But, seriously, Portlanders have, as a whole, been too long indifferent to the photographic works of Edward S. Curtis, and it is good news that the Curtis collection of photographs is to be exhibited here in the near future; and exhibited where all who care to inspect it may do so free of charge. The other day at a studio tea was displayed . . . Mr. Curtis' "Vanishing Race," representing a line of dim figures on horseback disappearing

The Vanishing Race (c. 1898), by Edward S. Curtis. Platinum print, 16 × 20 inches. Courtesy of Richard D. Rhoda. Photograph by Ken Wagner.

toward the hills in the gathering darkness, their shadows faintly cast upon the obscure path they are wending. . . .

It was a surprise to learn that many of those in the studio, nearly all of whom are lovers of art, were unfamiliar with this picture; which is only one of the gems of the collection. "Out of the Darkness," which portrays a group of Red men on horseback emerging from the shadows of the canyon into the broad, sunlit plain, is hardly less notable. "Before the Storm," calls up another mood. . . . There are dozens of equally effective examples of Mr. Curtis' art certain to appeal to the beauty lover.[33]

There are those who quibble with the ethnographic accuracy of Curtis's Indian photographs and photogravures and oppose the inherent perpetuation of stereotypes that the images often portray. But there is no ques-

tioning his expertise in creating a great body of work consistent with early twentieth-century thought and artistic photographic practices.[34]

Edward S. Curtis came with his family to the state of Washington in 1883 as a teenager. Growing up in Seattle, Curtis taught himself photography, an accomplishment not unusual at the time. By 1892 Curtis had an interest in a photo studio in Seattle, where his favorite subjects were Mount Rainier, the fast-changing cities of Washington, and local Indians. His brother, Asahel, also a photographer, had a long career providing commercial images for a wide variety of clients.

Through Edward's friendship with George

Homeward (c. 1898), by Edward S. Curtis. Orotone, 11 × 14 inches. Courtesy of James Flury, Jackson Street Gallery (Seattle). Photograph by Ken Wagner.

Bird Grinnell, an authority on Indians, and his experience as official photographer of the Harriman Alaska Expedition (1899) in association with C. Hart Merriam and John Muir, Curtis's interest in photographing Indians became an all-consuming passion.

Curtis's Indian photographs were considered artful, even by some avid defenders of the "only fine art is art" school, who at the time were skeptical and often derogatory about photography being considered art. The opinionated Frank V. DuMond consented to show a Curtis photograph in the Fine Arts Building at the Lewis and Clark exposition

(1905). Curtis had originally approached Du-Mond with an interest in displaying a large collection of his Indian photographs. In a letter to Henry E. Dosch, director of exhibits of the exposition, DuMond wrote:

Mr. Curtis, the photographer who is the specialist in Indian subjects and the great West, tells me that he has already had some kind of understanding about the exhibiting of a large collection of his photographs. He comes from the coast, Seattle, I think, and it is possible that through directly or indirectly a promise has been made him that he should have the necessary space for his exhibit. I have shown him the plans for the Art Gallery and it became perfectly evident to both of us that what ever your understanding was could not pertain to my collection or his collection would occupy about two of the seven rooms that make up the galleries. . . . He cannot exhibit in the Art Gallery and does not wish to exhibit a few only of his pictures. He will, therefore, require a great deal of space in some other department. Will you kindly give this matter your immediate attention and write Mr. Curtis, in my care, what he is to do.[35]

In his response, Dosch told DuMond that Curtis was told that he could have twenty to thirty feet of wall space in the exposition's Educational Department and that Curtis had only requested to show one or two of his best works in DuMond's Fine Arts Building.[36] DuMond must have granted that request, allowing Curtis to show a photograph titled *Indian Head* in the fine arts area, the only one to be shown outside of the collection of Photo-Secession photographs sent to the fair by Alfred Stieglitz at DuMond's request.[37] The rest of Curtis's collection of Indian photographs was displayed in the first and second balconies of the Forestry Building.

Curtis's "orotone," or gold-tone, Indian photographs, made by printing the image on glass with a gold-colored backing application, have become Arts and Crafts icons. Not only the images, but also the frame stock—referred to as "piecrust frames" in recent times—are considered synonymous with the period. Some paper labels on the back of piecrust-framed orotones bear the name of Schneider's Art Gallery in Seattle. It is almost certain that Lloyd Jensen, who was associated with Schneider's framing department as early as 1912, hand carved or molded from gesso many of

Many distinctive frames that came from A. E. Schneider's art and frame store in Seattle were more than likely carved or molded by Lloyd Jensen, who began to work there in 1912. Martin-Zambito Fine Art (Seattle).

the piecrust, bat-wing, and other equally attractive frame styles commonly used in the period that appear to have originated from the Seattle area.[38] Paintings, as well as artistic photographs, commonly used similar regional frames that rivaled, and often times exceeded, the work of national frame companies such as Newcomb-Macklin. These frames represent a major Northwest contribution to the Arts and Crafts aesthetic in the first two decades of the twentieth century.

Both the orotone process and the use of attractive Arts and Crafts–inspired frames were used by other Northwest photographers, such as James B. Barton, a photographer associated with Rainier National Park, and Edward S. Curtis's brother, Asahel. Norman Edson, whose beautiful color photographs of Washington's mountains and the Puget Sound area appear to have been popular for several decades, also presented his images in artistic frames.

Apart from these better-known photogra-

Mount Tacoma and Mirror Lake, Washington (1908), by James B. Barton. Barton advertised his gold-tone process as a Bartone. Private Collection. Courtesy of KaufmaNelson, Vintage Photographs (Bainbridge Island, Washington).

phers, there were many competent amateurs and professionals in Oregon and Washington producing images in the pictorialist style. Indians of the region were quite popular subjects for local photographers. Seattle photographer A. Benjamin Smith, probably after hearing of Curtis's inclusion in the Lewis and Clark exposition, wrote to Frank Vincent Du-Mond, the chief of the Department of Fine Arts: "I am very desirous of securing space in the department you are Director of, for an Artistic Display of Indian prints done in Carbon. . . . This exhibit is the equal in Artistic excellence of any proposed one of same na-

ture, and comprises representative types of all Tribes from Montana to Oregon." [39]

Another Washington photographer, O. E. Garland of Bellingham, was awarded a bronze medal for his photograph titled *Indian Camp*, shown as part of the state of Washington's exhibit at the Lewis and Clark exposition in 1905. Frank La Roche (1851–1934), a self-taught photographer who settled in Seattle, often photographed Indian subjects in Washington and Oregon, as did Walter Scott Bowman (1865–1938) and Thomas Leander "Major Lee" Moorhouse (1850–1926), both of the Pendleton, Oregon, area. These three prolific photographers of regional Indians often mounted their photographs in Curtis-like frames and sold them extensively throughout the Northwest.

Since many regional pictorialists were not professional photographers and had limited output, records of their work are scarce. Fortunately an increasing interest in regional photography continues to bring work to light. A group of outstanding images by Donald R. DeVoe, a photographer from the Seattle area, and a lone pictorialist photograph by a Mr. Jenks were discovered in the early years of the twenty-first century. Labels on the back of a few of DeVoe's photographs indicate that he showed in salons and exhibits in the early 1920s, but little else is known. [40] Jenks' soft-focus, dramatically lighted photo depicts a teary-eyed woman in a hooded robe. A penciled note on the back attributes the image to the Salem, Oregon, photographer c. 1918. George W. Libby Jr., a photographer in Spokane as early as 1909, produced some fine examples of soft-focus, nicely lit, sepia-tone portraits of children, many including Mission-style furnishings as studio props. Oswald L. P. Angvire, also of Spokane, did a series of studio portraits somewhat in the Curtis tradition of local Indians from the Coeur d'Alene tribe. Tinted, moody photographs by a Seattle-area photographer named McFarland (c. 1915) are occasionally found. It appears that in this period, most Northwest communities of any size had men and women taking stunning photographs in a manner consistent with Arts and Crafts precepts.

The magnificence of the Northwest landscape was a predominant inspirational theme for early twentieth-century regional photographers. Attractively framed, sepia-tone and color-tinted photographs of Mount Hood, Mount Rainier, the Puget Sound shoreline, the Columbia River Gorge, the Pacific Ocean, and Crater Lake were commonly seen.

Benjamin A. Gifford (1859–1936) came to the Northwest in the 1880s and probably photographed and sold more images of the regional landscape than any other photographer of the time. Working out of his studio in The Dalles, Oregon, and later Portland, Gifford photographed Indians and the beauty of the Columbia River. He produced several books of his scenic images, including *Snapshots on the Columbia* and *Art Work of Oregon*. His photographs also were used extensively in regional promotional brochures and by the railroads to promote tourism through the Columbia Gorge and in Oregon.[41] Gifford was only one of many photographers fascinated with the natural grandeur of the region. Visiting out-of-area photographers were also eager to capture the magnificence of the Northwest landscape. Even the nationally known Photo-Secessionist Oscar Maurer of

Curly Jim [a Spokane Indian] (c. 1905), by George W. Libby Jr. The edges of the photograph were intentionally curled up from the mount to resemble peeling bark. Northwest Museum of Arts & Culture, Eastern Washington State Historical Society (Spokane).

San Francisco traveled to Oregon and photographed along the Columbia River.

Seattle Camera Club

Shortly after World War I, a time that many claim coincides with the decline of the popularity of Arts and Crafts ideals and related artistic expressions, the Frederick & Nelson department store's Salon of Pictorial Photography energized photography in the Seattle area. In 1924, the Seattle Camera Club was founded. Ella E. McBride (1862–1965), who

Shirley Poppy (c. 1925), by Ella E. McBride. Chloride print, 9½ × 7⅜ inches. The national popularity of this photograph delighted the Rookwood Pottery Company because of the Rookwood vase in the composition. Martin-Zambito Fine Art (Seattle). Photograph by Ken Wagner.

had worked in Edward S. Curtis's studio in 1909, was a member of that new organization. So, too, was a group of Japanese Americans, particularly Dr. Kyo Koike (1878–1947), who is given credit for being the chief organizer and guiding spirit behind the creation of the Seattle Camera Club. Ella McBride became internationally known for her floral studies and she exhibited widely. During the 1926–1927 exhibition season, McBride was the sixth most exhibited pictorialist photographer in the world, with seventy-one different photographs exhibited in twenty-one interna-

tional salons. Dr. Koike, a trained physician who came from Japan in 1917, quickly became a widely exhibited Seattle photographer and a leading authority on Japanese aesthetics as applied to photography.

Other Japanese American photographers working in the Seattle area, including Frank A. Kunishige (1878–1960), Yukio Morinaga (1888–1968), and Soichi Sunami (1885–1971) helped bring international attention to the city. Sunami left Seattle in 1921 and eventually became the chief photographer for New York's Museum of Modern Art. A review of the

7:15 a.m. (c. 1920), by Frank Asakichi Kunishige. Bromoil
print, 13⅜ × 10⅛ inches. Martin-Zambito Fine Arts (Seattle).
Photograph by Ken Wagner.

Untitled [Smith Tower and waterfront, Seattle] (c. 1918), by Wayne Albee. Chloride print, 13½ × 10½ inches. Martin-Zambito Fine Art (Seattle). Photograph by Ken Wagner.

American Annual of Photography throughout the 1920s suggests that some of the most exhibited pictorialist photographers anywhere in the world were members of the Seattle Camera Club.[42]

Seattle pictorialist photographer Wayne Albee (1882–1937), a colleague of McBride and Kunishige's, was producing beautiful soft-focus photographs in the 1910s. Albee also went on to achieve international renown.[43]

Some of the same elements that lent themselves to a regional Arts and Crafts expression—the natural beauty and grandeur of the landscape, a close affinity and relationship to nature, and the regional Indian tribes—also inspired many photographers in Oregon and Washington. Those elements, coupled with aesthetic trends and design sensibilities coming from Japan, Europe, and other parts of the United States, influenced the work of Northwest photographers of the first quarter of the twentieth century and helped position them among the most artistic workers in American pictorialist photography.

TWELVE
Graphic Arts, Printing, and the Book

Founders and practitioners of the European and American Arts and Crafts, Art Nouveau, and Art Deco movements influenced the graphics, design, typography, and the aesthetic appearance of books and other printed pieces during the early twentieth century. There was strong American interest in the design of attractive, attention-getting posters and other forms of commercial art, printing, and publishing during this period. These forms of expression provided artists, designers, illustrators, printers, and craft workers the opportunity to use their creative talents while earning a commission or wage.

Graphic Arts

Artist-designed graphic posters published in France in the 1890s prompted American artists to work with commercial clients who wanted to sell or promote a product or service. Posters expressed

Nowland B. Zane, art instructor at the University of Oregon, was a frequent contributor of illustrated articles about graphic design to *Design: Keramic Studio*. The July-August 1924 issue of the journal featured his mountain and waterfall composition.

an idea or message in a quick glance that would make an immediate impression on the intended audience. Artist-educators Arthur Wesley Dow and, later on the West Coast, Pedro Lemos of California and N. B. Zane and Helen Rhodes working in the university systems of Oregon and Washington taught their students to understand basic design elements, the use of colors, the integration of text and graphics, and other components of a well-executed printed piece so that it attracted and held public interest.

Many posters produced during the Arts and Crafts period in the Pacific Northwest advertised events, such as the 1905 and 1909 expositions in Portland and Seattle, as well as Portland's annual Rose Festival beginning in 1907, Spokane's Interstate Fair, or special exhibitions. Others promoted Oregon and Washington travel and excursion destinations by steamship or railroad.

Newspaper and periodical reports on current events and commercial activities sometimes mentioned that a new poster had been produced as part of the overall attempt to attract out-of-area readers to visit or settle in the community. The posters particularly focused on activities that were boosterism efforts by boards of trade, commercial clubs, and chambers of commerce. Some of the regional graphic artists and designers of the pieces signed their work or were mentioned in the public announcement of a poster.

The Portland Rose Festival poster design winner in 1914 was Colista M. Dowling, who had studied at Drexel Institute in Philadelphia.[1] The 1916 Portland Rose Festival poster, which celebrated the scenic beauty of the Columbia River Highway, was designed by Fred C. Cooper, who had also designed the previous year's poster. Cooper's design was reproduced in four colors—orange, gray, green, and black. As reported: "This is the first publicity to go forth for the highway in the form of posters. The design will be issued in a few weeks, and will hang in railroad offices over the country to call attention to the dates of the 1916 festival, June 7, 8 and 9, and the national dedication of the Columbia River highway."[2]

Portland's Louis Conrad Rosenberg, who later became internationally known for his architectural renderings and etchings, signed his classic Arts and Crafts–design posters for early exhibitions of the Portland Architectural Club.

Many posters and broadsides of the period simply used imaginative typography to convey the message, foregoing artistic embellishment. Following the lead of firms from the East or California, job print shops acquired popular typefaces and the appropriate graphic symbols to be able to print items in the Arts and Crafts style. Regional print shops pursued approaches suggested by the work of Elbert Hubbard's Roycroft Press in East Aurora, New York, and print shops like Paul Elder's in the San Francisco area. As in other regions throughout the United States, having appropriate type styles did not necessarily mean that Pacific Northwest printers could do good presswork or come up with fine finished products. But they were prolific, regardless of their ability to design.

Advertising pieces and catalogs were printed for businesses wishing to showcase their products, and the drive to encourage people to move to Oregon and Washington resulted in the production of hundreds of varied promotional printed pieces. The effectiveness of the desired communication in an image or message often was directly proportional to the application of good graphic design principles. New printing technologies and color printing created many opportunities for graphic and commercial artists to partner with print-

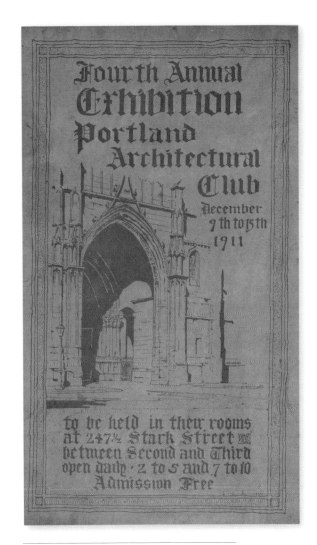

Several of the early Portland Architectural Club exhibit posters, like this one from 1911, were designed by Louis Conrad Rosenberg. 25¼ × 14 inches. Mason Collection. Photograph by Hermon Joyner.

ing firms to achieve desired results. The Ivy Press print shop in Seattle produced a series of nicely printed mottos of various sizes, each with a tagline at the bottom suggesting that the design, illustrations, and typography used comprised the kind of work they could do.

The 1908 exhibit catalog of the Portland Architectural Club contained the following ad: "Rhodes Advertising Agency, Specialists in the Writing, Arranging, and Printing of

The Ivy Press in Seattle printed several mottos on card stock to promote the company's design and printing capabilities (1904). 7⅞ × 4⅛ inches. Mason Collection.

High-Class Catalogues and Advertising Literature. Lovers of Artistic Printing will be interested in the good things done in our shops. We offer unusual facilities for the planning and making of tasty booklets, invitations, folders, announcements, etc. This Catalogue was planned & produced in our shops."[3] Attractive graphic ads for print shops were often included in city and county directories. During the first two decades of the twentieth century, Arts and Crafts–inspired design and typography were predominant in these advertisements.

Newspaper and periodical ads for Pacific Northwest businesses and services also incorporated Arts and Crafts design principles. Several smaller magazines modeled after the *Philistine* issued by the Roycrofters were produced in the region, including the *Comforter, A Magazine of Light, Hope and Inspiration*, published monthly in Portland beginning in 1914. Like the *Comforter*, the covers and pages of some of these publications had decorative borders, illustrated initials, and other period design features.

Miniature-size posters with gummed backs represented the most diminutive step down in size from huge billboard-size posters and the smaller French Maître d'Affiche posters which put the work of important graphic artists in the hands of the middle class. These "poster stamps" were very popular during the first two decades of the twentieth century in Europe and America. Often designed in an Arts and Crafts style, these stickers resembled postage stamps and promoted Northwest cities, events, and products. Regionally they were designed and printed by such firms as the Pacific Poster Stamp League and The Irwin-Hudson Company of Portland, the N.P. Bank Note Company of Tacoma, and the Ellis Publishing Company in Seattle. Some striking regional poster stamps were produced from approximately 1909 through the mid-1920s that were fine examples of effective use of color, negative space, and appropriate typography.

Northwest promotional postcards also embraced Arts and Crafts principles. The Portland Postcard Company of both Portland and Seattle produced attractively designed, full-color cards for the 1909 A-Y-P Exposition and

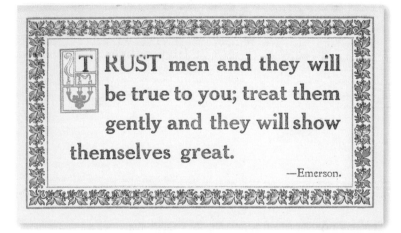

the 1911 Rose Festival. The Kubli-Miller Company printed a color poster-like postcard for the Elk's Grand Lodge 1912 Reunion in Portland. Other postcard companies such as the Hopf Brothers and the Enterprise Novelty Works in Seattle and the Spokane Book & Stationery Company printed popular greeting and motto cards with decorative borders, illustrated initials, and typography associated with Arts and Crafts printing and the work of the Roycrofters, Paul Elder, and the national postcard companies of P. F. Volland and A. M. Davis.

Regional high school and college monthlies and yearbooks during the early part of the twentieth century showed the influence of Arts and Crafts design instruction. Students in association with the school's fine art and manual arts departments often produced these publications. Woodblock print designs graced the covers, interior illustrations were by student artists, and the look and layout of

[top left] A popular affordable option to poster art was the poster stamp. This evocative view of Seattle from Elliott Bay with the moon rising behind the Smith Tower was likely produced to encourage attendees at the San Francisco and San Diego expositions in 1915 to include the Washington city in their travel plans. 2½ × 1⅝ inches. Mason Collection.

[top right] The N.P. Bank Note Company designed a series of poster stamps (c. 1920) to promote Tacoma's industrial potential in the scenic Northwest. 1½ × 2 inches. Mason Collection.

[above] Printed in Spokane by the Spokane Book & Stationery Company, this postcard (c. 1910) was no doubt influenced by the design and popularity of similar looking cards from the print shops of the Roycrofters, Paul Elder, and several national postcard-publishing companies. Mason Collection.

This student-designed cover for the February 1910 issue of Spokane's Lewis and Clark High School magazine *Orange and Black* took its graphic use of hearts and stylized lettering from British Arts and Crafts design. Steve Franks Collection.

an entire issue were practical applications of their design training. If the school had its own press, the printing and binding work may have been done by the students, too.

Printed Books

The attractively printed, limp leather-bound books of Elbert Hubbard's Roycrofters were well represented in the Pacific Northwest. This is hardly a surprise given the extent to which his writings, mottos, and personal appearances had attracted admirers and subscribers to the *Philistine*, and consequently to Hubbard's mass-marketing strategies to sell Roycroft books and other products. Even before Hubbard's 1904 lecture in Spokane,

Roycroft books were being sold in that city in John W. Graham's bookstore. A newspaper ad from December 1903 announced that John W. Graham & Company had received, "Direct From the Roycrofters—A choice line of their books, bound Roycrofty." A week later their ad read, "Pretty books bound Roycrofty. One thousand and one other holiday books in artistic bindings; many in limp leather; all marked lower than publisher's prices."[4] Four years later Graham & Company's book department was still advertising: "Elbertus Hubbard's New Roycroft Books, No Other Store Sells Them, the latest from the hands of the art crafters of East Aurora." The article listed many titles in the Little Journey series, plus individual books.[5]

By the 1920s, the catalog of *Roycroft Hand-Made Things* listed the stores in various Oregon and Washington cities that carried Roycroft books. The Oregon cities were Corvallis, Eugene, Independence, Lebanon, Marshfield, Medford, Pendleton, Portland, Roseburg, and Salem; Washington's cities were North Yakima, Pullman, Seattle (two stores), Spokane, Tacoma, and Walla Walla.[6] Judging from the number of similar looking books produced regionally, the design influence of Roycroft books and the output of their printing competitors made a tremendous impression on the printing industry and consumers in the Pacific Northwest.

In Seattle, Paul J. Smiley and Harry Spencer Stuff jointly owned and operated the Ivy Press between the years 1902 and 1904. In the 1902 Seattle city directory, their ad, bordered in gold and set off by a blue Gothic swash letter, reads, "A modern printing place doing things a bit better than the ordinary . . . at the sign of the Ivy Leaf . . . by neat, skilled, well paid and contented people."[7] While Harry Stuff was with the Ivy Press, the books *Cypress and Rose* and *Maurice and Other Stories* were printed and bound for Marion Frances Watt. The use of red ink for emphasis, the presence of a colophon, and binding in boards with gold leaf designs were all characteristics of the reach of national interest in attractive, well-designed, and finely printed books.

Harry Stuff went on to establish his own printing shop in 1906, with all his books bearing the "sign o' the dollar mark." One book issued by the Stuff Printing Concern in Seattle was Alice Harriman's *Songs o' the Sound*, printed that first year. After the first few copies were bound in boards, the rest were done in limp leather, each different from the other, including a copy with a metal dragon-form clasp and a brocade Chinese temple scene done up in a variety of colors under strips of leather.[8]

Many other books were printed and bound in an Arts and Crafts style by commercial firms in Oregon and Washington. *The Switzerland of America*, a book about the Healy Heights area in the southwest foothills of Portland with a view toward Mount Hood, was printed in 1912 by the House of Kilham in Portland. Published in tan suede leather, each page was illustrated with a common motif of stylized fir trees, initialed "LR" by the artist, most likely Louis C. Rosenberg, well known for his beautiful etchings of the period.

As early as 1905, the Irwin-Hodson Company of Portland was producing nicely printed books of prose and poetry that often included artist-designed graphics. *The Legend of Multnomah Falls* by Susan Williamson Smith, for

Pages in a 1912 promotional real estate development booklet for Healy Heights in west Portland featured illustrations with stylized borders that outlined the vistas. Signed "LR," the booklet's renderings were most likely the work of Louis C. Rosenberg. Mason Collection.

example, sported a color interpretation of the falls on the cover, plus interior reproductions of photographs of the Columbia River area by Lily White and other regional photographers, and was printed on fine, deckle-edged (untrimmed) paper and bound in paper wraps. Another Portland printing firm, F. W. Baltes and Company, produced several regional books that featured page decorations

This strong cover graphic illustration of Multnomah Falls along the Columbia River outside Portland no doubt attracted buyers to Susan Williamson Smith's book *The Legend of Multnomah Falls* (1905), published by the Irwin-Hodson Company, Portland. Mason Collection.

Gems of the Sound (1909) was bound at the studio of Mrs. S. B. Wilson in Seattle. A Washington scene was tooled into the leather. Thomas H. Wake Collection.

and covers with a Northwest theme, such as Kathleen MacNeal Durham's *Thoughts from Oregon to Greet a Friend* (1916), illustrated by Estelle Wallace Paris; Mount Hood was the cover image. The F. W. Baltes and Company also printed selections of verse from Oregon poets with illustrations by regional artists for the Art Room in the Oregon Building at the Panama-Pacific International Exposition in 1915.[9]

The Northwest had several printers doing work at what could be considered private presses. Usually all done by a single printer,

from the setting of type, design and layout, and binding, the creation of a private-press book embodies the Arts and Crafts spirit and intent of creating beautiful things by hand. *Gems of the Sound*, written and printed by Orrill V. Strapp at his Littlegables Craftshop in Seattle in 1909, was an artistic attempt in book printing. The book was bound in hand-tooled leather at the studio of Mrs. S. B. Wilson in the Boston Block, an artistic center in Seattle.

The printing of William Bryant's *Thanatopsis* in 1907, the only book produced by one of

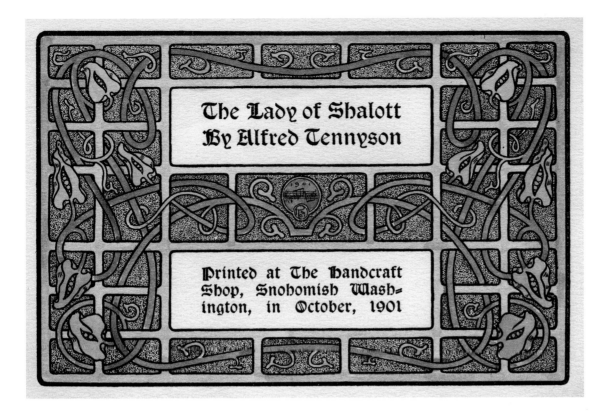

Will Ransom's 1901 printing of Alfred Lord Tennyson's *The Lady of Shalott* in Snohomish, Washington, is one of the finest examples of Arts and Crafts books printed in the Northwest. Title page, 5 × 7 inches. Mason Collection.

Seattle's first private presses, was significant for several reasons. First, the six-leaf work is notable for its typography and hand-illuminated initial letters. Second, the book is important as the only known piece designed and printed by John Julius Johnck, who two decades later would enjoy a reputation as one of California's best typographers. Johnck, a native of Iowa, came to Seattle about 1906, and worked with the Stuff Printing Concern. A year later he joined an independent job printer, Frank Montana West. Together, their private press issued that single volume. By 1908 Johnck had relocated to Portland.[10] While in Oregon, before moving to San Francisco around 1920, Johnck did the illumination of Samuel Simpson's poem *Beautiful Willamette*, which was printed by F. W. Baltes and Company and exhibited at the Panama-Pacific exposition.[11]

Will Ransom, author of the still highly regarded *Private Presses and Their Books*, published in 1929, first became interested in printing and fine books while living in the Pacific Northwest. As a high school student in Vancouver, Washington, he worked part-time as a typesetter for the *Columbian* newspaper. After a move to Snohomish, Washington, to take a position as a bookkeeper for the *Snohomish County Tribune*, Ransom began to produce hand-illuminated books, all written by hand. In September 1901, guided by only a few illustrations of William Morris's printing work, most likely from the *Inland Printer*, and several Roycroft books, Ransom founded the Handcraft Shop and began work on his first printed book. He did not have a physical print shop; he used the *Tribune*'s press during off hours and assembled the pages and did the binding in his hotel room and, later, a rented house.

The venture's first handcrafted book was Alfred Lord Tennyson's *The Lady of Shalott*, printed at the Handcraft Shop in October 1901.[12] Ransom explained his vision for the printing venture in the front of the book: "A love for beautiful books and a slight knowledge of the technical processes of their making have created in me a desire to build some volumes by the labor of mine own hands. The creative instinct has ever been strong within me, and while the possession of that instinct does not always imply the creative ability, it urges me to the effort, without thought for the result. Therefore have I established, in Snohomish, Washington, what it has pleased me to term The Handcraft Shop wherein, from time to time, I shall print by hand a few books, each one as beautifully as may lie in my power."[13]

The binding (with a few exceptions) was executed in brown sheepskin "ooze" (soft leather), with titles set in brown or blue silk labels. The choice of type, the decorative title page, and the use of illuminated initials, a colophon, and his Handcraft printer's mark all contributed to make *The Lady of Shalott* one of the finest Arts and Crafts–inspired books printed by any Oregon or Washington private press. Ransom's colophon page reads in part, "Speed you forth, little Book of my Handcraft, and if you do but add a moment's pleasure to the eye of some book-lover, then I shall not have builded you in vain. Peace and contentment go with you to all your readers."[14]

Ransom partially completed a second book near the end of 1902, Oscar Wilde's *Ave Imperatrix*. Because Ransom was preparing to move from Snohomish to Chicago while attempting to finish the production, he asked a friend, John Clancy, to do the drawings and write the book's foreword. That partnership allowed Ransom to spend more time with the presswork, illumination, and binding, which in turn, some critics claim, produced a book of even higher quality than *The Lady of Shalott*. Ransom relocated to Chicago in 1903, where he attended the Art Institute and became associated with Frederick Goudy, another icon of typography during the early part of the twentieth century. A third book, *A Vision: The Dream of Petrarca* (1904), was produced under the Handcraft Shop imprint, but it was done in Chicago, not Snohomish, Washington.[15]

Bookbinding

The appeal of many late nineteenth- and early twentieth-century books produced during the Arts and Crafts period often lay in the cover design or binding. In the craft's purest form, a book's cover would be created and embellished by hand, most often in leather. Bookbinding was a highly regarded applied art form, requiring a good sense of design and the necessary hand skills needed to execute the design in the chosen medium.

The communities of Portland and Seattle had been introduced to handcrafted bookbinding through Arts and Crafts exhibits, the Lewis and Clark Centennial Exposition, and the A-Y-P Exposition. Many of the best known leather bookbinders from Boston, New York, and San Francisco had exhibited and sold their handiwork in those two cities. Bindings from Boston included in the 1907 Portland exhibition were well received: "The display of the Arts and Crafts includes . . . leather, illumined and embossed in fine design and soft tones; volumes showing how beautiful books can be when art works with craft."[16] Included in the exhibit catalog were descriptions of a bound volume in full levant (fine, soft leather) of *Hand and Soul* by Margaret Danforth of Boston; three bound volumes of Balzac done in full dark blue levant with gold tooling by Mabel I. Mills; and two leather-bound books by May Howbert of Colorado Springs, one executed in full olive-green levant, the other in full dark blue, both gold-tooled.

The following year, four local Portland women were listed in the Arts and Crafts Society of Portland's exhibition catalog as exhibiting bound books: Miss F. Crocker, Georgina Burns, Miss C. A. O'Reilly, and Agnes G. Veasie.[17] Exhibition records and newspaper accounts continued to note a small number of craft workers, mostly women, in Oregon and Washington who were creating book bindings. In 1910 Cecilia O'Reilly's hardbound books exhibited in Portland were reviewed as "particularly artistic and found many admirers."[18] A year later the *Sunday Oregonian* reported, "Miss C. A. O'Reilly is exhibiting some of her excellent bookbinding. She shows among other books a very handsomely bound *Midsummer's Night Dream*, which is finished with gold tooling and inlay."[19]

Allen Eaton, in his Eugene book and art store, actively encouraged bookbinding. The May 24, 1908, *Sunday Oregonian* mentioned one of Eaton's apprentices in the craft: "The art store has indeed, been an inspiration to Arts and Crafts workers, as is shown the number of practical results gained. Chief among these is Mr. Eaton's bookbindery, where good work is being turned out. Here Miss Ruth Parkhurst, of Boston, served as an appren-

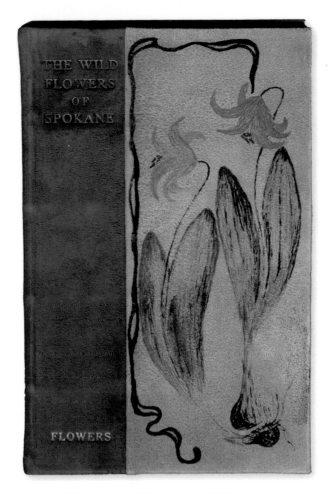

The Wild Flowers of Spokane (c. 1908), by Walter Flowers, with its handcrafted suede and painted floral cover, featured watercolor illustrations of local flora. Walter Flowers Collection, MsSC 127. Northwest Museum of Arts & Culture, Eastern Washington State Historical Society (Spokane).

tice, mastering the craft in its popular aspects. Miss Parkhurst intends to enter artistic book binding as a profession in which there is a large Western field almost untouched. Her work will undoubtedly be successful."[20]

Allen Eaton designed twenty portfolios for photographs and watercolors made from paper and cloth manufactured in Oregon, and a guestbook bound in Oregon sheepskin for the Art Room in the Oregon Building at the 1915 Panama-Pacific International Exposition. The designs were executed by A. B. Hansen.[21]

Two regional examples of the artistic combination of leatherwork and bookbinding are located in the research library of the Eastern Washington State Historical Society in Spokane. Both volumes contain illustrations of Spokane wildflowers, collected and drawn by Walter Flowers. The bindings were most likely executed by Flowers himself, or his friend artist Herbert Jackson.[22] Two yellow flowers, perhaps yellow fawn lilies indigenous to the Northwest, grace the cover of the leather binding, and raised gilt lettering conveys the title, *The Wild Flowers of Spokane*. Flowers later became an instructor of botany at Whitworth College in Spokane.

Book Design and Illustration

The change in bookmaking technology, particularly in Boston and New York, and the great increase in the production of books at the turn of the twentieth century prompted many printing firms to contract with artists and illustrators to design attractive covers, title pages, and interior decorations to enhance the sale of books. Someone within the printing firm using the latest technology most often completed the execution of an artist's design mechanically. Although the Arts and Crafts vision, which dictates that artists should be involved in the creative process all the way through from design to final execution, was not being met, the notion that the purpose of an object should be reflected in its decoration was still very much a part of book cover and illustration work.

Pacific Northwest booksellers proudly displayed books or periodicals with decorative covers or illustrations that reflected the imagery of the region or the talents of local artists and illustrators. Elizabeth Colborne, a Bellingham artist well known for her later color woodblock prints with regional themes of trees, mountains, and water, was cited as early as 1906 for her book illustrations in the May issue of the magazine the *Westerner: An Interpretation of the West*.[23] As late as 1924, Colborne illustrated Grace May North's book *Virginia's Romance*.[24] She also illustrated books published by Harper & Brothers, Reilly Lee, and Platt & Monk, the latter being a publisher of children's books.[25]

Portland was proud of its native daughter, Bertha Stuart, who was nationally recognized for her book cover designs and illustrations. In 1908 the Arts and Crafts Society of Portland featured a showing of several of her recent book covers, along with some of her bookplate designs, in the Shop of Fine Arts and Industries.[26] A year later her work was exhibited at the Portland Art Museum. The *Spectator* reported on the exhibition: "Miss Stuart, who is a Portland girl, has earned distinction in the East as a designer and maker of book covers. For several years she has been doing the cover and plate work for Dodd, Mead Company, and for Harper Bros. The reader of late fiction will find the original covers to many of his favorite novels in this exhibition. Among the latest books represented are *The Men of the Mountain* and *The Man in the Corner*, which has not yet come from the publishers."[27]

The exhibition was so popular that it was extended by the museum for an additional three weeks. The Portland Art Museum featured another exhibit of Stuart's book decoration work five years later in 1913. In 1915, fifteen book covers designed by Stuart, along

SOLITUDE.
O holy, blessed hour of solitude!
When, with the inner self the soul doth hold
Communion sweet; and the ecstatic thought
Upward soaring, touches the plane of God.
MARICE FREEMAN ROBERTS.

with two collections of her bookplates, were exhibited in Oregon's Art Room at the Panama-Pacific International Exposition.[28]

The newspaper article describing the 1913 exhibition indicated that although Bertha Stuart had lived in New York for most of the past thirteen years, the Chicago Art Institute and New York's Art Students League–trained artist and designer wanted to return permanently to Portland where she would enter the field of "designing for home decorating."[29] She did so shortly thereafter, and one of her commissions, c. 1915, was the interior design for the Pittock family mansion in Portland, now an historic house museum.

The Story the Crocus Told, written by Everett Merrill Hill, was an exemplary cloth-bound regional book in the Arts and Crafts style. Published in 1909 by the Uplook Publishing Company of Spokane in cooperation with the Lakeside Press of Chicago, the book featured a cover design by R. W. Little and title page decorations by Herbert Jackson, both from Spokane. The stylized cover design of this limited-edition signed book depicted three white crocus plants against a green-toned background.

Some local books, like John H. Williams's *The Mountain That Was God*, published in Tacoma in 1911, and *Puget Sound and Western Washington: Cities, Towns, Scenery*, written

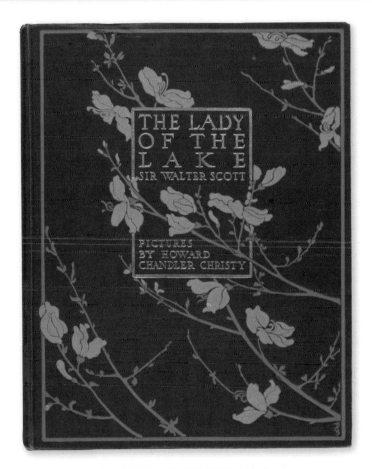

[top] "Solitude," by Maurice Freeman Roberts, illustrated by Elizabeth Colborne for the *Westerner* (1906), depicts the tranquil water and land features of the Pacific Northwest that drew people to the region. Seattle Public Library.

[above] Bertha Stuart's cover design for an edition of Sir Walter Scott's *The Lady of the Lake*, published by Bobbs-Merrill Company, Indianapolis, in 1910, was one of fifteen exhibited by the Portland artist at the Panama-Pacific International Exposition in San Francisco, 1915. Mason Collection. Photograph by Hermon Joyner.

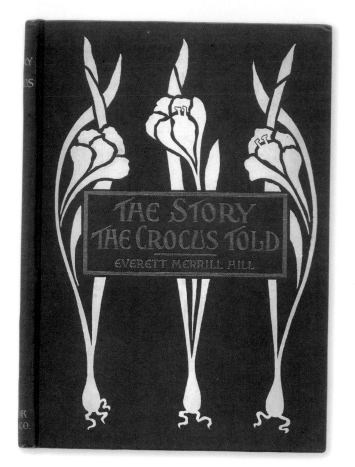

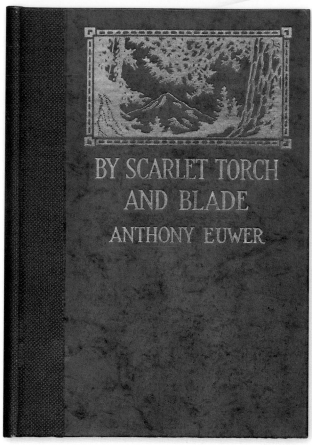

[top left] Everett Merrill Hill's *The Story the Crocus Told* (1909) was published in Spokane and Chicago by the Uplook Publishing Company in association with the Lakeside Press. The cover design was by R. W. Little of Spokane. Mason Collection.

[left] A classic Arts and Crafts graphic design for the cover of the book *Letters from an Oregon Ranch* (1905), published by McClurg & Co. in Chicago, was commissioned by the publisher to render an Oregon theme. Mason Collection.

[above] For *By Scarlet Torch and Blade* (1923), a book of Northwest poetry published by G. P. Putnam's Sons in New York, author Anthony Euwer's own artwork was used in the cover design and interior illustrations. Mason Collection.

and published by Robert A. Reid of Seattle in 1912, featured textured cloth covers illustrated with fir tree designs and containing color photo inserts of Pacific Northwest mountains. National publishers also drew upon the admired scenic beauty of the region when commissioning cover designs for books whose content, whether fact, fiction, or poetry, related to Oregon or Washington. One of the most vivid examples was *Letters from an Oregon Ranch*, published in 1905 by A. C. McClurg & Company of Chicago.

Anthony Euwer, a humorist, poet, illustrator, and artist who moved to Hood River around 1911, quickly became associated with the Pacific Northwest because of his illustrations of regional scenery included in his books of poetry. Prior to his arrival in Oregon, Euwer's illustrations and cartoons had been seen in the *New York Times*, *Harpers*, *Colliers*, and *Punch*. Even though his illustrated humorous book *The Limeratomy* was published several years after his arrival in Oregon, Euwer began to depart from that genre to focus his writings and artwork more and more on the rugged landscape of the region.[30] His later books of poetry, like *By Scarlet Torch and Blade*, published in 1923, often featured illustrations of Mount Hood, fir and pine trees, forest fires, and other Northwest scenes.

Bookplates and Illumination

In addition to their book work, Bertha Stuart and Anthony Euwer both designed bookplates. Bookplates were quite popular during the first several decades of the twentieth century. In a 1908 article about Bertha Stuart, the *Spectator* reported that, along with her book illustrating, she had been giving special

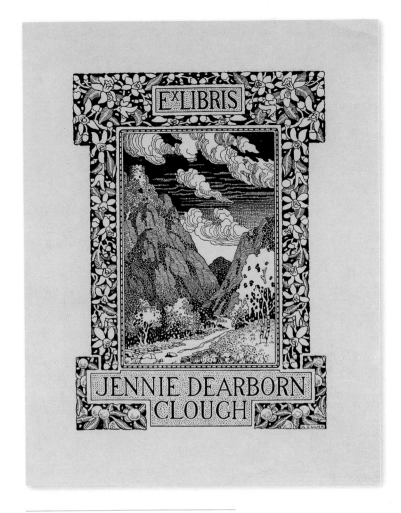

Bookplate for Jennie Dearborn Clough (c. 1920), by Anthony Euwer. Mason Collection.

attention to bookplates, and explained that interest: "In the East bookplates are considered one of the most appropriate of gifts at the holiday time, and for their variety and individuality offer a most attractive field for the collector."[31]

George W. Fuller, the librarian of the Spokane Public Library, wrote a book on bookplates that was published in 1921. Fuller assembled a collection of fine and rare books relating to printing that included titles and printers associated with the Arts and Crafts movement, and he also managed to acquire a full set of Edward S. Curtis's *Indians of North America* for the library. He was also a

From the Library of

Thomas W. Prosch

Bookplate for Thomas W. Prosch, c. 1910. Prosch was a Seattle newspaper man and regional historian. *Town Crier* (n.d.).

designer of bookplates. His bookplates were often in keeping with early twentieth-century designs that borrowed heavily from medieval illustrations. Three of his bookplates were illustrated in his book, *The Bookplate Annual for 1921.*[32]

Roi Partridge, the Centralia, Washington, artist who executed several magnificent etchings of Mount Rainier while living in Seattle with his wife, Imogen Cunningham, was quoted as saying, "I am not interested in bookplates, I don't like to make them, don't want to be connected with them by reputation or otherwise." Regardless of his sentiments, he was commissioned to do at least one bookplate for

businessman Paul Coates Harper, an art patron in Seattle. True to his interest in the naturalistic majesty of the Cascade Range, Partridge's bookplate is an image of Mount Rainier with fir trees in the foreground.[33]

The peaks of the Cascade Range were frequently incorporated into bookplates for book readers and collectors in Washington and Oregon. George W. Fuller designed a view of Mount Rainier for Clifford Cole Corbet. Annette Eden, who taught design at the University of Washington, created a bookplate for a colleague in Bellingham, Professor Glenn Hughes, that was of Mount Baker and Twin Sisters Mountain in the northern Cascades as seen from that city. Anthony Euwer often incorporated Mount Hood in his designs.[34]

Strength and simplicity in design were judged to be the primary goals of bookplate artists of the period. The artists wanted these bookplates to be decorative but not overly detailed. Besides the regional Northwest landscape, the artist often incorporated symbols of the occupation or interests of the intended owner into a bookplate design.[35]

Several Pacific Northwest artists and designers did hand-colored illumination for manuscript or calligraphy sheets of poetry and prose. Other artists designed and hand-illuminated initials that were used in the first word of a chapter or page in an artistically designed book. Trained in art and design, Anna B. Crocker, curator of the Portland Art Museum, produced a number of greeting cards and sheets c. 1910 to 1920, each illustrated and illuminated by her. Many of her extant pieces are reflective of the Arts and Crafts design teaching of New York artist-educator Arthur Wesley Dow.

MYNA AYRES RUSSELL

UNTO HIM WHO FINDS THEE HATEFUL, DEATH, THOU ART INHUMAN PAIN; BUT TO ME WHO DYING GAIN, LIFE IS BUT A TASK UNGRATEFUL

Portland artist Myna Russell (1884-1975) designed and lettered this 16 × 24 inch illuminated motto. Scott & Mary Withers Collection. Photograph by Hermon Joyner.

The regional production of book illustrations, illuminated mottos, decorative covers, poster designs, and regional printing done in the Arts and Crafts style is a fertile field for research. Examples continue to surface at a regular rate as the collecting of printed ephemera becomes more popular. Unfortunately, much of that material, like other examples of the work of regional artists, printers, and craftspeople, will remain anonymous until someone takes the time to dig into surviving printed sources and pursue family histories in an attempt to assign authorship to these examples of the Arts and Crafts movement's design and printing influence in the Pacific Northwest.

EPILOGUE

SCHOLARS DO NOT AGREE on a definitive end date for the Arts and Crafts movement in America. Some suggest it was already in demise when the New York Armory Show debuted Modern art in 1913. Others trace it from the onset of World War I in 1914, or from 1916 when *Craftsman* magazine discontinued publication, or to the sinking of the *Lusitania* in 1915 with Elbert Hubbard one of its casualties. Despite the fact that the 1920s were productive years for bungalow housing and allied industries, the spirit of the Arts and Crafts movement became watered down from its initial role as a life-changing philosophy to a mere decorating style, and was thus more vulnerable to changing tastes.[1]

The Arts and Crafts movement not only matured later in the Pacific Northwest than it did elsewhere in the country, but it lingered longer. The longevity of the movement's regional influence was perhaps due to several factors, including the fact that local timber resources continued to support the building of comfortable and inexpensive Craftsman houses and bungalows even as

Elizabeth Colborne's woodblock print of Mount Baker (c. 1920s). 4½ × 2¾ inches. Art Collection, Seattle Public Library.

351

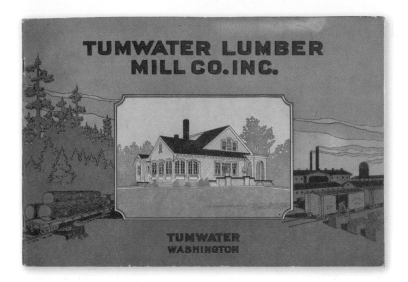

[top] The Tumwater Lumber Mill Company began showcasing Colonial Revival houses in its catalogs by the mid-1920s. Mason Collection.

[above] Ellsworth Storey's observation and fire tower of 1934 on Mount Constitution, Orcas Island, San Juan Islands, carried on the Arts and Crafts tradition of building sturdy and simple structures with local materials. Photograph by Larry Johnson.

building slowed during the Depression. Change was not something that happened quickly in the regional design and craft trades either. Manual arts programs were still producing Mission chairs in the 1920s, and some art and craft businesses continued to produce their popular items for the gift-buying public. For instance, Albert Berry's Seattle shop stocked hammered copper wares with few changes, well into the 1950s.

The style of Lake Quinault Lodge (1926) and Mount Baker Lodge (1927) reflected the earlier vocabulary of national park architecture, though one might argue that by this time, comfortable rusticity was being challenged by the increasingly sophisticated tastes of 1920s vacationers.

The culmination of the Arts and Crafts movement in Northwest architecture was expressed in two important projects outside of urban centers. The first project was in Washington: Ellsworth Storey's 1934 fire-watch and observation tower on Mount Constitution in Moran State Park on Orcas Island. It and a number of shelters and outbuildings constructed in the following years combined rough cut stone and logs in pleasing compositions that embraced locally found materials in structurally honest ways.

The second project, in Oregon, was Timberline Lodge, built as a Works Progress Administration project during 1936 and 1937 by the Forest Service from designs prepared by the firm of Gilbert Stanley Underwood. The basalt, wood, and shake-roof lodge was made of local building materials—stone, Douglas fir, native oak, pine, and cedar—along with recycled materials such as utility poles carved into newel posts and medallions and old iron railroad tracks transformed into andirons,

15-628 Timberline Lodge and Mt. Hood — Gov't Camp, Oregon

Steeply pitched shake roofs, a stone foundation, and shingled façades tied Oregon's Timberline Lodge (1936–1937) with earlier regional national park structures. Mason Collection.

15-598 Main Entrance – Timberline Lodge – Gov't. Camp, Oreg.

15-815 Main Dining Room – Timberline Lodge, Oregon

[left] Timberline's powerful timber portal, ram's head carved sentries, and entrance door with hand-hammered hardware prepared the visitor for the extraordinary artwork inside. Mason Collection.

[above] The dining room at Timberline Lodge was framed by hand-forged metal gates. Above the fireplace was an artist-carved frieze. Mason Collection.

hinges, window grilles, and even a weather-vane.[2] Timberline epitomized Arts and Crafts ideals through the employment of local artisans to carve wood, forge metal, and weave tapestries to embellish the interior spaces of the lodge. The lead interior designer in charge was Margaret Hoffman Smith, the daughter of Julia Hoffman, champion of Portland's Arts and Crafts Society two decades earlier.

Changes in the Works

In Pacific Northwest cities and towns and throughout America, the bungalow that was so popular in 1910 was not able to meet the expectations of homebuyers in the second half of the twentieth century. With rare exceptions, the bungalow had not been designed to accommodate large families or to house an automobile under its roof. Neither was the bungalow design able to adapt easily to technological and domestic advances that were to become commonplace and expected in new homes—dishwashers, refrigerator-freezers,

[top] A late edition of *Craftsman Bungalows*, under Edward L. Merritt, showed the move away from Arts and Crafts design toward English cottages and Colonial Revival housing. Kreisman Collection.

[center] This Craftsman house in Tacoma was probably a duplex when built (n.d.). But by April 1922, a sign on the property credits "Poe, the Rent Man" with making it into a number of apartments by raising it, slipping in a ground floor for more units, and adding stairs to a new veranda. Boland Collection, Washington State Historical Society (Tacoma), 5632.

[left] By the mid-1920s, this Bellingham department store window display encourages upgrades in lighting with the slogan "Why take a chance on your priceless sight with rates so low on electric light?" The Arts and Crafts slag glass lamp was "not old but out-of-date." J. W. Sandison Collection, Whatcom Museum of History and Art (Bellingham), 1460.

washers and dryers, televisions, and home shop equipment including power tools and gas-powered lawn mowers. As people became more affluent, their wardrobes grew, and the storage closets and built-ins of the cozy bungalow that had formerly met the needs of young couples just starting out failed miserably for a later generation of users.

Modernization was the answer. People enclosed open porches, added space to the back or side of the building, expanded dormers, or raised the entire roof for a full second floor. Post World War II homeowners paid little attention to matching the character-defining forms of an old building. Wood shingles and clapboard were sheathed with asbestos or vinyl siding. Decaying wood windows were replaced with aluminum frames.

Inside, the natural woodwork was painted white to lighten up the dark interiors, and built-in cabinets and colonnades were removed to open up the living and dining rooms and make them more closely resemble the popular family rooms touted in new construction. Brick and tile fireplaces were painted over or resurfaced with marble. Fir and oak floors were covered in carpet, and ceilings were sheathed with acoustical tile. Slag glass lighting fixtures were replaced with modern flush fixtures in clear or frosted glass or plastic that provided more—and whiter—light.

No bungalow was sacred. Even Jud Yoho's own Wallingford bungalow was modernized by later owners with orange shag carpeting, discount store lighting, and white paint throughout. What might Yoho say about this seeming desecration of the harmonious work of art that he had created? He was a practical man and at heart a promoter who encouraged people to appreciate and take advantage

BEAVER BOARD is easily put up when the simple instructions furnished to every user are carefully followed.

Just the Thing for Bungalows

Get away from the delay, litter, and inconvenience of lath and plaster. BEAVER BOARD is easily, quickly put up. Permanent, durable, crack-proof, it makes a room warmer in winter, cooler in summer. The beautiful pebbled surface is decorated by painting, thus doing away with unsanitary wall-paper.

Write for free, painted sample, and booklet "BEAVER BOARD for Bungalows." Many illustrations of beautiful bungalow and other interiors.

THE BEAVER BOARD COMPANIES

United States: 349 Beaver Road, Buffalo, N. Y.
Canada: 549 Wall St., Beaverdale, Ottawa
Great Britain: 4 Southampton Row, London, W. C.

BEAVER BOARD

Walls and Ceilings

An advertisement for Beaver Board in *Bungalow Magazine* (1918) promoted the new wall material's advantages over traditional lath and plaster methods. Seattle Public Library.

of new ideas. He had moved people successfully into embracing a style of living that was simple, compact, and domestically a step forward for women who did not have servants. Yoho might have taken the domestic changes of post–World War II America to heart and done exactly the same thing if he were still the owner of his bungalow, since he clearly embraced new materials. He did, after all, publish a story in the February 1918 issue of his magazine entitled "Fulfilling the Bungalow Spirit with Beaver Board."

A Shift in Attitude Toward Design

The demise of the common Arts and Crafts bungalow form was well on its way by the advent of World War I. The attendant patriotism and return to America's Revolutionary War roots had a huge impact on inspiring change. Small houses began to sport Colonial Revival exteriors and interiors. The 1926 *Craftsman Bungalow* catalog was, in fact, devoted exclusively to Colonial-style bungalows. Furniture stores found a ready market for reproduction Colonial Revival furniture in maple and mahogany. Draperies and upholstery fabrics that might have upholstered Sheraton and Chippendale settees in Colonial mansions found their way into the market.

The fall from grace of the Arts and Crafts movement was evident in the books and instruction on architecture and interior design and decorating during the 1920s. *The Practical Book of Interior Decoration*, published in 1919, provided evidence of this change in its chapter on color and color schemes: "We have previously inveighed against the deadness of many American homes; is it from simple inertia or from incapacity for any originality that so many rooms exist with walls of dead and dull mustard-colour oatmeal paper, which absorbs all light as a sponge does moisture; rugs and portieres in perhaps a darker and still duller shade, 'relieved' perchance with brown or sickly cream. Frequently added to this is Mission furniture in the dullest of oak, and leather cushions of the same hue, unrelieved by any ray of brightness, a veritable symphony of mud and mustard! If any reader is unfortunately possessed of such a room we trust he will make speed to import into it some notes of strong orange or blue."[3]

In its chapter on furniture, the authors were no less damning:

> The Mission style, which as the first attempt to escape from jig-saw and gingerbread is praiseworthy, is strictly utilitarian, heavy, unbeautiful, ungraceful, and with lines as antique as the ark. There is one thing to be said in its favour—it is admirable for a happy-go-lucky houseful of children, for it is almost impossible to destroy.
>
> In its lighter forms particularly it is much more attractive when painted and perhaps banded or treated with a few strong, modest decorations and upholstered in good virile style in solid comfortable fabrics not too fine for its texture, in strong stripes, or in a bold printed linen or cretonne with rather striking but tasteful colour. So done it is excellent furniture for the "newer" decoration.[4]

Lest one wonder why the stray Mission chair or chest found at a garage sale in the 1960s was painted, it is clear that this was done with the encouragement of the design community. As those authors concluded, "Mission furniture, so uninviting in its usual colouring, takes on new life and decorative value when painted in attractive colour."[5]

While changes in society and the economy may have signaled an end to the Arts and Crafts movement, this did not necessarily mean that the applied arts disappeared. Design transformed itself in response to the new challenges that industry set forth in the creation of new and improved products for the home and workplace. Seattle author Bernice S. Moore, in her post–World War II overview *Art in Our Community*, devoted an entire chapter to "Industrial Art in our Community: Art for the consumer":

Knowledge of art should be a part of everyone's education, for beauty enriches lives. Our homes are more artistic and well-designed than they were in the past decade. Today, one is able to purchase things of better design because there are persons with art training to design them; there is great need for more and better training.

Art is all about us. It is not something that is shut away in museums. One may get the same feeling for beauty from the smooth streamlines of an airplane or an electric iron that one may get from a beautiful piece of sculpture.[6]

In many ways, Moore's rhetoric echoed the founders of the Arts and Crafts movement. Although the manufacturing processes had changed, the message was clear—seek beauty and utility: "Life is changing. Art and beauty are becoming an intimate part of everyday life. When we go down to breakfast we take our milk from a modern electric refrigerator designed by an artist; we cook our bacon and eggs in a modern frying pan on a streamlined stove. We make coffee in the new-model percolator and cook our waffles on a beautiful waffle iron. Our toast is flipped out by a modern toaster designed by a famous artist; we ride to town in a streamlined automobile;

[top] The Colonial Revival housing of Edwin Ivey and others started to fill the pages of *Bungalow Magazine* from 1915 onward as World War I stimulated a reevaluation of American values.

[right] In 1937, *Practical Suggestions in House Improvement* encouraged remodeling of kitchens, bathrooms, and living rooms in response to the popularity of Colonial Revival features and furnishings. Mason Collection.

The Puget Sound ferry *Kalakala*, launched in 1935, became an icon for the new age of streamlined, modern design. Mason Collection.

take a streamlined ferry, or fly across the country in a stratoliner. How different life is from what it was thirty years ago when horseless carriages were the latest invention and street cars were drawn by mules."[7]

Revival of Arts and Crafts Ideas

Given the universal impact of the Arts and Crafts movement on America at the turn of the twentieth century, it is interesting to speculate on the phenomenon that has recently raised the value of the products of this movement with equal fervor and with a technological wizardry and marketing prowess that would have surprised and probably delighted Elbert Hubbard, Gustav Stickley, and Jud Yoho. What would Hubbard think were he to pick up the "New Homes Section" of the Saturday, May 21, 2005, *Seattle Times* and read: "Capturing the spirit of Seattle's early Arts and Crafts era—then adding fresh yet

reverent twists—the Roycroft Condominiums along Phinney Ridge have tapped into homebuyers' yearning to embrace the past, while enjoying the best of today. It's a fusion of what Jim Roberts of award-winning design firm Taylor Roberts calls 'a renaissance—a resurgence of naturalism.' This blend is already driving presales at Roycroft, where only five of 34 homes remain for today's grand opening."[8] Hubbard would probably be pleased and have no issue with the seemingly contradictory aspects of promoting sales and profits through evoking the idealistic imagery of returning to a simpler, more natural time.

Suburban development in the Pacific Northwest in the first decade of the twenty-first century seems driven by the return to the form and texture of early twentieth-century streetcar neighborhoods, complete with Craftsman houses. In many cases, beauty is only skin deep, with the battered stone pillars, barge boards, and brackets providing street appeal while behind the entrance door one finds the cathedral ceilings, spiral stairways, gas fireplaces, and gourmet kitchens and elaborate bathrooms that are a far cry from the simplicity of purpose of the original models. There are, however, a number of astute architectural firms that are passionate about period housing and specialize in well-detailed new bungalows and Craftsman houses, as well as the restoration and remodeling of older houses. At the same time, the gentrification of older city neighborhoods has brought new, more affluent homeowners whose interest in appropriately restoring bungalows and Craftsman houses has sparked the reintroduction of various Arts and Crafts products.

National furniture manufacturers have

taken their cues from the revival in interest in Arts and Crafts design. Author Jane Powell does a popular presentation "What Would Stickley do with a Computer?" in which she ponders whether the man would embrace the monitors and hard drives and show them plainly in sight or would hide them behind a suitably handsome quarter-sawn oak cabinet. The L. and J. G. Stickley Company continues the Stickley tradition with reissues of original designs. Their broad range of over 600 pieces of furniture in the Mission style includes pieces suitable for home entertainment centers and computer workstations. Perhaps L. and J. G. Stickley would have subscribed to the "hide the technology" camp.

The lighting fixture industry has also responded to public interest with slag glass, copper patina, and the appearance of hand hammering in everything from floor and table lamps to ceiling fixtures and wall sconces. The moniker "Tiffany" has been taken for products by any number of lighting companies wishing to evoke the spirit of luxury in leaded and stained glass of the master. Likewise, an increasing number of businesses create reproduction and Arts and Crafts–inspired ceramic tile, pottery, textiles, and accessories.

This revival has also helped to spawn resurgence in handcrafted work. Small, locally owned companies of artisans and designers in Washington and Oregon have established themselves in response to the marketplace. Their commitment to handwork and the satisfaction that comes from carrying through a design from start to finish reflects the tenets of the earlier Arts and Crafts movement. Some artisans have grown into businesses that have national reputations and, through Web sites and mail order, are able to send their work around the country.

The Arts and Crafts Contribution to the Pacific Northwest

As this study has revealed, there were certainly significant contributions made in Arts and Crafts–inspired buildings, furniture, and fittings, and the fine and applied arts in Washington and Oregon during the first quarter of the twentieth century. Entrepreneurs and businessmen distributed their products, along with those of the major manufacturers, throughout the Pacific and Mountain West. Artists, photographers, craftspeople, architects, and designers, most of whom did not gain national recognition, found personal satisfaction, a community of like-minded individuals, and occasional financial security in local and regional work. Not all the output was exceptional. However, some of it was certainly comparable to the work of their peers in the East and Midwest and in California.

Libraries, exhibitions, and publications made information on the Arts and Crafts movement easily available to Northwesterners who had interest in learning or applying what they learned through schools or self-teaching manuals and periodicals. The efforts of school children, hobbyists, laborers, society women, and art workers to express themselves with objects of beauty and utility would ultimately be more important than the products themselves, as craftspeople gained respect for handwork and self-taught skills. Ultimately, their view of the world changed as they became more attuned to the value of harmony, balance, color, and proportion in shaping a supportive environment.

NOTES

CHAPTER 1 (pages 17-44)

1. For a study of this entrepreneurial Arts and Crafts company, see Daryl Bennett, *Shapland & Petter Ltd. of Barnstaple: Arts and Crafts Furniture* (Barnstable, England: Museum of Barnstaple and North Devon, 2005).

2. *Seattle Post-Intelligencer*, January 8, 1909, 3.

3. C. R. Ashbee Journal, January 1909, fol. 12 (Cambridge, England: King's College Library; copies also at the London Library and Victoria and Albert Museum, London). See also "Through English Eyes: C. R. Ashbee and the American Arts and Crafts Movement," a lecture by James Elliott Benjamin for Historic Seattle at the Seattle Art Museum, June 26, 2003.

4. *Philistine* (East Aurora, New York), March 1906.

5. Charles Pierce LeWarne, *Utopias on Puget Sound 1885–1915* (Seattle: University of Washington Press, 1974), 168.

6. LeWarne, 194.

7. LeWarne, 200.

8. LeWarne, 153.

9. Robert Edwards, *Byrdcliffe: Life by Design* (Wilmington: Delaware Art Museum, 1984), 6.

10. *Homes and Gardens of the Pacific Coast* (Seattle: Beaux Arts Society, 1913).

11. Gideon Bosker and Lena Lencek, *Frozen Music: A History of Portland Architecture* (Portland: Oregon Historical Society, 1985), 45.

12. Leslie Freudenheim, *Building with Nature: Inspiration for the Arts & Crafts Home* (Salt Lake City: Gibbs Smith, 2005), 69.

13. Research by Donald Luxton in preparation for *Building the West: The Early Architects of British Columbia* (Vancouver, British Columbia: Talon Books, 2003). Also see Royal Architecture Institute of Canada Web site.

14. Eileen Boris, *Art and Labor: Ruskin, Morris, and the Craftsman Ideal in America* (Philadelphia: Temple University Press, 1986), 20.

15. Boris, 33.

16. Freudenheim, 35.

17. Boris, 54.

18. *Seattle Mail and Herald* 8, no. 37 (August 26, 1905): 4–5.

CHAPTER 2 (pages 45-61)

1. Some of these fairs included Atlanta's International Cotton Exposition (1881) and Piedmont Exposition (1887), the New Orleans Cotton Centennial (1885), the Chicago World's Columbian Exposition (1893), the Nashville Centennial (1897), the Trans-Mississippi Exposition in Omaha (1898), the Pan-American Exposition in Buffalo (1901), and the Jamestown Tercentennial in Norfolk, Virginia (1907).

2. The California Midwinter International Exposition in Golden Gate Park, San Francisco (1894) was held in a group of whimsical "permanent" pavilions. Portland and Spokane also held expositions during the 1890s. Tacoma architects Hermann Steinmann, Preusse & Zittel, and Proctor & Dennis designed massive wood-frame exhibition halls of permanent quality for that city's exhibits, and they were widely promoted and visited. Seattle, curiously, had no such venue.

3. Jeffrey Karl Ochsner, "In Search of Regional Expression: The Washington State Building at the World's Columbian Exposition, Chicago, 1893," *Pacific Northwest Quarterly* 86, no. 4 (fall 1995): 173.

4. Norman Bolotin and Christine Laing, *The World's Columbian Exposition* (New York: The Preservation Press, National Trust for Historic Preservation, 1992), 119.

5. Mildred Tanner Andrews, *Washington Women as Pathbreakers* (Dubuque, Iowa: Kendall, Hunt, 1989), 110.

6. *World's Work*, 8 (August 1904).

7. *Literary Digest*, 30 (June 17, 1905).

8. *Literary Digest*, 30 (June 17, 1905).

9. One notable exception was the Forestry Building that, surprisingly, was also the work of Whidden and Lewis. Carl Abbot, *Portland and the Lewis and Clark Exposition: The Great Extravaganza* (Portland: Oregon Historical Society, 1986), 24.

10. *Lewis & Clark Journal* 2, no. 4 (August 1904): 7.

11. *Westerner* 3, no. 2 (June 1905): 2.

12. *Lewis & Clark Journal* 3, no. 4 (April 1905): 10.

13. *Lewis & Clark Journal* 3, no. 6 (June 1905): 15.

14. "Foreign Craftsmen take much space," AYPE Seattle Scrapbooks #8 (May 23–June 13, 1909): 46, Special Collections Division, University of Washington Libraries (Seattle).

15. *Seattle Post-Intelligencer* (August 27, 1909), 151. Also see "Oriental Architecture at the AYP," *Pacific Builder and Engineer* 8, no. 32 (July 31, 1909).

16. The Spanish mission was also present in several exhibits, including the display of D. E. Fryer & Co. located in the main aisle of the Manufacturers Building. It consisted of a section of an old Spanish mission house built with Muerer's Spanish mission tile. "The unique appearance of this booth is worthy of note and it is attracting a great deal of attention. The design is the work of D. R. Huntington, architect. The firm of D. E. Fryer represents Eastern manufacturers of building materials." *Pacific Builder and Engineer* 21 (August 1909): 335. Daniel Huntington became a leading architectural voice in Seattle, serving as city architect and designing the concrete and brick infill Queen Anne retaining walls. This early example of the architect's interest in Mission architecture would be reflected years later. In 1927, he designed the Mediterranean Revival Piedmont Hotel on Seattle's First Hill, incorporating one of the largest installations of Malibu ceramic tile in the region.

17. "Arctic Brotherhood," AYPE Seattle Scrapbooks #8 (May 23–June 13, 1909): 44, Special Collections Division, University of Washington Libraries (Seattle).

18. James F. O'Gorman, "The Hoo Hoo House, Alaska-Yukon-Pacific Exposition, Seattle, 1909," *Journal of the Society of Architectural Historians* 19, no. 3 (October 1960): 123–25.

19. *Pacific Builder and Engineer* 7, no. 24 (May 22, 1909): 234.

20. Ironically, for all its intent to be a product of the Northwest, the official guide pointed out that "one of the special features of the Hoo Hoo building is the ladies' reception and waiting rooms where Japanese maids in native costume are in attendance during the progress of the fair." *Alaska-Yukon-Pacific Exposition Official Guide*, 53.

21. *Chehalis Building*, Alaska-Yukon-Pacific Exposition, publicity pamphlet file, Special Collections Division, University of Washington Libraries (Seattle).

22. *Lewis & Clark Journal* 3, no. 2 (February 1905): 13.

23. For an excellent discussion, see Jeanne Madeline Weimann, *The Fair Women* (Chicago: Academy, 1981).

24. *Seattle Times* (March 28, 1908) 11.

25. Karen Weitze, "Midwest to California," in *Substance of Style: Perspectives on the American Arts and Crafts Movement*, ed. Bert Denker (Delaware: Winterthur, 1996), 454–55.

26. Weitze, 459–60.

27. AYPE Seattle Scrapbooks #8 (May 23–June 13, 1909): 140.

28. *New York at the Alaska-Yukon-Pacific Exposition, Seattle, June 1–October 16, 1909. Report of the Legislative Committee from the State of New York to the AYP* (Albany: January 15, 1910), 32.

29. *Pacific Builder and Engineer* 7, no. 24 (May 22, 1909): 213.

CHAPTER 3 (pages 62–95)

1. The catalogs and other ephemera in the Myra Ballou Collection at the research library of the Northwest Museum of Arts & Culture, Eastern Washington State Historical Society, Spokane, have been cataloged as individual pieces. They include three descriptive brochures for porcelains by Adelaide Alsop Robineau; a four-page brochure from Tiffany Studios for shades for wax candles and miniature electric lamps; two catalogs from the *Craftsman* (c. 1909); a Weller Pottery catalog (c. 1905); catalogs illustrating art pottery from the Clifton Art Pottery (1906), Van Briggle Tile & Pottery Company (c. 1926), and Rookwood Pottery (c. 1898–1930); ten catalogs and mailers from Paul

Elder's Arts and Crafts Book Company in San Francisco (c. 1907–1917), and seventeen catalogs from the Roycrofters of East Aurora, New York, advertising books, furniture, copper, leather, and "hand made gifts" (1901–1926).

2. *Seattle Public Library Bulletin*, 1905, 1906, and 1907.

3. *Ashbee Journals*, regarding his Portland visit in March 1916, 362–63 (Cambridge, England: King's College Library).

4. *Ashbee Journals*, letter (April 1, 1916), from C. R. A. to J. E. A.

5. *Spokesman-Review* (Spokane), 1903 clipping, n.d.

6. Artistic Needlework Club Collection, Coos Historical & Maritime Museum (North Bend, Oregon).

7. Portland Art Association Archives, Portland Art Museum, Archives Box 2, File K-L-M, January 1905–November 1907, letter (April 11, 1905), from DuMond to Failing.

8. Portland Art Association Archives, letter (May 3, 1905), from DuMond to Failing.

9. *Official Catalogue of the Lewis and Clark Centennial* (Portland, Oregon, 1905).

10. Lewis and Clark Exposition Collection, Mss 1609, Research Library, Oregon Historical Society (Portland), Box 14M Folder 2, Fair Exhibitors, Louisiana.

11. Portland Art Association Archives, Archives Box 2, 1905–1907, letter (January 1907), from Failing to Hoffman.

12. Portland Art Association Archives, Archives Box 2, Folder F-G-H, March 1906–November 1907, letter (February 16, 1907), from Hoffman to Failing.

13. Portland Art Association Archives, letter (February 24, 1907), from Hoffman to Failing.

14. *Oregonian* (Portland), May 1, 1907.

15. *Oregonian*, May 3, 1907.

16. *Oregonian*, May 3, 1907.

17. *Spectator* 1, no. 8 (May 4, 1907): 5.

18. *Spectator* 1, no. 3 (March 30, 1907): 5.

19. Portland Art Association Archives, letter (April 30, 1906), from Hoffman to Failing.

20. Portland Art Association Archives, letter (February 15, 1907), from Hoffman to Failing.

21. Portland Art Association Archives, letter (February 23, 1907), from Failing to Hoffman.

22. Portland Art Association Archives, letter (March 1, 1907), from Hoffman to Failing.

23. Margery Hoffman Smith Collection, Mss 2660, Research Library, Oregon Historical Society (Portland), Box 2, Folder 19.

24. Portland Art Association Archives, Scrapbook #1.

25. Margery Hoffman Smith Collection, Mss 2660, letter (October 8, 1907).

26. Portland Art Association Archives, Bound Catalogs File 1 (1910).

27. *Spectator* VI, no. 25 (February 26, 1910): 8.

28. *Sunday Oregonian*, November 13, 1910.

29. *Spectator* (December 11, 1915).

30. *Spectator* (March 18, 1916).

31. *Spectator* IV, no. 19 (January 16, 1909): 6.

32. *Spectator* V, no. 3 (March 27, 1909): 9.

33. Oregon School of Arts & Crafts Collection, Mss 2983, Research Library, Oregon Historical Society (Portland), Scrapbook 1902–1929, clipping (c. October 1909).

34. Oregon School of Arts & Crafts Collection, Mss 2983, Scrapbook 1902–1929, clipping (c. October 1909).

35. *Spectator* VI, no. 4 (October 2, 1909): 9.

36. *Spectator* IV, no. 4 (October 3, 1908): 9.

37. *Spectator* IV, no. 7 (October 24, 1908).

38. Oregon School of Arts & Crafts Collection, Mss 2983, Scrapbook 1902–1929, Notice (June 18, 1915).

39. Oregon School of Arts & Crafts Collection, Mss 2983, Scrapbook 1902–1929, Notice (April 4, 1912).

40. Oregon School of Arts & Crafts Collection, Mss 2983, Scrapbook 1902–1929, *Report of the Portland Arts & Crafts Society for 1917–1918*.

41. Oregon School of Arts & Crafts Collection, Mss 2983, Scrapbook 1902–1929, Paper, "Arts and Crafts Society of Portland: The History of the Arts and Crafts Society of Oregon."

42. Oregon School of Arts & Crafts Collection, Mss 2983, Scrapbook 1902–1929, Broadside (c. June 1930).

43. Allen Hendershott Eaton Collection, Ms A263, Special Collections & University Archives, University of Oregon (Eugene), letter (Christmas 1952).

44. Portland Art Association Archives, letter (March 12, 1907).

45. Portland Art Association Archives, letter (March 15, 1907).

46. Portland Art Association Archives, letter (March 22, 1907).

47. Portland Art Association Archives, letter (March 24, 1907).

48. Portland Art Association Archives, letter (March 27, 1907).

49. *Sunday Oregonian*, May 24, 1908.

50. *Oregonian*, March 18, 1914.

51. *Spectator* VII, no. 1 (March 12, 1910): 6.

52. *Spectator* VII, no. 7 (April 23, 1910): 9.

53. *Spectator* VII, no. 8 (April 30, 1910): 8.

54. Prospectus, "The Art Room in the Oregon Building in the Panama-Pacific International Exposition" (Portland, 1915), Portland Art Association Archives, Scrapbook 2 (June 1911–March 1916).

55. Robert Lundberg, "The Art Room in the Oregon Building: Oregon Arts and Crafts in 1915," *Oregon Historical Quarterly* 101, no. 2 (summer 2000): 214–27.

56. Robert D. Clark, "Banning Allen Eaton," *Lane County Historian* (Eugene, Lane County Historical Society) 44, no. 3 (Fall 1999). Clark's article discusses in some detail the end of Eaton's political career in Oregon and his resignation from the University of Oregon.

57. *Seattle Mail and Herald* VI, no. 45 (September 19, 1903): 12.

58. *Seattle Mail and Herald* VII, no. 15 (January 2, 1904): 12.

59. *Seattle Mail and Herald* VII, no. 30 (June 4, 1904): 11.

60. *Seattle Mail and Herald* VII, no. 47 (October 1, 1904): 8.

61. *Seattle Mail and Herald* VIII, no. 31 (June 17, 1905): 5.

62. *Seattle Mail and Herald* IX, no. 18 (March 24, 1906): 7; and X, no. 19 (April 6, 1907): 9.

63. *Seattle Times*, clipping, 1908.

64. Dennis Andersen, unpublished notes regarding arts and artists in Seattle area from regional newspapers and other sources (n.d.).

65. *Seattle Times* (January 5, 1909).

66. Insert, *Homes and Gardens of the Pacific Coast* (Seattle) 1, republished by Christopher Laughlin, Historic Preservation Committee of Allied Arts of Seattle (1974).

67. *Westerner*, AYPE Issue X, no. 5 (May 1909).

68. *Olympia Record* (April 6, 1908).

69. *Catalogue of Fine Arts Gallery and Exhibit of Arts and Crafts, California Building, Exposition Grounds* (Seattle, 1909).

70. *Trail Blazer*, Oregon Agricultural College Bulletin (Corvallis), no. 200 (June 1915).

71. *The College Girl at O.A.C.* (Oregon Agricultural College, Corvallis, n.d.): 11.

72. Nowland B. Zane, "Mountain Themes in Decorative Landscapes," *Design: Keramic Studio* 26, no. 3 (July–August 1924).

73. Barbara Floyd, "The Skillful Hand, The Cultured Mind," *Style 1900* 14, no. 4 (November 2001).

74. Lewis and Clark Exposition Collection, Mss 1609, Research Library, Oregon Historical Society (Portland), CS Box 26.

75. *Sunday Oregonian*, May 23, 1909.

76. *Post-Intelligencer*, August 31, 1909.

77. *Northwest Journal of Education* XXI, no. 2 (October 1909).

78. AYPE Scrapbooks, Scrapbook #7 (April 12–May 27, 1909): 92, Special Collections Division, University of Washington Libraries (Seattle).

79. *Sunday Oregonian*, May 16, 1909, 5: 5.

80. *Sunday Oregonian*, March 29, 1914, 13.

81. *Oregonian*, May 29, 1915.

82. Portland Architectural Club, *First Annual Exhibition of the Portland Architectural Club*, 1908.

83. Portland Architectural Club, *Catalogue of the Second Annual Exhibition at the Museum of Art*, 1909.

84. *Pacific Builder and Engineer* (June 13, 1908).

CHAPTER 4 (pages 97–118)

1. *Fra* 4, no. 3 (December 1909): 60–61.

2. *Pacific Northwest Commerce* 4, no. 6 (June 1911): 17.

3. *Bungalow Magazine* (September 1913): 37–41.

4. *Pacific Builder and Engineer* 8, no. 50 (December 4, 1909): 478–79.

5. *Pacific Builder and Engineer* 9, no. 8 (February 26, 1910): 70.

6. *Weekend* 1, no. 9 (March 3, 1906): 14.

7. *Pacific Builder and Engineer* 9, no. 3 (January 15, 1910): 20–21.

8. *Oregon Country* (October 1914): 228.

9. *Pacific Builder and Engineer* 13, no. 2 (January 13, 1912): 36.

10. Henry C. Matthews, *Kirtland Cutter, Architect in the Land of Promise* (Seattle: University of Washington Press, 1998), 184–85.

11. Hotel Sorrento brochure, 90th Anniversary, 1909–1999.

12. *Pacific Builder and Engineer* 13, no. 19 (May 11, 1912): 404–5.

13. *Pacific Builder and Engineer* 12, no. 26 (December 23, 1911): 459.

14. *Pacific Builder and Engineer* 5, no. 45 (November 9, 1907): 16.

15. Woodbridge, 417; Matthews, 74–7. See Matthews for more thorough discussion of the work of Cutter and Malmgren throughout the Northwest using the Arts and Crafts vocabulary.

CHAPTER 5 (pages 119–151)

1. *Argus Annual* 2, no. 46 (December 17, 1904): 50.

2. Alan Gowens, *The Comfortable House: North American Suburban Architecture 1890–1930* (Cambridge: MIT Press, 1986), 48.

3. William Booth, *Carl Gould: A Life in Architecture and the Arts* (Seattle: University of Washington Press, 1995), 114–15.

4. A discussion of the development of Brookings is presented in Kenneth Cardwell's *Baynard Maybeck: Artisan, Architect, Artist* (Salt Lake City: Peregrine Smith, 1977). Only the hotel and one or two private houses are extant. The hotel, now called the Chetco Inn, was converted to a residential care facility. A Craftsman house reputed to be designed by Maybeck in 1917 for William Ward, hired by Brookings to survey the land and purchase land for the Brookings Land and Townsite Company, was converted to the South Coast Inn in 1993. See "History Lies Sleeping in Brookings Arts and Crafts Inn," *Sunday Oregonian*, July 27, 1997, T1: 4.

5. Terence O'Donnell and Thomas Vaughan, *Portland: A Historical Sketch and Guide* (Portland: Oregon Historical Society, 1976).

6. *Flowers We All Love Best in Mount Baker Park* (Seattle: Mount Baker Park Improvement Club, 1914). Reprint, Gerrard Beattie & Knapp, Realtors.

7. Portland Neighborhood Tour compiled by Leland M. Roth and Elizabeth Walton Potter for Historic Seattle, September 11, 2004.

8. *Pacific Builder and Engineer* 13, no. 24 (June 15, 1912): 50–51.

9. Real Estate and Building Review, *Seattle Times* July 20, 1901, 16.

10. *Craftsman* (October 1908): 119–20.

11. Unpublished research by Martin Eidelberg and Seattle interview with Lawrence Kreisman, October 27, 2005.

12. In 1927, the firm of Schack, Young and Myers designed the concrete garage, which was built into the slope with a tunnel connecting it to the house. Decorative tiles by Ernest Batchelder were incorporated into the concrete lintel above the garage doors.

13. Christine Carr, *The Seattle Houses of Ellsworth Storey: Frames and Patterns* (Seattle: University of Washington Master of Architecture thesis, 1994), 50.

14. Carr, 7–8.

15. Wes Hoffman, *The Historic "Contemporary" Houses of Denny Blaine*, ed. Lawrence Kreisman (Seattle: Seattle Architectural Foundation, 1997).

16. Carr, 7.

17. Henry C. Matthews, *Kirtland Cutter, Architect in the Land of Promise* (Seattle: University of Washington Press, 1998), 211.

18. *Pacific Builder and Engineer* 6, no. 20 (May 16, 1908): 192–93.

19. *Pacific Builder and Engineer* 7, no. 3 (January 16, 1909): 21.

20. *Pacific Builder and Engineer* 7, no. 7 (February 13, 1909): 49.

21. Jeffrey Karl Ochsner, ed., *Shaping Seattle Architecture* (Seattle: University of Washington Press, 1994), 80.

22. *Pacific Builder and Engineer* 5, no. 50 (December 14, 1907): 14–15.

23. *Pacific Builder and Engineer* 12, no. 24 (December 9, 1911): 421.

24. In 1892 the street railways of the communities of Bellingham Bay united and Victor A. Roeder was named treasurer of the new street railway commission. He served as Whatcom County Treasurer from 1896 to 1900. In 1904 he was involved with the formation of the Bellingham National Bank and was elected president, serving in that capacity until his death in 1939.

25. *Roeder Home History* (Bellingham: Whatcom County Parks and Recreation Department, n.d.).

26. *Bellingham Herald*, August 28, 1909.

27. Sally Woodbridge, *A Guide to Architecture in Washington State* (Seattle: University of Washington Press, 1980), 444–45; Jeffrey G. Condit, *The Ramsay House: Its Architecture and History* (Salem), unpublished paper, 1995.

28. Lawrence Kreisman, *Westhome Historic Overview and Tour* (Seattle: Historic Seattle, 2003).

29. John Fahey, *Shaping Spokane: Jay P. Graves and His Times* (Seattle: University of Washington Press, 1994), 44.

30. Information provided by Linda Yeomans, architectural historian and preservation planner, Spokane, May 31–June 1, 2005.

31. Ann Brewster Clarke, *Wade Hampton Pipes: Arts and Crafts Architect in Portland, Oregon* (Portland: Binford & Mort Publishing, 1986), xv, 7, 27. Clarke's book is a valuable monograph on Wade Hampton Pipes.

32. Clark, 8.

33. Clark, 16, 20, 23.

34. Clark, 42.

35. Ruth Mullen, "Searching for Emil Schacht," Homes

& Gardens of the Northwest, *Oregonian*, September 27, 2001. See also Jim Heuer and Roy Roos, *The Emil Schacht Houses in Willamette Heights: The Cradle of Arts and Crafts Architecture in Portland* (draft 2g, October 2, 2003).

36. William J. Hawkins III and William F. Willingham, *Classic Houses of Portland* (Portland: Timber Press, 1999), 372. This comprehensive study provided valuable background information for the Portland architectural firms and their work in the Arts and Crafts style.

CHAPTER 6 (pages 152-182)

1. *Seattle Daily Bulletin*, July 7, 1902, 3.

2. *The Land of Opportunity Now: The Great Pacific Northwest* (Chicago: Burlington & Quincy Railroad, Northern Pacific Railway, and Great Northern Railway, 1924), 18.

3. Norman H. Clark, *Mill Town: A Social History of Everett, Washington* (Seattle: University of Washington Press, 1970), 80.

4. *Coast* 12, no. 4 (October 1906): 213–14.

5. *Craftsman Bungalows* (Seattle: Jud Yoho, 1916 edition deluxe).

6. "Spring-time is Bungalow Time: Pleasing Designs for Western Homes," *Westerner* (April 1912): 8, 24.

7. Conversation with Ray Stubblebine, who provided research gathered for his new book, *Gustav Stickley's Craftsman Homes* (Salt Lake City: Gibbs Smith, 2006); and Paul Dorpat, *Pacific Northwest* Magazine, *Seattle Times* (January 30, 2004): 22.

8. *A Tour of Early 20th Century Residences, Historic Irvington* (Portland: National Trust for Historic Preservation Conference, 2005), 12.

9. *Coast* 9, no. 1 (January 1906): 86.

10. James Massey and Shirley Maxwell, *Arts & Crafts Design in America* (San Francisco: Chronicle Books, 1998), 11.

11. Cheryl Robertson, "House and Home in the Arts and Crafts Era: Reforms for Simpler Living," in Wendy Kaplan, *The Art that is Life* (Boston: Museum of Fine Arts, 1987): 348. See also *Bungalow Magazine* (September 1912): 5.

12. *Pacific Builder and Engineer* 15, no. 25, (June 21, 1913): 381.

13. *Bungalow Magazine* (September 1912): 7–16.

14. *Bungalow Magazine* (September 1912): 25–30.

15. *Bungalow Magazine* (December 1913): 28, 38.

16. *Bungalow Magazine* (April 1915): 201.

17. *Bungalow Magazine* (August 1915): 505–9.

18. *Bungalow Magazine* (January 1916): 3.

19. *Bungalow Magazine* (March 1916): 137–48.

20. *Bungalow Magazine* (March 1916): 149–57.

21. *Pacific Builder and Engineer* 10, no. 17 (October 22, 1910): 160–61.

22. *Pacific Builder and Engineer* 6, no. 35 (August 29, 1908): 316.

23. *Coast* 11, no. 1 (January 1906): 81–82.

24. *Pacific Builder and Engineer* 17, no. 3 (January 17, 1914): 397.

25. W. W. DeLong and Mrs. W. W. Delong, *Seattle Home Builder and Home Keeper* (Seattle: Commercial Publishing, 1915). For their comments on interior design, see Chapter 8.

26. DeLong and DeLong, 22–23.

27. DeLong and DeLong, 25.

28. DeLong and DeLong, 25.

29. *Roberts Home Builder* (Portland: Roberts & Roberts, 1909).

30. *Pacific Builder and Engineer* 17, no. 3 (January 17, 1914): 37.

31. *Westerner* (March 1913).

32. Lottie Roeder Roth, *History of Whatcom County* (Seattle: Pioneer History, 1926), 74.

33. Some information about Spokane properties was provided by Linda Yeomans, preservation consultant, May 2005.

34. Paul C. Murphy, *Laurelhurst and Its Park* (Portland: Paul C. Murphy, September 1916), 19, 20.

35. *Anybody's Magazine* 2, no. 1 (spring 1911): 12–13.

36. One such plan-book house for Dr. J. H. Cook (c. 1909) was from, or adapted from, T. E. O'Neill's *Fancher's Craftsman Book of Bungalows*, 2nd ed. (c. 1911–1919). Janice Williams Rutherford, *The Bungalow Aesthetic: The Social Implications of a Nationwide Phenomenon* (master's thesis, Portland State University, 1981), 198, 117.

37. Rutherford, 113, 119.

38. Rutherford, 153.

39. *Bend Old Mill Neighborhood* (Bend: Deschutes County Historical Society, 2003), 4.

40. *Bend Old Mill Neighborhood*, 15.

41. *Bend Old Mill Neighborhood*, 3.

42. *Bend Old Mill Neighborhood*, 10.

43. *Heritage Walk* (Bend: Deschutes County Historical Society, n.d.).

44. *Bungalow Magazine* (April 1917): 203.

45. *Pacific Builder and Engineer* (August 7, 1915): 60. There is no photographic evidence that this building was constructed.

CHAPTER 7 (pages 183–203)

1. *Oregon Country* 21, no. 4 (October 1914): 231.

2. *Oregon Country* 21, no. 4 (October 1916): 171.

3. One example was Tacoma artist Abby Williams Hill. She studied at the Art Students League in New York City. Beginning in the 1890s, she received commissions from the State of Washington and from both transcontinental railways to paint landscape scenes illustrating the beauty of the Northwest. While her husband, Dr. Frank Hill, stayed home, she took her children for lengthy camping trips to Puget Sound islands, the rugged North Cascades, and Northwest Indian reservations. In her "painting tent-studio" she finished each canvas on site in the tradition of *plein air* artists who were well known in California. Both Great Northern and Northern Pacific Railroad companies exhibited her work in other parts of the country to attract tourists and real estate developers to Washington, notably at the Louisiana Purchase Exposition in St. Louis in 1904. Possibly because it was socially unacceptable for a doctor's wife to work for pay, Hill requested only complimentary travel tickets and the return of her paintings, which she kept. Despite her achievements, her work was rarely exhibited after 1909. Mildred Tanner Andrews, *Washington Women as Path Breakers* (Dubuque, Iowa: Kendall, Hunt Publishing, in cooperation with the Junior League of Tacoma, 1989), 110. Her son's widow donated her collection to the University of Puget Sound. See Ronald M. Fields, *Abby Rhoda Williams Hill, 1861–1943: Northwest Frontier Artist* (Tacoma: Washington State Historical Society, 1989).

4. *The Built Environment Image Guide for the National Forests and Grasslands* (Washington, D.C.: United States Department of Agriculture Forest Service, FS-710, September 2001).

5. Christine Barnes, *Great Lodges of the West* (Bend: W. W. West, 1997), 71.

6. Sarah Allabeck, "Anything but Natural: The Rustic Furniture Movement & Mount Rainier National Park," *Columbia* 8 (fall 1999): 12–13.

7. *Seattle Mail and Herald* 6, no. 29 (May 30, 1903): 2.

8. *Seattle Mail and Herald* 8, no. 37 (August 26, 1905): 4–5.

9. Lawrence Kreisman, "Prairie Meets the Sound," *Pacific Northwest* Magazine, *Seattle Times* (February 20, 2000), 22–24.

10. Florence K. Lentz, "Centennial Snapshots," *Seattle Times/Post-Intelligencer*, December 11, 1988, D1.

11. Lawrence Kreisman, *The Stimson Legacy: Architecture in the Urban West* (Seattle: Willows Press, 1992), 87.

12. *Town Crier*, October 10, 1914. The farm was acquired in 1975 by the Chateau Ste. Michelle winery, which placed additional buildings on the site, razed a number of dairy buildings, and painted the exterior and interior of the house white. The property is maintained as a banquet facility.

13. The Moran estate is described in Christopher M. Peacock, *Rosario Yesterdays* (Eastsound, Washington: Rosario Productions, 1985).

14. *Westerner* (June 1903): 5; (May 1905): 37.

15. *Bungalow Magazine* (July 1915): 7.

16. *Bungalow Magazine* (July 1916): 423–28.

17. Stephen Dow Beckham, *The Simpsons of Shore Acres* (Portland: Arago Books, 1971), 25–26.

18. *Sunday Oregonian*, May 9, 1909, 6: 4.

19. *Bungalow Magazine* (July 1913): 13. See also interview with an original community member, James Sanderson Ditty (age 81) in 1961 in Beaux Art Village file, Eastside Heritage Center, Bellevue, Washington.

20. See Janet Ore's in-depth article about this house, "Pagodas in Paradise: Clancey Lewis's Craftsman Bungalow and the Contradictions of Modern Life," in *Pacific Northwest Quarterly* 92 (summer 2001): 115–26. Also see her master's thesis, *Constructing the Modern Home: Domestic Architecture and Cultural Change in Seattle Neighborhoods, 1890–1940* (Seattle: University of Washington, 1993), which examines several bungalows in neighborhoods north of the Ship Canal. The July 1913 issue of *Bungalow Magazine* also included advertisements for the Western Academy of Beaux Arts, Home Craft, Home Study.

21. *Bungalow Magazine* (August 1913): 32–33.

22. Louis Dechmann, photograph album, Qui Si Sana, Lake Crescent, c. 1913, K0092, Collection #169, Special Collections Division, University of Washington Libraries (Seattle).

CHAPTER 8 (pages 205–243)

1. *Pacific Builder and Engineer* 5, no. 37 (September 14, 1907): 10.

2. W. W. DeLong and Mrs. W. W. DeLong, *Seattle Home Builder and Home Keeper* (Seattle: Commercial Publishing, 1915), 11.

3. DeLong and DeLong, 49.

4. *Pacific Builder and Engineer* 12, no. 11 (September 9, 1911): 118.

5. *Bungalow Magazine* (January 15, 1915): 45.

6. *Bungalow Magazine* (January 15, 1915): 45.

7. *Pacific Builder and Engineer* 12, no. 11 (September 9, 1911): 118.

8. Helen Hawthorne, "Realm Feminine," *Oregon Daily Journal*, March 2, 1907.

9. *Spokesman-Review*, September 14, 1909.

10. *Sunday Oregonian*, May 2, 1909.

11. Ladd & Tilton Bank, *Book of Facts and Information about Portland* (Portland: F. V. Parsons, 1917), 5.

12. *Carman Manufacturing Co. Catalogue No. 20, 1911 and 1912* (Tacoma, 1911), 57, 138–40, 147–48, 157, 161, 178–79.

13. *Carman Manufacturing Co. Catalogue No. 27, 1918 and 1919* (Tacoma, 1918), 37, 127–29.

14. *Pacific Northwest Commerce* 2, no. 5 (May 1910): 12.

15. *Oregon Furniture Manufacturing Co.* (Portland, c. 1910), 3–4.

16. *Oregonian*, April 4, 1907.

17. *Sunday Oregonian*, May 9, 1909.

18. *Oregonian*, February 16, 1914.

19. *Oregonian*, February 23, 1914.

20. *Pacific Builder and Engineer* 13, no. 19 (May 11, 1912): 404–5.

21. Coos Historical & Maritime Museum, #965-132.

22. Robert Lundberg, "The Art Room in the Oregon Building: Oregon Arts and Crafts in 1915," *Oregon Historical Quarterly* 101, no. 2 (summer 2000): 218.

23. Lundberg, 219.

24. *The Art Room in the Oregon Building at the Panama-Pacific International Exposition: A brief statement of the plans issued for those who may be able to help by their interest or work* (Oregon, 1915), 2.

25. *Peters Manufacturing Co., Makers of Genuine Solid Oak Mission Furniture, Sold Direct, Factory to Home* (Portland, c. 1915), 2.

26. *Peters Manufacturing Co.*, 2.

27. *Peters Manufacturing Co.*, 1.

28. *Peters Manufacturing Co.*, 17.

29. *Pacific Builder and Engineer Year Book 1909, Part II* 7, no. 13 (March 27, 1909): 108.

30. *Pacific Builder and Engineer* 6, no. 17 (April 25, 1908): 162–63.

31. Lundberg, 220, 224.

32. Portland Art Association, *First Annual Exhibition of Artists of the Pacific Coast* (1913).

33. Portland Art Association, *First Annual Exhibition of the Arts and Crafts Society of Portland* (1908).

34. Portland Art Association, *Third Annual Exhibition of the Arts and Crafts Society of Portland* (1910).

35. Coos Historical & Maritime Museum, collection #980-50.

36. *Bungalow Magazine* (June 1913): 72.

37. *Pacific Builder and Engineer* 7, no. 24 (June 12, 1909): 234.

38. Portland Architectural Club, *First Annual Exhibition of the Portland Architectural Club* (1908), 67, 106.

39. Portland Architectural Club, *Second Annual Exhibition [of the] Portland Architectural Club* (1909), 12.

40. *Spokesman-Review*, April 18, 1906, 5.

41. *Spokesman-Review*, November 1, 1909.

42. *Pacific Builder and Engineer* 7, no. 4 (January 23, 1909).

43. *Pacific Builder and Engineer* 7, no. 4 (January 23, 1909).

44. *Pacific Builder and Engineer* 4, no. 12 (March 24, 1906): 3.

45. *Grants Pass City Directory, 1912–1913* (Grants Pass, Oregon: City Directory Company, 1912).

46. *Town Crier*, clipping (n.d.).

47. *Pacific Builder and Engineer* 10, no. 17 (October 22, 1910): 160–61.

48. Portland Architectural Club (1908), 17, 94.

49. *Pacific Builder and Engineer*, 6, No. 24 (June 13, 1908): 228–29.

50. Portland Architectural Club (1909), 16.

51. Portland Architectural Club, *Portland Architectural Club Year Book 1910*.

52. *Pacific Builder and Engineer* 11, no. 4 (January 28, 1911): 42.

53. *Pacific Builder and Engineer* 11, no. 4 (January 28, 1911): 42.

54. *Pacific Builder and Engineer* 11, no. 8 (February 25, 1911): 100.

55. *Bungalow Magazine* (May 1913): 19.

56. Unattributed newspaper clipping, "Arts and Crafts Well Nourished in Seattle Life" (Seattle, c. mid-1910), Art Department, Seattle Public Library.

57. DeLong and DeLong, 56.

58. *Spectator* IV, no. 17 (January 2, 1909): 24.

59. *Northwest Architect* (June 1910).

60. *Sunday Oregonian*, March 24, 1912, 3: 10.

61. Portland Architectural Club, *The Architectural League of the Pacific Coast and Portland Architectural Club Year Book 1913*.

62. *The Architectural League of the Pacific Coast and Portland Architectural Club Year Book 1913*.

63. *Spokane City Directory, 1911* (R. L. Polk & Co., 1911), 1298.

64. Jack Nisbet, "The Washington Brick and Lime Company," *The Inlander* (April 25, 2002): 16–21.

65. Washington Brick, Lime & Sewer Pipe Company, *Catalogue of WACO Tile Products* (Spokane, c. 1925), 1.

66. Washington Brick, Lime & Sewer Pipe Company, 22.

67. Washington Brick, Lime & Sewer Pipe Company, 22.

68. Nisbet, 16–21.

69. *Spokesman-Review*, April 23, 1911.

70. Janice Williams Rutherford, *The Bungalow Aesthetic: The Social Implication of a Nationwide Phenomenon Viewed from the Perspective of a Small Town* (Portland: Portland State University, master's thesis, 1981).

71. Ballard Plannery Company, *The Modern Bungalow* (Spokane, c. 1910), 111.

72. DeLong and DeLong, 33.

73. DeLong and DeLong, 32.

74. *Sunday Oregonian*, 1905 (clipping without specific date).

75. *Spokane Ornamental Iron and Wire Works* (Spokane, c. 1910s).

76. Maria Pascualy, e-mail correspondence with Larry Kreisman, February 12, 2006.

77. Stephen Dow Beckham, *Lewis and Clark College* (Portland: Lewis and Clark College Press, 2001). To view color photographs of Bach's work on Frank's "Fir Acres Estate," go to the Friends of Oscar Bach Web site.

78. DeLong and DeLong, 50–51.

79. *Town Crier*, clipping (n.d.).

80. Unattributed newspaper clipping, "Arts and Crafts Well Nourished in Seattle Life" (Seattle, c. mid-1910).

81. *Pacific Builder and Engineer* 7, no. 24 (June 12, 1909): 234.

82. *Pacific Builder and Engineer* 5, no. 25 (June 22, 1907): 6.

83. Michael McCary lecture on Povey Brothers (Portland: Bosco-Milligan Foundation, April 30, 2005). Glass researcher and craftsman Michael McCary has worked on many Povey windows and period glass installations.

84. Portland Architectural Club (1908).

85. Portland Architectural Club (1909).

86. Portland Architectural Club (1910).

87. Portland Architectural Club (1913).

88. Lundberg, 219, 224.

89. C. C. Belknap Company, *Leaded Art Glass* (Seattle, n.d.).

90. Ballard Plannery Company, 114.

91. Marsha Rooney, Curator of History, Northwest Museum of Arts & Culture, Eastern Washington State Historical Society, Spokane, e-mail correspondence with Glenn Mason, February 7, 2006, regarding collection #2962.24.

CHAPTER 9 (pages 244–281)

1. Portland Art Association Archives, Portland Art Museum, Archives Box 2, Folder F-G-H, March 1906–1907, letter, April 11, 1905, DuMond to Henrietta H. Failing, Curator of the Portland Art Museum.

2. *Sunday Oregonian*, May 24, 1908.

3. *Sunday Oregonian*, May 24, 1908.

4. In our research into the Arts and Crafts movement in Oregon and Washington, we have been particularly frustrated in our inability to discover many works by some of the best-known craft workers of the period. There could be many reasons for this paucity of available objects for study: perhaps the work was just not signed, or still remains in the private homes, or has been melted down, or even thrown away as tastes in decorative and applied arts change over time. Hopefully, as those interested in the regional expression of the Arts and Crafts movement become acquainted with these almost forgotten artists' names, more of the works will surface.

5. *Spokesman-Review*, November 4, 1906.

6. *Sunday Oregonian*, May 24, 1908.

7. Portland Art Association, *Exhibition of Applied Art April 30–May 18, 1907: Catalogue of Examples of Handicraft from the Recent Exhibition of the Society of Arts and Crafts, Boston, Shown with a Small Loan Collection by the Portland Art Association* (1907).

8. Biographical information about Albert Berry came from several sources. His earlier work in Alaska was the subject of an article by David Paul, "Quaint Conceits, Illustrating Alaska Lore Fashioned in Metal and Ivory by Cunning Craftsman," in the April 1916 issue of *Bungalow Magazine*. The *Town Crier* featured Berry's Handcraft Shop in its December 10, 1921, issue. Erwina Jeanneret Berry was the focus of a feature article in the *Seattle Times*, April 1, 1951. More recent articles about Berry were Jeffrey Hill, "Albert Berry: A Northwest Craftsman," *Arts & Crafts Quarterly* 2, no. 4, 4–5; and Joe Farmarco, "Berry Picking: A Personal Pursuit of the Craft of Albert & Erwina Berry," *Style 1900* 11, no. 2 (spring–summer 1998): 64–70.

9. *Town Crier* (December 10, 1921): 11–12.

10. Albert Hansen, *The Century Vase* (Seattle: Albert Hansen, 1909).

11. Dorothy T. Rainwater, *Encyclopedia of American Silver Manufacturers* (New York: Crown, 1975), 106.

12. Jos. Mayer, Inc., catalog and pricelist (Seattle, 1921).

13. *Oregonian*, May 3, 1907.

14. Portland Art Association Archives, Box 2, Folder W-Z, September 1905–April 1907, letter, April 20, 1907, Wisner to Failing.

15. Margery Hoffman Smith Collection, Mss 2660, Oregon Historical Society, Box 1, Folder 1900–1907, letter, November 3, 1907, Julia Hoffman to Margery Hoffman.

16. *Sunday Oregonian*, May 24, 1908.

17. *Sunday Oregonian*, May 24, 1908.

18. Margery Hoffman Smith Collection, Mss 2660, Box 1, Folder 1910, letters, March 12–May 9, 1910, Julia Hoffman to Margery Hoffman.

19. Caroline Couch Burns Hoffman Collection, Mss 2546, Oregon Historical Society, Wedding Gift Registry.

20. *Sunday Oregonian*, November 13, 1910.

21. *Sunday Oregonian*, December 10, 1911.

22. Two letters in the Margery Hoffman Smith Collection at the Oregon Historical Society written by Wisner in September and October 1908 are on his stationery. The letterhead bears a logo of the intertwined initials "JNW" above the text "John Nelson Wisner, Handicraftsman, Oregon City, Oregon." His services and materials are listed on the letterhead.

23. Oregon School of Arts & Crafts Collection, Mss 2983, Oregon Historical Society, Scrapbook 1902–1929, letter, March 7, 1912, Gebelein to Hoffman.

24. *Oregon Daily Journal*, September 16, 1916.

25. *Sunday Oregonian*, December 10, 1911.

26. *Spectator* XII, no. 6 (October 15, 1912).

27. *Oregon Daily Journal*, September 16, 1916.

28. Portland Art Association Archives, Box 2, Folder F-G-H, March 1906–November 1907, letter, February 23, 1907, Failing to Hoffman.

29. Portland Art Association Archives, letter, February 26, 1907, Failing to Hoffman.

30. *Sunday Oregonian*, May 24, 1908.

31. *Spectator* IV, no. 3 (September 26, 1908): 15.

32. *Spectator* IV, no. 9 (November 7, 1908): 5.

33. *Spectator* VI, no. 11 (November 20, 1909): 10.

34. Margery Hoffman Smith Collection, Mss 2660, Box 1, Folder 1909, letter, January 21, 1909, Julia Hoffman to Margery Hoffman.

35. Margery Hoffman Smith Collection, Mss 2660, Box 1, Folder 1909, letter, February 16, 1909, Julia Hoffman to Margery Hoffman.

36. Margery Hoffman Smith Collection, Mss 2660, Box 1, Folder 1909, letter, May 3, 1909, Julia Hoffman to Margery Hoffman.

37. Oregon School of Arts & Crafts Collection, Mss 2983, Scrapbook 1902–1929.

38. *Spectator* VII, no. 7 (April 23, 1910): 9.

39. *Spectator* VII, no. 9 (May 7, 1910): 9.

40. Arts and Crafts Society of Portland, *Third Annual Exhibition of the Arts & Crafts Society of Portland*, "Exhibition of the Arts and Crafts Society," Museum of Art, April 14–April 28, 1910.

41. Margery Hoffman Smith Collection, Mss 2660, Box 1, Folder 1908, letter, November 29, 1908, Julia Hoffman to Margery Hoffman.

42. Margery Hoffman Smith Collection, Mss 2660, Box 1, Folder 1908, letter, December 6, 1908, Julia Hoffman to Margery Hoffman.

43. *Sunday Oregonian*, November 13, 1910.

44. Margery Hoffman Smith Collection, Mss 2660, Box 2, Folder 31, letter (n.d.), Alice Robbins to Margery Hoffman.

45. Margery Hoffman Smith Collection, Mss 2660, Box 1, Folder 1900–1907, letter, November 16, 1907, Julia Hoffman to Margery Hoffman.

46. Margery Hoffman Smith Collection, Mss 2660, Box 1, Folder 1909, letter, March 22, 1909, Julia Hoffman to Margery Hoffman.

47. Margery Hoffman Smith Collection, Mss 2660, Box 1, Folder 1910, letter, January 31, 1910, Julia Hoffman to Margery Hoffman.

48. Margery Hoffman Smith Collection, Mss 2660, Box 1, Folder 1910, letter, February 15, 1910, Julia Hoffman to Margery Hoffman.

49. *Spokesman-Review*, December 8, 1907.

50. *Sunday Oregonian*, May 24, 1908.

51. Oregon School of Arts & Crafts Collection, Mss 2983, Scrapbook 1902–1929, Notice, March 1914.

52. Robert Lundberg, "The Art Room in the Oregon Building: Oregon Arts and Crafts in 1915," *Oregon Historical Quarterly* 101, no. 2 (summer 2000): 219, 227.

53. *Spectator* XVI, no. 21 (January 23, 1915): 9.

54. *Oregonian*, May 9, 1917.

55. *Sunday Oregonian*, May 13, 1917.

56. *Sunday Oregonian*, December 10, 1911.

57. Allen Hendershott Eaton Collection, Ms A263, Special Collections and Archives, University of Oregon, letter, Christmastime 1952.

58. Lundberg, 227.

59. Allen Hendershott Eaton Collection, Ms A263, letter, Christmastime 1947.

60. *Spectator* XVII, no. 17 (July 3, 1915).

61. Oregon School of Arts & Crafts Collection, Mss 2983, Scrapbook 1902–1929, unattributed newspaper clipping, December 1, 1915.

62. For an introductory discussion of the history of china painting in America, see Dorothy Kamm's two books, *American Painted Porcelain* (Paducah, Kentucky: Collector Books, 1977) and *American Painted Porcelain With Values* (Norfolk, Virginia: Antique Trader Books, 1999).

63. *Spectator* VI, no. 2 (September 18, 1909): 17.

64. *Oregonian*, July 9, 1905.

65. *Keramic Studio* (May 1910).

66. *Keramic Studio* (June 1910).

67. *Seattle Mail and Herald* VII, no. 30 (June 4, 1904): 11.

68. *Seattle Mail and Herald* VIII, no. 29 (June 3, 1905): 6.

69. *Seattle Mail and Herald* IX, no. 18 (March 24, 1906): 7.

70. *Weekend* 1, no. 6 (February 10, 1906): 14.

71. *Weekend* 1, no. 12 (March 17, 1906): 11.

72. *Catalogue of Fine Arts Gallery and Exhibit of Arts and Crafts, California Building, Exposition Grounds* (Seattle: Alaska-Yukon-Pacific Exposition, 1909).

73. *Keramic Studio* (August 1911).

74. *Sunday Oregonian*, May 27, 1917.

75. *Keramic Studio* XV, no. 1 (May 1913): 2.

76. Unattributed clipping, January 2, 1923.

77. For informative sources on Arts and Crafts textiles, read Dianne Ayers et al., *American Arts and Crafts Textiles* (New York: Abrams, 2002); Ann Wallace, *Arts & Crafts Textiles* (Salt Lake City: Gibbs-Smith, 1999); and Chris Walther, "Sources & Identification of American Arts & Crafts Needlework Kits," *Style 1900* 12, no. 3, (summer-fall 1999).

78. *Spectator* IV, no. 11 (November 21, 1908): 15.

79. *Spectator* V, no. 22 (August 7, 1909): 15.

80. *Spectator* IV, no. 8 (October 31, 1908): 15.

81. Margery Hoffman Smith Collection, Mss 2660, Box 1, Folder 1910, letter, December 7, 1910, Julia Hoffman to Margery Hoffman.

82. Oregon School of Arts & Crafts Collection, Mss 2983, Scrapbook 1924–1964, various notices and clippings.

83. For a useful discussion of Oregon's competing woolen mills and of Indian blankets, see Robert W. Kapoun with Charles J. Lohrmann, *Language of the Robe: American Indian Trade Blankets* (Salt Lake City: Gibbs Smith, 1992).

84. *Spectator* IV, no. 5 (October 10, 1908): 15.

85. *Spectator* VII, no. 7 (April 23, 1910): 9.

86. Alaska-Yukon-Pacific Exposition (1909) Scrapbooks Collection, Special Collections Division, University of Washington Libraries (Seattle).

87. *Julia E. Hoffman: A Family Album* (San Francisco: San Francisco Museum of Modern Art, 1977), 12, 20.

88. *Spokane Chronicle*, April 13, 1908.

89. *Spectator* VII, no. 11 (May 23, 1908): 16.

90. Margery Hoffman Smith Collection, Mss 2660, Box 2, Folder 9, letter, February 26, 1922, Deenie Robbins to Julia Hoffman.

91. Margery Hoffman Smith Collection, Mss 2660, Box 2, Folder 9, letter, December 12, 1922, Deenie Robbins to Julia Hoffman.

92. Margery Hoffman Smith Collection, Mss 2660, Box 2, Folder 9, letter, March 13, 1925, Deenie Robbins to Julia Hoffman.

93. *Sunday Oregonian*, May 24, 1908.

CHAPTER 10 (pages 283–310)

1. *North-Western Industrial Exposition, Spokane Falls, Official Catalogue* (Spokane, 1890).

2. Ginny Allen and Jody Klevit, *Oregon Painters: The First Hundred Years (1859–1959)* (Portland: Oregon Historical Society, 1999). We used Allen and Klevit's index and biographical dictionary of Oregon artists extensively in beginning our research on artists who painted with an Arts and Crafts aesthetic. We also found of great help the introductory essays by Robert L. Joki and Jack D. Cleaver for understanding the chronology of Oregon art and artists.

3. W. E. Rollins, "Art and Its Possibilities in the Northwest," *Pacific Monthly* 2, no. 1 (May 1899): 18–19.

4. *Spokane City Directory, 1912* (R. L. Polk Co., 1912), 154.

5. Margaret E. Bullock, *Childe Hassam: Impressionist in the West* (Portland: Portland Art Museum, 2004). Bullock's book provides insight into the relationship between Hassam and C. E. S. Wood and their painting excursions. Both artists' works are illustrated.

6. *Spectator* IV, no. 12 (November 18, 1908): 9.

7. Lewis and Clark Exposition Collection, Mss 1609, Oregon Historical Society, letter, April 17, 1905, DuMond to Dosch.

8. Lewis and Clark Exposition Collection, Mss 1609, letter, April 25, 1905, Dosch to DuMond.

9. Lewis and Clark Exposition Collection, Mss 1609, letter, May 12, 1905, DuMond to Dosch.

10. Lewis and Clark Exposition Collection, Mss 1609, letter, April 22, 1905, DuMond to Dosch.

11. Portland Art Association, *First Annual Exhibition, Artists of Portland and Vicinity* (1912).

12. *Seattle Post-Intelligencer*, October 8, 1915.

13. Robert Lundberg, "The Art Room in the Oregon Building: Oregon Arts and Crafts in 1915," *Oregon Historical Quarterly* 101, no. 2 (summer 2000): 214–27.

14. *Spectator* VI, no. 25 (February 26, 1910): 11.

15. Allen and Klevit, 266.

16. Allen and Klevit, 323.

17. *Spectator* VI, no. 25 (February 26, 1910): 11.

18. *Spectator* V, no. 3 (March 27, 1909): 9.

19. Arts and Crafts Society of Portland, *First Annual Exhibition of the Arts and Crafts Society of Portland* (1908).

20. *Sunday Oregonian*, December 3, 1911, 5: 4.

21. *Spectator* VI, no. 25 (February 26, 1910): 11.

22. Ginny Allen and Gregory L. Nelson, "Impressions of Oregon: The Art of Reverend Melville Thomas Wire," *Oregon Historical Quarterly* 105, no. 4 (winter 2004).

23. Lundberg, 226.

24. Michael Munk, "The Portland Period of Artist Carl Walters," *Oregon Historical Quarterly* 101, no. 2 (summer 2000).

25. *Spectator* XV, no. 17 (June 27, 1914): 9.

26. *Oregon Daily Journal*, August 16, 1914.

27. *Spectator* IV, no. 18 (January 9, 1909): 9.

28. Portland Art Museum, *Fiftieth Anniversary Exhibition 1909–1959* (1959).

29. Allen and Klevit, 153–54.

30. Dennis Andersen, Notes (n.d.). Andersen, while working with the University of Washington's Special Collections, compiled a series of notes gathered from newspapers and other sources regarding art and artists in the Seattle area and throughout Washington. Copies of those notes, which are in our possession, were used extensively to piece together the chronology of Washington's art scene during the Arts and Crafts period, as well as the activities of the artists. If we do not provide a citation in this text after a reference to an artist, exhibition, or art organization, that is because it came either from Andersen's notes or a second source of information about Washington artists, the biographical index compiled by Dode Trip and Sherburne F. Cook Jr., *Washington State Art and Artists, 1850–1950* (Olympia: Sherburne Antiques and Fine Art, 1992).

31. *Spokesman-Review*, February 12, 1909, 10.

32. Unattributed newspaper clipping, 1904, Northwest Museum of Arts & Culture, Eastern Washington State Historical Society (Spokane).

33. Andersen, 32.

34. Andersen, 69–70.

35. Kitty Harmon, ed., *The Pacific Northwest Landscape: A Painted History* (Seattle: Sasquatch Books, 2001), 134. Harmon's book includes biographies of many Northwest artists painting in the early twentieth century. The text and color plates make this book a valuable reference for understanding the role the natural landscape played in Northwest art.

36. *Spokane Daily Chronicle*, September 2, 1912.

37. Doris Ostrander Dawdy, *Artists of the American West*, vol. 2 (Chicago: Sage Books, 1981), 170.

38. Melissa Webster, *McDermitt's View: An Affair with the Land* (Pullman: Washington State University Museum of Art, 1996).

39. Trip and Cook, 146.

40. Andersen, 59–61.

41. Harmon, 49, 141.

42. Nancy E. Green and Jessie Poesch, *Arthur Wesley Dow and American Arts & Crafts* (New York: American Federation of Arts in association with Harry N. Abrams, 1999), 58.

43. Portland Art Association Archives, Portland Art Museum, File 2, 1911–1929.

44. Allen and Klevit, 312–3.

45. *Spectator* VI, no. 4 (October 2, 1909): 9.

46. *Spectator* VI, no. 8 (October 30, 1909): 10.

47. *Spectator* VI, no. 13 (December 4, 1909): 16.

48. W. Corwin Chase, *TePee Fires* (Burley, Washington: Coffee Break Press, 1981), 51.

49. David Martin, e-mail correspondence with Glenn Mason, February 9, 2006.

50. *Descendents of James Harper*, a Web site maintained by Rick Harper. Whatcom Museum of History & Art, Bellingham, has a collection of Elizabeth Colborne's color woodblock prints. Only a few private collections own examples of her work.

51. Andersen, 25–28.

CHAPTER 11 (pages 311–332)

1. Eastman Kodak Company, *The Modern Way in Picture Making*, revised edition (Rochester, New York: Eastman Kodak Co., 1907), 29–30.

2. Lewis and Clark Centennial Exposition, *Official Classification and Rules of Exhibit Department* (Portland, 1905).

3. Lewis and Clark Exposition Collection, Mss 1609, Research Library, Oregon Historical Society, letter, May 19, 1905, Stiegltiz to DuMond.

4. Lewis and Clark Centennial Exposition, *Catalogue of the Fine Arts Exhibit, Lewis and Clark Centennial Exposition* (Portland, 1905), 72–73. The other Photo-Secessionist photographers included in the exhibit were Dugmore Radcliffe, R. Eickemeyer Jr., Benedict F. Herzog, George H. Seeley, Sarah C. Sears, Frank Eugene, Mary Devens, and Joseph Keiley.

5. *Catalogue of Fine Arts Gallery and Exhibit of Arts and Crafts, California Building, Exposition Grounds, Seattle* (Alaska-Yukon-Pacific Exposition, 1909), 28–30.

6. *Spectator* III, no. 26 (September 5, 1908): 8.

7. For a brief biography of William B. Dyer, see Weston Naef, *The Collection of Alfred Stieglitz: Fifty Pioneers of Modern Photography* (New York: Viking Press in association with the Metropolitan Museum of Art, 1978), 340–41.

8. Portland Art Association Archives, Portland Art Museum, Box 3, 1908–1910, A–Z, letter, August 30, 1908, Dyer to Failing.

9. Portland Art Association Archives, Box 3, 1909 A–Z, 1909–1910, A–Z, letter, September 15, 1908, Dyer to Failing.

10. Robert Lundberg, "The Art Room in the Oregon Building: Oregon Arts and Crafts in 1915," *Oregon Historical Quarterly* 101, no. 2 (summer 2000): 226.

11. Lundberg, 226–27.

12. Oregon Camera Club, *Thirteenth Annual Print Exhibit* (Portland, 1907).

13. *Spectator* V, no. 3 (March 27, 1909): 8.

14. *Spectator* VII, no. 6 (April 16, 1910): 5.

15. Thomas Robinson, *Oregon Photographers: Biographical History and Directory, 1852–1917* (Portland: Thomas Robinson, 1992). Photography historian Tom Robinson's comprehensive study of Oregon photographers is a compilation of newspaper articles and other references, based primarily on Robinson's reading of sixty-five years of Oregon newspapers. The information on Berger and some of his Oregon Camera Club colleagues is extensive. Since there is no pagination in this publication, references to photographers are under their surnames.

16. *Spectator* IV, no. 25 (February 27, 1909): 8–9.

17. Portland Society of Photographic Art, *Catalogue of The First American Photographic Salon* (New York and Portland, 1904–1905).

18. *Seattle Mail and Herald* X, no. 19 (April 6, 1907): 9.

19. David Martin, *Pioneer Women Photographers* (Seattle: Frye Art Museum, 2002): 7–9.

20. *Pacific Builder and Engineer* 7, no. 20 (May 15, 1909).

21. Carole Glauber, *Witch of Kodakery: The Photography of Myra Albert Wiggins, 1869–1956* (Pullman: Washington State University Press, 1997). This book, along with Clauber's article, "Myra Albert Wiggins: Arts and Crafts Photographer" (in *Style 1900* 12, no. 2, spring–summer 1999), and David Martin's *Pioneer Women Photographers* provide an overview of the life and work of Wiggins in Oregon and Washington, her national reputation, and her contributions as a photographer and an artist.

22. Robinson (see under Gatch, Helen P.).

23. Terry Toedtemeier's foreword to Glauber's book on Wiggins provides some information about Ladd and White.

24. Sidona V. Johnson, "Houseboating in the Pacific Northwest," *Pacific Monthly* (August 1906): 219–220, 224.

25. *Sunday Oregon Journal*, October 18, 1914.

26. *Town Crier* VII, no. 16 (April 20, 1912): 9.

27. The information on the life and activities of Cunningham in the Northwest is derived primarily from Dennis Andersen's notes and David Martin's *Pioneer Women Photographers*, 9–14.

28. Martin, 9–13.

29. Andersen, 20.

30. Andersen, 20.

31. *Argus*, December 25, 1915, 2–3.

32. Martin, 13.

33. *Spectator* V, no. 22 (August 7, 1909): 9.

34. Rod Slemmons, *Shadowy Evidence: The Photography of Edward S. Curtis and His Contemporaries* (Seattle: Seattle Art Museum, 1989). While there are many books chronicling Edward Curtis's career, Slemmons's essay in this museum exhibition catalog is one of the most thoughtful about Curtis's photography.

35. Lewis and Clark Exposition Collection, Mss 1609, letter, April 22, 1905, DuMond to Dosch.

36. Lewis and Clark Exposition Collection, Mss 1609, letter, April 28, 1905, Dosch to DuMond.

37. Lewis and Clark Centennial Exposition, *Catalogue of the Fine Arts Exhibit* (Portland, 1905), 72–73.

38. David Martin, e-mail correspondence with Glenn Mason, September 6, 2005.

39. Lewis and Clark Exposition Collection, Mss 1609, letter, May 13, 1905, Smith to DuMond.

40. KaufmaNelson, dealers in vintage and artistic photographs, Bainbridge Island, Washington, represent the work of DeVoe.

41. Robinson, (see under Gifford, Benjamin A.).

42. David Martin, "Photographs of the Seattle Camera Club," *American Art Review* XII, no. 1 (2000): 164–69. See also Martin's essay on McBride in *Pioneer Women Photographers*, 15–16; and the essay by Robert D. Monroe, "Light

and Shade: Pictorial Photography in Seattle, 1920–1940, and the Seattle Camera Club," in *Turning Shadows into Light: Art and Culture of the Northwest's Early Asian Pacific Community*, Mayumi Tsutakawa and Alan Chong Lau, eds. (Seattle: Young Pine Press, 1982), 8–32.

43. Martin, 16.

CHAPTER 12 (pages 333–349)

1. *Sunday Oregonian*, January 11, 1914.

2. *Spectator* XVIII, no. 24 (February 12, 1916): 4.

3. Portland Architectural Club, *First Annual Exhibition of the Portland Architectural Club* (1908).

4. John W. Graham & Company Records, Ms 12, Eastern Washington State Historical Society, Northwest Museum of Arts & Culture, unidentified newspaper clippings dated December 6 and December 13, 1903. The scrapbook of advertising in the Graham & Company's manuscript collection contains many references to Arts and Crafts period products, such as Teco pottery and Apollo Studios art metal.

5. *Spokesman-Review*, December 8, 1907.

6. *Roycroft Hand-Made Things* catalog (East Aurora, New York, c. 1920).

7. Willis Armstrong Katz, *A Historical Survey of Washington Publishers and Printers from 1842 to 1956* (Seattle: University of Washington, master's thesis, library science, 1956), 133.

8. Katz, 135–36.

9. Robert Lundberg, "The Art Room in the Oregon Building: Oregon Arts and Crafts in 1915," *Oregon Historical Quarterly* 101, no. 2 (summer 2000): 227.

10. Katz, 200–2.

11. Lundberg, 227.

12. Michael Anderson, "That Man from Snohomish," *North West Book Arts* 1, no. 5 (March–April 1981): 11–16.

13. Alfred Lord Tennyson, *The Lady of Shalott* (Snohomish, Washington: The Handcraft Shop, 1901), printed by Will Ransom in an edition of 100 copies, 95 of which were actually bound and completed.

14. Tennyson.

15. Anderson, 14.

16. *Spectator* I, no. 8 (May 4, 1907): 6

17. Arts and Crafts Society of Portland, *First Annual Exhibition of the Arts and Crafts Society of Portland, Exhibition of the Arts and Crafts Society together with a Loan Collection of Applied Arts* (1908).

18. *Sunday Oregonian*, November 13, 1910.

19. *Sunday Oregonian*, December 10, 1911.

20. *Sunday Oregonian*, May 24, 1908.

21. Lundberg, 223.

22. Walter Flowers Collection, MsSC 127, Eastern Washington State Historical Society, Museum of Northwest Arts & Culture (Spokane).

23. *Westerner* (May 1906): 11, 13.

24. Grace May North, *Virginia's Romance* (New York: Burt, 1924).

25. Dode Trip and Sherburne F. Cook Jr., *Washington State Art and Artists 1850–1950* (Olympia, Washington: Sherburne Antiques and Fine Arts, 1992), 40.

26. *Spectator* IV, no. 10 (November 14, 1908): 9.

27. *Spectator* VI, no. 3 (September 25, 1909): 7.

28. Lundberg, 224.

29. *Sunday Oregonian*, November 9, 1913.

30. Ginny Allen and Jody Klevit, *Oregon Painters: The First Hundred Years (1859–1959)* (Portland: Oregon Historical Society Press, 1999).

31. *Spectator* IV, no. 10 (November 14, 1908): 9.

32. Alfred Fowler, *The Bookplate Annual for 1921* (Kansas City: Alfred Fowler, 1921).

33. *Quarterly of the Book Club of Washington* XV, no. 3 (fall 1997): 8–9.

34. Frederick Starr, *Washington Bookplates* (Seattle, 1927), 22, 46.

35. Starr, 8–9.

EPILOGUE (pages 351–359)

1. For a discussion of changing attitudes, see Eileen Boris's excellent study, *Art and Labor: Ruskin, Morris, and the Craftsman Ideal in America* (Philadelphia: Temple University Press, 1986). Also see Lionel Lambourne, *Utopian Craftsmen: The Arts and Crafts Movement from the Cotswolds to Chicago* (London: Astragal Books, 1980) and Patricia Poore's commentary, "The Bungalow and Why We Love It So," *The Old-House Journal* 13, no. 4 (May 1985).

2. Harvey H. Kaister, *Landmarks in the Landscape* (San Francisco: Chronicle, 1997), 70.

3. Harold Donald Eberlein, Abbot McClure, and Edward Stratton Holloway, *The Practical Book of Interior Decoration* (Philadelphia: J.B. Lippincott, 1919), 201.

4. Eberlein, 207.

5. Eberlein, 211.

6. Bernice S. Moore, *Art in Our Community* (Caldwell, Idaho: Caxton Printers, 1947), 31.

7. Moore, 40–41.

8. "New Homes Section," *Seattle Times*, May 21, 2005, 1.

SELECTED BIBLIOGRAPHY

This work is only a first step in research needed on the Arts and Crafts movement in the Pacific Northwest. It is our hope that others will take up where we left off and fill in the gaps with additional, new investigations. This bibliography includes all works cited in the text as well as other useful period references in ten sections:

Books and Pamphlets
Articles
Theses, Dissertations, Research Papers
Exhibition Catalogs
Product Catalogs
City Directories
Newspapers
House Plan Books
Periodicals and Trade Journals
Manuscript Collections

BOOKS AND PAMPHLETS

Alaska-Yukon-Pacific Exposition Official Guide. Seattle, 1909.

Allen, Ginny, and Jody Klevit. *Oregon Painters: The First Hundred Years (1859–1959)*. Portland: Oregon Historical Society, 1999.

Andrews, Mildred Tanner. *Washington Women as Path Breakers*. Dubuque, Iowa: Kendall, Hunt Publishing Co. in cooperation with the Junior League of Tacoma, Washington, 1989.

Arctic Club: Our New Home, Souvenir Book. Seattle: Metropolitan Press, 1916.

Art, Carl W., and R. A. Wegner. *Seattle: World City that Had To Be!* Seattle: Metropolitan Press, 1930.

Ashland Commercial Club. *Ashland, Oregon: The City Beautiful*. n.d.

Ayers, Dianne, et al. *American Arts and Crafts Textiles*. New York: Abrams, 2002.

Barnes, Christine. *Great Lodges of the West*. Bend, Ore.: W. W. West, 1997.

Batchelder, Ernest A. *Design in Theory and Practice*. New York: Macmillan, 1910.

Bend Old Mill Neighborhood. Bend, Ore.: Deschutes County Historical Society, 2003.

Bennett, Daryl. *Shapland & Petter Ltd. of Barnstaple: Arts and Crafts Furniture*. Barnstaple, England: Museum of Barnstaple and North Devon, 2005.

Bolotin, Norman, and Christine Laing. *The World's Columbian Exposition*. New York: Preservation Press, National Trust for Historic Preservation, 1992.

Booth, T. William, and William H. Wilson. *Carl F. Gould: A Life in Architecture and the Arts*. Seattle: University of Washington Press, 1995.

Boris, Eileen. *Art and Labor: Ruskin, Morris, and the Craftsman Ideal in America*. Philadelphia: Temple University Press, 1986.

Bosker, Gideon, and Lena Lencek. *Frozen Music: A History of Portland Architecture*. Portland: Oregon Historical Society, 1985.

Bowman, Leslie Greene. *American Arts & Crafts: Virtue in Design*. Los Angeles: Los Angeles County Museum of Art, 1991.

Brunsman, Laura, and Ruth Askey, eds. *Modernism and Beyond: Women Artists of the Pacific Northwest*. New York: Midmarch Arts Press, 1993. See especially essay by Lynn McAllister, "Stirrings of Modernism in the Northwest," 3–16.

Bullock, Margaret. *Childe Hassam: Impressionist in the West*. Portland: Portland Art Museum, 2004.

Calhoun, Anne H. *A Seattle Heritage: The Fine Arts Society*. Seattle: Lowman & Hanford, 1942.

California Heritage Museum. *California Tile: The Golden Age 1910–1940, Hispano-Moresque to Woolenius*. Atglen, Pa.: Schiffer Publishing, 2004.

Cardwell, Kenneth H. *Bernard Maybeck: Artisan, Architect, Artist*. Salt Lake City: Peregrine Smith, 1997.

Chase, W. Corwin. *TePee Fires*. Burley, Wash.: Coffee Break Press, 1981.

Clark, Norman H. *Mill Town: A Social History of Everett, Washington*. Seattle: University of Washington Press, 1970.

Clark, Rosalind. *Architecture: Oregon Style*. Portland: Professional Book Center, 1983.

Clarke, Ann Brewster. *Wade Hampton Pipes: Arts and Crafts Architect in Portland, Oregon*. Portland: Binford & Mort, 1986.

Comerford, Jane. *At the Foot of the Mountain: An Early History*. Portland: Dragon Fly Press, 2004.

Corvallis, City of. *Corvallis in the New Century: The Dawn of the Motor Age, 1900–1929*. Historical narrative on City of Corvallis, Oregon, Web site.

Dawdy, Doris Ostrander. *Artists of the American West*, vol 2. Chicago: Sage Books, 1981.

DeLong, W. W., and Mrs. W. W. DeLong. *Seattle Home Builder and Home Keeper*. Seattle: Commercial Publishing, 1915.

Doty, Robert. *Photo Secession: Photography as a Fine Art*. Rochester, N.Y.: George Eastman House, 1960.

Duncan, Kate C. *1001 Curious Things: Ye Olde Curiosity Shop and Native American Art*. Seattle: University of Washington Press, 2000.

Eastman Kodak Company. *The Modern Way in Picture Making: Published as an Aid to the Amateur Photographer* (revised edition). Rochester, N.Y.: Eastman Kodak Company, 1907.

Eberlein, Harold Donald, Abbot McClure, and Edward Stratton Holloway. *The Practical Book of Interior Decoration*. Philadelphia: J.B. Lippincott, 1919.

Edwards, Robert. *Byrdcliffe: Life by Design*. Wilmington: Delaware Art Museum, 1984.

Eugene: The Midway Metropolis of Western Oregon. Eugene, 1909.

Fahey, John. *Shaping Spokane: Jay P. Graves and His Times*. Seattle: University of Washington Press, 1994.

Fowler, Alfred. *The Bookplate Annual for 1921*. Kansas City, Mo.: Alfred Fowler, 1921.

Freudenheim, Leslie. *Building with Nature: Inspiration for the Arts & Crafts Home*. Salt Lake City: Gibbs Smith, 2005.

Gibbs, Harry F. *The Advantages and Opportunities of Washington, "The Evergreen State," For Homebuilders, Investors and Travelers*. Olympia, Washington, 1920.

Gidley, M. *The Vanishing Race: Selections from Edward S. Curtis's The North American Indian*. Seattle: University of Washington Press, 1987.

Glauber, Carole. *Witch of Kodakery: The Photography of Myra Albert Wiggins, 1869–1956*. Pullman: Washington State University Press, 1997.

Gowens, Alan. *The Comfortable House: North American Suburban Architecture, 1890–1930*. Cambridge, Mass.: MIT Press, 1986.

Greater Seattle, Pictorial Souvenir. Seattle: Art Publishing Company, c. 1909.

Green, Nancy E., and Jessie Poesch. *Arthur Wesley Dow and American Arts and Crafts*. New York: American Federation of Arts with Abrams, 1999.

Green, Nancy E., ed. *Byrdcliffe: An American Arts and Crafts Colony*. Ithaca, N.Y.: Herbert F. Johnson Museum of Art, Cornell University, 2004.

Hansen, Albert. *The Century Vase*. Seattle: Albert Hansen, 1909.

Harless, Susan E., ed. *Native Arts of the Columbia Plateau: The Doris Swayze Bounds Collection*. Seattle: University of Washington Press with the High Desert Museum, 1998.

Harmon, Kitty, ed. *The Pacific Northwest Landscape: A Painted History*. Seattle: Sasquatch Books, 2001.

Hawkins, William J. III, and William F. Willingham. *Classic Houses of Portland*. Portland: Timber Press, 1999.

Heritage Walk. Bend, Ore.: Deschutes County Historical Society, n.d.

Hoffman, Wes. *The Historic "Contemporary" Houses of Denny Blaine*, Lawrence Kreisman, ed. Seattle: Seattle Architectural Foundation, 1997.

Homer, William Innes, and Catherine Johnson, eds. *Stieglitz and the Photo-Secession, 1902*. New York: Viking Studio, 2002.

Homes and Gardens of the Pacific Coast. Vol. 1: *Seattle.* Beaux Arts Village, Lake Washington: Beaux Arts Society Publishers, 1913.

James, George Wharton. *Indian Basketry and How to Make Indian and Other Baskets.* New York: Henry Walkan, 1903.

Julia E. Hoffman: A Family Album. San Francisco: San Francisco Museum of Modern Art, 1977.

Kaister, Harvey H. *Landmarks in the Landscape.* San Francisco: Chronicle, 1997.

Kamm, Dorothy. *American Painted Porcelain: Collector's Identification and Value Guide.* Paducah, Ky: Collector Books, 1977.

———. *American Painted Porcelain, with Values.* Norfolk, Va.: Antique Trader Books, 1999.

Kaplan, Wendy. *The Arts and Crafts Movement in Europe and America: Designing the Modern World 1880–1920.* Los Angeles: Los Angeles County Museum of Art, 2004.

———. *The Art that is Life: The Arts & Crafts Movement in America, 1875–1920.* Boston: Museum of Fine Arts, 1987.

Kapoun, Robert W., with Charles J. Lohrmann. *Language of the Robe: American Indian Trade Blankets.* Salt Lake City: Gibbs Smith, 1992.

Kardon, Janet, ed. *The Ideal Home: The History of Twentieth-Century American Craft, 1900–1920.* New York: Abrams with American Craft Museum, 1993.

Karlson, Norman. *The Encyclopedia of American Art Tiles: Region 4, Region 5.* Atglen, Pa.: Schiffer Publishing, 2005.

Kovinick, Phil. *The Woman Artist in the American West 1860–1960.* Fullerton, Calif.: Muckenthaler Cultural Center, 1976.

Kreisman, Lawrence. *Apartments by Anhalt.* Seattle: Office of Urban Conservation, 1978.

———. *Made to Last: Historic Preservation in Seattle and King County.* Seattle: Historic Seattle Preservation Foundation with the University of Washington Press, 1999.

———. *The Stimson Legacy: Architecture in the Urban West.* Seattle: Willows Press, 1992.

Lambourne, Lionel. *Utopian Craftsmen: The Arts and Crafts Movement from the Cotswolds to Chicago.* London, England: Astragal Books, 1980.

Lancaster, Clay. *The American Bungalow: 1880–1930.* New York: Abbeville, 1985.

The Land of Opportunity Now: The Great Pacific Northwest. Chicago: Burlington & Quincy Railroad, Northern Pacific Railway, Great Northern Railway, 1924.

Lemos, Pedro J. *Applied Art: Drawing, Painting, Design and Handicraft Arranged for Self-Instruction of Teachers, Parents, and Students.* Mountain View, Calif.: Pacific Press Publishing, 1920.

LeWarne, Charles Pierce. *Utopias on Puget Sound 1885–1915.* Seattle: University of Washington Press, 1974.

Lewis and Clark Centennial Exposition. *Official Classification and Rules of Exhibit Department.* Portland: Lewis and Clark Centennial Exposition, 1905.

Livingstone, Karen, and Linda Perry. *International Arts and Crafts.* London: Victoria & Albert Museum, 2005. See especially essay by Ted Bosley, "Western North America: Nature's Spirit."

Maddex, Dianne. *Bungalow Nation.* New York: Abrams, 2003.

Mann, Margery. *California Pictorialism.* San Francisco: San Francisco Museum of Modern Art, 1977.

Massey, James, and Shirley Maxwell. *Arts & Crafts Design in America.* San Francisco: Chronicle, 1998.

Martin, David. *An Enduring Legacy: Women Painters of Washington 1930–2005.* Bellingham, Wash.: Whatcom Museum of History and Art, 2005.

———. *Pioneer Women Photographers: Myra Albert Wiggins, Adelaide Hanscom Leeson, Imogen Cunningham, Ella E. McBride.* Seattle: Frye Art Museum, 2002.

Matthews, Henry. *Kirtland Cutter: Architect in the Land of Promise.* Seattle: University of Washington Press, 1998.

Meyer, Marilee Boyd, et al. *Inspiring Reform: Boston's Arts and Crafts Movement.* New York: Abrams with the Davis Museum and Cultural Center, 1997.

Moore, Bernice S. *Art in Our Community.* Caldwell, Idaho: Caxton Printers, 1947.

Murphy, Paul C. *Laurelhurst and Its Park.* Portland: Paul C. Murphy, September 1916.

Naef, Weston J. *The Collection of Alfred Stieglitz: Fifty Pioneers of Modern Photography.* New York: Viking Press with the Metropolitan Museum of Art, 1978.

Ochsner, Jeffrey Karl, ed. *Shaping Seattle Architecture: Seattle, A Historical Guide to the Architects.* Seattle: University of Washington Press, 1994.

O'Donnell, Terence, and Thomas Vaughan. *Portland: A Historical Sketch and Guide.* Portland: Oregon Historical Society, 1976.

Official Classification and Rules of Exhibit Department. Portland: Lewis & Clark Centennial Exposition, 1905.

Oregon Agricultural College. *The College Girl at O.A.C.* Corvallis: Oregon Agricultural College, 1924.

Peacock, Christopher M. *Rosario Yesterdays.* Eastsound, Wash.: Rosario Productions, 1985.

Peterson, Christian A. *After the Photo-Secession: American Pictorial Photography, 1910–1955*. New York: W. W. Norton with the Minneapolis Institute of Arts, 1997.

Portland Architectural Club. *The Architectural League of the Pacific Coast and Portland Architectural Club Year Book, Oregon Chapter of the American Institute of Architects and the Architectural League of the Pacific Coast with the Fifth Annual Exhibition, at Lipman Wolfe & Company, June 2–21, 1913.*

———. *Portland Architectural Club Year Book, Second Annual Exhibition in Portland of the Architectural League of the Pacific Coast, Galleries of the Museum of Fine Arts, June 3–19, 1910.*

———. *Portland Art Association, Portland Architectural Club Year Book, Second Annual Exhibition, Galleries of the Museum of Fine Arts, March 22–April 10, 1909.*

Puget Sound Summer Resorts: A Guide to the Summering Places on Puget Sound. Seattle: Puget Sound Navigation, n.d.

Rainwater, Dorothy T. *Encyclopedia of American Silver Manufacturers*. New York: Crown, 1975.

Rhoades, Lynette. *The Roycroft Shops, 1894–1915: A Propelling Force of the American Arts and Crafts*. Erie, Pa.: Erie Art Museum, n.d.

Ritz, Richard Ellison. *Architects of Oregon: A Biographical Dictionary of Architects Deceased, Nineteenth and Twentieth Centuries*. Portland: Lair Hill Publishing, 2003.

Robinson, Thomas. *Oregon Photographers: Biographical History and Directory, 1852–1917*. Portland: Thomas Robinson, 1992.

Roos, Roy E. *The History & Development of Portland's Irvington Neighborhood*. Portland: Irvington Book Committee, 1997.

Royal Architecture Institute of Canada, Web site.

Schlick, Mary Dodds. *Columbia River Basketry: Gift of the Ancestors, Gift of the Earth*. Seattle: University of Washington Press, 2002.

Seattle: Mistress of the North Pacific, Souvenir Book. Buffalo, N.Y.: W. G. MacFarlane, n.d.

Sharylen, Maria. *Artists of the Pacific Northwest: A Biographical Dictionary, 1600s–1970*. Jefferson, N.C.: McFarland & Company, 1993.

Slemmons, Rod. *Shadowy Evidence: The Photography of Edward S. Curtis and His Contemporaries*. Seattle: Seattle Art Museum, 1989.

Smith, Bruce, and Yoshiko Yamamoto. *The Beautiful Necessity: Decorating with Arts & Crafts*. Salt Lake City: Gibbs Smith, 1996.

Snohomish County, Washington: Past Achievements, Present Status, Future Possibilities. Snohomish, Wash.: James Lewis, 1914.

Starr, Frederick. *Washington Bookplates*. Seattle, 1927.

Swope, Caroline T. *Classic Houses of Seattle: High Style to Vernacular, 1870–1950*. Portland: Timber Press, 2005.

Trapp, Kenneth R. *The Arts and Crafts Movement in California: Living the Good Life*. New York: Abbeville with the Oakland Museum, 1993.

Trip, Dode, and Sherburne F. Cook Jr. *Washington State Art and Artists 1850–1950*. Olympia, Wash.: Sherburne Antiques and Fine Art, 1992.

Tsutakawa, Mayumi, and Alan Chong Lau. *Turning Shadows into Light: Art and Culture of the Northwest's Early Asian Pacific Community*. Seattle: Young Pine Press, 1982. See especially Robert D. Monroe, "Light and Shade: Pictorial Photography in Seattle, 1920–1940, and the Seattle Camera Club."

Varnum, William H. *Arts & Crafts Design: A Selected Reprint of Industrial Arts Design*. Salt Lake City: Gibbs Smith, 1995.

Wallace, Ann. *Arts & Crafts Textiles*. Salt Lake City: Gibbs Smith, 1999.

Webster, Melissa. *McDermitt's View: An Affair with the Land*. Pullman: Washington State University, Museum of Art, 1996.

Weimann, Jeanne Madeline. *The Fair Women*. Chicago: Academy, 1981.

Weisberg, Gabriel P., Edwin Becker, and Evelyne Posseme, eds. *The Origins of l'Art Nouveau: The Bing Empire*. Amsterdam: Van Cough Museum, 2004.

Wilson, Michael, and Dennis Reed. *Pictorialism in California: Photographs 1900–1940*. Malibu, Calif.: J. Paul Getty Museum and Henry E. Huntington Library and Art Gallery, 1994.

Winter, Robert. *The California Bungalow*. Los Angeles: Hennessey & Ingalls, 1980.

Woodbridge, Sally B., and Roger Montgomery. *A Guide to Architecture in Washington State*. Seattle: University of Washington Press, 1980.

ARTICLES

Adams, Harriet Dyer. "The Undiscovered Photo-Secessionist: William B. Dyer." *History of Photography: An International Quarterly* 12, no. 4 (October–December 1988): 281–93.

Allaback, Sarah. "Anything But Natural: The Rustic Furniture Movement and Mount Rainier National Park."

Columbia: The Magazine of Northwest History (fall 1999): 8–14.

Allen, Ginny, and Gregory L. Nelson. "Impressions of Oregon: The Art of Reverend Melville Thomas Wire." *Oregon Historical Quarterly* 105, no. 4 (winter 2004): 588–603.

Anderson, Michael. "That Man from Snohomish." *North West Book Arts* 1, no. 5 (March–April 1981): 11–16.

Bonansinga, Kate. "Julia Hoffman and the Oregon School of Arts and Crafts." *Style 1900* 8, no. 4 (fall–winter 1995–1996): 30–32.

Farmarco, Joe. "Berry Picking: A Personal Pursuit of the Craft of Albert and Erwina Berry." *Style 1900* 11, no. 2 (spring–summer 1998): 64–70.

Hill, Jeffrey J. "Albert Berry: A Northwest Craftsman." *Arts & Crafts Quarterly* 2, no. 4: 4–5.

Hill, Jeffrey J., and Kathryn B. Hill. "Arts and Crafts in the Pacific Northwest." *Antiques West Newspaper,* May 1988, 25, 29.

Hopkins, Virgil Elizabeth. "Joseph Knowles." *Cowlitz Historical Quarterly* XXXIII, no. 4 (1991): 3–40.

Johnson, Sidona V. "Houseboating in the Pacific Northwest." *Pacific Monthly* (August 1906): 219–20, 224.

Lundberg, Robert. "The Art Room in the Oregon Building: Oregon Arts and Crafts in 1915." *Oregon Historical Quarterly* 101, no. 2 (summer 2000): 214–27.

Martin, David F. "Photographs by the Seattle Camera Club." *American Art Review* XII, no. 1 (January–February 2000): 164–169.

Mellin, Barbara Rizza. "Frank Vincent DuMond." *American Art Review* XIII, no. 3 (May–June 2001): 98–105.

Mullen, Ruth. "Searching for Emil Schacht." "Homes & Gardens of the Northwest," *Oregonian,* September 27, 2001.

Munk, Michael. "The Diaries of Helen Lawrence Walters." *Oregon Historical Quarterly* 106, no. 4 (winter 2005): 594–615.

———. "The 'Portland Period' of Artist Carl Walters." *Oregon Historical Quarterly* 101, no. 2 (summer 2000): 134–61.

Nisbet, Jack. "Leno's World: Leno Prestini Revisited." *Inlander,* April 25, 2002, 16–21.

O'Donnell, Anne Stewart. "Amy M. Sacker: Designer and Teacher, A Link in an Arts & Crafts Chain." *Tabby* 2, no. 1 (spring 2005): 20–53.

O'Gorman, James F. "The Hoo Hoo House, Alaska-Yukon-Pacific Exposition, Seattle, 1909." *Journal of the Society of Architectural Historians* XIX, no. 3 (October 1960): 123–25.

Ore, Janet. "Pagoda in Paradise: Clancey Lewis's Craftsman Bungalow and the Contradictions of Modern Life," *Pacific Northwest Quarterly* 92 (summer 2001): 115–26.

Paul, David. "Quaint Conceits Illustrating Alaska Lore Fashioned in Metal and Ivory by Cunning Craftsman." *Bungalow Magazine* (April 1916).

Poore, Patricia. "The Bungalow and Why We Love It So." *The Old-House Journal* XIII, no. 4 (May 1985): 71, 90–93.

Quarterly of the Book Club of Washington xv, no. 3 (fall 1997): 8–9.

Rhodes, Helen. "The Linoleum Cut in a University." *Design: Keramic Studio* XXVI, no. 8 (January 1925): 157–59, 167.

Rollins, W. E. "Art and Its Possibilities in the Northwest." *Pacific Monthly* 2, no. 1 (May 1899): 18–19.

Rust, Robert C. "Art for the Bungalow Dweller, Part One: Photography." *Craftsman Homeowner Club Newsletter* 1, no. 4 (winter 1990): 9–11.

"Special Specimens of Spokane Architecture." *Western Architect* (September 1908): 35–38.

Walther, Chris. "Sources and Identification of American Arts & Crafts Needlework Kits." *Style 1900* 12, no. 3 (summer–fall 1999): 44–51.

Zane, Nowland B. "Decorative Landscape in Pen-and-Ink." *Design: Keramic Studio* XXVI, no. 4 (September 1924): 78–79.

———. "Mountain Themes in Decorative Landscapes." *Design: Keramic Studio* XXVI, no. 3 (July–August 1924): 46–49.

THESES, DISSERTATIONS, RESEARCH PAPERS

Andersen, Dennis. Notes on art and artists of Seattle and Washington from many sources arranged chronologically by year.

Carr, Christine. "The Seattle Houses of Ellsworth Storey: Frames and Patterns." Master's thesis, University of Washington, 1994.

Christen, Richard S., and Thomas G. Greene. "Surviving the City: The Arts and Crafts Society of Portland, Oregon (USA)." University of Portland, 2001.

Condit, Jeffrey G. "The Ramsey House: Its Architecture and History." Salem, 1995. Ellensburg Public Library.

Heuer, James, and Roy Roos. "The Emil Schacht Houses in Willamette Heights: The Cradle of Arts and Crafts Architecture in Portland." Draft #2g, Portland, October 2, 2003.

Katz, Willis Armstrong. "A Historical Survey of Washington Publishers and Printers from 1842 to 1956." Master's thesis, University of Washington, 1956.

Lakin, Kimberly Keir. "The Life and Work of John Hunzicker, Architect." Master's thesis, University of Oregon, 1982.

Luxton, Donald. Background research notes for his book *Building the West: The Early Architects of British Columbia*. Vancouver, B.C.: Talon Books, 2003.

Roth, Leland, and Elizabeth Walton Potter. "Portland Neighborhood Tour Notes," Historic Seattle, September 11, 2004.

Rutherford, Janice Williams. "The Bungalow Aesthetic: The Social Implication of a Nationwide Phenomenon Viewed from the Perspective of a Small Town." Master's thesis, Portland State University, 1981.

Steele, Harvey, and Richard Pugh. "Oregon China Painters." Wilsonville, Ore.: Northwest Pottery Research Center, 1998.

Thomas, Ronald. "Arts & Crafts: A Movement for the 21st Century." Manuscript, Seattle, n.d.

EXHIBITION CATALOGS

Affirmation and Rediscovery: A Centennial Exhibition and Sale, Objects from the Society of Arts and Crafts, Boston. Boston: JMW Gallery, 1997.

Annual Exhibition of the Arts and Crafts Society of Portland, June 10 to September 15, 1915. Portland: Arts & Crafts Society of Portland, 1915.

The Art Room in the Oregon Building at the Panama-Pacific International Exposition: A brief statement of the plans issued for those who may be able to help by their interest or work. Oregon, 1915.

Arts and Crafts Interiors: Furnishings from Portland Collections, Photographs by Julia Hoffman. Portland: Oregon School of Art & Craft, 1995.

Catalogue, Department of Fine Arts, Section B, Including Painting, Watercolors, Pastels, also Original Illustrations and Sketches from Nature, Under the Auspices of the Portland Art Association at the Museum of Art. Portland, 1905.

Catalogue of a Loan Exhibition of Paintings (September 22–November 22, 1912), Museum of Art, Portland. Portland: Portland Art Association, 1912.

Catalogue of Educational Exhibits in the Washington Education Building, Alaska-Yukon-Pacific Exposition (Seattle, 1909). Compiled by Dora Belle Craig and issued by Henry B. Dewey. Olympia, Washington, 1909.

Catalogue of Fine Arts Gallery and Exhibit of Arts and Crafts, California Building, Exposition Grounds. Seattle: Alaska-Yukon-Pacific Exposition, 1909

Catalogue of the Art Room in the Oregon Building at Panama-Pacific International Exposition, San Francisco, California, 1915. Panama-Pacific International Exposition, 1915.

Catalogue of the Fine Arts Exhibit, Lewis and Clark Centennial Exposition, Portland, Oregon, June 1 to October 15, 1905. Portland: Lewis and Clark Centennial Exposition, 1905.

Catalogue of the First American Photographic Salon. New York & Portland: Portland Society of Photographic Art, 1904.

Exhibition of Applied Art, April 3–May 18, 1907, Portland, Catalogue of Examples of Handicraft from the Recent Exhibition of the Society of Arts and Crafts, Boston, Shown with a Small Loan Collection by the Portland Art Association. Portland: Portland Art Association, 1907.

Fifth Annual Exhibition of the Works of Artists of the Pacific Northwest (November 14–December 10, 1916), Museum of Art. Portland: Portland Art Association, 1916.

First Annual Exhibition, Artists of Portland and Vicinity, March 9–April 8, 1912. Portland: Portland Art Association, 1912.

First Annual Exhibition of Artists of the Pacific Coast, Portland Art Association, Portland, March 1–31, 1913. Portland: Portland Art Association, 1913.

First Annual Exhibition of the Arts and Crafts Society of Portland, Together with a Loan Collection of Applied Arts (Museum of Art, May 19 to June 9, 1908). Portland: Arts & Crafts Society of Portland, 1908.

First Annual Exhibition of the Portland Architectural Club, Portland, Oregon, in the Galleries of the Museum of Fine Arts, Fifth & Taylor Streets, January 6 to 18, Inclusive. 1908. Portland: Portland Architectural Club, 1908.

The Margo Grant Walsh 20th Century Silver and Metalworks Collection. Portland: Portland Art Museum, n.d.

Museum Art School: Fiftieth Anniversary Exhibition 1909–1959. Portland: Portland Art Association, 1959.

North-Western Industrial Exposition, Spokane Falls, Official Catalogue. Spokane: North-Western Industrial Exposition, 1890.

Official Catalogue of the Lewis and Clark Centennial. Portland, 1905.

Portland Architectural Club, Catalogue of the Second Annual Exhibition at the Museum of Art, March 22 to April 10, 1909. Portland: Portland Architectural Club, 1909.

The Seattle Architectural Club Year Book 1910, Published in Connection with the First Annual Exhibition in Seattle of the Architectural League of the Pacific Coast, Held in the

Gallery of the Washington State Art Association, Public Library, April 16 to 30, 1910, Seattle. Seattle: Seattle Architectural Club, 1910.

Sixth Annual Exhibition of the School of the Portland Art Association at the Museum of Art, May 15–May 31, 1915. Portland: Portland Art Association, 1915.

Third Annual Exhibition of the Arts & Crafts Society of Portland, Museum of Art, April 14 to April 28, 1910. Portland: Arts & Crafts Society of Portland, 1910.

Thirteenth Annual Print Exhibit. Portland: Oregon Camera Club, 1907.

PRODUCT CATALOGS

Carman Manufacturing Company. Catalogue No. 20 Furniture, 1911 and 1912. Tacoma, Seattle, Spokane, Portland, 1911.

Carman Manufacturing Company. Catalogue No. 27 Furniture, 1918 and 1919. Tacoma, Seattle, Spokane, Portland, 1918.

Catalog of Pacific Coast China Co.: White China, Colors, and Materials for the China Decorator. Seattle, n.d.

Jos. Mayer, Inc., Manufacturing Jewelers and Silversmiths, Seattle, USA. 1921.

Oregon Furniture Manufacturing Co. Portland, 1910.

Peters Manufacturing Co., Makers of Genuine Solid Oak Mission Furniture, Sold Direct, Factory to Home. Portland, 1915.

Povey Brothers Glass Company. Art in Glass, Illustrated, 1903. Portland, 1903.

Shope Brick Company. Shope Concrete Brick: Its Origin, Uses and Methods of Manufacture. Portland, c. 1923.

Spokane Ornamental Iron and Wire Works. Spokane, n.d.

Tull & Gibbs, Catalogue [of] Furniture, Spokane's Greatest Housefurnishing Store. 1914.

Washington Brick, Lime & Sewer Pipe Company. Catalogue of WACO Tile Products, Seattle, Portland, Spokane. Spokane, c. 1925.

CITY DIRECTORIES

Astoria City and Clatsop County Directory. R. L. Polk & Co., 1908–1909, 1910, 1915, 1925.

Baker City, Sumpter, Huntington, Haines, Union, La Grande, and Pendleton Directory. R. L. Polk & Co., 1908–1909.

Eugene City Directory. R. L. Polk & Co., 1905–1920.

Everett City and Snohomish County Directory. R. L. Polk & Co., 1910–1925.

Grants Pass City Directory. 1912–1913. Grants Pass: City Directory Co., 1912.

Oregon and Washington Gazetteer. R. L. Polk & Co., 1919–1920.

Portland City Directory. Portland: R. L. Polk & Co., 1900–1925.

Roseburg City Directory 1909–1910. Roseburg: Roseburg Directory Co., 1909.

Salem City and Marion County Directory. Portland: R. L. Polk & Co., 1905, 1907–1908, 1911, 1913.

Seattle City Directory. R. L. Polk & Co., 1895–1930.

Spokane City Directory. R. L. Polk & Co., 1895–1925.

NEWSPAPERS

Argus, Seattle, Washington.

Baker Herald, Baker, Oregon.

Eugene Register, Eugene, Oregon.

Inlander, Spokane, Washington.

Oregon Daily Journal and Sunday Oregon Journal, Portland, Oregon.

Oregonian and Sunday Oregonian, Portland, Oregon.

Portland Daily Journal, Portland, Oregon.

Portland Telegram, Portland, Oregon.

Register-Guard, Eugene, Oregon.

Seattle Daily Bulletin, Seattle, Washington.

Seattle Mail and Herald, Seattle, Washington.

Seattle Post-Intelligencer, Seattle, Washington.

Seattle Times, Seattle, Washington.

Spokane Daily Chronicle, Spokane, Washington.

Spokesman-Review, Spokane, Washington.

HOUSE PLAN BOOKS

30 Homes of Distinction by Fenner. Portland: Fenner Manufacturing Company, 1925.

Bungalows Designed and Built by the Bungalow Company, Seattle, Washington, n.d.

Catalogue Number Five, 1925, The Tumwater Lumber Mills Company, Manufacturers of Ready Cut Homes. Tumwater, Wash.: Tumwater Lumber Mills Company, 1925.

Craftsman Book of Bungalows, 2nd edition. Portland: Bungalow Book Publishing Company, n.d.

Craftsman Master Built Homes. Seattle and Portland: Take Down Manufacturing Co., c. 1915.

Cruse, Frank. The Seattle Building & Investment Company. Seattle: Seattle Building & Investment Company, n.d.

Harden, D. L. Northwest Bungalow Book. Eugene: D. L. Harden, Architect, n.d.

Merritt, Edward L. Craftsman Bungalows: A Collection of the Latest Designs, Dedicated to "The Lover of a Convenient Home," 16th edition. Seattle: Edward L. Merritt, n.d.

Millmade Signifies Economy, Quality, Service, When Applied to Ready-Cut and Portable Houses and Garages. Portland: Millmade Construction Company, n.d.

The Modern Bungalow: A Treatise on the Construction and Arrangement of the Modern Bungalow (Illustrated), Showing Floor Plans and Exterior Views as Designed and Arranged by the Ballard Plannery Co., 2nd edition. Spokane: The Ballard Plannery Company, c. 1910.

Porter, A. L., and W. J. Ballard. *Ideal Homes: A Select Collection of Attractive Designs for Modern Homes, Combining, in Exceptional Degree, Convenience, Beauty and Economy of Construction, An Inspiration for the Building of Better Dwellings.* Spokane: A. L. Porter and W. J. Ballard, c. 1915.

Roberts & Roberts, Architects. *Roberts Home Builder.* Portland: Roberts & Roberts, c. 1909.

———. *Roberts Home Builder: Bungalows, Flats & Apartments.* Portland: Roberts and Roberts, n.d.

Voorhees, V. W. *Western Home Builder.* Seattle: V. W. Voorhees, c. 1907.

Yoho, Jud. *Craftsman Bungalows: Edition Deluxe, A Collection of Latest Designs.* Seattle: Jud Yoho, 1914.

PERIODICALS AND TRADE JOURNALS

American Bungalow
Anybody's Magazine
Argus Annuals
Beautiful Homes
Bungalow Magazine
Coast
Columbia (The Magazine of Northwest History)
Comforter
Cowlitz Historical Quarterly
Craftsman Magazine
Fra (A Journal of Affirmation)
Inland Empire Architect (Hyslop and Wescott, Architects, 1911–1912)
Keramic Studio (or *Design: Keramic Studio*)
Lewis & Clark Journal
Northwest Journal of Education
Northwest Magazine (An Illustrated Magazine)
Oregon Country
Out West
Pacific Builder and Engineer
Pacific Monthly
Pacific Northwest Commerce
Philistine
Seattle Public Library Bulletin

Seattle Mail and Herald (A Social and Critical Journal of the Northwest)
Spectator
Sunset
Tabby (A Chronicle of the Arts & Crafts Movement)
Touchstone Magazine
Town Crier
Weekend
Western Architect
Westerner (An Interpretation of the West)
World's Work

MANUSCRIPT COLLECTIONS

Coos Historical & Maritime Museum (North Bend, Oregon):
Artistic Needle Work Club of Marshfield
Eastern Washington State Historical Society, Northwest Museum of Arts & Culture (Spokane, Washington):
Ms 49. Cutter, Kirtland K.
Ms 12. Graham, John W., & Company
MsSC 127. Flowers, Walter
King's College Library (Cambridge, England):
C. R. Ashbee Journals
Oregon Historical Society (Portland):
Mss 1609. Lewis & Clark Centennial Exposition
Mss 2546. Hoffman, Caroline Couch Burns
Mss 2660. Smith, Margery Hoffman
Mss 2983. Oregon School of Arts & Crafts
Mss 6000. Pacific Northwest Regional Promotional Brochures
Oregon State University (Corvallis):
Oregon State University Archives
Portland Art Museum:
Portland Art Association Archives
Seattle Public Library:
Elizabeth Colborne Collection
University of Oregon (Eugene):
Ms A263. Eaton, Allen Hendershott
University of Washington (Seattle):
Alaska-Yukon-Pacific Exposition Scrapbooks
HT 1188. Raymond Nyson Glass Company
E. T. Osborne
PH Coll 340. Andrew Willatsen
Washington State Historical Society (Tacoma):
MsSC 46. Baird, Bella
Whatcom Museum of History & Art (Bellingham):
Colborne, Elizabeth A., collection

INDEX

HILLSBORO PUBLIC LIBRARIES
Hillsboro, OR
Member of Washington County
COOPERATIVE LIBRARY SERVICES